Principles of Premium Auditing

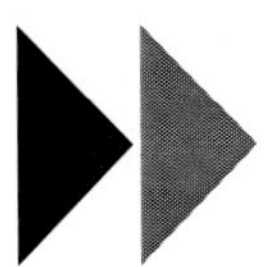

Principles of Premium Auditing

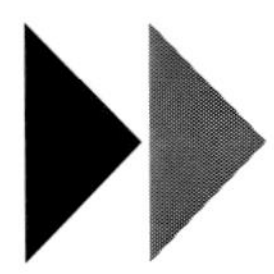

Everett D. Randall, CPCU, CLU, APA
Vice President, Examinations
The Institutes

Coordinating Author

Lowell S. Young, CPCU, CLU, APA
Director of Curriculum
The Institutes

4th Edition • 11th Printing

The Institutes
720 Providence Road, Suite 100
Malvern, Pennsylvania 19355-3433

Unless otherwise apparent, examples used in The Institutes materials related to this course are based on hypothetical situations and are for educational purposes only. The characters, persons, products, services, and organizations described in these examples are fictional. Any similarity or resemblance to any other character, person, product, services, or organization is merely coincidental. The Institutes are not responsible for such coincidental or accidental resemblances.

This material may contain Internet Web site links external to The Institutes. The Institutes neither approve nor endorse any information, products, or services to which any external Web sites refer. Nor do The Institutes control these Web sites' content or the procedures for Web site content development.

The Institutes specifically disclaim any implied warranties of merchantability or fitness for a particular purpose. No warranty may be created or extended by sales representatives or written sales materials.

The Institutes materials related to this course are provided with the understanding that The Institutes are not engaged in rendering legal, accounting, or other professional service. Nor are The Institutes explicitly or implicitly stating that any of the processes, procedures, or policies described in the materials are the only appropriate ones to use. The advice and strategies contained herein may not be suitable for every situation.

4th Edition • 11th Printing • October 2010

Library of Congress Control Number: 2005931419

ISBN 978-0-89463-264-8

Foreword

The Institutes are the trusted leader in delivering proven knowledge solutions that drive powerful business results for the risk management and property-casualty insurance industry. For more than 100 years, The Institutes have been meeting the industry's changing professional development needs with customer-driven products and services.

In conjunction with industry experts and members of the academic community, our Knowledge Resources Department develops our course and program content, including Institutes study materials. Practical and technical knowledge gained from Institutes courses enhances qualifications, improves performance, and contributes to professional growth—all of which drive results.

The Institutes' proven knowledge helps individuals and organizations achieve powerful results with a variety of flexible, customer-focused options:

Recognized Credentials—The Institutes offer an unmatched range of widely recognized and industry-respected specialty credentials. The Institutes' Chartered Property Casualty Underwriter (CPCU) professional designation is designed to provide a broad understanding of the property-casualty insurance industry. Depending on professional needs, CPCU students may select either a commercial insurance focus or a personal risk management and insurance focus and may choose from a variety of electives.

In addition, The Institutes offer certificate or designation programs in a variety of disciplines, including these:

- Claims
- Commercial underwriting
- Fidelity and surety bonding
- General insurance
- Insurance accounting and finance
- Insurance information technology
- Insurance production and agency management
- Insurance regulation and compliance
- Management
- Marine insurance
- Personal insurance
- Premium auditing
- Quality insurance services
- Reinsurance
- Risk management
- Surplus lines

Flexible Online Learning—The Institutes have an unmatched variety of technical insurance content covering topics from accounting to underwriting, which we now deliver through hundreds of online courses. These cost-effective self-study courses are a convenient way to fill gaps in technical knowledge in a matter of hours without ever leaving the office.

Continuing Education—A majority of The Institutes' courses are filed for CE credit in most states. We also deliver quality, affordable, online CE courses quickly and conveniently through our newest business unit, CEU.com. Visit www.CEU.com to learn more.

College Credits—Most Institutes courses carry college credit recommendations from the American Council on Education. A variety of courses also qualify for credits toward certain associate, bachelor's, and master's degrees at several prestigious colleges and universities. More information is available in the Student Services section of our Web site, www.TheInstitutes.org.

Custom Applications—The Institutes collaborate with corporate customers to utilize our trusted course content and flexible delivery options in developing customized solutions that help them achieve their unique organizational goals.

Insightful Analysis—Our Insurance Research Council (IRC) division conducts public policy research on important contemporary issues in property-casualty insurance and risk management. Visit www.ircweb.org to learn more or purchase its most recent studies.

The Institutes look forward to serving the risk management and property-casualty insurance industry for another 100 years. We welcome comments from our students and course leaders; your feedback helps us continue to improve the quality of our study materials.

Peter L. Miller, CPCU
President and CEO
The Institutes

Preface

Principles of Premium Auditing is the textbook used for the APA 91 course. It is one of the textbooks used to obtain the APA designation. The APA program is designed to provide a program of professional education in the specialized field of premium auditing.

This textbook describes a systematic process that can serve as a framework for all premium audits. The following summarizes the eleven chapters of *Principles of Premium Auditing*:

Chapter 1 provides an overview of insurance premium auditing and discusses the vital role premium auditors play in the insurance business.

Chapter 2 covers insurance law and the rights of premium auditors to audit the financial and other pertinent records of insureds.

Chapter 3 emphasizes the importance of planning and preparation to a successful audit and describes how premium auditors can prepare.

Chapters 4 and 5 describe the process a premium auditor should use to review an insured's operations and classify an insured's employees. The chapters also indicate the types of financial information that are needed in a audit.

Chapters 6 and 7 cover evaluation of accounting systems to obtain necessary audit information and the importance of comprehensive audit program procedures as a significant part of the audit process.

Chapters 8 sets out a framework for data verification and analysis to ensure that data collected are sufficient, accurate, reasonable, and complete.

Chapter 9 describes the goals of an audit report and presents a format for systematically preparing the report.

Chapter 10 describes the importance of communication during a premium audit and provides suggestions on about how premium auditors can more effectively communicate.

Chapter 11 stresses the importance of professionalism in premium auditing, which requires rigorous educational qualifications, technical proficiency, high performance standards, and a dedication to ethical standards.

The Institutes appreciate the following individuals who served in an advisory capacity or reviewed one or more chapters of the book:

Marilyn J. Atkins, APA, CPIW

David G. Baker, APA

James C. Boone, APA

Sharon L. Carney, APA, CIPA

Raymond F. Cass, CPCU, APA, AU

Anthony J. Iacono

Gregory E. Jensen

Donna L. Marquette, APA, CIPA

Diana L. McCarthy, APA, ARM

James F. Mendyk, CPCU, APA, CIPA

Jeanette K. Pagano, CPCU, CLU, APA

Laura A. Pieters, APA

Donald S. Sutton, CPCU, APA, CIPA

Their thoughtful review of the material has contributed to making this text more relevant to current industry conditions. The Institutes remain equally thankful to individuals who contributed to the earlier development of texts for this course, although they are too numerous to name here. The current updated and revised text still reflects the valuable insight of these insurance professionals.

For more information about The Institutes' programs, please call our Customer Service Department at (800) 644-2101, e-mail us at customerservice@TheInstitutes.org, or visit our Web site at www.TheInstitutes.org.

Lowell S. Young

Contributing Authors

The Institutes and the authors acknowledge with deep appreciation the work of the following contributing authors:

Robert J. Gibbons, PhD, CPCU, CLU
International Insurance Foundation

Ann E. Myhr, CPCU, ARM, AIM
The Institutes

Contents

Direct Your Learning 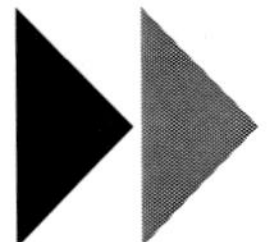

Overview of Premium Auditing

Educational Objectives

After learning the content of this chapter and completing the corresponding course guide assignment, you should be able to:

- Explain why premium auditing is a growing field.
- Explain how premium audits contribute to the following:
  - Correct premium
  - Ratemaking data collection
  - Adherence to regulatory requirements
  - Fraud deterrence and detection
  - Insureds' confidence
  - Complete policyholder information
- Describe the stages of the premium auditing process.
- Describe the various organizations and reporting relationships of the premium audit function.
- Explain why the integrity of the audit process is important.
- Explain how auditors contribute to the insurer's marketing and underwriting functions and the insurer's financial position.
- Define or describe each of the Key Words and Phrases for this chapter.

OUTLINE

Develop Your Perspective

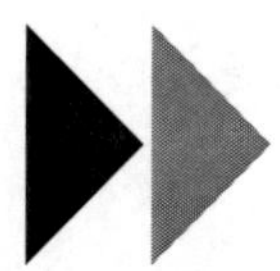

What are the main topics covered in the chapter?

This chapter introduces the premium audit function and the stages in the premium auditing process.

Describe the steps in the premium auditing process.

- What is the importance of premium auditing?
- What are the steps or processes necessary for premium auditing?

Why is it important to learn about these topics?

Premium auditing involves a systematic investigation of the policyholder's operations and records. The purpose of the investigation is to determine the correct premium charge for the policy period.

Consider why premium audits are necessary in property-casualty insurance.

- Explain the necessity and advantages that arise from premium audits.
- What are the consequences of premium audit errors?

How can you use what you will learn?

The advantages of performing premium audits presume a high degree of care and accuracy in the performance of a premium audit.

- What are the standards of performance expected of all premium auditors?
- What is the importance of making a thorough and accurate premium audit?

Overview of Premium Auditing

Premium auditors play a vital role for the insurance industry. With their knowledge of insurance principles, accounting procedures, and particular state regulations, they can obtain the information needed to calculate premiums accurately and to collect data that are used to establish future insurance rates for insurers. By safeguarding the accuracy of the information on which insurance premiums are based, premium auditors help to make the insurance mechanism work as it is intended. Demands for controls and accountability in the insurance business are increasing. The importance of accurate and detailed premium audits has grown considerably over the years as the importance of all kinds of audits has grown.

AUDITING AND PREMIUM AUDITING

An **audit** is a systematic investigation of records, documents, systems, and operations performed for various reasons. The auditing of systems has become more common with the increased use of electronic data and is likely to continue to gain importance.

Audit
A systematic investigation of records, documents, systems, and operations.

Businesses routinely audit their operations and procedures. For example, most insurance companies conduct underwriting audits to determine whether underwriting decisions reflect the company's underwriting policy. Generally, large corporations employ internal auditors to verify the information reported by employees and to ensure compliance with applicable laws and company policies. The external audit performed by auditors not employed by the company, which government regulations require of all public corporations and many other organizations, is perhaps the most elaborate kind of audit. Federal securities laws require that external financial audits be performed by independent certified public accountants (CPAs). These CPAs issue opinions indicating whether the corporations' financial statements fairly present their financial position in conformity with generally accepted accounting principles (GAAP). For whatever reason they are performed, all audits have in common a systematic investigation procedure that includes an independent analysis by persons not involved in the activity being audited.

INSURANCE PREMIUM AUDITING

Premium
An insured's periodic payment for insurance coverage, determined by multiplying the applicable insurance rate by the number of exposure units.

Insurance premium audit
An examination of an insured's operations, records, books of account, electronic data, and computer systems to determine the insured's actual exposures under the coverages provided.

In an insurance policy, the insurer promises to indemnify the insured for certain kinds of losses during the specified policy period. In return, the insured pays a **premium**, that is, a periodic payment for coverage determined by multiplying the applicable insurance rate by the number of exposure units involved.

An **insurance premium audit** is a methodical examination of an insured's operations, records, books of account, and electronic data and computer systems. It is performed to determine the insurer's actual exposure under the coverages provided. The report of the findings of the premium audit provides the information needed to set an accurate premium.

The need for a premium audit arises because some insurance policies have adjustable premiums. For these kinds of insurance policies, loss exposure varies substantially by individual insureds. A standard premium rate might be far from reflecting an insured's actual exposure to loss. When entering an adjustable premium contract, the insured pays a standard premium, which is adjusted the following year based on the actual loss exposure determined by the first year's loss experience. Adjustable premium policies include a clause that allows the insurer to perform premium audits to determine the actual amount of exposure units on which the premium will be based.

Exposure base, or **premium base**
A variable that approximates the loss potential of a type of insurance.

An **exposure base**, or **premium base**, is a variable that approximates the loss potential of a type of insurance. For example, payroll is a good indicator of the loss potential for workers' compensation insurance because disability payments depend heavily on the injured worker's wages. Therefore, payroll is the exposure base for workers' compensation.[1] In fire insurance, the exposure base is the amount of insurance. Other exposure bases include gross sales, area, admissions, and total cost of a contract.

Exposure unit
A unit of measurement of the exposure base used to calculate an insurance premium.

An **exposure unit** is a unit of measurement of the exposure base used in premium calculations. For example, the exposure unit in workers' compensation insurance is each $100 of payroll (or sales). The exposure unit is chosen based more on common sense, convenience, or computer requirements than for any statistical reason. That is, there is no real statistical difference in using each $100 of payroll or each $1,000 of payroll (or sales). The only difference is that the insurance rate would be different by a factor of ten. The final premium the insured pays would be the same. In fact, the exposure unit in workers' compensation is each $100 of payroll, and in general liability insurance, it is each $1,000 of payroll.

Rate
The price of insurance per exposure unit that, when multiplied by the number of exposure units, determines a premium.

The insurance **rate** is the price of insurance per exposure unit that, when multiplied by the number of exposure units, determines a premium. Each rating classification has a different rate, depending on the probability of loss for that classification. Exhibit 1-1 shows how an insurance premium is calculated.

Insureds cannot know in advance exactly what their gross sales or payroll will be for the coming policy period. Yet the insurance premium they pay is based on gross sales or payroll for that period. If, instead, a flat premium

were charged, insureds could pay more or less than their loss exposure would dictate. To avoid that, insurers set insurance rates per exposure unit, and at the end of the policy period they determine the exact number of exposure units (for example, each $100 of payroll) developed for the policy period. The insured's final premium is based on that number of exposure units. For some cases, the insurer allows the insured to submit a report of its exposure units developed during the coverage period. In other cases, a premium auditor determines exposure units during an audit of the insured. If a premium auditor goes to the insured's office or the insured's CPA's office to review the insured's books and records, the audit is called a **field audit**.

Field audit
An audit conducted by a premium auditor at the insured's office or at the insured's CPA's office.

EXHIBIT 1-1

Calculation of Insurance Premiums

Assume that the exposure base is gross sales and that the exposure unit is each $1,000 of gross sales. The insurance rate for the insurance coverage is $1.35 per exposure unit. ABC Company has $3,500,000 in gross sales.

ABC has 3,500 exposure units ($3,500,000/1,000). ABC's premium is calculated as follows:

$$\begin{aligned}\text{Premium} &= \text{Insurance rate} \times \text{Number of exposure units}\\ &= \$1.35 \times 3{,}500\\ &= \$4{,}725.\end{aligned}$$

The premium audit has some similarities to the independent audit performed by a CPA, but its scope and purpose are different. Whereas the CPA performs a public function, the insurance premium auditor performs an insurer function by exercising a condition of the private contract (insurance policy) between the insurer and the insured. In fact, the insurance premium auditor need not address the reliability of the insured's overall financial statements except to the degree that they relate to the insurance exposures. On the other hand, the premium auditor must make an extremely detailed and precise determination of those items that relate to the insurance exposures. To thoroughly make that determination, the auditor might examine the same records and use many of the same auditing techniques as a CPA. In addition, a premium auditor uses many other techniques applicable strictly to premium auditing.

Growth and Complexity of Premium Auditing

Premium auditors play an increasingly important role in the commercial insurance business because of the number and the size of policies now written on an adjustable premium basis. According to an industry survey conducted by the Premium Audit Advisory Service in 2004, insurers developed more than $528 million dollars in net additional premium by premium auditing. The total auditable written premium for the same time frame was $17.761 billion dollars; therefore, the percentage of net additional premium to auditable written premium was 2.97 percent.[2] This additional premium is

a result of performing premium audits. To develop the correct premium for the loss exposures assumed on an adjustable premium policy, premium auditors need technical skills and knowledge. They must be experts on rating manual rules and classifications, continually assimilating the latest changes. Because premium auditors have access to sensitive financial information, they must behave discreetly and professionally. Their findings must be recorded and communicated thoroughly and precisely because they serve as the basis of premium billings as well as future ratemaking statistics. The audit can also be a valuable opportunity to gain insight into the policyholder's operations and to establish a mutually beneficial relationship between insurer and insured. Therefore, the skills required of premium auditors are as diverse and challenging as they are for any career in the insurance field.

Workers' compensation and employers' liability insurance policies were the first to use adjustable premiums. Premium audits arose because of the difficulty of obtaining the payroll information needed to set accurate premiums. Eventually, other types of insurers adopted the practice of premium auditing.

In policies other than workers' compensation, the premium might be based on any number of items other than payroll. General liability coverages are written on an adjustable premium basis using gross sales, payroll, or other measures of fluctuating exposure bases. Business auto policies, if audited, require premium auditors to verify a schedule (listing) of covered vehicles or to determine the amount paid to lease autos. Reporting forms used with fire or marine insurance can be audited at the insurer's discretion. Some policies provide for an audit to adjust the premium for locations or operations added or discontinued during the policy term.

There are several reasons for the increased complexity of premium auditing. The large number of exposure bases used for calculating premiums has increased. Businesses have become larger and more complex, requiring more extensive investigations. Perhaps the greatest reason, however, is the enormous increase in the records that businesses are required to maintain.

The increasing complexity of premium auditing has presented both an opportunity and a burden to premium auditors. The additional records that businesses are required to keep have greatly facilitated the task of verifying premium audit findings because they provide more than one source of information. Unemployment insurance laws and Social Security laws, for example, require employers to maintain employee payroll records to file the necessary tax returns. Those records provide premium auditors with additional information to verify actual payrolls. To take advantage of those additional sources of information, however, premium auditors have had to become far more knowledgeable about general accounting procedures as well as the specific financial reporting requirements of various kinds of businesses.

Reasons for Premium Auditing

The reasons for performing premium audits are the following:

- Determining the correct premium
- Collecting ratemaking data
- Meeting regulatory requirements
- Deterring and detecting fraud
- Reinforcing confidence of insureds
- Obtaining additional information

Determining the Correct Premium

The primary reason for premium auditing is to determine the correct premium for the policy period. The insurer bears a responsibility to determine the premium correctly. Unless premiums are sufficient for the loss exposures covered, the insurer cannot operate profitably. If, however, the insurer overcharges the insured, it will certainly encounter negative reactions when the error is discovered and will probably lose the business. The insurer's interest and obligation, therefore, requires as much certainty and precision in the premium determination as possible. A premium audit provides that accuracy.

When a policy is written subject to audit, an accurate premium can be calculated only at the end of the policy term when the exact number of exposure units developed during the policy period is known. In most cases, the applicable manual for the type of insurance involved has rules that strictly define the procedure to be followed, specifying inclusions and exclusions in the premium base and defining distinct rating classifications. For example, for workers' compensation coverage, manual rules specifically indicate how to assign payroll for clerical office employees. Mastering those rules requires considerable effort and practice.

The fundamental rule in collecting information is: the closer to the information source, the more reliable the information. Even if the insured's ability to provide the premium data is not in question, the insurer can gain confidence in the data's accuracy by physically inspecting the insured's original books of account and verifying the data obtained.

Collecting Ratemaking Data

Insurance advisory organizations collect ratemaking data, and in most cases, project the costs of future losses (loss costs). **Loss costs** are the portion of an insurer's rate, provided by a statistical organization, that covers projected costs of future losses and loss adjusting expenses. To these loss costs insurers add their own expense component to determine a final insurance rate.

Loss costs
The portion of an insurer's rate, provided by a statistical organization, that covers projected costs of future losses and loss adjusting expenses.

Bureau
A statistical organization that collects data to provide insurance industry rates and other information for workers' compensation.

Bureaus, also called service bureaus or rating bureaus, are insurance advisory organizations for workers' compensation insurance. Although the term bureau is widely used in premium auditing to refer to all insurance advisory organizations, this text applies the term only to those in workers' compensation.

The National Council on Compensation Insurance (NCCI) prepares workers' compensation insurance rate and loss cost recommendations for thirty-seven states and the District of Columbia. Other states, such as California, Delaware, Massachusetts, Michigan, New Jersey, New York, Pennsylvania, and Texas, have their own workers' compensation bureaus. The NCCI assists many of those individual state bureaus in gathering and processing data. An additional five states—North Dakota, Ohio, Washington, West Virginia, and Wyoming—are considered monopolistic states. A monopolistic state allows only the state to administer insurance. No other insurance companies may write insurance in those states.

Calculating actuarially credible rates begins with data about claim payments, earned premiums, and insured exposure amounts for each classification. Although claim reports reveal the necessary information on claims for a given period, the premium volume and total insured exposure amounts by class cannot be determined with any degree of certainty without compiling data from premium audits. The detailed classification breakdown of exposure units obtained by a premium audit is needed to generate the insurer's report for the advisory organization and for billing purposes. Actuaries can project future loss costs only when the organization has compiled data showing the premiums, losses, and the total insured exposure units for each classification.

The compiled data are primarily important for the Unit Statistical Plan used in reporting workers' compensation experience. Every state bureau, whether independent or part of the NCCI, requires a Unit Statistical Plan. Similar plans compile data for other types of insurance.

Unit Statistical Plan
A statistical report that includes payroll, manual premium, and incurred losses, by classification and by state, for each insured.

The **Unit Statistical Plan** is a statistical report that includes payroll, manual premium, and incurred losses, by classification and by state, for each insured. Incurred losses, used to project future loss costs, include loss amounts paid plus loss amounts reserved. Losses are valued at eighteen months after the policy's effective date and must be reported to the bureau twenty months after the policy's effective date. If any of the losses reported at that time are open (loss amount has not been finalized), or if a closed claim has been reopened and settled for a loss amount different from that shown in the evaluation eighteen months after the policy's effective date, the insurer must submit a follow-up report to the applicable bureau. That procedure is implemented annually (from the date of original loss valuation) for up to five years. Equally important is the audit exposure portion (payroll by code and state) of the Unit Statistical Plan. Exposures must also be reported twenty months after the policy's effective date. As with changes in claims, revised audits require a resubmission of data to the bureau for the same time period. The data contained in the individual units are sent monthly to the applicable bureau. Premium auditors are often asked to assist in assigning the proper code to a

specific type of injury as part of the audit process. Assigning the code also allows the premium auditor to discover loss exposures not shown on the policy or possible misuse of existing classifications.

Losses are identified by type of injury. The major types of injury are death, permanent total disability, permanent partial disability, temporary total or temporary partial disability, medical only, and contract medical, used when the insurer has established contracts with physicians or hospitals for treating injured employees covered by the insurer's policies. For each injury involving disabilities, unit statistical reports show medical benefits separate from the wage loss benefit.

Whenever an Anniversary Rating Date (ARD) exists, that is, the anniversary of the effective date of the policy, it is usually but not always accompanied by experience modification change, and the payrolls must be reported separately as of the effective date of the change. The payroll report must also show the premium for each rate classification. The information about payroll and premium by classification comes from premium audit reports.

Meeting Regulatory Requirements

Although requirements vary by state, premium audits are often required to meet workers' compensation insurance regulations. Compared with other types of insurance, workers' compensation regulation tends to be much more restrictive because of the compulsory nature of its coverage. It can be argued that in requiring such insurance coverage, the state has also assumed an obligation to guarantee its availability and to administer the coverage equitably. Therefore, uniform workers' compensation rules and rates are usually prescribed even in states allowing open competition on other types of insurance. As an added protection for insureds, the rules prevailing in some states stipulate that the insurer must audit the records of policyholders meeting certain criteria (usually related to premium size or type of business within specific time frames, such as every three years).

Deterring and Detecting Fraud

Premium auditing tends to deter fraud. Insureds are far less likely to submit erroneous information to an insurer when they know it will be checked and independently verified by a premium auditor. Therefore, even when performed randomly, premium audits are an effective control on the integrity of the premium computation and collection process.

Although uncovering fraud is not the primary purpose of premium auditing, premium auditors have occasionally discovered evidence of massive fraud during routine audits. Such discoveries can lead to a maze of falsified or missing records. An insured attempting to defraud an insurer might also attempt to defraud the Internal Revenue Service, other tax authorities, or even customers and stockholders. Massive frauds often result from desperate efforts to hide a dishonest act or report.

Premium auditors cannot deal with such massive frauds on their own, nor can they make accusations of fraud without fear of legal complications, no matter how strong their suspicions. Their responsibility is to obtain accurate premium data, and if they cannot do so, to explain why not.

Insureds who deliberately try to mislead or defraud the insurer are usually far less cooperative in providing records that the auditor requires. The prospect of a protracted billing legal dispute makes it especially important for the auditor to proceed carefully and systematically, thoroughly documenting every step of the investigation. Legal action by the insurer to collect the premiums due is time consuming and expensive. The insurer's usual recourse is not to renew the policy. However, any such decision depends on accurate and precise information from the auditor.

Reinforcing Confidence of Insureds

Competent premium audits can contribute to insureds' confidence in their insurers and in the accuracy of premiums. The auditor has the opportunity to explain the auditing procedure to the insured during the audit so that the premium bill generates less surprise when it arrives.

The auditor's professionalism can result in long-term benefits for the insurer. A policyholder with a favorable impression of the insurer is less likely to look for another insurer at renewal or when the need for additional coverage arises. As a result of the auditing procedure, an insured might have a greater understanding of how the premium is determined. This knowledge might encourage the insured to keep better records, especially in situations in which properly segregated records will reduce the premium. The insured might also be more receptive to loss control advice or other services the insurer can provide. In the atmosphere of a mutually beneficial relationship, the insured is more likely to seek help from an insurer when other questions or problems arise.

Premium audits can improve insurer certainty about the actual loss exposures assumed, the proper classification of loss exposures, the amount of premium earned, and the ability to collect those premiums. The insured may become more aware of the benefits of its relationship with the insurer, the protection the insurer provides, and the fairness of the cost of insurance coverage. Similarly, advisory organizations and bureaus may have more confidence in the validity of their rate calculations.

Obtaining Additional Information

A premium auditor's skills in communication, observation, and judgment can generate additional information about the insured. That information can be useful to the underwriter in determining whether to renew the policy. Generally, the policy is renewed about sixty days before expiration. The audit is not done until about thirty to sixty days after expiration. Information collected from several audits can support an analysis of insurer underwriting

policy or overall operations. Information gathered can also identify insurer marketing opportunities. Finally, the information gathered can be a source of feedback about the insurer's image and effectiveness.

Example of a Premium Determination

Suppose a small firm specializing in residential carpentry employs five full-time carpenters covered by workers' compensation insurance. The classification given in the NCCI *Basic Manual for Workers' compensation and Employers Liability Insurance* is Code 5645, which carries a rate of $17.50 in that state. The carpentry firm estimates its payroll for the policy period to be $75,000.00. The insurer estimates the premium as shown in Exhibit 1-2.

The insured pays $13,125.00 as the deposit premium. Near the end of the year, however, extra business requires the firm to add another carpenter. The workers' compensation and employers' liability insurance policy automatically covers the additional employee. At the end of the policy period, the insurer determines the actual remuneration earned by employees, and the insurer issues an adjusted premium bill for $1,002.05 as shown in Exhibit 1-3.

EXHIBIT 1-2

Estimated Premium

Classification of Operations:

CARPENTRY—DETACHED one or two family DWELLINGS; Code 5645

Rate per $100 of payroll	$17.50
Total estimated payroll	$75,000.00
Estimated Annual Premium ($75,000÷100) × $17.50	$13,125.00

EXHIBIT 1-3

Adjusted Premium Bill

Rate per $100 of payroll	$17.50
Total actual payroll	$80,726.00
Total earned premium ($80,726÷100) × $17.50	$14,127.05
Less deposit premium	($13,125.00)
Additional premium due	$1,002.05

PREMIUM AUDITING PROCESS

The extent to which others rely on the work of premium auditors depends on the accuracy and completeness of the audit information. To ensure that their information is accurate and complete, premium auditors should follow a systematic process for each audit.

Of course, no single method produces a perfect audit every time. At each stage of the auditing process, premium auditors must make judgments about the particular situation and decide how to proceed. Sometimes they need more information about the insured's operations, sometimes additional records, and sometimes an explanation for an apparent discrepancy. Premium auditors concerned only with following instructions, no matter how good the instructions are, may produce impressive-looking audits that are inadequate to meet the insurer's goals.

The premium auditing process emphasized throughout this text can be applied to all premium audits, large or small, regardless of the coverages involved. The stages of the auditing process provide a framework for organizing the many individual decisions auditors must make.

As with many other processes, each stage of the premium auditing process is not necessarily a clearly defined step. The process is a continuum, and many of the stages blend together. The following stages in the premium auditing process are covered in this section:

- Planning
- Reviewing operations
- Determining employment relationships
- Finding and evaluating books and records
- Auditing the books and records
- Analyzing and verifying premium-related data
- Reporting the findings

Planning

Insurers cannot afford the expense of auditing every auditable policy every year, so they must select the policies to be audited. Once the decision is made to conduct a field audit, auditors must judge how long each audit will take and decide how to schedule their audit appointments efficiently. For each audit, they must anticipate the classification and loss exposure questions that might be involved. They must determine the exposure base and predict any possible problems in its measurement.

In planning how to perform the audit, the premium auditor must consider what records to use, where they are located, whom to contact, and what questions to ask. A critical portion of this advance planning is a review of the insurance policy itself. To conduct a proper audit, an auditor must know the coverage provided.

Reviewing Operations

Premium auditors can learn much about the insurer's characteristics by direct observation. Even before conducting the audit, the auditor can review the insurer's books and records to determine the form of business ownership and to obtain a general idea of the insured's operations.

From the moment they arrive at the insured's premises, premium auditors make important observations. They determine the nature of the insured entity. They observe the nature of the operation and compare it to similar enterprises. They look for classifications that might not be shown on the insurance policy. They assess the quality and cooperation of the management to judge how to proceed with the audit. Premium auditors note changes in the organization and new loss exposures and are alert to other clues about the nature and trend of the insured's business. They report significant information about any of these issues to the appropriate departments.

Determining Employment Relationships

After analyzing the insured's operations, premium auditors must determine who the insured's employees are. Although the employees' payroll might constitute the premium base for both workers' compensation and general liability policies, the definition of "employee" is not necessarily the same for both policies. The question becomes especially complex when employees must be identified according to the applicable workers' compensation laws, which vary by state. If the premium base is not payroll, employment status loses much of its significance for the premium auditor, but it can still be a clue to the nature of the insured's operations.

Finding and Evaluating Books and Records

Premium auditors can examine any of the insured's books or records that relate to insurance premiums. They must decide, however, what records will provide the necessary information in the most efficient and reliable manner. They must determine any alternative information sources that would confirm the premium data obtained. To a large extent, the condition of the insured's accounting records and the accounting system as a whole can reflect the quality of management. Poorly kept records can reduce an auditor's confidence in their reliability and accuracy. The premium auditor should take special care to verify any information derived from those records.

Auditing the Books and Records

When examining an insured's accounting books and records, a premium auditor must select a procedure for obtaining the premium-related information as efficiently as possible. How much evidence is needed to ascertain the classifications and the number of exposure units must be determined with a reasonable degree of confidence. If the evidence is not readily available, the

auditor must balance the time and expense of locating it against its potential benefit to the audit. Reliable audit tests or comparisons might allow premium auditors to rely on more readily available books and records.

When the insured uses an automated accounting system, the premium auditor must evaluate the system's capabilities and the accounting process's reliability and must decide what output to accept for premium determination purposes and what additional data to request. If the output does not include all the necessary information, they must determine the steps to take to obtain the information. Time spent at the beginning of the audit arranging for the computer to produce the necessary data can save significant overall auditing time.

Analyzing and Verifying Premium-Related Data

Once premium auditors have obtained the necessary information for calculating the premium, they must decide whether the information is reasonable. Some questions the premium auditor asks are as follows:

- Are the data logical?
- Do the data seem complete?
- Do the data reflect enough detail for the insured's operations?
- Are the data consistent with industry averages? For example, are the ratios of payroll to sales or labor to materials reasonable considering the nature of the insured's operation?
- Can deviations from expected amounts be explained?

Premium auditors should verify premium-related data against the general accounting records and should reconcile any discrepancies. Considerable judgment is required in analyzing and verifying premium-related data to ensure the validity of the audit findings.

Reporting the Findings

No premium audit is complete until the results are submitted. The premium-related data should be recorded and the billing information clearly summarized so that the audit can be processed and billed without delay. In addition, premium auditors must show in their reports how they obtained the data so as to enable others to retrace the audit steps. They should succinctly describe the insured's operations, explaining deviations from operations typical for that type of business. Other significant information obtained during the audit should be identified and communicated to the appropriate people, such as underwriters.

The successive stages of this systematic premium auditing process (discussed in subsequent chapters) form the core of this textbook. Because premium auditors work exclusively in an insurance context, this text also considers the insurer's overall goals and functions, the process of underwriting insurance policies, and the nature of those policies. Understanding the ramifications of their work enables premium auditors to make sound judgments that conform to uniform standards of premium auditing.

PREMIUM AUDIT FUNCTION

For insurers writing policies with premiums based on a variable premium base, the premium auditing function is an essential part of insurance operations. Premium auditing can significantly affect the insurer's overall performance. Unless the premium auditor accurately determines actual earned premium, the insurer's underwriting results are adversely affected.

Organization of the Premium Audit Function

Premium auditors must know the reporting relationships and lines of communication within their organization so that they can readily share important information. They should also be aware of how the premium audit function fits into the insurer's overall structure so that their efforts support insurer goals.

The organization of the premium audit function varies by insurer. The typical structures for premium audit include the following:

- A separate department
- Combined with the loss control department
- A division of the underwriting department
- A part of an administrative department
- Subcontracted to an independent audit service firm

As a Separate Department

Some insurers establish the premium audit function as a separate department with its own line staff and management control. Under this structure, the premium audit department is at the home office and is responsible for premium auditing throughout the insurer's organization. Depending on the management structure, the head of nationwide premium audit at the home office might be a vice president, perhaps reporting to an executive vice president.

For a large national insurer with many regional and branch offices, the premium audit department has lines of authority and responsibility at the regional and branch office levels. Each branch reports to the home office department. Exhibit 1-4 outlines such a structure. Field premium auditors, audit reviewers, and premium audit support personnel in the branch report to the premium audit manager. If the insurer is large enough to warrant it, the branch premium audit manager reports to the regional premium audit manager. If not, the branch premium audit manager reports directly to the premium audit vice president in the home office. The branch premium audit manager may also report to the branch manager. That dual reporting is

characteristic of insurer branch organizations. Branch underwriting and claim managers have similar reporting relationships. Exhibit 1-5 shows that type of branch organization.

EXHIBIT 1-4

Premium Auditing as a Separate Department—Premium Audit Reporting Relationships

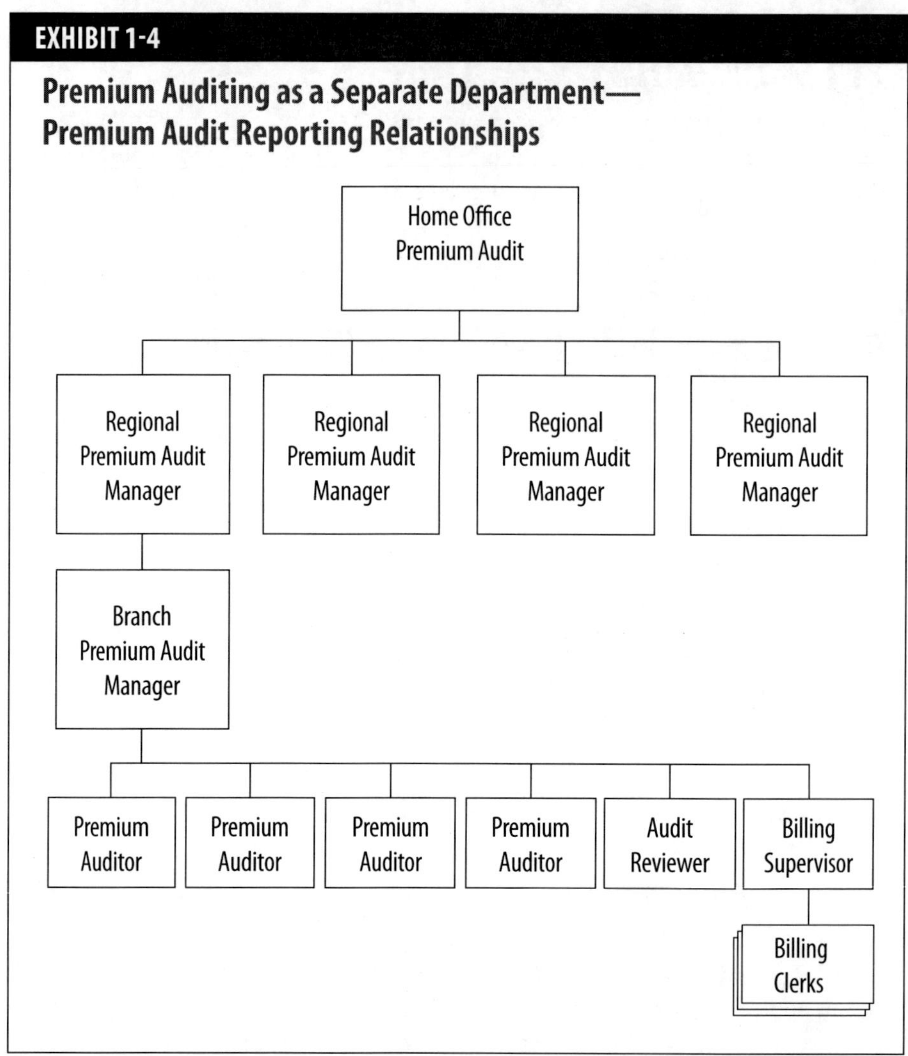

Occasionally, the premium auditor and the underwriter have different perceptions of the appropriate classification for a particular insured. In branch organizations, the premium auditor and the underwriter can appeal to their respective managers, who can then take the conflict directly to the branch manager for resolution.

In some insurance organizations, the premium audit manager also has responsibility for the credit function. That combined responsibility can lead to better coordination of premium billing and collection. One disadvantage of that arrangement, however, is that it may not always provide adequate internal controls. However, the few insurers that combine those responsibilities rely on other controls.

EXHIBIT 1-5

Branch Office Organization—Premium Audit as a Separate Department

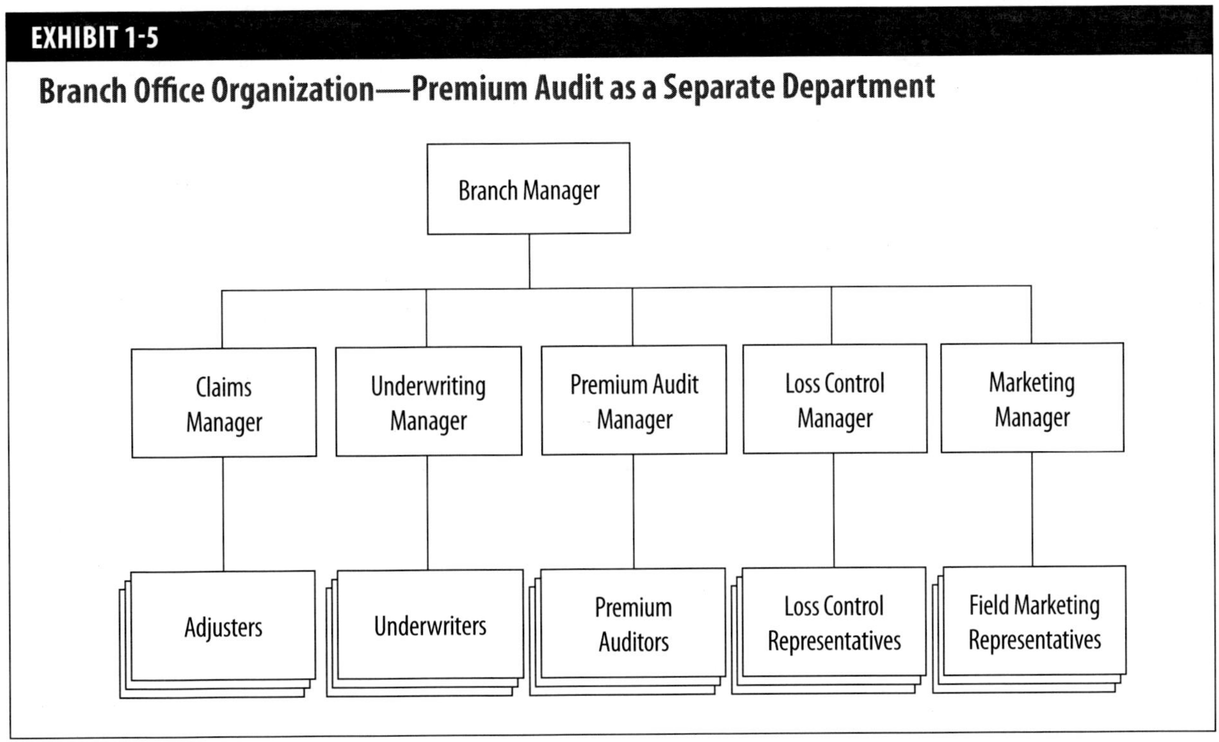

Combined With Loss Control

An alternative form of organization of the premium audit function combines premium audit with loss control. At the branch office level, the insurer might call such a department a "policyholder services department." In that organizational structure, the policyholder service manager supervises those employees who most frequently call on the insurer's commercial customers. Both loss control representatives (LCRs) and the premium auditors provide technical services to the policyholder. The training and duties for those two functions are, however, substantially different. Furthermore, the policyholder service unit manager is likely to have a background in one or the other of the functional areas but not in both. One disadvantage of such an arrangement is the differing technical knowledge required to effectively manage each function. The manager might be unable to understand the particular problems of the field personnel in discharging their duties when the manager is less familiar with one of the two areas. In addition, policyholder service managers might favor the specialty area in which they have expertise.

Some insurers, when restructuring for operational efficiencies, have blended the loss control and premium audit functions. That is, these insurers have begun asking premium auditors to perform relatively simple loss control inspections. LCRs, in return, have been asked to perform uncomplicated premium audits or advance premium audits at the time of the initial loss control inspection.

Reporting to Underwriting

With some insurers, the premium audit function falls within the underwriting department. If the insurer divides underwriting into specialized departments, then premium audit is usually part of the commercial insurance or commercial liability department. At the branch office level, premium audit departments report to the branch office underwriting manager. Branch loss control personnel may also report to the branch underwriting manager.

The independence of the audit function may vary among insurers that place the premium audit function within the underwriting department. Some insurers consider premium audit and loss control as functional areas that serve the underwriting department by obtaining underwriting information and ascertaining premium values. A disadvantage to this arrangement may be loss of the auditing department's autonomy, that is, the underwriter and the premium auditor can differ in their interpretation of the appropriate classification for a particular insured. Although making classification determinations is part of underwriters' jobs, their resources for assigning correct classifications may be limited. Auditors have the advantage of direct observation and other information gathered on field visits to insureds' operations. With that additional information, they can more accurately assign appropriate classifications.

As Part of Administrative Department

Some insurers prefer to combine the premium audit function with such administrative functions as accounting and credit. That structure serves the needs of small insurers or those with a relatively small proportion of commercial business requiring premium auditors as well as insurers who rely heavily on independent auditing service firms.

Subcontracted to Independent Auditing Service Firms

Independent auditing service firms perform premium audits for insurers as subcontractors rather than as employees. The independent auditing service firm is similar to an independent claim adjusting service used by insurers. Some insurers rely heavily on independent auditing service firms. On the whole, independent auditing service firms have been estimated to perform as many as half of all premium audits. The restructuring for operational efficiencies of insurers in recent years has increased the volume of premium audits that are performed by independent auditing service firms. In some cases, insurers have disbanded their audit departments and transferred the function entirely to such firms.

Insurers with the widest territorial spread of business tend to use independent auditing service firms the most, to audit commercial accounts located some distance from their nearest branch or regional offices. For insureds in territories with a low volume of auditable policies, an insurer can make significant savings by using an independent auditing service firm.

Another reason for using independent auditing service firms is to provide additional auditing capability to meet peak-level demands for audits when adding full-time staff premium auditors is not warranted. Independent auditing service firms are also used to meet auditing requirements during periods when the insurer's auditing staff is diminished because of employee vacations, illness, or turnover.

Integrity of the Audit Process

For complex adjustable policies, determining the correct earned premium requires the efforts of a skilled premium auditor. By definition, an audit is "an *independent* examination and report." It is not subject to compromise or negotiation. The auditor should derive the classification and premium basis from the information developed during the premium audit. The marketing or underwriting departments might contribute additional information supporting a different classification. Insurers can resolve disagreements about the results of an audit by a review, further explanation, or even another audit. For the premium audit process to be effective, however, it must be autonomous.

The responsibility of the premium audit function is to determine the proper exposure so the correct earned premium can be billed. Depending on the insurer, the premium audit function may or may not include the billing. Usually various credits and debits that are not addressed by the field auditor are applied to the bill. However, because any adjustment in the premium is a result of the audit, the premium adjustment should be considered a part of the premium audit function.

If underwriting or marketing considerations lead to a concession, the insurer might bill the insured a lesser amount and record the difference as a waiver of premium or a write-off. That write-off is different, though, from showing the incorrect classification or exposure basis on the audit. The correct Unit Statistical Report information is often provided to the bureau, so that correct payroll and loss information is used in ratemaking and in the development of the insured's experience modification factor.

To ensure accurate premium audits, the auditor must be free of pressures that jeopardize the audit process and affect the accuracy of the audit. Whatever the insurer's organizational structure, the reporting relationships must respect the integrity of the premium audit process.

Premium Auditors' Contributions to Marketing and Underwriting

Effective insurer management capitalizes on the opportunities for premium auditors to contribute to marketing and underwriting goals. Frequently, the premium auditor is the only insurer representative to meet the insured and to see the insured's operations. That direct contact not only significantly influences the insured's impression of the insurer but also provides a channel of communication.

Occasionally, policyholders mention plans to expand operations or erect new buildings. They might be considering an employee benefits plan or business interruption insurance, or they might have obvious gaps in present coverages that the auditor notes during the audit. All of those situations present new marketing opportunities for the insurer. Generally, auditors should refrain from discussing coverages with insureds, but they should note the essential information and convey it to the appropriate insurer staff. Auditors must not violate the confidentiality of the audit by divulging information without the insured's permission. In many cases, however, the auditor can benefit both the insured and the insurer by referring the insured to the marketing or underwriting department.

Delay of a return premium that is due to an insured can adversely affect the insurer's future marketing efforts. In a complex audit, some delay might be unavoidable, but information explaining the delay can reduce the insured's concerns about it. Whether the audit results in an additional premium or a return premium, the insurer's long-term interest requires making the adjustment as accurately and expeditiously as possible.

Advance audits or pre-audit surveys can have significant public relations value. Insureds appreciate a visit from insurer personnel for a reason other than to perform an audit, whose purpose the insured is likely to view as to collect additional premiums. Auditors can help insureds set up accounting records to take advantage of any manual rules that might apply to save the insured money. Improved recordkeeping also benefits the insurer by making audits easier to conduct. Helping insureds improve recordkeeping before the audit can prevent a raise in premium caused by inadequate records.

Premium audits can also assist the insurer's monitoring process. When evaluating a producer, for example, insurer personnel can analyze premium audit reports to reveal the quality of producer information. A producer who consistently gives low premium base estimates or misclassifies the insured's operations in an apparent effort to obtain a lower premium quotation can require premium auditors to continually revise premiums upward. Comparing premium audit reports with producers' applications might reveal a pattern of inaccurate or deficient information from a particular producer, which, when corrected, can improve future underwriting decisions.

The premium auditor can potentially contribute more directly to the underwriting process. While on the insured's premises, an auditor can become aware of physical, moral, and morale hazards. The auditor's impression of the insured's efficiency and managerial ability also constitutes useful underwriting information. For example, the audit itself can reveal a moral hazard if the insured uses questionable accounting practices.

Advance audits, or pre-audit surveys, also support underwriting decision making by ensuring that insurers issue policies based on correct business classifications and exposure bases. The auditor meets with the insured's contact to discuss the insured's operations (covered entities and recordkeeping procedures) and to determine if the final audit should be performed at the insured accountant's office. Auditors can gain valuable underwriting information during those advance audits—information that might change an underwriter's opinion of a risk's desirability. There may also be interim audit requests, usually after three or six months, to determine a projection of the annual exposures, particularly if the prior year's audit developed a large additional or return premium.

Premium audits can also contribute to evaluating underwriting efforts because they provide a comparison of anticipated loss exposures and actual loss exposures. In a smoothly functioning insurance operation, the cases in which the auditor discovers a substantially different loss exposure should be rare. Ideally, unless the policyholder has changed the business operations, the auditor's assessment at the end of the policy term should correspond with the underwriter's assessment at the beginning of the policy term.

Effect on Insurer's Financial Position

The premium audit function also significantly affects the insurer's balance sheet. Because of field auditors' accounting background, some insurers have expanded the premium audit function to include financial analysis and business interruption analysis. A prompt and accurate premium audit can benefit the insurer's financial position in the following three ways:

1. The resulting premium is commensurate with the loss exposures assumed.
2. Cash flow is improved.
3. The resulting earned premiums become immediate additions to policyholders' surplus.

Premium Commensurate With Loss Exposures

As previously noted, accurate classification of loss exposures is important to ensure equitable and accurate insurance rates. Determining the correct earned premiums is also important to obtain adequate premium for the loss exposures assumed. Misclassifying hazardous business into a lower-rated classification results in loss of premium volume, which might make an otherwise profitable policy unprofitable. Similarly, the insurer might unintentionally insure additional loss exposures overlooked in a carelessly conducted audit.

Cash Flow

Financial managers emphasize the importance of short-term money management. Even an additional day of float on funds can have a measurable effect on an organization's cash flow position, particularly during periods of high interest rates. Timely premium audits have a direct effect on an insurer's cash flow management efforts.

The premium audit is the foundation of the premium collection process for auditable commercial business. An insurer cannot collect a premium before billing the insured, and it cannot bill the insured before it has determined the actual premium by audit. Delay in audits and the resulting billing delay can have a significant effect on the firm's cash flow. Even more important is the effect of increasing the deposit premium for a renewal policy on the basis of the premium audit. Keeping the deposit premium at a realistic level provides additional cash at policy inception and prevents any later collection problem. A timely audit can also improve collection efforts by indicating to the insured that the insurer considers promptness important. Motivating an insured to pay any additional premium promptly is difficult if the premium adjustment notice arrives late.

Influence of Earned Premiums on Surplus

Premium that has been developed by audit is fully earned and, consequently, has an immediate effect on profit and policyholders' surplus. The size of the policyholders' surplus determines the insurer's ability to write new business. Insurers try to hold written premiums in proportion to policyholders' surplus, often using a three-to-one ratio as a guide. Therefore, the flow of earnings into policyholders' surplus is important to the insurer's financial strength. Because losses, which add liabilities to the balance sheet, continue to accrue regardless of the level of premium collection, the timely collection of earned premiums is essential for policyholder surplus growth.

ENSURING CONSISTENCY IN PREMIUM AUDITING

Although premium auditors make individual judgments at each stage of the process, following a systematic process that conforms to uniform professional standards can enhance insureds' confidence in the fairness of the audit process and in the final results. The importance of adherence to uniform standards contributes directly to the proper functioning of the insurance mechanism. Repeated overlooking or misclassification of substantial loss exposures can ultimately distort the underwriting practices, pricing, and profitability of the insurance business.

Because the additional premium—the amount by which the actual earned premiums developed by audit exceeds the deposit premium—increases an insurer's profitability, one might assume that insurers use additional premium as the primary measure of the value of the premium audit. That assumption is not true in and of itself, and it minimizes the real importance of premium audits. The size of the additional premium does not necessarily demonstrate the proficiency of the premium auditing staff. Instead, it might indicate that producers or underwriters have underestimated the covered exposure bases and set the deposit premiums too low. A large additional premium might also indicate that the insured purposely underestimated the exposure base or had unanticipated growth. Regardless of the reason, the premium auditor's responsibility is not to develop more billable premium, but rather to develop the correct premium.

Consequences of Premium Audit Errors

Although the insurance mechanism relies on premium auditors to measure and classify loss exposures correctly, premium auditors can make mistakes. A **loss exposure** is any condition or situation that presents the possibility of a financial loss, whether or not loss occurs. A premium audit error can have lasting and far-reaching consequences. The previous section on collecting ratemaking data explained how premium audit data are used in determining future appropriate insurance rates. Consequently, mistakes in premium audits can cause significant financial problems for both the insurer and insured. Correcting mistakes requires considerable time and effort, and a single error can have long-term and far-reaching effects.

Loss exposure
Any condition or situation that presents the possibility of a financial loss, whether or not loss occurs.

An equitable insurance premium requires that similar loss exposures be priced similarly. Therefore, all insureds presenting similar loss exposures belong in the same rate classification. Lack of consistency in audit classification of loss exposures causes inequity not only in the level of the current premium paid but also in the resulting distortion of the classification loss results, which determine the future insurance rates. Particularly in workers' compensation insurance, in which a large volume of the business is audited, the results of premium audits substantially affect insurance rate equity and accuracy. No matter what ratemaking method is used to develop the rates for the various workers' compensation classifications, the accuracy of the underlying classification rate can be no better than the data provided by the premium audits.

Premium audits affect the equity and accuracy of rates in two ways. The first is in the consistency and accuracy of classification determinations. If a premium auditor considers a particular insured's operations to be in Classification X, when Classification Y is the correct classification, then the resulting loss data for *both* classifications are distorted. Losses and premiums that should be assigned to Classification Y would be assigned to Classification X. In addition, Classification Y data would be incomplete. That misclassification and misassignment would lead to inequitable future insurance rates for all insureds in both classifications.

The second way in which premium audits affect the equity and accuracy of rates is the measurement of the exposure base. An auditing error, not in classification but in determining the number of exposure units, also distorts the insurance rate. However, rate distortions resulting from misreporting of exposure units are likely to be minor relative to distortions resulting from misclassification. That conclusion is supported by the statistics collected in advisory organization or bureau test audit programs described subsequently in this chapter.

Consequences for the Insured

If audit errors slip past insurers and insureds undetected, insureds end up paying the wrong premium for their insurance. Some insureds pay more than their proportional share for the loss exposures covered; others pay less than their share. Insureds paying excessive insurance premiums are placed at a competitive disadvantage and can experience financial problems. Other

insureds are placed at a competitive advantage. They might continue to operate despite unusually hazardous working conditions because audit errors can lead to a subsidy in the form of underpriced insurance coverage. Insureds can also experience problems if their financial planning decisions are based on erroneous past audits. A later, more accurate audit can result in a substantial difference in premium.

Errors in audits also result in incorrect experience modifications. Experience rating bases an insured's current premium on the insured's past experience (exposure units and losses). If those exposure units and losses are incorrect, the experience modification is incorrect, and so are any future premiums. In addition, if an error in an audit is detected, the bureau cannot calculate the correct experience modification until it receives the correct audit data. Depending on the modification (that is, whether the correct modification is higher or lower than the one being used), the insured is either overpaying or underpaying for insurance until the bureau calculates the final, correct modification.

Finally, errors in premium can reduce insureds' confidence in auditors and in the insurance mechanism in general, making them reluctant to buy insurance or to cooperate with insurers in the future.

Consequences for the Insurer

Incorrect or incomplete premium audits negatively affect the insurer in a variety of ways. Each audit error impairs the efficiency of an insurer's operations even when the errors are corrected. Although some errors might be invisible, the more obvious errors are the following:

- *Improper Charges*. When an audit is incorrect, an insurer collects the inappropriate premium for the loss exposures covered, and that can result in either better or worse underwriting results than should have been experienced. Undetected premium audit errors can cause some policyholders that are overcharged to switch to another insurer to obtain coverage at a lower premium. Policyholders that are undercharged are likely to remain with their insurers. Consequently, the insurer loses premium volume and underwriting results deteriorate.
- *Loss of Goodwill*. As previously mentioned, when insureds discover errors in the premium audit, they lose confidence in the insurer's competence and may consider switching to another insurer. Some insureds may lose confidence in the insurance mechanism as a whole, and may, instead of buying insurance, self-insure by retaining their loss exposures. Insureds that continue their coverage despite their consternation over an incorrect audit might be unwilling to cooperate in a claim investigation or to implement loss prevention measures. Perhaps the biggest costs, however, are the marketing and underwriting efforts needed to secure the business lost because of mistakes in premium audits.

- *Extra Work*. Incorrect or incomplete audits can cause extra work for several insurer departments. Redoing the audit drains the resources of the

premium audit department. Other departments may become involved in attempting to explain the error and reassure the insured. Underwriters may have to correct records and may be drawn into any controversy. The accounting department may have to adjust entries and issue a corrected bill. The marketing department could also have extra work to regain the insured's confidence.

- *Premium Collection Problems.* Insureds are less likely to pay premium bills they suspect to be incorrect. Even when a problem is eventually resolved, the insurer's cash flow suffers as a result. For example, suppose that a prompt audit of a policy expiring December 31 leads to a January 23 billing for an additional premium of $10,000, payable within forty-five days. On March 25 the producer reports a substantial error in the premium audit, requiring a re-audit of the insured's records. The insured refuses to pay until the error is corrected. The re-audit, conducted on April 2, reveals a correct additional premium of $8,000. That amount is billed on April 20 and is due within forty-five days. At this point, the insurer has lost the use of $8,000 for approximately eighty-five days. If the audit had been conducted properly, the bill for $8,000 would have been due on March 10. The amended bill of $8,000 was not due until June 4.

Test Audit Programs

Many workers' compensation bureaus, including the NCCI, have test audit programs. Each state decides if it will implement a test audit program. A **test audit** is an audit conducted by the bureau to check the accuracy of insurers' premium audits. The overriding purpose of test audit programs is to ensure uniformity in the application of classifications, rating plans, and manual rules. In the states in which such programs exist, auditors from the bureau audit the records of a random sample of insureds and compare the results of their audits to those obtained by the insurer's premium auditors. Most bureaus select insurance policies for test audits in proportion to the insurer's premium volume and/or the number of policies written by the insurer in the state. The test audits are usually distributed over the entire state in the same proportion as the insurer's total workers' compensation premium writings.

Test audit
An audit conducted by an insurance advisory organization or bureau to check the accuracy of insurers' premium audits.

Most test audit programs compile the results and compute the error ratio for each insurer operating in the state. Error ratios are reported to insurers on a quarterly basis. Some test audit programs also require the insurer to adjust its billing or at least the unit statistical report in accordance with the bureau's test audit if the results of an individual audit differ materially. The insurer has the right of appeal to try to justify its audit. Usually, a material difference is defined as an amount greater than two percent of the actual premium and/or $300. This can vary by state. Even when the premium does not differ materially, some test audit programs require the insurer to file a revised unit statistical report if the loss exposures have been substantially misclassified or if one difference found (even if offset by other differences) would, in itself, cause a significant difference in premium.

Test audit programs help to protect insureds against possible overcharging, but they are not intended to monitor individual premium auditors. In fact, premium auditors with reason to disagree with a test audit can communicate any relevant information supporting their views to the bureau. Such communication promotes greater consistency in auditing practices, which is clearly a mutual goal.

For insurers with consistently high error ratios, however, sanctions are a possibility in some states. In extreme cases, fines could result, and the license to write business in the state could even be jeopardized. At the least, it is an embarrassment for an insurer to have a high error ratio in a test audit program. A high error ratio also indicates possible deficiencies in the skills of an insurer's premium auditing staff. In response to such indications, some insurers have dramatically improved their performance by strengthening their educational efforts for premium auditors.

Quality Control Programs

Some insurers also attempt to identify and correct deficiencies through their own audit review or through quality control procedures. Procedures vary widely among insurers. They might be highly formalized or almost entirely discretionary. Some programs concentrate on the performance of new auditors. Others extend to the performance of the entire auditing staff.

Exhibit 1-6 shows the checklist used in a formalized quality control program. For each audit report submitted, a reviewer checks the items on the list and records the total number of items checked "yes." Those numbers are accumulated for each premium auditor over a period of time. Dividing the total number of "yes" items by the number of audits performed during the period produces an average score, a quantitative measure of an auditor's performance in the areas covered by the checklist.

Such quality monitoring procedures can detect incomplete audits and lead to clearer audit reports, but they do not necessarily improve the quality of the auditor's investigation. Most of the items checked involve matters of format rather than of judgment. Although premium audits based on a thorough examination and sound judgment usually produce clear worksheets and complete audit summaries, the reverse is not necessarily true.

Programs to review quality and judgment are generally much less formal. For example, an audit manager may review the audit report and raise questions about additional matters that the premium auditor might have investigated. A quality control worksheet, such as that shown in Exhibit 1-7, can be used to review specific audits. Although an audit manager might want to test a sample of each auditor's work, such reviews usually focus on the work of new premium auditors to help them increase their knowledge and judgment.

Some insurers even conduct another premium audit for the same policy to compare the results, reasoning that the only true test of a premium audit's quality is another premium audit. Nevertheless, only a tiny fraction of all

EXHIBIT 1-6

Quality Control Checklist

QUALITY CONTROL

	1		2		3		4		5		6	
AUDITOR SUMMARY SHEET AUD-3170	YES	NO	YES	NO	YES	NO	YES	NO	YES	NO	YES	NO
1. Summary sheet printed												
2. Heading complete												
3. State shown												
4. Code number and classification shown												
5. One line between each classification												
6. Five lines between each state												
7. Signature of auditor and date completed												
AUDITOR WORKSHEET—AUD 2826/3077												
1. Heading complete												
2. Gross payroll shown per month												
3. Audit period within 15 days of policy period												
4. Columns labeled (Code #, nature of work, location)												
5. Signature of insured or representative												
6. Auditor's signature and date audit completed												
7. Principals of business named, actual salary, code #, included												
8. Two sources of records checked												
9. Brief description of operations												

ORIGINAL TO H.O. PREMIUM AUDIT CONTROL

EXHIBIT 1-7

Quality Control Work Sheet

Policyholder's Name ______________________ Auditor Chase Nelson ______________

Type of Business ______________________ Initial ________ Renewal ________ Expiration Date ________

1. Approximate Premium __________ WC $ ______________ GL $ ______________ Auto $ ______________
2. Records used: ____

____

____

3. Acceptable verification? ____________ (a) If answer is "no," was a report submitted? ______________
4. Work sheet acceptable? ____
5. Overtime deducted? ______________________ Two tests? ______________________
6. Payroll limitation allowed? ______________________ Did policyholder prepare schedule? ______________
7. (a) Classifications properly applied? ____

   (b) Test of policyholder summaries? ____
8. Other premium bases (hired trucks, equipment rental, subs, pieceworkers, additional insureds) ______________

____

____

9. Audit reports (written when necessary and including a description of the operations) ______________

____

____

10. Additional premium $ ____
11. Is audit time reasonable? ____
12. Other comments: ____

____

____

premium audits are double-checked by either insurer reviews or bureau test audits. Because of the nature of premium auditors' work, reviewing every audit is simply not feasible. The assurance of completeness and accuracy must come from premium auditors themselves through their dedication to professionalism. To a large extent, premium auditors must govern themselves by establishing and maintaining high standards of technical competence and ethical conduct.

SUMMARY

Demands for controls and accountability in the insurance business are increasing. The importance of accurate and detailed premium audits has grown as the importance of all kinds of audits has grown. The number and size of insurance policies written on an adjustable premium basis, and therefore subject to audit, have grown significantly in recent years.

Insurers have developed measures to ensure accurate premium audits in an effort to ensure fair and equitable treatment to the insurer and the insured. The auditor determines an exposure or premium base approximating the loss potential of a type of insurance and then determines the number of exposure units of that base. The adjustable insurance premium is calculated by multiplying the insurance rate times the average number of exposure units for the period.

The reporting of workers' compensation and other loss experience by insurers to various statistical organizations is essential to obtaining reliable loss cost and other rating information. Every state, whether independent or a part of the NCCI, requires insurers to submit an annual Unit Statistical Plan, reporting payroll, manual premium, and incurred losses by classification.

Compared with other types of insurance, the regulation of workers' compensation tends to be much more restrictive because of the compulsory nature of its coverage. Uniform workers' compensation rules and rates are usually prescribed even in states allowing open competition on other types of insurance. Some states require insurers to audit the records of policyholders meeting certain premium size or type of business within certain time frames.

Premium audits are an effective control on the integrity of the premium computation and collection process. Uncovering fraud is not the primary purpose of premium auditing; however, when fraud is discovered, the insurer's usual recourse is not to renew the policy.

Competent premium audits can contribute to insureds' confidence in their insurers and in the accuracy of the premium calculations. In the atmosphere of a mutually beneficial relationship, the insured is more likely to seek help from an insurer when other questions or problems arise. A premium auditor's skills in communication, observation, and judgment can generate additional information about the insured that can be useful to the underwriter in determining whether to renew the policy.

The stages of the premium auditing process include (1) planning, (2) reviewing operations, (3) determining employment relationships, (4) finding and evaluating books and records, (5) auditing the books and records, (6) analyzing and verifying premium data, and (7) reporting the findings.

The organization of the premium audit function varies by insurer. Typical structures include premium audit as a separate department, a combination with loss control functions, a division of underwriting, part of an administrative department, or subcontracted to an independent audit service firm.

Maintaining the integrity of the audit process is important to derive the proper classification and premium basis from the information developed during the premium audit. The results should not be subject to compromise or negotiation. These audits become useful tools to the marketing and underwriting departments to aid decision making.

Prompt and accurate premium audits help to ensure a premium commensurate with the loss exposures assumed and improve cash flow. The earned premiums become immediate additions to policyholders' surplus. Consistency and accuracy in premium auditing also ensure the proper functioning of the insurance mechanism. Most states have test audit programs and encourage quality control programs and checklists for the benefit of insureds and insurers to help alleviate the problems and consequences associated with audit errors.

CHAPTER NOTES

1. Technically, the exposure base is remuneration, but the workers' compensation manual defines "remuneration" as payroll.
2. Premium Audit Advisory Service, "Net Additional Premium," Premium Audit Advisory Service survey, January 2004.

Direct Your Learning 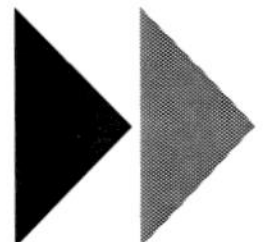

Insurance Law

Educational Objectives

After learning the content of this chapter and completing the corresponding course guide assignment, you should be able to:

- Describe the distinctive features of insurance contracts.
- Given a case, justify whether a binding contract exists.
- Given a case, determine the rights, duties, and options available to each party according to contract law.
  - Summarize the principles of contract interpretation and assignment.
  - Explain how contracts may be discharged.
  - Describe the remedies available in case of a breach of contract.
- Analyze the nature of the relationship characterized by a person acting on behalf of another, and describe the duties owed, authority possessed, and liability created by both parties.
  - Describe the ways in which an agency can be created.
  - Describe the duties of each party to an agency.
  - Describe the scope of and the limits on the authority of a person acting or purporting to act in the capacity of an agent.
- Apply the principles of agency law to insurance auditors.
- Define or describe each of the Key Words and Phrases for this chapter.

OUTLINE

Develop Your Perspective

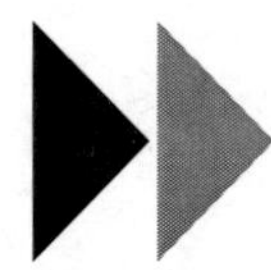

What are the main topics covered in the chapter?

Insurance policies are contracts bound by the relevant principles of insurance contract law. Agency relationship are also defined by basic legal concepts regarding the relationship of principals and agents. Premium auditors' actions are framed by these foundational legal concepts.

Identify the relevant legal principles that apply to insurance law.

- What principles apply to insurance contacts that also apply to other contracts?
- How does a court interpret ambiguities with respect to insurance contracts?
- What are the remedies available if one of the parties breaches a contract?
- Why must premium auditors be familiar with contract law?

Why is it important to learn about these topics?

Because insurance policies constitute legal contracts, an understanding of insurance law is important. Because a contract can be executed by an agent, an understanding of agency law is also important.

Consider the importance of insurance law to premium auditors.

- How can premium auditors be considered agents?
- How might agency law be helpful for a premium auditor in examining an insured's operations?
- Why does an insurer have the right to send premium auditors to an insured?

How can you use what you will learn?

Analyze the premium auditor's contractual duties and rights contained in insurance policy provisions.

- What are an insurer's rights to have a premium auditor make an audit of an insured's operations?
- What are the limitations of a premium auditor's rights with respect to making an audit of an insured's operations?

Insurance Law

To a great extent, the laws of contract and agency, and their specific application to insurance, define the framework within which premium auditors work.

Insurance policies are legal contracts. Therefore, although they have distinctive features, they fall under the general principles of contract law. Because premium auditors perform a function contemplated within the context of the insurance contract, they must understand the essentials of contract law and how it applies to insurance contracts.

The principles of agency law are also important in the premium audit function because most premium auditors act on behalf of an insurer in an agency relationship.

FUNDAMENTALS OF INSURANCE CONTRACTS

A **contract** is a legally enforceable agreement between two or more parties. Contracts arise out of various situations and take many different forms, but they always involve a set of promises binding on each party. An insurance contract is much like any other contract. However, the insurance business involves a public interest because it affects the lives and property of many people. Therefore, over the years it has been subject to much more governmental regulation and much stricter treatment from the courts than most ordinary businesses. Much of regulation applies specifically to the insurance contract.

Contract
A legally enforceable agreement between two or more parties.

Legislatively prescribed insurance contracts have existed since 1873, when Massachusetts adopted the first standard fire policy. Since then, all states have passed laws prescribing insurance policy provisions for nearly every kind of insurance. Many states have also enacted legislation requiring that policy wording be "simple and readable."

Elements of a Contract

An insurance contract, called a **policy**, is an agreement between the insurer and the insured. An insurance policy must meet the same requirements as any other valid contract.

Policy
A complete written contract of insurance.

If a dispute arises between the parties to a contract, a court will enforce only valid contracts. The validity of a contract depends on the following four essential elements:

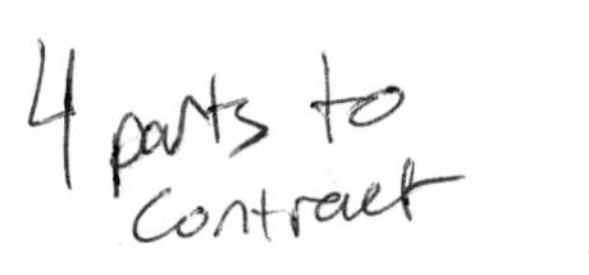

1. Agreement (offer and acceptance)
2. Capacity to contract
3. Legal purpose
4. Consideration

If a court cannot confirm the presence of all four elements, it will not enforce the contract.

Agreement (Offer and Acceptance)

One essential element of a contract is that the parties to the contract must be in agreement. One party must make a legitimate offer and another party must accept the offer. In legal terms, there must be "mutual assent."

In the case of insurance, the process of achieving mutual assent generally begins when someone who wants to purchase insurance completes an insurance application—an offer to buy insurance. The details on the application describe the exposures to be insured and indicate the coverage the applicant requests.

In an uncomplicated case, an insurer underwriter (or an agent, acting on behalf of an insurer) accepts the application and agrees to provide the coverage requested at a premium acceptable to both the insurer and the applicant. The premium is the payment by an insured to an insurer in exchange for insurance coverage. At this point, agreement exists; the insurer has accepted the applicant's offer to buy insurance.

In a more complicated case, the underwriter may not be willing to meet all the requests of the applicant. One of the underwriter's options is to accept the application with modification. The underwriter may be willing to provide coverage, but only on somewhat different terms. For example, the underwriter may insist on a higher deductible than the applicant had requested. When the underwriter communicates the proposed modifications to the applicant, these modifications constitute a counteroffer. Several offers and counteroffers may be made before both parties agree to an exact set of terms. If the other essential elements of a contract exist, the mutual assent of the insurer and the applicant forms a contract.

To be enforceable, the agreement cannot be the result of duress, coercion, fraud, or a mistake. If either party to the contract can prove any of these circumstances, a court could declare the contract to be void.

Capacity to Contract

For the contract to be enforceable, all parties must have the legal capacity to make the agreement binding. In other words, each party must be legally

competent. Individuals are generally considered to be competent and able to enter into legally enforceable contracts, unless they are one or more of the following:

- Insane or otherwise mentally incompetent
- Under the influence of drugs or alcohol
- Minors (persons not yet of legal age)

However, minors are sometimes considered competent to purchase auto insurance, especially when auto insurance qualifies as a necessity. State laws vary in regard to issues involving minors.

Another aspect of legal capacity is that, in most states, an insurer must be licensed to do business in the state. If an insurer mistakenly writes a policy in a state where that insurer is not licensed, the insured might later argue that the contract is not valid and demand the return of the premium. This demand would be based on the fact that the insurer did not have the legal capacity to make the agreement.

Legal Purpose

An enforceable contract must also have a legal purpose. The courts may consider a contract to be illegal if its purpose is against the law or against public policy (as defined by the courts). For example, an agreement to pay a bribe to a government official in exchange for receiving a government job would not be enforced by the courts because such activities are against public policy.

Although most insurance policies do not involve a question of legality, certain situations do exist that may invalidate an insurance policy. Courts will refuse to enforce any insurance policy that is illegal or that tends to injure the public welfare. Insurance contracts must involve a legal subject matter. Property insurance on illegally owned or possessed goods is invalid. For example, property insurance covering illegal drugs would be illegal and therefore unenforceable. If fireworks are illegal in a particular state, then an insurance policy covering fireworks would be illegal in that state. In addition, no insurance contract will remain valid if the wrongful conduct of the insured causes the operation of the contract to violate public policy. Thus, arson by an insured would render a property insurance policy unenforceable and would preclude recovery by the insured under the policy for a building the insured intentionally burned.

Consideration

Consideration is something of value bargained for and exchanged by the parties to a contract. For example, when an auto is purchased, the buyer gives money (consideration) to the seller who, in turn, provides the car (which is also consideration).

Consideration
Something of value bargained for and exchanged by the parties to a contract.

Some contracts do not involve the exchange of one tangible item for another, but instead involve performance. For example, an author may sign a contract agreeing to write a book in exchange for payment by the publisher.

Performance can also involve a promise to perform some act in the future that is dependent on a certain event occurring. In the case of an insurance contract, the insurer's consideration is its promise to pay a claim in the future *if* a covered loss occurs. If no loss occurs, the insurer is still fulfilling its promise to provide financial protection even though it does not pay a claim. In insurance contracts, the following two types of consideration are involved:

- The *insured's* consideration is the payment of (or the promise to pay) the premium.
- The *insurer's* consideration is its promise to pay claims for covered losses.

Special Characteristics of Insurance Contracts

In addition to having the four essential elements of all contracts, insurance contracts have certain special characteristics. An insurance policy is all of the following:

- A conditional contract
- A contract involving fortuitous events and the exchange of unequal amounts
- A contract of the utmost good faith
- A contract of adhesion
- A contract of indemnity
- A nontransferable contract

Conditional Contract

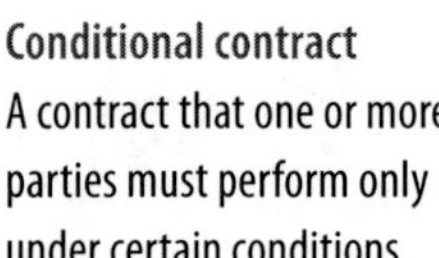

Conditional contract
A contract that one or more parties must perform only under certain conditions.

An insurance policy is a **conditional contract** because one or more of the parties must perform only under certain conditions. Whether the insurer pays a claim depends on whether a covered loss has occurred. In addition, the insured must fulfill certain duties before a claim is paid, such as giving prompt notice to the insurer after a loss has occurred.

A covered loss might not occur during a particular policy period, but that fact does not mean the insurance policy for that period has been worthless. In buying an insurance policy, the insured acquires a valuable promise—the promise of the insurer to make payments if a covered loss occurs. The promise exists, even if the insurer's performance is not required during the policy period.

Contract Involving Fortuitous Events and the Exchange of Unequal Amounts

While noninsurance contracts involve an exchange of money for a certain event, such as the provision of goods or services, insurance contracts involve

an exchange of money for protection upon the occurrence of fortuitous events. A **fortuitous event** is an event occurring by chance. Insurance contracts involve an exchange of unequal amounts. Often, there are few or no losses and the premium paid by the insured for a particular policy is more than the amount paid by the insurer to, or on behalf of, the insured. If a large loss occurs, however, the insurer's claim payment might be much more than the premium paid by the insured. It is the possibility that the insurer's obligation might be much greater than the insured's that makes the insurance transaction a fair trade.

Fortuitous event
An event occurring by chance.

For example, assume an insurer charges a $1,000 annual premium to provide auto physical damage coverage on a car valued at $20,000. The following three situations may occur:

1. If the car is not damaged while the policy is in force, the insurer pays nothing.
2. If the car is partially damaged, the insurer pays the cost of repairs, after subtracting a deductible.
3. If the car is a total loss, the insurer pays $20,000 (minus any deductible).

Unless, by chance, the insurer's obligations in a minor accident total exactly $1,000, unequal amounts are involved in all three of these cases. However, it does not follow that insureds who have no losses—or only very minor losses—do not get their money's worth or that insureds involved in major accidents profit from the insurance.

The premium for a particular policy should reflect the insured's share of estimated losses that the insurer must pay. Many insureds have no losses, but some have very large losses. The policy premium reflects the insured's proportionate share of the total amount the insurer expects to pay to honor its agreements with all insureds having similar policies.

Contract of Utmost Good Faith

Because insurance involves a promise, insurance contracts are considered contracts of **utmost good faith**, requiring complete honesty and disclosure of all relevant facts from both parties. Both parties to an insurance contract—the insurer and the insured—are expected to be ethical in their dealings with each other.

Utmost good faith
An obligation to act in complete honesty and to disclose all relevant facts.

The insured has a right to rely on the insurer to fulfill its promises. Therefore, the insurer is expected to treat the insured with utmost good faith. An insurer that acts in bad faith, such as denying coverage for a claim that is clearly covered, could face serious penalties under the law.

The insurer also has a right to expect that the insured will act in good faith. An insurance buyer who intentionally conceals certain information or misrepresents certain facts does not act in good faith. Because an insurance contract requires utmost good faith from both parties, an insurer could be released from a contract because of the insured's concealment or misrepresentation.

Concealment
An intentional failure to disclose a material fact.

Concealment is an intentional failure to disclose a material fact. Courts have held that the insurer must prove two things to establish that concealment has occurred. First, it must establish that the failure to disclose information was intentional, which is often difficult. The insurer must usually show that the insured knew that the information should have been given and then intentionally withheld it. Second, the insurer must establish that the information withheld was a **material fact**—information that would affect an insurer's underwriting or claim settlement decision. In the case of an auto insurance applicant, for example, material facts include how the applicant's autos are used, who drives them, and the ages and driving records of the drivers. If an insured intentionally conceals the material fact that a sixteen-year-old son lives in the household and is the principal driver of one of the cars, that concealment could void the policy.

Material fact
For insurance purposes, any information that would affect an insurer's underwriting or claim settlement decision.

Insurers carefully design applications for insurance to include questions regarding facts material to the underwriting process. The application includes questions on specific subjects to which the applicant must respond. These questions are designed to encourage the applicant to reveal all pertinent information.

An insured's misrepresentation can also release an insurer from a contract. In normal usage, a misrepresentation is a false statement. In the insurance context, a **misrepresentation** is a false statement of a material fact on which the insurer relies. The insurer does not have to prove that the misrepresentation is intentional.

Misrepresentation
In insurance, a false statement of a material fact on which the insurer relies.

For example, an applicant for auto insurance is assumed to have had two speeding tickets during the eighteen months immediately before submitting the application for insurance. When asked if any driving violations have occurred within the past three years (a question found on most auto insurance application forms), an applicant giving either of the following answers would be making a misrepresentation:

- "I remember having one speeding ticket about two years ago."
- "I've never been cited for a moving violation—only a few parking tickets."

The first response provides incorrect information, and this false statement may or may not be intentional. The false statement made in the second response is probably intentional. The direct question posed in the application requires a full and honest response from the applicant because the insurer relies on the information. Anything less is a misrepresentation, whether intentional or not.

As with a concealment, if a material fact is misrepresented, the insurer could choose to void the policy because of the violation of utmost good faith.

Contract of Adhesion

The wording in insurance contracts is usually drafted by the insurer (or an insurance advisory organization), enabling the insurer to use preprinted forms

for many different insureds. Because the insurer determines the exact wording of the policy, the insured has little choice but to "take it or leave it." That is, the insured must adhere to the contract drafted by the insurer. Therefore, insurance policies are considered to be **contracts of adhesion**, which means one party (the insured) must adhere to the agreement as written by the other party (the insurer). This characteristic significantly influences the enforcement of insurance policies.

Contract of adhesion
A contract to which one party (the insured) must adhere as written by the other party (the insurer).

If a dispute arises between the insurer and the insured about the meaning of certain words or phrases in the policy, the insured and the insurer are not on an equal basis. The insurer either drafted the policy or used standard forms of its own choice; in contrast, the insured did not have any say in the policy wording. For that reason, if the policy wording is ambiguous, a court will generally apply the interpretation that favors the insured.

Contract of Indemnity

The purpose of insurance is to indemnify an insured who suffers a loss. To indemnify is to restore a party who has had a loss to the same financial position that party held before the loss occurred. Most property and liability insurance policies are contracts of indemnity. With a **contract of indemnity**, the insurer agrees, in the event of a covered loss, to pay an amount directly related to the amount of the loss.

Contract of indemnity
A contract in which the insurer agrees, in the event of a covered loss, to pay an amount directly related to the amount of the loss.

Property insurance generally pays the amount necessary to repair covered property that has been damaged or to replace it with similar property. The policy specifies the method for determining the amount of the loss. For example, most auto policies, both personal and commercial, specify that vehicles are to be valued at their actual cash value (ACV) at the time of a loss. If a covered accident occurs that causes a covered vehicle to be a total loss, the insurer will normally pay the ACV of the vehicle, less any applicable deductible.

Liability insurance generally pays to a third-party claimant, on behalf of the insured, any amounts (up to the policy limit) that the insured becomes legally obligated to pay as damages because a covered liability claim, as well as the legal costs associated with that claim. For example, if an insured with a liability limit of $300,000 is ordered by a court to pay $100,000 for bodily injury incurred by the claimant in a covered accident, the insurer will pay $100,000 to the claimant and will also pay the cost to defend the insured in court.

A contract of indemnity does not necessarily pay the full amount necessary to restore an insured who has suffered a covered loss to the same financial position. However, the amount the insurer pays is directly related to the amount of the insured's loss. Most policies contain a policy limit that specifies the maximum amount the insurer will pay for a single claim. Many policies also contain limitations and other provisions that could reduce the amount of recovery. For example, a homeowners policy is not designed to cover large amounts of cash. Therefore, most homeowners policies contain a special

limit, such as $200, for any covered loss to money owned by the insured. If a covered fire destroys $1,000 in cash belonging to the insured, the homeowners insurer will pay only $200 for the money that was destroyed.

Principle of indemnity
The principle that insurance policies should compensate the insured only for the value of a loss but should not provide a benefit greater than the loss.

According to the **principle of indemnity**, insurance policies should provide a benefit no greater than the loss suffered by the insured. That is, the insured should not be better off financially after the loss than before. Insurance policies usually include certain provisions that reinforce the principle of indemnity. For example, policies generally contain an other insurance provision to prevent an insured from receiving full payment from two different insurance policies for the same claim. Insurance contracts usually protect the insurer's subrogation rights, as discussed earlier. Other insurance provisions and subrogation provisions clarify that the insured cannot collect more than the amount of the loss. For example, following an auto accident in which the insurer compensates its insured when the other driver is at fault, the subrogation provision stipulates that the insured's right to recover damages from the responsible party is transferred (subrogated) to the insurer. The insured cannot collect from both the insurer and the responsible party.

Another factor enforcing the principle of indemnity is that a person usually cannot buy insurance unless that person is in a position to suffer a financial loss. In other words, the insured must have an insurable interest in the subject of the insurance. For example, property insurance contracts cover losses only to the extent of the insured's insurable interest in the property. This restriction prevents an insured from collecting more from the insurance than the amount of the loss he or she suffered. A person cannot buy life insurance on the life of a stranger, hoping to gain if the stranger dies. Insurers normally sell life insurance when there is a reasonable expectation of a financial loss from the death of the insured person, such as the loss of an insured's future income that the insured's dependents would face. Insurable interest is not an issue in liability insurance because a liability claim against an insured results in a financial loss if the insured is legally responsible. Even if the insured is not responsible, the insured could incur defense costs.

Valued policy
A policy in which the insurer pays a stated amount in the event of a specified loss (usually a total loss), regardless of the actual value of the loss.

Some insurance contracts are not contracts of indemnity but valued policies. When a specified loss occurs, a **valued policy** pays a stated amount in the event of a loss, regardless of the actual value of the loss. For example, a fine arts policy may specify that it will pay $250,000 for loss of a particular painting or sculpture. The actual market value of the painting or sculpture may be much smaller or much greater than $250,000, but the policy will pay $250,000 in either case. In most valued policies, the insurer and the insured agree on a limit that approximates the current market value of the insured property.

Nontransferable Contract

The identities of the persons or organizations insured are important to the insurer, which has the right to select those applicants with whom it is willing to enter into contractual agreements. After an insurance policy is in effect, an insured may not freely transfer the policy to some other party (a practice

called "assignment"). If such a transfer were allowed to take place, the insurer would be legally bound to a contract with a party it may not wish to insure. Most insurance policies contain a provision that requires the insurer's written permission before an insured can transfer a policy to another party.

Traditionally, insurance textbooks used language stating that "insurance is a personal contract" to indicate its nontransferable nature, and cited clauses in property policies to illustrate the principle. The policy language does differ between typical property and liability policies, but in both types, the intention is to prohibit the insured from transferring the policy to another party without the insurer's consent.

Interpretation of Contracts

When determining the meaning of a contract, courts review the entire contract and attempt to determine the parties' common intent. Courts assign regular meanings to contract wording. However, local language usage can modify that rule. For example, the ordinary or dictionary definition of a word might have one meaning, but local custom or usage might give the word a different meaning. The local usage applies if both parties were aware of it. If a contract uses technical words, a court would give the words their technical meaning because that is usually why the contract drafters used them in the first place.

Courts correct obvious mistakes in writing, spelling, and grammar. They also give words with two or more meanings the interpretation that makes the contract valid. All contracts incorporate existing law that affects them.

Whole Agreement

Courts interpret all parts of a contract together; they give no disproportionate weight to any particular word, sentence, or provision. Of course, the parties can specifically provide in the contract that a certain word or phrase is to be given precedence over all other provisions. However, the entire contract must be considered in arriving at its meaning and intent.

Ambiguities

Courts also construe ambiguities most strictly against the party who introduced the ambiguous term into the contract. That rule is especially applicable to insurance contracts because they are contracts of adhesion. When the language is ambiguous and the ordinary meaning is unclear, the words are construed in favor of the insured because it was the insurer who used the ambiguous language. Consequently, if a court can interpret language used in an insurance policy in two ways, then the one that allows greatest indemnity governs.

AKA favors insured

Doctrine of Reasonable Expectations

The rationale of the **doctrine of reasonable expectations** is that an insured is entitled to the coverage that may be reasonably expected under a given policy.

Doctrine of reasonable expectations
A rule of insurance contract interpretation based on the rationale that an insured is entitled coverage that may be reasonably expected under a given policy.

It also means that, to be effective, any exclusions or qualifications affecting a situation in which the insured might otherwise expect coverage must be conspicuous, plain, and clear. A policy means what a reasonable buyer would expect it to mean; that approach protects the weaker party's expectations at the expense of the stronger party's.

Parol Evidence Rule

Parol evidence rule
A rule of evidence that limits the terms of a contract to those expressed in writing.

The **parol evidence rule** limits the terms of a contract to those expressed in writing. The rule requires that, once the parties have reduced the terms of a contract to writing, parol (oral) evidence will not be admitted to vary the terms of the written instrument. The parol evidence rule, strictly speaking, is not a rule of contract interpretation but a rule of evidence. However, it is important to any contract interpretation.

In insurance cases, the parol evidence rule arises most frequently because of policy ambiguities. For example, a property policy covered "tanks and structures" at a specified premises. Tanks were located both inside and outside the building. The policy contained a coinsurance clause, and if all the tanks were included, a coinsurance penalty would apply. The insurer took the position that "tanks" was an all-inclusive term.

The court, however, permitted parol evidence to determine that the parties intended to include only inside tanks in determining the values for coinsurance purposes. The court made this determination under an exception to the parol evidence rule, which allows parol evidence to show the parties' intentions when the terms of a written contract can have more than one interpretation or when the provisions are unclear.

Assignment

Assignment
A written transfer of a contract interest from one party to another.

Assignment is a written transfer of a contract interest from one party to another. Under current assignment rules, both rights and duties may be assigned under a contract unless it is a personal contract. Traditionally, the insurance contract has been a personal contract. An insured cannot assign its coverage because the insurer has a right to know, and an interest in knowing, who is being insured. The insurer might be willing to insure one person and unwilling to insure another for numerous reasons. A property insurance contract is a contract created to indemnify the named insured against loss and does not attach to the property. Therefore, selling the property does not automatically transfer the seller's insurance to the buyer. A contract of insurance is so peculiarly personal that neither party can assign rights under the policy without the other's consent.

In addition to the common-law rule applying to assignment, practically all property and liability policies specifically prohibit assignment without the insurer's consent. In some such clauses, any assignment without the insurer's consent renders the policy void, and in others the assignment is considered invalid.

Although a majority of courts still adhere to the "personal contract—nonassignment" concept, a growing body of law agrees that if the risk is unchanged and the insurer concedes that it would have routinely approved the assignment if it had known of it in advance, then the assignment does not void the policy. That concept is based on the doctrine of reasonable expectation and the doctrine of purpose.

Discharge of Contracts

Contracts can be discharged in the following five ways:

1. Performance—The contract's terms are completed.
2. Breach—One or more of the parties does not perform as required.
3. Impossibility—For some reason the contract cannot be completed.
4. Operation of law—Rules of law operate to discharge the contract.
5. Agreement—Parties agree to terminate a prior contract.

Performance

The first way a contract can be discharged is by performance. It is important to distinguish between performance that discharges both parties from their rights and liabilities and performance that discharges only one of the parties.

If both parties fully perform all contracted conditions or promises, nothing further needs to be performed under the contract. However, if the contract consists of a promise for a promise, and if only one party performs the contract by carrying out its promise, the other party is not discharged. The contract is still in existence and must be discharged in one of the other ways.

Property insurance policies are usually discharged by performance. Included within the term "performance" as used here is policy expiration, because that constitutes full performance under the contract. Performance by the insurer by payment of either partial or total loss does not necessarily discharge the policy. Sometimes a total loss, in the absence of any contract provision, does discharge the policy. However, almost all policies have "loss clauses" or "automatic reinstatement clauses" that reinstate the policy to its full limit again after a loss. Thus, performance is completed only when the property insurance policy has expired.

Most liability policies are also discharged by performance. In those policies, performance could be completing the policy period without any claim, incurring a potential claim requiring a defense of the insured, or incurring a claim that requires payment to a third party. Here again, the payment of a claim, even up to the policy limit, does not discharge the contract.

Normally, if a loss does not occur, the only action the insured needs to take to discharge the contract is to pay the premium. However, when the policy is written on a deposit, advance, or provisional premium basis, the provision for the premium adjustment at the end of the policy term forms part of the entire

contract. The contract, therefore, is not discharged until the insurer completes this premium adjustment and the insured pays the amounts due to the insurer or the insurer pays any return premium to the insured.

Breach

Breach of contract
The failure of a party to a contract, without legal excuse, to perform all or part of the contract.

Another way a contract can be discharged is by a breach. A breach of the contract by one of the parties generally discharges the other party. A **breach of contract** is the failure of a party to a contract, without legal excuse, to perform all or part of the contract. If one party informs the other of an intention not to perform some or all of the contract and in fact does not perform it, the other party is excused from any further performance and can sue immediately for breach of contract. A voluntary act making performance of the contract impossible also constitutes a breach. For example, if A agrees to sell a rare book to B for a sum of money and then sells it to C before delivery to B is due, B is entitled to sue A immediately for breach of contract.

A breach of an insurance contract, like any other contract, involves non-performance by one of the parties. However, because of the nature of the contract and the fact that it normally continues in effect until expiration, breach of an insurance contract has some special connotations.

As discussed, payment of the premium, in the absence of a policy condition, does not have to occur to create a binding insurance contract. Therefore, nonpayment does not constitute a breach unless the policy states otherwise. To put the other party in default, the insurer must request payment or must take an affirmative step to cancel the policy pursuant to its conditions.

Breaches of contract by insureds usually involve fraud, misrepresentation, or concealment rather than nonpayment of premium.

At common law, any contract, including an insurance contract, is breached by the fraud of one of the parties. The elements of common-law fraud are as follows:

- Misrepresentation of a fact
- Materiality of the fact misrepresented
- Knowledge or reckless indifference that the representation was false
- Intent to deceive
- Justifiable reliance of the other party on the representation
- Resulting damage sustained by the other party

In the absence of statutory language or policy language defining fraud, all of the foregoing elements must be proven before the innocent party can avoid the contract. Statutes in some states have defined fraud differently from common-law fraud. The specific fraud clause contained in most policies also modifies the common-law definition.

Some state statutes provide that misrepresentation, omission, or incorrect statements do not prevent recovery unless they were material to the insurer's acceptance of the risk. That is, the insurer would not have written the policy

if it had known the facts. In some respects, that type of statute is stricter than the common law because it permits the insurer to void the contract when the insured makes misstatements, even if made in good faith and without knowledge of falsity.

Fraud in insurance contracts also differs from fraud in other contracts in that the insurer frequently invokes fraud after the fortuitous event under the contract has occurred. For example, if an insured willfully and fraudulently lists property not possessed or not damaged in a proof of loss statement or if the insured places a false or fraudulent value on the property listed, then the insurer can treat that act as a breach that discharges the contract.

With liability policies, misrepresentation or concealment are the usual grounds for claiming a breach rather than fraud. A misrepresentation in insurance law can be either an oral or written statement, and, as discussed previously, the fact must be material. Misrepresentation voids the contract, regardless of the intent with which the insured made it. The insurer needs to show only that the misrepresentation was false and material in that it changed the nature, extent, or character of the risk. Essentially, the question is whether the insured misled the insurer, and by doing so, affected the insurer's underwriting and policy decisions.

The law does not require the insurer to determine the truth of representations made to it. In other words, failure to recheck the correctness of the applicant's statements does not prevent the insurer from pleading misrepresentation. On the other hand, the applicant for insurance has no duty to volunteer information that the insurer does not request. Thus, for example, the applicant has no duty to advise an insurer of a potential lawsuit incurred before the insurer issued the policy if the insurer does not ask for this information.

In insurance, concealment is misrepresentation by silence. The insurer has a duty to inquire about matters it believes to be material to the risk, and the applicant is entitled to a presumption that information not requested is not material. Consequently, when the insurer has not inquired about a matter the applicant has allegedly concealed, the insurer can void the policy only by proving that the concealment was material and that the concealment was intentional and fraudulent.

Another kind of breach is breach of warranty. A **warranty** is a written or oral statement in a contract that certain facts are true. In insurance law, a warranty is a statement made by an insured that a certain situation relating to the risk exists or that some act relating to the risk will be performed. For example, an insured might warrant that the building to be insured is protected by an automatic sprinkler system. The stated situation must be true; likewise, any act the insured is to perform must be done. If not, the policy is void, regardless of whether there is any connection between the warranted action and the loss. An insured must comply with any warranties before being able to file suit on the policy.

Warranty
A written or oral statement in a contract that certain facts are true.

Most states' statutes essentially provide that all statements in any application made by or on behalf of an applicant or insured are considered representations,

not warranties. If courts treated all statements as warranties, any misstatement would void the policy regardless of how material it was to the risk. If a statement is treated as a representation, then the statement voids the policy only when it is material to the risk assumed.

Impossibility

In addition to performance and breach, a contract can be discharged by impossibility of performance. If an event occurring after contract formation is not the promisor's fault, and if the event renders objective performance impossible, the obligation of performance is removed. For example, either death or disability of the promisor in a personal service contract discharges that party's obligation.

Normally, impossibility of performance is not a factor in the discharge of insurance contracts. One exception is if the insurer becomes insolvent and is therefore unable to perform its part of the contract. Usually, a conservator takes over the insurer and operates much like a trustee in bankruptcy. The insured's rights, such as receiving payment for claims covered under the policy, would then be similar to a creditor's rights in a bankruptcy case. All states have created guaranty funds that make good, to a varying extent, on the promises of an insolvent insurer so far as claims are concerned.

Normally, bankruptcy does not discharge insurance contracts because the insured has already performed by paying its premium, and the admitted insurer can usually liquidate its assets to pay claims. Nonadmitted insurers do not benefit from state guaranty funds. If the assets of an admitted insurer are insufficient to pay its claims, a guaranty association pays the claims as mentioned previously. In addition, most liability policies protect third-party claimants by providing that bankruptcy of the insured does not release the insurer from liability. For advance premium policies, if additional premium is due and the insured is bankrupt, then the insurer has a claim like any other creditor. However, the insurer may cancel the policy for nonpayment of premium should this occur.

Operation of Law

A fourth way a contract can be discharged is by operation of a law; that is, the provisions of a law serve to discharge the contract. That possibility might occur in several ways, but the two most important are supervening illegality and bankruptcy. **Supervening illegality**, that is, passage of a law that makes the contracted act illegal, discharges performance unless the contract contemplated assumption of that risk.

Supervening illegality
Passage of a law that makes performance of a contract illegal, thus discharging its performance.

Agreement

A fifth way for a contract to be discharged is by agreement. Types of agreements include the following:

- *Termination provisions*. In the original agreement, the parties can stipulate that if a certain event occurs or does not occur within a given time, then

the contract will be terminated. The happening or nonhappening of the stated event automatically discharges the contract. Insurance contracts might contain several conditions that discharge the contract. The expiration date is one such condition, that is, the arrival of the expiration date terminates the contract. Although it is not usually so stated, this condition is implied in the contract. Another such condition is the cancellation clause, a discharge condition, which permits either party to terminate the contract. Also, certain policies provide that they become void if assigned, so an unauthorized assignment discharges them.

- *Rescission.* The parties can also agree to rescind a prior contract. **Rescission** is the complete unmaking of a contract. The subsequent contract must have all of the elements of a valid contract, including independent consideration. The parties to insurance contracts seldom use contractual rescission.

Rescission
The complete unmaking of a contract.

- *Novation.* **Novation** is an agreement to replace an original party to a contract with a new party. In insurance, novation usually arises in cases of assignment, when the insurer agrees to accept the assignee as the insured in place of the assignor.

Novation
An agreement to replace an original party to a contract with a new party.

- *Accord and satisfaction.* The parties may substitute a different type of performance for the performance required under the original agreement. **Accord** is an agreement to substitute performance other than that in the contract, and **satisfaction** is the carrying out of that agreement. Accord and satisfaction are the basis of many loss settlements. If the amount due under the contract or the insurer's liability is disputed and the parties reach an agreement settling these points, this constitutes an accord and satisfaction.

Accord and satisfaction
An agreement (accord) to substitute performance other than that required in a contract and the carrying out of that agreement (satisfaction).

Remedies to a Breach of Contract

When a breach of contract occurs, several remedies are available to the injured party. The following are the available remedies:

- Damages
- Specific performance
- Rescission
- Declaratory judgment
- Summary judgment
- Reformation

Damages

The payment of damages is a remedy for a breach of contract. The primary obligation of an insurance contract is the payment of money. The general rule at common law is that the damages for breach of a contractual obligation should cover the amount due plus interest. In insurance contracts, that general rule limits the amount recoverable as specified by policy provisions. In recent years, courts have been permitting additional recoveries for breach of insurance contracts, such as compensatory damages and punitive or exemplary damages. A contract might also provide for liquidated damages.

Compensatory damages
A payment awarded by a court to indemnify a victim for actual harm.

Compensatory damages are awarded to indemnify a victim for actual harm. They may include payment for out-of-pocket expenses, loss of time, mental suffering, attorney fees, and similar expenses not covered under the policy provisions but deemed necessary to fully compensate the insured. Those damages are sufficient to put the injured person in the same situation as if the insurer had performed the contract. The damages must be those directly resulting from the breach and readily foreseeable as a natural result of the breach.

Punitive damages, or **exemplary damages**
A payment awarded by a court to punish a defendant for a reckless, malicious, or deceitful act or to deter similar conduct; need not bear any relationship to a party's actual damages.

A court levies **punitive damages**, or **exemplary damages**, to punish a defendant for a reckless, malicious, or deceitful act or to deter similar conduct. Punitive damages need not bear any relationship to a party's actual damages.

Two common questions arise relating to compensatory and punitive damages in insurance:

- Whether an insured's liability policy covers punitive damages

- Whether an insurer that has acted improperly in claim settlement is liable for compensatory or punitive damages over and above the contractual limit of liability

Liquidated damages
A reasonable estimation of actual damages, agreed to by contracting parties and included in the contract, to be paid in the event of a breach or for negligence.

In certain cases, a contract specifies liquidated damages, the amount to be paid in the event of default. **Liquidated damages** are a reasonable estimation of actual damages, agreed to by contracting parties and included in the contract, to be paid in the event of a breach or for negligence. They are specified when computing the actual damages would be difficult or impossible. A court will enforce a liquidated damages clause as long as the amounts are reasonable and are not so large as to constitute a penalty.

Liability insurance raises special issues. Most courts recognize that the rights of an insured go deeper than the surface of the written contract. These courts rule that if a liability insurer acts in bad faith and fails to settle a claim against the insured within policy limits, the insurer will be liable for the total amount of the judgment because the insurer, not the insured, has the right and duty to control the claim. The excess amount over the policy limit is considered compensatory damages.

Some courts hold an insurer liable for the amount of the final judgment as compensatory damages any time the insurer has received an offer to settle within the policy limits and has rejected it, regardless of whether bad faith was involved.

These courts reason that every contract of insurance has an implied covenant of good faith and fair dealing that prevents either party from doing anything to injure the other's rights. An insurer's refusal to settle a claim when it would be in the insured's interest to do so constitutes a breach of that implied covenant and is grounds for compensatory damages.

To justify an award of punitive damages, an insurer must be guilty of oppression, fraud, or malice. The insurer must have acted with the intent to injure or annoy the insured and with conscious disregard of the insured's rights. For example, an insurer might pay an insured under a disability policy for several

years and then stop payments because of an alleged preexisting condition. Also, an insurer's bad-faith refusal to make payments under the policy, coupled with false and threatening communications to the plaintiff designed to force him to settle his claim disadvantageously, is essentially tortious in nature and could be the basis for punitive damages.

In property insurance, a significant number of courts have now adopted the opinion that an insurer's failure to perform its implied obligation to pay an insured's claim in good faith constitutes a tortious breach of the implied covenant of good faith and fair dealing. That breach allows recovery of compensatory and punitive damages.

For example, an insured who had suffered a substantial fire loss advises the insurer that he is in desperate need of funds to settle financial problems. Over two years, the insurer makes no offer to settle, although coverage was obviously afforded by the policy. This conduct amounts to heedless disregard of the consequences, malice, gross fraud, and oppressive conduct likely sufficient to support an award of punitive damages.

Specific Performance

In the usual contract case, the injured party is entitled to money damages only. In some situations, money damages alone cannot compensate insureds for their losses. Another remedy to a breach of contract is **specific performance**, a court-ordered equitable remedy requiring precise fulfillment of a legal or contractual obligation when money damages are inappropriate or inadequate. Courts might direct specific performance in two situations.

Specific performance
A court-ordered equitable remedy requiring precise fulfillment of a legal or contractual obligation when money damages are inappropriate or inadequate.

The first situation involves subject matter that is unique. A common example of a contract involving unique subject matter is one to purchase real estate. The law regards every piece of land as unique. Therefore, in a suit for breach of contract to sell land, either party can usually compel specific performance. Unique personal property, such as works of art, falls into this same category.

The second situation in which a court might direct specific performance occurs when special features of the contract make it impossible to arrive at a financial measure of damages. Examples include employment of singers, architects, and other professionals whose skills are unique. The problem is how to make them perform when they do not want to perform. The usual method is by a mandatory injunction, but this cannot guarantee the quality of the work they will eventually deliver.

Because the subject matter of an insurance contract is not unique, specific performance rarely arises as a contract remedy in insurance cases. The most common situation is a suit to compel the insurer to defend the insured under a liability policy.

Rescission

Rescission is another remedy to breach of contract. When an insurer encounters fraud or misrepresentation, the usual procedure is to cancel the policy.

However, if a claim or loss has occurred before cancellation, the insurer must start an action to rescind the contract, either as an original action or as a counterclaim. The effect of rescission is to void the contract from the beginning, thus relieving the insurer of any necessity to perform its part of the contract.

If an insurer tries to rescind after a loss has occurred, the insured will attempt to defeat it on the basis of the facts, on the basis that the insurer waived the breach, or on the basis that the insurer is estopped to assert its defense. The doctrines of waiver and estoppel extend to practically every ground on which an insurer can deny liability.

Waiver
The intentional relinquishment of a known right.

Express waiver
A statement relinquishing a right that arose because of a breach of contract.

Implied waiver
A clear, unequivocal, and decisive act by a party showing intent to waive that party's rights.

A **waiver** is an intentional relinquishment of a known right. A waiver can be either express or implied. An **express waiver** is an oral or written statement specifically relinquishing a right that arose because of the breach. An **implied waiver** occurs when a party has pursued a course of conduct that exhibits an intention to waive his or her rights. A waiver is implied only when the party performs a clear, unequivocal, and decisive act showing an intent to waive the right.

In insurance, a waiver is generally not expressed or intentional but is implied from the conduct of the insurer or its agent. The insurer must have knowledge of the breach of condition before waiving it. However, once having knowledge, the insurer must act immediately to disclaim the breach, or a court will deem the insurer to have waived it. Whether someone has waived a right depends on the facts in each case. A request for information about a loss after the expiration of a clause in the policy requiring all suits be brought within one year does not constitute a waiver of the suit clause. When an insurer has denied liability and refused to pay a claim, that action waives the policy requirement of filing a proof of loss. An insurer that has denied liability on a given ground cannot thereafter deny liability on a different ground.

In an effort to confine all waivers to the "express" type, most liability policies contain a clause reading as follows:

> Notice to any agent or knowledge possessed by any agent or by any other person shall not effect a waiver or a change in any part of this policy or estop the company from asserting any right under the terms of this policy; nor shall the terms of this policy be waived or changed, except by endorsement issued to form a part of this policy.

Most property policies have a similar clause.

Estoppel
A legal principle that bars a party from asserting a claim or right that contradicts what the party has done previously.

An **estoppel** is a legal principle that bars a party from asserting a claim or right that contradicts what the party has said or done previously. An estoppel can occur when the following three conditions are met:

- A breach of a condition of the policy occurs.
- An insurer with knowledge of the breach by its conduct leads the insured to believe the insurer continues to recognize the policy's validity and considers the insured still protected by it.
- The insured, thereby, incurs expense.

If the above conditions are met, the insurer is deemed to have waived the forfeiture of a right and is estopped from using the forfeiture as a defense. Even the act of bringing suit against the insurer is sufficient "incurred expense" by the insured to trigger this rule.

Declaratory Judgment

Parties can also seek a declaratory judgment as a remedy to a breach of contract. A **declaratory judgment** is a declaration by a court of the rights of the parties under a contract. Parties to insurance contracts, particularly insurers, frequently use this remedy to a possible contract breach. The parties can use it only when there is a question of contract construction involving no argument about the facts. An insurer may use it, for example, to determine whether it is obligated to proceed with defending its insured under a liability policy when no such obligation is stated in the contract. Of course, the insurer could merely refuse to defend, but in such cases, it might be liable for punitive damages if it turns out that the insurer did owe the insured a defense.

Declaratory judgment
A declaration by a court of the rights of the parties under a contract.

Summary Judgment

A party may also move for a summary judgment as a remedy to a breach of contract. A trial is necessary only when the facts are in dispute. A **summary judgment** (or a judgment on the pleadings) may apply in any case, including a declaratory judgment action, in which material fact is not an issue and the party making the motion is entitled to judgment as a matter of law. For example, the parties may agree on the facts, but one party questions whether the law provides a remedy, given those facts. Insurers frequently request summary judgments when the insured brings suit after expiration of a year, under a policy with a clause requiring that suit be brought within one year. That is, the insurer does not dispute any of the facts but wants the court to dismiss the action because the party bringing the action did not file suit within one year as the policy requires.

Summary judgment
A final judgment by a court, based on the pleadings and discovery in a case, that no material fact is at issue and that the party making the motion is entitled to judgement as a matter of law.

Reformation

A reformation, by which a court modifies a contract to reflect the parties' intent, is another remedy to a breach of contract. As with rescission and declaratory judgment, reformation is used only after the fortuitous event has occurred and a claim is filed under the policy. Reformation usually involves a situation in which the insurer alleges that no meeting of the minds occurred or when the insured alleges that the contract as written does not truly express the agreement of the parties.

AGENCY

Agency is a fiduciary relationship, created by contract or by law, in which one party can act on behalf of another party, the principal, and can bind that other party by words or by actions. A principal can authorize an agent to do anything that the principal might do on its own behalf. In fact, sometimes a principal can act only through an agent, such as when an organization is legally required to deal only with licensed insurance or realty agents.

Agency is a fiduciary relationship that requires the highest degree of mutual trust between the principal and the agent. There are two essential elements to every agency relationship:

1. Authority on the agent's part to act for the principal
2. Control of the agent's actions by the principal

If either of those elements is missing, there is no agency. For example, a real estate agent, A, purports to be the agent to sell P's house and enters into a contract with T. If P has not granted authority to A, then there is no agency, and the contract is not binding on P. Conversely, the mere performance of an act for another with permission does not necessarily create an agency. For example, P takes a lawn mower to A's repair shop to be repaired. A has no authority to do anything other than repair the mower. Because P has retained no control over how the repairs are to be made, the element of control is missing, and there is no agency.

Creation of Agency

Agency can be created only by the consent of the principal or by operation of law and is generally a voluntary act on the principal's part. A party acting unilaterally as a purported agent cannot create the agency relationship. The agency relationship can be created by express appointment, ratification, estoppel, or operation of law.

Express appointment
An oral, written, or expressed contract in which the principal authorizes an agent to act in the principal's behalf.

Express appointment is the most common method of creating an agency. That is, one person authorizes another to act in his or her behalf, and the second person assents to the appointment. The contract may be in writing, it may be oral, or it may arise from the conduct of the parties.

Ratification
An agency relationship created when a principal adopts the act of another who has purported to act for the principal and has neither power nor authority to perform the act for the principal.

Ratification, another way to create an agency relationship, occurs when a principal adopts an act of another who has purported to act for the principal and who had neither power nor authority to perform such an act for the principal at the time. Every act that a principal could have authorized in advance can be adopted by ratification. A valid ratification requires the following elements:

- The purported agent must have professed to have done the act for the principal.
- The principal must know all of the material facts concerning the act.
- The principal must ratify the entire act. In other words, a principal cannot ratify only the favorable parts of an act and reject the unfavorable.
- The principal must ratify the purported agent's agreement before the third party elects to withdraw from the agreement.

Ratification becomes effective when made; the ratification date does not revert to the date the agent made the contract. Ratification once made is irrevocable and generally has the same legal effect as a prior authorization.

An **agency by estoppel** is created when a principal's words or conduct cause a third party to reasonably believe that an agency exists. Estoppel[1] is another way to create an agency relationship. In those cases, the principal is estopped (prevented) from denying the agency. The underlying reason for agency by estoppel is that one should be bound by one's words and conduct if another person has materially relied on those words and conduct.

Agency by estoppel
An agency relationship created by a principal's words or conduct that cause a third party to reasonably believe that an agency exists.

Operation of law can also create an agency relationship, that is, the agency relationship is created, or implied, by existing law. Thus, even though not specified in the partnership agreement, a partnership itself confers on each partner the authority to act as an agent in the ordinary course of partnership business, and each partner accepts the corresponding liability for the acts of the other partners. Similarly, a parent has a duty to provide necessities for his or her child. If the parent fails in that duty, the child can purchase necessities on the parent's credit, and the law sees the transaction as having been made on the parent's behalf.

Operation of law
A change that occurs automatically or that is implied because of existing law.

Authority of Agents

Any acts of the agent that are within the agent's express, implied, or apparent authority bind the principal. **Express authority** is the actual authority conferred by a principal on an agent through specific instruction, including acts incidental to carrying out those instructions. In addition, an agent has implied authority to perform such additional acts as are necessary to accomplish the agency's goals. **Implied authority** is the actual authority implicitly conferred on an agent by custom, usage, or a principal's conduct indicating the intention to confer such authority. Finally, the agent can have **apparent authority**, the authority that a reasonable person could believe that an agent has to act on a principal's behalf. Therefore, an agent under an express contract to purchase an article for a principal would have the implied authority to enter into a contract to purchase it and the apparent authority to put such terms in the contract as are normally contained in such contracts of purchase. Except for an express written contract, the courts liberally construe the authority of an agent.

Express authority
The actual authority conferred by a principal on an agent through specific instruction, including acts incidental to carrying out those instructions.

Implied authority
The actual authority implicitly conferred on an agent by custom, usage, or a principal's conduct indicating the intention to confer such authority.

A third person, without actual notice or reason to believe otherwise, cannot be expected to know of any unusual limitations on the agent's express, implied, or apparent authority. Notice of a limitation on the agent's authority can be by direct information, circumstances, custom, or requirement of law. Consequently, the court would assume that a third party would know that an agent under an oral agency agreement could not enter into a contract to sell or purchase land.

Apparent authority
The authority that a reasonable person could believe that an agent has to act on a principal's behalf.

Degrees of Authority

Some agents have more power to bind their principals than other agents. The agent's powers can be as broad as the principal's so that the agent can perform any act that the principal can perform, or it can be limited.

Principals frequently authorize agents to transact their business of a particular kind, or business in a particular place. For example, corporation *P* might appoint A to transact all of its business in a given territory. To third parties, A really is the corporation, although fully disclosed as an agent. Such an agent is frequently called a **general agent**.

General agent
An agent authorized to transact a principal's business of a particular kind or in a particular place.

Limited agent, or **special agent**
An agent with the power to perform specified acts only or acts limited to a particularly small, defined area.

A **limited agent**, or **special agent**, can have power to perform specified acts only or can have authority limited to a particularly small, defined area. Most employees would fall into this category. The principal authorizes them to carry out their particular jobs, but they do not have authority to act generally on behalf of their principals.

Insurance Agents and Brokers

The insurance agent is the insurer's representative, with broadly defined powers to transact their business. The courts generally consider the usual insurance agent to be a general agent. The insurer is bound by all acts within the agent's apparent authority. Agents are licensed by the states in which they work.

An insurance broker is a limited agent who has authority from a prospective insured to obtain an insurance policy. Brokers are under no obligation to place the policy with any particular insurer. Their only duty is to obtain the best possible contracts for the insureds. A broker's actions, therefore, are not binding on an insurer.

Subagents

Generally, an agent does not have the power to appoint subagents unless the agency contract allows it or unless it is necessary to carry out the object of the agency.

The authorized employment of subagents or solicitors by general agents is common in the insurance business. The general rule is that the insurer is bound by the acts or knowledge of the subagent to the same extent as though the party were a general agent. Unless the agency contract specifies otherwise, the agent is primarily liable for the acts of unauthorized subagents.

Duties of the Parties

An agency relationship imposes duties on both the agent and the principal. Courts consider the agency relationship a fiduciary relationship, even when the principal does not reimburse the agent. The agent owes full obedience to the orders of the principal, except for illegal or immoral acts. The agent is expected to use, in good faith, the utmost skill and diligence in carrying out

the agency. The agent owes a duty to account to the principal and cannot exercise dominion over the principal's property, for example, by putting the principal's money in the bank solely in the agent's name. Also, the agent cannot use information obtained in the principal's business for personal gain beyond that intended under the agency relationship.

Because of the fiduciary relationship, the agent can represent only one party in a transaction unless both parties knowingly consent to having the agent act for both of them. Any contract made by a person acting as agent for both parties without the permission of both can be voided by any party that was unaware of the dual representation. The usual insurance transaction does not violate that principle because the agent represents only the insurer and not the insured. It is sometimes said that the insurance agent owes a fiduciary duty to the insured, but this responsibility arises out of public policy considerations rather than out of an agency relationship.

Principals also have duties to their agents. The first obligation of the principal is to compensate the agent. However, unless the contract provides otherwise, the agent is not entitled to remuneration until the objective of the agency has been fully accomplished. The principal also owes a duty to reimburse the agent for any necessary expenses incurred in carrying out the agency. If a third party sues the agent in connection with a contract or other activities entered into by the agent on behalf of the principal, the principal is bound to indemnify the agent for any liability incurred. The principal is not bound to reimburse the agent for liability incurred for acts that were unauthorized or illegal, even though the principal might be liable to others for such acts.

Liabilities to Third Parties

Unintended liabilities to third parties can arise because of an agency relationship. The principal is liable for all acts of the agent, including illegal acts committed in carrying out the purpose of the agency, provided they were within the scope of the agent's authority. This is so even if the acts directly violated express instructions from the principal. For example, when the terms of the agency contract require the agent to notify the insurer before entering into any contract, a binder issued by the agent is valid and binding on the insurer even when the agent did not give the insurer prior notice.

Even though liable to the third party under the contract, the principal still has a right of action to recover from the agent for a loss resulting from an unauthorized act. For example, an insurer tells its agent not to renew a policy, but the agent disregards the instruction and renews it. Although the insurer is liable to the insured for a subsequent loss, the insurer can recover that loss amount from the agent.

Any information acquired by an agent is imputed to the principal. Thus information acquired by an insurance agent can estop the insurer from asserting a defense. For example, an agent has visited insured property on several occasions over a five-year period. The insurer wants to void the policy, asserting a

business occupancy on the property violates the policy. The insurer is estopped from voiding the policy because the agent's knowledge of the occupancy, acquired during visits to the site, is imputed to the insurer. The insurer is considered to have consented to the business occupancy.

The principal is not liable to third parties when the agent has completely departed or deviated from the agency purpose. In such a case, the agent becomes primarily liable because the element of the principal's control is missing. It is hard to tell when the acts of the agent are private acts and when they are for the principal's benefit. Actions are within the scope of the agency if the agent, in performing the act, was motivated, at least in part, by a desire to serve the principal and if the act was not an extreme deviation from the normal conduct of an agent in similar circumstances. For example, an agent's interpretation of coverage under the policy binds the insurer when the interpretation does not blatantly conflict with the policy condition even though the condition might not be legally ambiguous.

The agent is ordinarily discharged from any contractual liability when acting for a disclosed principal. However, suits by third parties against principals often also name the agent because of the possibility of limitations on the agent's authority or other factors. An agent who has acted properly is entitled to indemnification from a principal in such situations.

A court can hold an agent who acted for an undisclosed or partially disclosed principal primarily liable on the contract. The agent could then take action against the undisclosed principal for indemnification.

Agents are individually liable for torts they commit against third parties, even if committed within the scope of the agency. That liability is in addition to the liability of the principal for such acts. The agent is also primarily liable for the acts of subagents. If the principal is also held liable, the principal would be entitled to recover damages from the agent.

Termination

An agency relationship can be terminated or discharged in the same manner as a contract. So agreement of the parties or the accomplishment of the purpose of the agency can terminate an agency. The lapse of time can also terminate an agency. That time might be stated in the agreement; if not, it will be a reasonable time, depending on the circumstances. Because agency is a personal relationship, the incapacity of either party, such as by insanity or death, terminates it. A breach of the agency contract, such as revocation of authority by the principal or renunciation by the agent, can terminate an agency relationship. Because of the personal nature of the relationship, the principal has the power to revoke the agent's authority at any time, even though the agent might sue the principal for breach of contract.

Auditors as Agents of Insurers

The authority of a premium auditor to act as an agent of an insurer depends to some extent on the relationship to the insurer. Generally, auditors are

either insurer employees, rating bureau employees, or independent auditing service firm employees. Courts consider an auditor who is directly employed by an insurer to have limited agency status because the insurer has the right to direct and control the auditor's actions.

The agency status of an auditor employed by a rating bureau is different. The insurer might be a member or subscriber of the bureau, but that does not necessarily make the bureau or its employees agents of the insurer. Usually, a bureau auditor examines the insured's records to test the payroll, the premium calculations, and the classifications shown on the insurer's audit report to determine that they conform to bureau filings. It can be argued that in such cases no agency relationship exists because that test audit is a policing operation contrary to the interests of, and not under the control of, the insurer. Therefore, it would appear difficult in most cases to establish a principal-agent relationship with a bureau auditor.

When an insurer retains an independent auditing service firm to conduct audits, the relationship may be considered that of an independent contractor. The independent contractor relationship is similar to an attorney-client relationship and constitutes a limited agency. Based only on the public interest nature of insurance, courts may find that an agency relationship existed.

Right of Auditor to Conduct Audit

Without a specific contract provision, the insurer and its agent are not ordinarily authorized to conduct an audit. But if such a contract provision exists, it is enforceable, and the insurer can delegate the duty to an agent. As previously mentioned, a corporation can act only through agents, and therefore it can exercise its right to audit through an agent, including an independent auditing service firm.

It is uncertain whether bureau auditors have the right to conduct an audit because they are not agents of the insurer. However, this would be an issue only in workers' compensation insurance, and the audit provision of that policy provides that insurance rating bureaus have the same rights as the insurer to audit the insured's records.

Authority of Auditor to Bind Insurer

The authority of an auditor employed by the insurer to bind the insurer is governed by the general rules of the agency previously reviewed. The auditor has the power to bind the insurer on any matter within the auditor's apparent authority. This is so even if the auditor, acting on behalf of the insurer, has information that the insurer does not have. For example, if an auditor sent by an insurer to perform an audit incidentally acquires knowledge about the insured's operations, that would not necessarily impute that knowledge to the insurer. In the absence of a showing that such knowledge was within the auditor's authority, an auditor's knowledge about a change in the personnel of the insured partnership is not imputed to the insurer. In general, a bureau auditor has no authority to bind the insurer.

Alteration of Contract by Auditor

Under the general rules of agency and the contract provisions requiring the insurer's written permission to alter the policy, the auditor has no authority to alter an insurance contract. However, as reviewed previously, an alteration can be accomplished by waiver or estoppel in certain situations.

Hypothetically, an auditor could alter the books and records provision of a policy because this provision is in the auditor's field of authority. There are no cases on that point specifically, but cases involving similar agency situations might apply. When the insurer or its agent approves the system of bookkeeping employed by its insured, the insurer cannot later evade liability because of an unsuitable or faulty bookkeeping system. Therefore, it would appear that if the insured alters or modifies the requirements of the audit provision of the policy, the insurer is bound if the auditor agrees to the alteration or modification. The insurer would be estopped from later claiming that the requirements approved by the auditor did not comply with policy requirements. The same rules would also apply to auditors from independent auditing service firms.

INSPECTION AND AUDIT CONDITIONS

As explained earlier, the right of an insurer or its agent to inspect or audit the insured's premises, books, and records is not implied under the usual insurance contract. The amount of the premium can be ascertained only from the contract. For a policy to require an audit, the contract must specifically provide for it, or some special condition must imply the insurer's right to audit.

Normally, the premium payment constitutes contract performance by the insured. However, when the insurer writes a policy with a variable premium base, the insured's performance is not complete under the contract until the insurer computes and the insured pays the final premium. Therefore, an "advance premium" provision in a variable premium policy implies a right to audit. In practice, insurers include express audit provisions in policies they want to audit.

Rating bureau auditors do not have the same interest in the premium that the insurer has; and, therefore, they have no implied right to make an audit. However, the National Council on Compensation Insurance *Basic Manual* states: "The bureau has authority to conduct test audits and to require corrections in accordance with the results of the test audit."[2] The workers' compensation policy adopts the manual forms a part of the policy. Some of the state compensation bureaus have similar provisions that go even further and permit bureaus to conduct an audit at any time during the policy period or within three years thereafter to promulgate changes in classifications or ratings for an insured.

Two additional factors must be considered. First, the standard workers' compensation policy contains a specific provision indicating that insurance

advisory organizations have the same rights to conduct an audit as the insurer. Second, the insurance rating laws imply such a right as a matter of public policy. Rating law articulates a perceived public policy to do the following:

1. Maintain insurer solvency
2. Protect insureds against excessive rates
3. Guard against rebates, discrimination, and favoritism

To accomplish those ends, the bureau is deemed to have the right to audit.

Recent manual rule changes have limited the rights of insurers to change rating classifications after a policy has been in force for a certain number of days. However, those limitations do not alter an insurer's right to conduct the audit and to collect the additional premium resulting from an increase in the exposure base.

Specific Policy Terms

The insurer's right to conduct premium audits depends on two separate provisions found in most policies with a variable premium base: The provision for an advance premium and the provision for a final computation according to insurer or bureau rules. The wording and detail of those provisions, as well as their locations, vary widely among policies.

The advance premium provision stipulates that the insured's initial premium payment is not final. The insurer might call the initial payment an advance or an estimated, provisional, or deposit premium. Those terms help to distinguish the advance premium from the earned premium calculated at the end of the policy term. That distinction alerts the insured that the premium adjustment will occur.

The second essential provision in auditable policies describes the method of determining the premium adjustment. That provision often appears in the same paragraph of the policy as the inspection provision, which concerns the insurer's physical inspection of hazards. Separating the two essential audit provisions in many policies can be a source of confusion. Even so, explicit policy wording should leave no doubt about the insurers' right to audit. The audit provisions of the workers' compensation and general liability policies are described below.

Workers' Compensation Policy

Part Five of the Standard Workers' Compensation Policy clearly provides for an advance premium and a subsequent audit. The policy includes the following paragraph under the "Final Premium" section:

> The premium shown on the Information Page, schedules, and endorsements is an estimate. The final premium will be determined after this policy ends by using the actual, not the estimated, premium basis and the proper classifications and rates that lawfully apply to the business and work covered by this policy.[3]

Under "Audit" the policy contains the following wording:

> You will let us examine and audit all your records that relate to this policy. These records include ledgers, journals, registers, vouchers, contracts, tax reports, payroll and disbursement records, and programs for storing and retrieving data. We may conduct the audits during regular business hours during the policy period and within three years after the policy period ends. Information developed by audit will be used to determine final premium.[4]

Commercial General Liability Policy

The Common Policy Conditions for commercial insurance policies includes the following paragraph regarding "Examination of your books and records:"

> We may examine and audit your books and records as they relate to this policy at any time during the policy period and up to three years afterward.[5]

Therefore, any commercial policy that provides for an advance premium and includes the Common Policy Conditions gives the insurer the right to audit. The Commercial General Liability Coverage Form, however, is particularly explicit in the following "Premium Audit" condition:

> a. We will compute all premiums for this Coverage Part in accordance with our rules and rates.
>
> b. Premium shown in this Coverage Part as advance premium is a deposit premium only. At the close of each audit period we will compute the earned premium for that period. Audit premiums are due and payable on notice to the first Named Insured. If the sum of the advance and audit premiums paid for the policy term is greater than the earned premium, we will return the excess to the first Named Insured.
>
> c. The first Named Insured must keep records of the information we need for premium computation, and send us copies at such times as we may request.[6]

Court Interpretation of Audit Provisions

There is no question about the retrospective effect of an audit on the premium, whether the insurer's auditors, independent audit service firm's auditors, or the rating bureau's auditors conduct the audit. Court cases appear to be unanimous in that respect. The insured is liable for additional premium found due as the result of audit and reclassification by the rating bureau. That result is in accordance with the policy provision indicating that the premium stated in the declarations was estimated and, on termination, the earned premium would be computed in accordance with the rate manual. The insured cannot claim that the insurer increased the premiums without consent at the end of the policy year. The insured has consented by agreeing to policy language that permits initial payments of estimated premiums based on estimated exposure units but requires determination of actual premium based on actual exposure units at the end of policy year, after audit and with appropriate refund of payment of additional premium. The right to recover is not affected

by the fact that the insurer incorrectly computed the advance premium or by a dispute about the party responsible for the original incorrect classification. That rule applies even to third parties, such as banks that have made loans to finance premiums, if the party knew of the audit requirement or was aware of facts that made it the party's duty to inquire.

Although the policy provisions regarding the audit are fairly broad, auditors do not have complete freedom. Auditors are limited regarding the books and records that can be used, the confidentiality of those records, the time and place the audit can be conducted, and how soon the audit must be conducted.

Books and Records

Some audit provisions are very detailed about naming the books and records the auditor can review, while others are more general. The workers' compensation policy provision is probably the most complete because it includes items that otherwise might be questionable, such as tax reports. With a detailed provision, auditors should have no problems in obtaining any necessary information. However, when the policy limits the requirement to "books and records," such as in the simplified commercial lines policies, a question might arise about what records the insurer can demand.

No reported court decisions directly concern which books and records auditors can examine. The closest analogous situation involves the provisions found in fire and burglary policies regarding examination of books and records after a loss. In such policies, substantial and reasonable compliance is sufficient compliance with provisions requiring the insured to keep records in such a manner that the insurer can determine from them the amount of loss. The law entitles an auditor to review any insured's records that would enable the insurer to determine the proper premium with reasonable accuracy.

The right to review the insured's records is actually limited to verifying certain information bearing on the insurance. Having a limited license, the auditor has no right to use the information for any purpose, other than that for which it was given. The auditor should not ordinarily disclose information to any person other than the insurer.

It can also be argued that much of the information available to an auditor could be labeled a trade secret, which, by accepted legal definition, includes business information that would give competitors an opportunity to obtain an advantage over competitors that do not have the information. Unauthorized disclosure of a trade secret creates a liability on the part of the discloser.

The workers' compensation policy states that the insurer will perform the audit "during regular business hours." However, even in the absence of a specific provision, the courts may impose such a requirement. Most policies do not specify a place. In that case, the courts may also require that records be examined at a reasonable place. For example, an insurer could not compel an insured, and conversely, an insured could not compel an insurer, to review the records at a remote and inconvenient location.

Most commercial policies permit an examination within three years after policy expiration. No court cases have held that this period is unreasonable.

Compliance with the Audit Provision

An insured's failure to comply with the audit provision presents some problems to the insurer, because failure generally occurs after the policy term and possibly after the insurer has adjusted any losses covered by the policy. A failure occurring during the policy term is a breach of contract for which the insurer could cancel or bring an action to rescind. Courts have held that the insured's failure to produce books and records to be a valid defense for an insurer in a suit for a loss under the policy if the policy's loss settlement provision required such production. In those cases, the insurer can merely refuse to pay the claim, and the insured must then take affirmative action to recover. But when the insured refuses to permit an audit after the policy has expired, most losses have been paid, and the insurer does not have the leverage of withholding a loss payment.

Those cases can be divided into two situations: when the insured will not permit any audit and when the insured has permitted the audit but refuses to pay any additional premium.

To compel the insured to comply with the policy conditions and permit an audit, the insurer could request a court injunction. The insurer could also start an action for the premium alleging that the defendant owes the plaintiff a stated amount for premiums on insurance policies and showing numbers of policies, effective dates, and premium due. In a state in which a complaint must allege the amount of damages, starting the action for the premium would require obtaining sufficient facts from outside sources to approximate the premium owed. Under such a suit, through the discovery process, the court and the insurer would then be able to ascertain the proper additional premium.

If the insured refuses to pay an additional premium, the insurer has a valid cause of action for the additional premium. The burden is on the insurer to prove the additional amount of the premium due. The insurer cannot recover if the evidence does not show the exact amount due, pursuant to policy provisions. If the policy bases premium on total wages, the use of payrolls based on average number of employees is not admissible. The award must be based on proper evidence, and estimates or surmises about the amount of the payroll are not sufficient. When the additional premium is the result of the application of a retrospective rating plan, the insurer must show that the claims paid were reasonable and paid in good faith.

SUMMARY

Insurers have contractual rights to audit insureds if the policy has been written subject to audit. The policy constitutes a binding contract between the insurer and the insured, and the principles of contract law apply to this

relationship. Each party to the contract makes certain promises that are enforceable in a court of law.

A legal contract exists only when all the essential elements are present, including the following:

- An agreement (offer and acceptance)
- Capacity to contract
- Legal purpose
- Consideration

In insurance contracts, underwriters establish contract terms that make the transaction acceptable to the insurer. Although the fundamental principles of contract law apply, the distinctive features of insurance contracts influence contract interpretation. Insurance contracts, as distinguished from other contracts are the following:

- Conditional contracts
- Contracts involving fortuitous events and the exchange of unequal amounts
- Contracts of the utmost good faith
- Contracts of adhesion
- Contracts of indemnity
- Nontransferable contracts

All of these requirements apply to all contracts, including insurance contracts.

When a dispute arises between the parties to a contract, courts interpret the contract according to well-established rules. The court examines the entire contract to determine the intention of the parties in that context. Particularly important in the interpretation of insurance contracts is that they are contracts of adhesion; therefore, courts usually interpret ambiguities against the insurer, because the agreement was drafted by and presented to the insured on a take-it-or-leave-it basis. The unequal bargaining strength of insurers and insureds makes the utmost care on the part of insurers critical. Another rule, the parol evidence rule, prohibits the use of oral or parol evidence to modify a written agreement, although many exceptions are now made to this rule.

The rights and duties under a contract can be assigned to third parties in some cases, but limitations in this regard apply to insurance contracts.

Performance, breach, impossibility, operation of law, or agreement can discharge a contract. Although most insurance contracts are discharged by performance, they can be breached by fraud, misrepresentation, or failure to perform what was promised. The usual remedies for such breach include damages and rescission. Insureds who are sued for breach may raise the defenses of waiver and estoppel, that the insurer had waived a condition of the contract or is estopped from enforcing it. Other contract remedies—specific performance,

declaratory judgments, summary judgments, and reformation—are infrequent in insurance cases. Courts usually restrict recovery under an insurance contract to the limit of liability. However, if the insurer has acted improperly, the court might award compensatory and, possibly, punitive damages to the insured.

Rather than enter into the contract directly, either party can act through an agent. An agency requires authority for the agent to act on behalf of the principal and requires control of the agent's actions by the principal. Although the degree of authority depends on the situation, the agent owes the principal full obedience, and the principal is liable for all authorized acts of the agent. Premium auditors are the insurer's agents, exercising the insurer's contract right to audit the insured's records.

The right to audit is explicitly included as a contract condition in most policies with a variable premium base. The wording varies considerably among policy forms, but a provision for an advance or estimated premium and a stipulation about the calculation of the final earned premium at the end of the policy term together constitute a right to audit. The insurer is then entitled to the proper premium even if the insurer calculated the advance premium incorrectly. The right to audit can cover virtually any of the insured's records relating to the insurance premium, but it is limited by the duty of confidentiality as well as by the requirement that the audit occur at a reasonable time and place and within a stated time. If the insured fails to comply with the audit provision, the insurer can bring suit, but the burden is on the insurer to prove the amount of premium due. An understanding of the legal context of premium auditing provides a framework within which the auditor can plan the audit.

CHAPTER NOTES

1. Technically, estoppel does not create an agency, but it only prevents the third party from suffering a loss that would result if the principal successfully denied the agency. The practical legal effect, however, is the same to the third party as if the principal had appointed the agent.
2. *Basic Manual for Workers Compensation and Employers Liability Insurance*, Copyright, National Council on Compensation Insurance, 1999, Effective January 1, 2000, page AA2 of Appendix A, IV.
3. Workers Compensation and Employers Liability Insurance Policy, WC 00 00 00 A, Part Five–Premium, Clause E, Page 5 of 6, Copyright, National Council on Compensation Insurance, Inc., 1991.
4. Workers Compensation and Employers Liability Insurance Policy, WC 00 00 00 A, Part Five–Premium, Clause G, Page 5 of 6, Copyright, National Council on Compensation Insurance, Inc., 1991.
5. Common Policy Conditions, Clause C, IL 00 17 11 98, Copyright, Insurance Services Office, Inc., 1998.
6. Commercial General Liability Coverage Form, CG 00 01 12 04, Section IV, 5, page 12 of 15, Copyright, ISO Properties, Inc., 2003.

Direct Your Learning 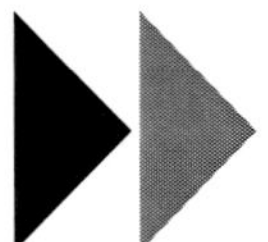

Premium Audit Planning

Educational Objectives

After learning the content of this chapter and completing the corresponding course guide assignment, you should be able to:

- Evaluate the justification for a premium audit, given a particular situation.
  - Describe the possible approaches to determining the earned premium on policies subject to audit.
  - Describe the factors an insurer must consider in determining which policies to audit.
  - Describe the circumstances in which a premium auditor's visit to the insured's premises might be useful for reasons other than the determination of earned premium.
- Describe the factors a premium auditor should consider and the steps a premium auditor should take in scheduling an audit.
- Given a case, apply the steps a premium auditor should take in preparing for a premium audit.
- Analyze an insurance policy according to a systematic procedure.
- Describe the various sources of information that premium auditors can use in planning a premium audit.
- Given a case, compile information concerning the insured for use in a premium audit.
- Define or describe each of the Key Words and Phrases for this chapter.

OUTLINE

Develop Your Perspective

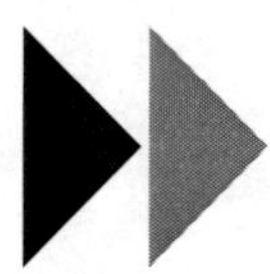

What are the main topics covered in the chapter?

Effective planning by a premium auditing department increases the efficiency and effectiveness of the tasks staff members must do to complete the premium adjustments on all insurance policies subject to audit.

Identify the complications that might occur with variations from a regular premium audit.

- When might a premium audit be waived or a voluntary report be requested?
- When might an auditor make a preliminary visit to an insured before the regular premium audit?
- What considerations may be evaluated in scheduling a premium audit?

Why is it important to learn about these topics?

Combined with the knowledge of a premium auditor's own company policies, procedures, and requirements, an auditor must schedule appointments for auditable policies and plan those audits with confidence.

Consider why proper planning is essential in premium auditing.

- What are the steps that should be taken in planning a premium audit?
- Why is it important to understand the insurance policy when preparing for a premium audit?
- Why is it important to plan an audit?

How can you use what you will learn?

Evaluate your own organization's audit requirements.

- What is the nature of change in operations in your organization?
- What classifications will be involved?
- What records will be needed?

Premium Audit Planning

An insurance contract is executed when the final premium is paid. If the insurer writes the policy with a variable premium base, the premium audit department is responsible for completing the premium adjustment. Because of the volume of policies processed and the time required for each premium audit, carrying out that responsibility requires careful planning.

The premium planning process encompasses two broad areas. The first area covers the period before an insurer assigns a policy for field audit and might be thought of as audit management planning. The second area covers the field auditor's preparation for the audit visit. In both areas, planning minimizes nonproductive auditing time and uses the auditing staff most effectively.

Efficiently managing the audit function requires understanding the benefits and limitations of several possible approaches. At this stage in the process, the audit department also interacts with other departments that might ask for assistance. That cooperation among departments contributes to the insurer's overall success.

A premium auditor can increase the likelihood of a successful audit through careful and thorough planning before examining the insured's records. Premium auditors can apply the specific techniques and procedures discussed in this chapter to facilitate this audit planning process.

AUDIT DEPARTMENT RESPONSIBILITIES

Planning an insurance premium audit begins when the audit department receives notice that the insurer has written a policy with a variable premium base. If the underwriter sees a need for a pre-audit survey for a policy, the underwriting department notifies the audit department. Some insurance companies set a minimum premium threshold for a pre-audit survey. Every new policy with a variable premium base that exceeds this threshold is assigned for a pre-audit survey. However, not all pre-audit surveys are initiated by the underwriting department. The premium audit department may also have specific criteria established for determining when a pre-audit survey will be conducted.

The premium auditor conducts a pre-audit survey early in the policy period to gather information, ensure that classifications and loss exposures are correctly identified, and assist the insured in proper recordkeeping. A pre-audit survey can also resolve procedural questions, secure additional information for underwriters, and confirm the adequacy of deposit premiums, thereby reducing the possibility of large premium adjustments at expiration.

If a pre-audit survey is not needed, the method of notifying the audit department about a policy with a variable premium base varies, depending on whether the insurer issues its policies electronically or manually. With a manual system, the audit department receives either a copy of the policy or some other notice of coverage when the underwriting department issues the policy. The audit department then establishes a diary system to have the policy assigned for audit at policy expiration. The audit department's major responsibilities during the policy period include receiving and filing policy copies and endorsements, handling inquiries, and preparing the policies for premium adjustment and final billing.

With an electronic system, the audit department receives computer notification before the policy expires or is canceled. The premium audit department need not maintain a paper copy of the policy because any information needed can be accessed electronically when necessary to conduct the audit. Therefore, the audit department does not have to know about a variable premium policy unless a pre-audit survey has been suggested or unless the insured or the producer requests assistance before the policy's expiration.

Making Premium Adjustments

After a policy written with a variable premium base expires or terminates, the audit department must complete the premium adjustment. Exhibit 3-1 is an example of a premium adjustment issued after an audit has determined the correct earned premium. Because conducting a field audit on every policy is impracticable because of the expenses involved, the audit manager must decide which one of the following is most appropriate at the premium adjustment stage:

- Waive the audit
- Request a voluntary report (either manual or electronic) from the insured
- Conduct a telephone audit
- Make an office adjustment
- Conduct a field (physical) audit

The percentage of auditable policies on which insurers actually conduct field audits varies considerably by insurer and by the type of business the insurer writes.

EXHIBIT 3-1

Statement of Premium Adjustment

STATEMENT OF PREMIUM ADJUSTMENT

NAME AND ADDRESS OF INSURED	NAME AND ADDRESS OF COMPANY	
Country Estate Construction Company 546 Bellbrook Road Easton, Maryland 21601	Chesapeake Casualty Company Chesapeake Square Baltimore, MD 21201	
NAME AND ADDRESS OF AGENCY	**Policy Number** WC 5678	**Kind of Policy** Workers' Comp.
Tidewater Agency 111 Main Street Easton, MD 21603	**Policy Period** 5-1-X5 to 5-1-X6	**Date** 5-25-X6
	Audit Period 5-1-X5 to 5-1-X6	**Type of Audit** Field

Code	Description/ Location	Premium Base Amount	Rate	Premium	Previously Billed	Additional Return
State 19						
5645	Carpentry—detached dwelling	$488,817	8.71	$42,576		
5606	Executive supervisors	31,600	5.45	1,722		
8742	Salespersons, outside	31,600	0.65	205		
8810	Clerical office employees, NOC	17,300	0.34	59		
	TOTAL			$44,562	$41,000 (deposit)	$3,562 Additional premium due
		Experience Mod	×	1.00 $44,562		

Waive the Audit

When the rules of the advisory organization or bureau having jurisdiction allow, an insurer might decide that performing a field audit is not necessary. If the insurer decides to waive the audit, then the premium adjustment reflects the estimated premium stated by the policy and subsequent endorsements. Advisory organizations or bureaus still might require a final audit invoice to generate the statistical information they need.

An insurer usually waives an audit based on two factors: (1) when the premium falls below a pre-established amount and (2) when the policy's rating classifications are those whose exposure bases traditionally are not very volatile. As an example of a volatile exposure base, payroll for contractors often fluctuates tremendously by year depending on the local economy, so audits are generally not waived for contractors' accounts. However, insurers should consider other factors as well in considering whether to waive an audit.

The insurer should waive an audit only after carefully reviewing the policy and its endorsements, previous audit reports, and voluntary reports from the insured. Completing any premium adjustment without performing an audit could result in an incorrect statement of the earned premium. Such errors also distort the premium information that is supplied to rating bureaus and that is used to determine insurance rates and experience modifications.

Request a Voluntary Report

Voluntary report
A policyholder's reply to an insurer's request for the information necessary to adjust the premium for an expired policy period.

If a policy premium is below the insured's established guideline for conducting a field audit, the insurer might request a voluntary report by mail or e-mail. A **voluntary report** is the policyholder's reply to the insurer's request for the information necessary to adjust the premium for the expired policy period. Some insurers call a request for such a report a "mail request," a "mail report," or even just a "voluntary."

The instructions sent with the request for a voluntary report should be relatively simple, explaining inclusions and exclusions to the classifications and the premium bases that the policyholder should report. Exhibit 3-2 is an example of a voluntary report form.

If the insurer decides to issue a premium adjustment based on a voluntary report, the following three alternatives are available:

1. Assign the policy for subsequent verification by an auditor. The insurer might consider this when the information on the voluntary report differs substantially from the estimated premium basis.
2. Assign the policy for a field audit the following year. For example, the insurer might use a voluntary report for the Year 1 policy year but might assign the Year 2 policy for a field audit. At the expiration of the Year 2 policy, the auditor would prepare a premium adjustment for that policy period. If the figures used on the voluntary report for Year 1 are comparable to the figures obtained by the auditor's examination for Year 2, the auditor might recommend accepting the prior year's premium adjustment based on the voluntary report as final. On the other hand, if the auditor discovers a material discrepancy, then some insurers insist on auditing the prior year's exposure base amounts as well and issuing a corrected premium adjustment. Other insurers believe it is more important for customer relations that a voluntary report, once accepted, stands.
3. Accept the voluntary report as reasonable and accurate and consider the premium adjustment completed.

EXHIBIT 3-2

Policyholder's Voluntary Report

POLICYHOLDER'S REPORT

Your Insurance Policy was issued on an **estimate** of the premium bases listed below. We now need the **actual amounts** so we can figure the premium. Please fill in the amounts for the period of time shown in the section called **Reporting Period**. If you have any questions **please contact your agent**. We will appreciate your response by the **due date. Thank you.**

NAME AND ADDRESS OF AGENT	NAME AND ADDRESS OF COMPANY		
Elliott B. Arnold Agency P. O. Box 1224 AGENCY CODE 3207 Atlanta, GA 30301	Spring Insurance Company P. O. Box 1000 Springton, PA 19809		
NAME AND ADDRESS OF INSURED	POLICY NUMBER WC 1234	KIND OF POLICY Workers' Compensation	
John's Sporting Goods, Inc. 1972 Olympic St. Atlanta, GA 30301	POLICY PERIOD MONTH-DAY-YEAR TO MONTH-DAY-YEAR 6-6-X5 to 6-6-X6		DATE 6-7-X6
	REPORTING PERIOD 6-6-X5 to 6-6-X6		DUE DATE 7-6-X6

CODE	DESCRIPTION/LOCATION	PREMIUM BASE	AMOUNT	RATE	PREMIUM
8017	Retail Stores N.O.C.	Remuneration		3.73 per $100	

☐ COMPLETE ☐ DO NOT COMPLETE THIS SECTION EXECUTIVE OFFICERS PARTNERS/PROPRIETORS

TITLE	NAME	SPECIFIC DUTIES	EARNINGS
			DO NOT INCLUDE IN UPPER SECTION

Who keeps your records? ____________ (NAME) Signature ____________ Title ____________

Where are they kept? ____________ (ADDRESS) Phone Number ____________ Date ____________

RETURN TO ☐ COMPANY ☐ PRODUCER

Conduct a Telephone Audit

In some cases, contacting the policyholder by telephone and requesting some information to assist in making the premium adjustment can be quicker and less expensive than inspecting or visiting the insured's premises. Telephone audits are useful when the policyholder is too far away to make an audit visit practicable or when the insurer believes that a telephone audit will secure more up-to-date and accurate information than a voluntary report. The telephone audit might also be appropriate when an insured has failed to return a voluntary report or has returned a questionable voluntary report.

Telephone audits allow the auditor to ask more questions or delve more deeply than a voluntary report does. In a telephone interview, the auditor can ask follow-up questions to clarify and expand on information given. The interviewer must obtain an accurate description of the operations and considerable detail regarding activities of the owner, partners, or officers to justify the classifications used. It is also important for the interviewer to ask about casual, contract, or subcontract labor and about any changes in operations or additions to operations over the past year. Auditors can follow up on telephone interviews with e-mail exchanges to document audit information.

Make an Office Adjustment

Office adjustment
A premium adjustment for an expired policy period based on estimates of an insured's exposure units.

In some situations, an insurer might make what some insurers call an office adjustment. An **office adjustment** is a premium adjustment for an expired policy period based on estimates of an insured's exposure units. The insurer estimates the premium adjustment rather than performing any kind of audit. Insurers sometimes use estimated figures when the insured fails to supply information necessary or does not allow access to the information or when the insurer is making short-term adjustments.

Many state insurance departments allow the insurer to adjust the estimated exposure units if an insured refuses to allow a field audit and refuses to complete a voluntary report. The insured might refuse an audit when a claim has not been paid. Also, premium adjustments frequently occur when insurers cancel policies. If the insurer has reason to believe that the estimated number of exposure units in the policy was low, the insurer can increase the number through the office adjustment and bill the insured for the additional premium.

An insured that is uncooperative about the audit might also be unwilling to pay the additional premium. The insured in that situation becomes a debtor, and the insurer uses means similar to those used by other businesses to collect funds due from borrowers. State regulations vary about whether the insurer can cancel or nonrenew the current policy when the prior term's audit is being disputed. Some states view the two policy terms as separate and stipulate that the insurer cannot cancel or refuse to renew the current term's policy for nonpayment of the premium for the previous policy period.

In some cases, an insured, after receiving a bill for additional premium resulting from an office adjustment, becomes willing to allow a field audit. With the results of the audit, the insured may willingly pay the additional premium.

The following illustrates another situation in which an office adjustment would be appropriate. The auditor has just completed an extensive trip to a rural area to complete audits. In the month after an audit, an audited policyholder submits a request to terminate its policy. If the necessary adjustment is not overly complex and the insurer does not expect the number of exposure units to fluctuate widely, the insurer (assuming state law allows it to do so) might prorate the figures from the recently completed audit.

Some states require insurers to pay any return premium within thirty days of the policy cancellation date or be subject to fine. That short period generally does not allow enough time to conduct a field audit, especially because many insurers back-date cancellations before the date the insurer actually learns of the insured's intent to cancel. That is, on January 15 an insured might return a policy for cancellation effective January 1. In this example, fifteen of the insurer's thirty days have already elapsed, limiting the insurer's ability to conduct a field audit.

Conduct a Field (Physical) Audit

If an insurer does not handle a policy written with a variable premium base in one of the preceding ways, it assigns the policy to a field auditor (or to an independent auditing service firm). Some insurers call this examination a physical audit. However, because by definition an audit involves physically examining books and records prepared by someone else, the term "physical audit" is redundant.

A field audit might also be used (1) if claim activity from classifications not shown on the policy has occurred, (2) at the insured's or producer's request, or (3) because of any unusual activity noted by the underwriting or loss control departments. A subsequent section of this chapter describes those situations in more detail.

A field audit requires considerable time and skill. Both audit managers and field auditors must plan carefully to make the best use of auditors' time. Because insurers do not audit as many small policies as they previously did, the number of field audits has decreased in recent years, while the average size of an audited account has increased. In a 2001 survey conducted by the Premium Audit Advisory Service (PAAS),[1] the average number of policies audited was 523 and the average billable hours was 1,438. Therefore, the average physical audit took approximately 2.7 hours to complete. The length of time varies significantly, however, depending on the complexity of the audit.

Once assigned an audit, the auditor becomes responsible for scheduling the audit appointment, determining which records should be examined, traveling to the insured's premises, obtaining and classifying the necessary information, verifying the information, and reporting the results.

In addition to insurer guidelines on when the insurer assigns a policy for a field audit, the audit manager must adhere to applicable state or bureau requirements. The following section describes those requirements.

Determining Which Policies to Audit

To remain cost effective, audit departments must screen policies carefully to determine which ones to audit. Policies selected for field audit should be those with the greatest potential deviation from the estimated premium and contemplated loss exposure. In some cases, state insurance statutes may require specific policies to be audited.

When making field audit assignments, the audit manager should consider such factors as statutory requirements, premium size, the insured's operations, prior audit experience, the type of coverage, the direct cost of the audit, geographical factors, and staff workloads and skills. Many insurers begin screening policies sixty, or even ninety, days before expiration so that they can select policies for audit and can plan accordingly.

Considerations in Determining Policies to Audit

- Statutory requirements
- Premium size
- Insured's operations
- Prior audit experience
- Type of coverage
- Direct costs of audit
- Geographical factors
- Audit staff workload and skills
- Other considerations

Statutory Requirements

Sometimes, certain regulatory requirements determine whether to perform a field audit. That is the case primarily in workers' compensation, for which regulation is generally stricter than in other types of commercial insurance, because of the compulsory nature of workers' compensation.

The rules of workers' compensation rating bureaus generally require field audits for all policies involving an annual premium above a specified amount. In some jurisdictions, policies must be audited at least once every three years, regardless of the premium amount. The bureau might allow a voluntary report if the insured submits certain payroll records (for example, unemployment payroll tax reports) to verify the accuracy of the data used to determine premium. Bureau rules in some states also limit the time during which an insurer can bill the insured as the result of the audit, generally within 180 days after policy expiration.

Workers' compensation rules also apply to filing unit reports. The Unit Statistical Plan enables insurers to convey pertinent information from the premium audit adjustment to the bureau. The classification information also shows the premium base established by the auditor and the applicable rates used to calculate the premium. Insurers can be fined for late filing and for inaccurate reports.

The information disclosed by a Unit Statistical Report filing includes the following:

- Insurer's name
- Named insured
- Policy number
- Losses experienced during the policy period by classification
- Premium charged by classification

As previously discussed, the information the insurer files with the various state workers' compensation bureaus or the National Council on Compensation Insurance serves as the statistical basis for actuarially determining rates by state and for determining the insured's experience modification. Errors in reported data can lead to errors in each of those determinations.

Field audits may also be required for the various residual market or "assigned risk" plans that provide a market for businesses that would not otherwise be able to obtain workers' compensation insurance. An employer may not be able to get insurance in the voluntary market because of failure to meet an insurer's underwriting requirements, unusually poor loss experience, adverse credit experience, and inadequate premium in relation to overall loss potential. Organizations that have uncontrollable, high-risk workplace hazards, such as mining, asbestos abatement, or police work, also go to the involuntary market.

Because businesses usually need workers' compensation insurance to operate, insurance regulators established residual market plans to make coverage available while allocating losses fairly among insurers. Such plans operate under rigid rules and describe the requirements for performing a field audit (including both a pre-audit survey and a final audit). The requirements relate to premium size, classification codes, and the insured's operations. Requirements differ between new and renewal policies. Policies for which the insurer does not conduct a field audit must have a voluntary or telephone audit performed. The insurer must maintain adequate documentation for its decisions on voluntary and telephone audits.

Residual market plans also prescribe the period following policy expiration within which an insurer must perform an audit and adjust premiums. A common requirement is that the audit be completed, billed, and recorded on the insurer's records within ninety days of policy expiration.

Premium Size

One of the major factors in determining whether to audit a policy is the amount of premium involved. Obviously, an insurer cannot afford to annually audit a policy generating a small premium. However, premium size alone should not prevent an underwriter from requesting and receiving a field audit. Certain types of coverages, classes of business, or individual insureds may necessitate an audit, regardless of premium size.

Most insurers have established guidelines specifying the premium amount requiring an audit. For example, a large insurer might require an audit on all workers' compensation policies generating an annual premium of $5,000 or more and on all general liability policies generating a premium of $10,000 or more. On small policies, the insurer might accept voluntary reports or waive the audit, but guidelines vary by insurer.

Such guidelines should be flexible allowing for specific circumstances. For example, the estimated workers' compensation premium for a recently established building contractor could be $4,500, but the actual earned premium developed by an audit could be $10,000. On the other hand, a somewhat larger account that has consistently reported its exposure bases correctly over a long period might not need an annual audit.

Insured's Operations

For several reasons, audits of contractors engaged in general construction, logging and lumbering, trucking, or home improvement require a more extensive examination of the insured's records than audits involving mercantile or manufacturing businesses. As a result of the more complicated manual provisions applicable to policyholders engaged in the former operations, the underwriter usually assigns the classifications, and the auditor confirms them at the time of the audit. In addition, many of those businesses tend to hire people who operate in the grey area between employee and independent contractor. Determining employment status and allocating the exposure base amounts among several classifications, such as construction classifications, usually require examining a large volume of records. Depending on the insured's particular operations, the audit could result in many hours of detailed work.

Insureds in any type of contracting work have traditionally had greater fluctuations in the number of exposure units than manufacturing or mercantile risks. Those fluctuations, along with the difficulty in determining if workers are employees or independent contractors, may tempt some insureds to circumvent manual rules in an attempt to pay a lower premium. Field auditors can usually detect circumvention attempts.

Prior Audit Experience

In determining the need for a field audit, the audit manager should consider the policyholder's prior audit experience. Auditors can obtain such information from the audit history or reference sheets from previous audits. An audit history sheet includes the location of the policyholder's records, if other than the policy address, directions to the records' location, and sometimes specific information about the format of the policyholder's records or special accounts that should be examined. It also contains such routine information as the names of executive officers, their corporate capacity, their compensation classification as to the type of work done, names of policyholder personnel to contact for the audit, the amount of time required for the audit, and the travel time required to reach the location of the insured's records. Occasionally,

audit history sheets disclose an auditor's treatment of audit problems the policyholder might have or references to major reclassifications of payroll that were necessary as a result of policyholder recordkeeping. The prior audit file should include information about any unusual or substantial premium changes that the previous auditor reported to the underwriter on the policy then in force. All of that information helps the audit manager determine whether a field audit on the present policy is warranted.

Because no prior audit experience is available for new business, many insurers have different guidelines for new business and for renewal business. Some insurers use pre-audit surveys for new business. The survey confirms the validity of the classifications and reinforces the insured's understanding of the audit process at policy inception rather than at the end of the first policy period. If any problems arise, the insurer can handle them immediately, not after it has provided coverage for a year. Once the insurer is satisfied about classifications, exposure amount estimates, and the insured's understanding of the audit process, voluntary reports might be appropriate.

Type of Coverage

Although insurers issue different types of policies using a variable premium base, the insurer does not audit all policies with the same frequency. For example, insurers regularly audit workers' compensation policies. On the other hand, a variety of property coverages are written with a variable premium base, and most insurers think that the full reporting clause in such policies adequately protects against underreporting. Therefore, regular audits are not necessary. Commercial general liability policies fall somewhere in between workers' compensation and property insurance policies. Most insurers consider many of the other factors described here when determining whether to audit commercial general liability policies.

Direct Costs of Audit

The insurer must balance the benefits derived from an audit against its cost. An insurer cannot afford to audit too many policies for which the audit cost exceeds any expected additional premium to be generated. However, cost alone should not prevent an underwriter from requesting an audit.

The insurer must decide if the audit's anticipated expense is likely to be less than the additional premium or additional information the insurer will probably receive. But putting a dollar figure on the additional information the auditor gathers in the field audit is very difficult. The audit department's payroll costs, including employee benefits, are the biggest expense. The cost of a field auditor's time also includes the time expended in unsuccessful audit visits, for example, when the auditor cannot contact the right people at the time of the audit. Unsuccessful audits can occur despite efforts to reduce them.

Two costs to consider, in addition to the time expended conducting the audit, are the auditor's travel time and travel expenses. Any time spent

traveling is time not spent conducting an audit and thus should be minimized wherever possible. Auditors can reduce travel time by conducting several audits while in a given area. Audit managers must also consider travel expenses such as transportation, meals, and lodging. The insurer may find it more cost-effective to hire an independent auditing service firm to conduct audits of distant organizations.

Some auditing benefits are difficult to quantify, such as the goodwill generated by the visit, the assistance provided to insureds in keeping their records properly, and the possibility that the audit will lead to a more accurate estimate of exposure units and classifications of loss exposures at policy inception. Such benefits should be considered when comparing the costs and benefits of auditing.

Geographic Factors

Geographic factors affect the decision to conduct a field audit. A geographic concentration of policyholders facilitates the audit process by reducing travel time and expenses. Often audits must be performed at addresses other than those indicated on the policy. For example, many businesses receive mail at post office boxes. Some insureds keeps their records at accountants' offices rather than on their business premises. When scheduling several audits in the same area, premium auditors should be sure their plans include the real location of the records.

To afford full-service coverage in a state or region, an insurer might write policies for insureds in remote locations or for subsidiaries of corporations located in different sections of the country, where records are located. In such cases, the insurer might either send one of its staff auditors to perform all of the audit work in that area on a quarterly basis or assign the audit to an independent auditing service firm near the location of the records or the insured. Sending auditors to remote locations is practical only if several audits are to be done. When using a staff auditor for a remote location, the insurer can monitor the number of policy expirations in that geographical area and ensure that all bureau requirements are met. Use of an independent premium auditing service may be more feasible and cost effective if only one or a very few audits are required in an area.

Many insurers are arranging for their auditors to work out of their homes rather than out of the local branch or field office. The insurers reduce their overhead by not having an office for every auditor; such offices in many cases remain unused most of the time (while the auditor is in the field). Auditors working out of their homes are generally more geographically dispersed and can often service insureds in locations remote from the branch office.

Audit Staff Workload and Skills

Assigning audits also depends on auditor availability at a given time. The insurer might have to eliminate some marginal audits (in terms of the need

for the audit) when the audit staff is short-handed. Some insurers use retired auditors to help when the workload exceeds the current staff's capacity.

Sometimes a particular auditor, by reason of overall experience or familiarity with a certain industry, might be better suited for a specific audit. Some industries, such as mining, logging, and agriculture, are unique to one region of the country. In addition, some insurers assign specialists or executive premium auditors to handle large or special types of loss exposures. Those auditors handle audits in all parts of the country.

Other Considerations

The insurer might consider the audit's cost in some situations as a public relations cost. That is, the primary benefit derived from the audit is not additional premium but goodwill. The insurer may have little chance of receiving any additional premium to recover the audit costs but may decide to conduct an audit for marketing reasons. For example, suppose a producer has promised the insured that an audit would be conducted. In order not to lose the insured's confidence, the producer asks the insurer to conduct an audit. The insurer might decide the audit is valuable from a public relations or marketing standpoint.

Another consideration in deciding which policies to field audit is the claim activity that has occurred under the policy. If claims on a policy have arisen from classifications not shown on the policy, an underwriter would likely request a field audit to determine if the insured's operations have changed since it issued the policy. Although the claims may have arisen from a one-time job, they may instead indicate a shift in the insured's operations. The underwriter needs that information to properly evaluate the loss exposure's desirability.

Additional Audit Assignments

An auditor can visit an insured for reasons other than the premium determination. The most common reason is the pre-audit survey, also called the preliminary audit, audit request, or sample audit. Unlike the premium audit itself, no fixed rules govern the pre-audit survey. Traditionally, those surveys have assisted the insured in some way relating to the eventual audit or have assisted those responsible for marketing, underwriting, credit, or claims in performing their jobs.

More recently, insurers have used pre-audit surveys as a substitute for or complement to the annual policy audit. That is, some insurers conduct pre-audit surveys when they write policies and then may request voluntary reports from insureds at the end of the policy periods. Insurers often do this because of regulations or bureau restrictions regarding changes in classifications after a policy has been in force some minimum period and because of the costs of an annual audit. The pre-audit survey is used to verify classifications and exposure unit estimates at policy inception, especially for risks with exposure

units that are not expected to fluctuate widely in number. An insurer might conduct a field audit only once every four or five years, if at all, unless the exposure units and classifications submitted raise any questions. Other insurers use the pre-audit survey for the same reasons but still conduct the annual audit at the end of the policy period.

If the insurer plans to conduct a field audit at the end of the policy period, the audit manager must be sure the premium volume generated by the policy can support both a pre-audit survey and a final audit. Consequently, pre-audit surveys are more common on policies having risks that generate a sizable amount of premium (which varies by insurer). For many insurers, conducting pre-audit surveys has become almost standard operating procedure for policies with large premium volume. In fact, the pre-audit survey has become part of the service that large policyholders expect.

Because pre-audit surveys extend beyond the responsibility of the premium adjustment, they can help to accomplish the insurer's overall goals. Audit managers must keep these goals in mind when evaluating the potential benefits from that use of an auditor's time.

In addition to audit department benefits, insurers use the pre-audit survey to provide assistance to their marketing and underwriting staffs. However, premium auditors can also be of assistance to claims, loss control, and accounting/collection/credit departments.

Marketing Assistance

Some insurers encourage their auditors to visit their producers, a practice that promotes goodwill on the behalf of the insurer. Auditors can explain any significant changes in auditing procedures that would affect the producer. As part of maintaining good producer relations and supporting the marketing function, auditors also visit prospective insureds at the request of producers.

Because conducting an audit is an insurance policy condition, a prospective insured might have questions about the audit before purchasing the policy. The producer answers most questions directly but occasionally refers insureds to the audit department if the questions are complex, or beyond the producer's expertise. Sometimes a visit from an auditor to explain audit rules and procedures can help to sell a good account.

Policyholders' questions about the manual rules and interpretations specific to their industries can be answered during an auditor's visit. For example, the auditor can explain to a prospective insured when "split" payrolls can be split and when they cannot, according to manual rules.

Prospective insureds occasionally request an auditor's visit to determine the adequacy of their records under the manual rules. A new business's public accountant can usually determine the recordkeeping requirements of manual rules. However, with the increasing complexity of insurance coverages in

recent years, a new business might need additional information about the records it should keep. Requests for an auditor's visit to discuss recordkeeping can also come from insureds that have been in business for years and have had personnel changes in their accounting department.

The premium auditor should point out to insureds when a change in accounting methods is either required to conform to the manual rules or is likely to reduce the insured's premium. However, the auditor must be aware of the costs of such a change. To avoid encroaching on the accountant's responsibility, premium auditors should limit their suggestions to records required for insurance purposes, and even then they should recognize alternative possibilities. The auditor should record in writing any suggestions made for future reference.

In addition to manual rules interpretation and recordkeeping advice, policyholders may request a meeting with the premium auditor to discuss audit procedures and to familiarize themselves with their obligations under the insurance policy. Such meetings, usually with the policyholder's insurance or accounting representative, open lines of communication between the parties, especially for complex policies covering extensive business operations. Knowing whom to contact makes it easier for the auditor to answer questions that might arise during day-to-day operations. The auditor should provide a written summary of the discussions held during those meetings, for the audit records.

Early communication between auditor and insured can also clarify the insurer's billing procedures. For example, an insurer may require monthly or quarterly voluntary reports to compute interim premium bills. Policyholders unfamiliar with those reports might request an explanation of how to prepare them.

Underwriting Assistance

Auditors also provide information and assistance to the underwriting department. The underwriter must judge whether a particular policy is likely to yield a premium proportional to the loss exposures assumed. Many considerations are involved in that decision, some within the premium auditor's area of expertise. Auditors use the pre-audit survey to confirm that the classifications and exposure unit estimates are correct.

Another underwriting consideration is whether an accurate premium adjustment is feasible for a particular policy. When the complexity of the loss exposures or information received from the producer makes an accurate adjustment unlikely, the underwriting department might request a premium auditor to visit the prospective insured as part of a pre-audit survey. The premium auditor can then determine whether the insured maintains sufficient records for an accurate premium adjustment and can help to resolve any difficult classification questions. Such a visit could also help to estimate the deposit premium's adequacy.

Accounting/Collection/Credit Assistance

Occasionally, the insurer's accounting department may request assistance from a premium auditor. For example, accounting personnel might question a policyholder's periodic report because of a seemingly inappropriate classification or faulty premium calculations. In such a case, the premium auditor's expertise can help eliminate confusion.

When an insurer or insured cancels policies midterm, regardless of the reason, an outstanding premium balance could be due. The balance could represent renewal premium deposits due or endorsement premium adjustments due. In many of those cases, the policyholder withholds payment in anticipation of the auditor's final adjustment. With outstanding premium balances on the books, not all of which are necessarily earned, the accounting department must obtain audit adjustments to clear the accounts. Consequently, the credit department frequently works with the audit department.

A disputed premium bill can be very difficult to settle. A policyholder with complete confidence in the accuracy of its records might not be able to reconcile those records with the insurer's premium computations. The insurer cannot easily resolve such a problem. When a bill has remained outstanding for over ninety days, it becomes a nonadmitted asset of the insurer, that is, the insurer can no longer show the premium as an asset on its balance sheet, according to statutory accounting rules. Premium auditors can help resolve such problems.

Many audit disputes can be resolved if the notes from the audit explain why people have been classified in the way they were, or why classes were added or deleted. Often the audit sheets are used in court when the collection matter cannot be resolved. Without documentation, the insurer may have difficulty collecting.

Sometimes as a part of their assistance to the accounting department, auditors become involved in premium fraud investigations. Many different departments can handle such investigations, depending on how the insurer is organized. Many large insurers have established separate fraud investigation divisions. Because of their knowledge of accounting, familiarity with insureds' records, and expertise in classification, auditors are important participants in those investigations.

Claim Assistance

Auditors can also assist the claim department. The claim department must assign each claim to the proper classification. When the claim department needs to verify information from the policyholder's records, a premium auditor can sometimes do so more conveniently. The claim department, for example, might question payment of benefits for accidents involving executive officers. Information from an auditor about the insurance classification of such officers can resolve those problems. If the claim department is not able to clearly determine the classification code it should assign to a particular accident in a

claim report, the auditor usually can determine the classification code because of knowledge of the policyholder's operations.

Another area in which the auditor can assist the claim department is claim auditing. A **claim audit** is an audit performed to determine the amount of loss the insurer should pay on a particular policy. An auditor's assistance might be requested in cases involving fidelity, fire, burglary, or cargo losses; contractors' installation floaters; loss of business income or rental value; coinsurance compliance, and so forth. Auditors can also verify employment status and payroll amounts for workers' compensation claims. When the claim department requests assistance, the auditor reviews the policyholder's proof of loss in light of the records and makes a report to the claim department on the validity of the claim. Some insurers assign that responsibility to claim auditing specialists.

Claim audit
An audit performed to help the claim department determine the amount the insurer should pay for a covered loss.

Loss Control Assistance

Many insurers cross-train their premium auditors in loss control activities so that they can perform relatively uncomplicated loss control inspections. Many small insureds benefit from a loss control inspection, but their operations do not warrant the time and expense of sending out a loss control specialist. The auditor assists in those cases.

Insurers may cross-train to control employee numbers by using personnel in the most efficient manner possible. Cross-training premium auditors in the basics of loss control leverages auditors' knowledge of various operations.

SCHEDULING FIELD AUDITS

After deciding which policies to field audit, as well as which other requests for an auditor's time are warranted, the audit manager delegates assignments to individual field auditors. The audit manager typically assigns field audits at least two weeks before the policy expiration date.

Audit Schedules

An auditor should schedule field audits for at least a one-week period, beginning with the highest priority audits according to expiration date or some other criterion. The auditor should identify the locations of the audits on a map, determine the most efficient route, and record the estimated time for each. If the resulting schedule exceeds the planning period, the auditor should give the audit manager an opportunity to change the schedule. If the schedule leaves significant slack time at the end, then the auditor or audit manager should revise the schedule to include additional audits from the next priority class of audits.

The auditor should place any audits that cannot be performed during the scheduled period in the highest priority class for the next planning period. That method of scheduling ensures prompt completion of audits while minimizing travel.

Audit Scheduling Factors

1. Policy expiration or cancellation date
2. Estimated audit time
3. Audit location
4. Extraordinary circumstances

Policy Expiration or Cancellation Date

The first consideration in audit schedules is the policy expiration or cancellation date. Most insurers strive to issue a premium adjustment notice within sixty days of policy expiration or cancellation. Conducting audits promptly is beneficial for several reasons. It can help maintain good relations with the insured and maintain the insurer's reputation of efficient service.

Prompt auditing also encourages prompt premium payment. The insurer needs the premium to pay claims and operating expenses and to improve cash flow. In addition, the sooner the insurer enters the earned premium on its books, the faster the insurer can write new business, while still meeting solvency requirements. Other information that the auditor obtains for the benefit of underwriters or other departments rapidly loses its value when audits are delayed.

Reporting and regulatory requirements also necessitate prompt audits. For example, an insurer must file the National Council on Compensation Insurance (NCCI) unit statistical report within eighteen months of the effective date of a one-year policy. As previously mentioned, residual market plans also have rules about the time within which an insurer must conduct the premium audit and bill the insured.

Because the insured might normally need two or three weeks to complete the recording of transactions (for example, if employees are paid every two weeks, it could take up to two weeks to have completed payroll records for the policy period), the optimal time to make an audit is from twenty to forty days after policy expiration or cancellation. Scheduling should allow time for unexpected delays.

Estimated Audit Time

The second consideration in scheduling audits is estimated audit time. To achieve a smooth work flow, the auditor must reasonably estimate the time a given audit might require. Previous audits of the insured, if available, can provide some record of the time required for the audit, which can be used as a guide.

The auditor must consider several factors in estimating audit time, including the following:

- *The number of policies and types of coverage involved and the policy periods.* For example, three policies covering the same period are ordinarily easier to audit than three policies each having a different policy period because in the latter case the auditor must determine a separate number of exposure units for each period.

- *The nature of the policyholder's business.* A governmental entity using unfamiliar accounting procedures requires more time because the auditor must learn the accounting system. General building contractors require longer audit times than mercantile or manufacturing operations because of the difference in records and the verification required. In addition, a general building contractor is generally not as busy in the winter months as in the summer. During those slow times, the auditor can more easily locate the contractor and establish a convenient audit time.
- *The nature and condition of the records.* The general contractor's records might include a job cost ledger recording material, labor, and overhead expenses for each job the contractor has been awarded. The premium auditor must determine the labor expended for each job performed during the year. If the books record direct labor by job, they usually record payments to subcontractors similarly.
- *The location of the records.* Having the records for all locations in the same place is most efficient for the auditor. If the insured has several locations, accounting entries may be recorded by location, and the auditor might have to visit all locations.
- *The time required for an audit.* The majority of premium audits require from one or two hours (excluding travel time) to approximately three days. In rare cases, certain audits might require an entire month or more.

Audit Location

The third consideration in audit schedules is the location of the audit. Once the auditor identifies the audits required in a certain period and the probable time required for each, the auditor should list those audits in the order that minimizes travel time from one location to another. Travel time, of course, depends to a considerable degree on the nature of the auditor's territory. Territorial differences might influence the choice of planning periods, which may be any convenient period such as a week or a month.

Extraordinary Circumstances

The fourth consideration in audit schedules is any extraordinary circumstances. Certain circumstances, such as the following examples, may require that an audit be performed quickly.

- If the insurer has nonrenewed the policy or the exposure amounts significantly change (and, therefore, a large additional premium will be due), the auditor must conduct the audit as quickly as possible. The longer the insurer takes to conduct the audit, the greater the chance of collection problems.
- If the insured is experiencing financial problems, the insurer may want to conduct its audit as soon as possible, especially if an additional premium is likely. In those cases, the insured might be paying its bills on a first-come, first-served basis until it runs out of money.

- The producer might be a preferred producer who has requested that the audit be conducted quickly to avoid possible problems. Or a producer who knows that the insured will be receiving a return premium may want to get that money to the insured as soon as possible.
- The insured might be undergoing its own audit or an IRS audit and must have the final premium determined quickly.
- The insured's availability might also be a factor. An insured may prefer to work with an auditor who is available only at certain times. Or, the insured's workload might make an audit on a certain day or during a certain week more convenient. Trying to accommodate such requests often goes a long way toward obtaining the insured's cooperation during the audit.
- A valuable account might ask for a quick audit. An insurer usually does all it can to comply with such requests.

Audit Appointments

After determining the optimal schedule for the next planning period, the auditor should arrange appointments with each policyholder. Although making unexpected visits might occasionally uncover significant information about the insured's operations, this practice generally wastes time because the insured does not have a chance to prepare for the auditor's visit. The insured may resent the intrusion and may not cooperate with the auditor in getting the correct information. Policyholders who expect the auditor on a specific date are more likely to cooperate and to have the necessary records available.

Depending on the size and complexity of the risk, a personal phone call by the auditor to the risk manager or accountant to set up the appointment might be appropriate. In most cases and with the majority of insureds, insurers use form letters or audit appointment cards to notify insureds of an upcoming audit. Exhibit 3-3 shows an example of such an appointment card. The card should provide sufficient information to allow the insured either to accommodate the auditor or to reply with a request for clarification or for different arrangements. That information should generally include:

- Insurer name
- Date of appointment
- Auditor's name, address, and phone number
- Policy(ies) to be audited—including the named insured, the name and address of the firm(s) to be audited, a street address if the policy shows a post office box, and the address of the location at which records are kept if not at the insured's address
- Policy period
- A list of specific records or information needed, which would include 1099 tax forms, overtime records, sales tax returns, certificates of insurance for subcontractors, and vehicle lists

EXHIBIT 3-3

Audit Appointment Card

Etchley Insurance Company
111 Elm Road
Malvern, PA 19355

Named Insured ____________________

I will call on ____________________ to obtain the data required to adjust the premium on your:

- ❑ Workers' compensation
- ❑ General liability
- ❑ Property insurance
- ❑ Auto liability
- ❑ Garage liability

Unless otherwise notified, I will conduct the audit at your address indicated on the policy, which is: ____________________

____

Firms to be audited (if other than named insured indicated above):

____

Please have the records indicated below available for the period:

____________________ to ____________________

- ❑ Payroll ❑ FICA
- ❑ Overtime payroll
- ❑ Individual earning cards/reports
- ❑ Job cost records
- ❑ Cash disbursements
- ❑ Certificates of insurance from all subcontractors
- ❑ Gross vehicle weight as specified by the manufacturer (This information is obtained from the vehicle identification plate, which is usually located in the doorjamb of the vehicle.)
- ❑ General ledger
- ❑ Monthly financial reports
- ❑ Sales journal/cash receipts
- ❑ Inventory
- ❑ Accounts receivable
- ❑ Auto registration/titles
- ❑ Other. See letter of ________.
- ❑ State unemployment reports
- ❑ Sales tax reports
- ❑ 1099s

____________________ Phone # ____________________

Auditor

Thank you for your cooperation.

The audit appointment card is usually sent by mail one to two weeks before the audit. Some auditors then confirm the appointment by telephone. That step is especially important when the audit entails significant travel time. Any specific scheduling and notification preferences of the insured should be noted in the audit history file for future audits.

Exhibit 3-4 is a sample follow-up to the appointment card for an insured contractor asking that the applicable certificates of insurance be made available.

Insureds sometimes refer the premium auditor to their public accountants or bookkeeping services, which often are more familiar with the records than the insured. However, accountants may lack information about employees' specific job duties; therefore, the auditor would need to call or visit the insured's place of business to obtain the information. Visits to the insured's place of business give the auditor the opportunity to see the operations first hand and make observations that could yield information valuable to the audit, such as product brochures in the waiting area, pictures of operations on the wall, and functions being performed by certain personnel.

EXHIBIT 3-4

Pre-Audit Notice—Request for Contractor's Certificates of Insurance

Etchley Insurance Company
111 Elm Road
Malvern, PA 19355

Contractor's Notification

Named Insured ____________________
Address ____________________
Policy Number ____________________

As you were recently notified, an audit will be made on your Etchley Insurance Company workers' compensation insurance policy listed above. To facilitate this audit, please have available a Certificate of Insurance indicating workers' compensation insurance for each subcontractor to whom you have subcontracted work during the policy period ____________ to ____________.

The certificates should indicate the insurer, the policy period, the applicable states, and the limit of liability for the employers' liability insurance.

Should you find that there are subcontractors for whom you do not have certificates, kindly contact the subcontractor for a certificate to be used during this audit. You should obtain the certificate prior to the scheduled audit because we will make a premium charge for each subcontractor for whom you do not have a properly completed certificate of insurance.

Thank you for your cooperation.

Yours truly, Date ____________

____________ Phone # ____________

Auditor

PREMIUM AUDIT PREPARATION

Before each audit, the auditor should analyze the policy, review the available information about the insured, and identify any additional audit questions the auditor must answer.

Analyze the Policy

Familiarity with the policy terms and the specific coverage provided is a prerequisite to an effective audit. By asking what the policy coverage is, an auditor can develop exposure base and classification information and information on potential loss exposures and hazards.

An insurance policy might be a self-contained, single, standard printed form or an original manuscript policy specifically drafted and typed. Premium auditors most often encounter policies assembled by combining two or more standard forms to tailor the coverage to the insured's needs. In that case, the policy includes various coverage parts, endorsements, information pages, declarations, or other forms. The insurer might also incorporate collateral documents into the policy by specific reference. For example, the sentence, "All premium for this policy will be determined by our manuals of rules, rates, rating plans, and classifications," means that those manuals constitute part of the contract to which the insurer and the insured have agreed. Similarly, a reference to "the workers' compensation laws" incorporates those statutes into the contract.

The auditor must obtain all necessary information about the policy terms, including all coverage parts, declarations pages, and endorsements containing information specific to the insured. The auditor must also obtain a rating work sheet, if it exists, or any other information about the policy terms not shown on the policy itself.

Having a systematic framework for analyzing insurance policies can help a premium auditor understand a policy thoroughly before making the audit. That framework consists of asking a series of questions about the policy's coverage. Exhibit 3-5 lists those questions.

EXHIBIT 3-5

Questions to Ask to Analyze Coverage

- What persons or interests are insured?
- What property, activity, or situation is insured?
- What places or locations are insured?
- During what period is coverage provided?
- What causes of loss (perils) are insured?
- What kinds of losses are insured?
- What are the limits on the amounts of coverage?
- What miscellaneous clauses affect the coverage provided?

What Persons or Interests Are Insured?

Most policies have one named insured. On other policies, however, determining who is an insured or even the named insured can be confusing. Determining the insured has been an issue in many premium audit fraud cases in which insureds have tried to hide payroll or sales by using multiple corporations. It is critical for an auditor to understand who all the named insureds are under the policy and the relationship of any additional insureds to the named insured.

The declarations or information page shows the named insured. The auditor should determine whether it is an individual, a partnership, a corporation, or some other form of entity. If there is a subsidiary corporation, the insured entity might be the parent, the subsidiary, or both. Different businesses sometimes operate from the same location or use the same accountant.

The auditor must also be alert to the possibility that the policy extends coverage to persons or interests beyond those specifically named. For example, are there additional partners, and if so, does the policy cover them?

The address shown on the declarations or information page helps to identify the insured, but it does not necessarily give the location of the operation or the records. When an insured uses a post office box as a mailing address, the auditor should note the location of the insured's operations and records. On new business, the loss control report might show this information. On renewal business, previous audit reports should show the address. If not, the auditor must ascertain the insured's actual location by other means.

What Property, Activity, or Situation Is Insured?

The premium auditor must know which of the insured's operations or activities are covered by a liability policy. Frequently, all operations are covered because the policy is comprehensive. The auditor should also be aware of policy exclusions. If an insurer has assigned a property policy for audit, it is usually because the covered property is stock subject to fluctuation during the policy term.

What Places or Locations Are Insured?

The answer to this question can become quite complicated. The insured might have operations in different states, which the policy might cover, depending on the policy declarations and endorsements. Some operations insured for workers' compensation might come under the jurisdiction of the U.S. Longshore and Harbor Workers Compensation Act. A general liability policy usually covers all locations and operations unless specifically excluded.

During What Period Is Coverage Provided?

In examining the insured's records, the auditor must determine the exposure units during the policy term. Sometimes several accounting adjustments are necessary to match the audit period to the policy period.

Most insurers issue policies for a one-year period. However, some insurers offer three- and five-year policy terms, but this option is declining in popularity. As an accommodation, insurers may extend the policy term for a particular insured, such as when a home is being sold two days after the policy's expiration.

In most cases, the reason an insurer writes a policy with a period other than one year is to change the policy expiration date. A policy might contain an odd expiration date, such as the 17th or the 23rd, because the insured initially obtained the policy on that date. Accountants or policyholders might ask the insurer to adjust the policy to a more convenient date, such as the end of a month, the end of a calendar quarter, or the end of the insured's fiscal year. The insurer extends the policy by issuing a new policy for a one-year period from the desired date. Such an adjustment usually simplifies the audit as well.

If the insurer has endorsed the policy after inception, the auditor must observe the endorsement's effective date. The endorsement can change the insurance rate for the period it is in effect, requiring the auditor to determine the exposure base separately for the part of the policy period when the endorsement is in effect. The endorsement can also cover a loss exposure with a different exposure base, which the auditor must determine. Many audit errors result from the auditor's neglect of an endorsement and failure to adjust the premium accordingly.

If a policy has been canceled, the auditor should determine the reason for cancellation. When an insured cancels a policy because the business ceases operations, the records should remain available for a reasonable time in the custody of a former principal of the business, the public accountant, or the firm's attorney. In bankruptcy cases, the records might be with a court-appointed receiver. However, because a business usually packs and moves its records when it closes, completing the audit adjustment as quickly as possible is advisable, in order to ensure that records or personnel needed for this audit are still available. The likelihood of collecting any additional premium also decreases as time passes.

A policy canceled and rewritten to change the expiration date or to combine coverages requires adjustments to determine the exposure base for the policy period. However, future audits will be simpler as a result.

If the insured canceled the policy because of dissatisfaction with the insurer's service, the premium auditor might not get the insured's cooperation during the audit. If the insurer canceled the policy for nonpayment of premium or failure to submit interim reports, the auditor should anticipate some difficulty in completing the audit satisfactorily.

What Causes of Loss (Perils) Are Insured?

An insurance policy defines the causes of loss covered by (1) naming specified causes of loss, (2) providing coverage for all causes of loss except those specifically excluded, or (3) including groups of causes, such as "perils of the sea." Liability policies cover a named cause of loss, that is, legal liability arising out

of stipulated activities. The premium auditor must know which coverages the policy includes and to which of the insured's operations the coverages apply.

What Kinds of Losses Are Insured?

Insured losses might be loss of property, loss of the use of property, or a liability loss. Liability losses include amounts the insured becomes legally obligated to pay, the expense of investigating and defending claims against the insured, and miscellaneous related costs. Losses insured under a workers' compensation policy depend on the benefits provided to employees according to applicable state laws. Except when assisting the claim department with valuation or classification problems, a premium auditor generally does not become involved in adjusting losses.

What Are the Limits on the Amounts of Coverage?

Another question about policy provisions relates to the amount of recovery for an insured loss. The amount of recovery depends not only policy limits but also on several other possible factors. The limit can be per-person or per-occurrence, and the policy might divide the limits into classes as shown on a schedule. There might also be sublimits, blanket limits, or reporting form limits. Some policies provide additional insurance to supplement the basic coverage. Of course, workers' compensation coverage has no specific limit, only the promise to pay the amounts required by law.

Analyzing coverage limits is particularly important to the premium auditor if the insurer has increased or decreased the limits during the policy term. Consequently, calculating the earned premium might require segregating the premium base before and after the change. The limits on a liability policy for a contractor might vary by job. If so, the auditor must separate the exposure amounts on the audit because the rates vary with the limits.

What Miscellaneous Clauses Affect the Coverage Provided?

Specific policies might include additional language clarifying or modifying the coverage provided. They might stipulate conditions voiding or suspending coverage. An automobile liability policy, for example, might suspend coverage for an automobile used beyond the designated territory. By systematically analyzing the policy, the auditor prepares to adjust the premium according to the coverage actually provided by the policy.

Determine Basis of Premium

In addition to analyzing the coverage provided by the policy, the auditor must determine the basis of premium to complete the audit. Because there are occasional variations, however, the auditor must examine the policy rather than assume that the usual premium base is accurate.

The auditor should also review the results of the coverage analysis to determine its effect on the premium base. Should officers or active partners be

included in the payroll? Do any endorsements require the auditor to split the premium base? Only when those and similar questions have been answered does the auditor know how to determine the premium base.

Review Information About the Insured

Familiarity with the insured's operations before an audit helps the auditor obtain the necessary information during the audit and classify the data. Understanding the nature of the insured's business or operations helps the auditor determine whether the classifications shown on the policy are the correct ones. The auditor must know each employee's functions to allocate the payroll to various classifications. The auditor also needs to know what functions or processes to expect in such an operation to discover additional loss exposures. Rather than assume that the classifications shown on the policy are complete and accurate, the auditor should develop the habit of challenging the given information and reaching an independent judgment.

Audit preparation, therefore, should include reviewing all available information about the insured. The sources of such information include the following:

- Audit files
- Other company files
- Experience rating worksheet
- Bureau inspection reports
- Producer's observations
- Insured's publications
- Financial rating service reports
- Public records

Audit Files

Insurers organize their files in various ways. In most cases the premium audit department maintains some sort of file recording all audit activity. The file might include a summary called an audit history or an audit reference sheet, reports of previous premium audits, and memoranda about any pre-audit survey visits to the insured.

Exhibit 3-6 shows a sample audit history sheet. Such standard forms summarize the more detailed field audit reports and are useful in pinpointing significant information about audit procedures. When the audit history is maintained, each subsequent auditor can quickly determine the location of the insured's records, the nature of the records, the name of the accountant, and the approximate time required for the audit. If the policyholder has requested that the insurer use a special audit procedure for billing purposes, the audit history sheet should describe that procedure.

Reports of previous audits provide information beyond what the audit history sheet provides. However, auditors should not simply retrace the same steps of a previous audit. The auditor should treat every audit as if it were a new audit.

EXHIBIT 3-6

Audit History Sheet

TO NEXT AUDIT **AUDIT HISTORY—REFERENCE**

NAME OF INSURED: Maryland Mfg. Co., Inc. ACCOUNT NO. 044347

ADDRESS: 1234 Main St., Baltimore, MD 21020-0005 TELEPHONE NO. 301-692-5823

RECORDS LOCATED: Policy Address (Arrange appt. with treasurer Mrs. J. Smith)

PERIOD AUDITED: Workers' Compensation	10/1/X2-X3	10/1/X3-X4	10/1/X4-X5	10/1/X5-X6	
General Liability					
Automobile					
Other					
DATE OF PAYROLL CUT-OFF	9/25/X3	10/1/X4	9/30/X5	9/30/X6	

EXECUTIVE OFFICERS CLASSIFICATION	CODE NUMBER	CODE NUMBER	CODE NUMBER	CODE NUMBER	CODE NUMBER
Pres. Dale Stone	8810	S	Same	S	
Vice Pres. Wm. Fine	8742	A	(Retired 1/1)		
Sec. Harold King	2501	M	Same	A	
Treas. Joan Smith	8810	E	Same	M	
V.P. E. Simpson	—	—	8742 Eff. 1/1	E	

RECORDS AUDITED	General Ledger EDP P/R Sum. Fed'l 941's	Same	Same	Same	
INFORMATION FURNISHED BY	Anne Marie Lane (Acct)	Same	Same	Reid Thompson (Acct)	
AUDIT TIME (hours)	6 hours	7 hours	5½ hours	5 hours	
AUDITOR AND DATE AUDIT COMPLETED	11/30/X3 E. Johnson	12/12/X4 D. Havens	12/12/X5 L. Stevens	11/27/X6 D. Havens	

Remarks and Instructions

1. See General Ledger A/C #172 for "Homeworkers." These payments are not included in payroll (to be included on audit).
2. Policyholder wants audit conducted in November or December each year.

For example, the audit report should include a description of the insured's operations indicating the classifications involved. Of course, the auditor must be alert to the possibility of changes in the operations that add new classifications for loss exposures since the last audit. The auditor should note the date of the previous audit and the period audited. The more recent the previous audit, the more reliable a guide to the current operations it is likely to be. The audit history sheet should indicate whether the previous auditor encountered any unusual difficulties in making the audit. If so, the new auditor should watch for the same problems and check to see if the insured has taken corrective action. If the previous audit revealed substantial overtime or significant additional loss exposures, the auditor should expect and prepare for those situations again.

If the insured has submitted interim reports of the loss exposures covered by the policy, those reports will reveal characteristics of the insured's business, such as seasonal fluctuations, that might justify special attention during the audit.

As previously discussed, pre-audit surveys provide useful information for field audit planning. The pre-audit survey might result in an agreement on procedures to guide the audit after policy expiration. The auditor should place a memorandum recording the substance of such an agreement in the audit file, for review during audit planning. Exhibit 3-7 shows an example of such a memorandum.

Other Company Files

Other insurer departments, such as underwriting, claims, and loss control, maintain files about insureds for their own needs. Those files can provide the auditor with insight into the nature of the insured's operations and may also contain information relevant to the audit.

Underwriting files can include the insured's original application, financial rating service reports, loss control inspection reports, and experience modification work sheets. In addition, correspondence among the insured, the producer, the underwriter, and other insurer personnel can provide useful information. Occasionally, copies of letters or memoranda that should be in the audit file show up in the underwriting file.

Underwriting files contain experience modification worksheets if the insured is eligible for experience rating. The auditor can compare actual payrolls and classification codes on those worksheets with estimates shown on the policy. An interstate (more than one state) experience modification should alert the auditor to the possibility of operations in multiple states. Similarly, the auditor can use reports from financial rating services, which this section subsequently describes.

Useful information might also be found in files maintained by the claim department. Although the claim file is generally a less useful source of information than other departments' files, sometimes information on a specific claim can support the audit. Some insurers provide premium auditors with

EXHIBIT 3-7

Memorandum of Pre-Audit Survey

April 19, 20X6

To: William Smith—Mid-Atlantic Audit Manager

From: Paul Johnson—Baltimore Audit

Re:	Maryland Drilling Company, Inc. (MDC)	WC	2219-00-059630
	1205 Carpenter Drive	CGL	2229-00-059630
	Bowie Junction, MD 96241	Auto	2229-02-059630

AUDIT SERVICE PROGRAM CALL

E.W. Williams, field audit manager; Dave Lewis, producer; and this auditor made, at the request of Mr. Ron Smith, Baltimore sales producer, a visit to the above-captioned new policyholder at 1:00 p.m. on April 12, 19X6.

The purpose of our visit was to introduce Mr. Williams and myself and to explain to Mr. Paul Franklin, corporate treasurer, the audit services provided by our company, and what records we will need to perform our audit and also to answer any questions he might have.

We had in our possession, at the time of our visit, the audit copies of the three policies captioned above. Prior to making the visit, Mr. Williams and I had reviewed the policies to determine the coverages provided, as well as other terms of the contract.

Our meeting was conducted exclusively with Mr. Paul Franklin, treasurer. Mr. George Barlow, president, had hoped to be present but was called out of town unexpectedly on business.

The following items were discussed:

ACCOUNTING RECORDS

The insured keeps accounting records on a calendar-year basis and maintains these at the address on the policy. We reviewed the following methods of the insured's record keeping:

N.C.R. accounting machine	Cash disbursement journal	Cash receipts journal	A.D.P. tab runs
General ledger	Voucher register	Sales journal	Hourly payrolls—weekly
			Salary payrolls—semimonthly

MANUFACTURING OPERATIONS

Policyholder manufactures a line of drilling supplies and equipment, of which approximately 30% are used by MDC on its own jobs. The insured sells the remaining supplies to several water drilling companies in Maryland and surrounding states. Supplies are transported by common carrier. A separate area on the ground floor of the main building is set aside for that operation, and there is no interchange of labor with drilling operations. Approximately seven (7) employees work in manufacturing operations.

DRILLING OPERATION

We briefly discussed the water drilling operation, at which time we determined that the policyholder maintains contractors' permanent yards at three (3) locations in Maryland and one location in Virginia. Since the liability policy did not include a contractors' yard code, Baltimore Sales was advised, and an endorsement adding same is now in process. MDC generally bids on large projects beyond the capability of most of its customers (i.e., the customers can handle only smaller jobs) for its drilling supplies.

CORPORATE OFFICERS	STATUS FOR W.C.
President—George Barlow	Active Clerical
Treasurer—Paul Franklin	Active Clerical
V.P. & General Manager—John Smith	Active Clerical
Secretary—Mrs. George Barlow	Nonactive—Nonsalaried

GENERAL DISCUSSION

Because the W.C. and C.G.L. policies are set up on a monthly reporting basis, we reviewed with Mr. Franklin the proper way of preparing this report and answered the few questions he had regarding same. We advised him that in connection with any work being performed on or about navigable waterways, a separate record of payroll is required for Longshore coverage.

The importance of obtaining certificates of insurance indicating all coverages and adequate general liability limits from any subcontractors who are employed by the insured was discussed. We also discussed the rules regarding hired haulers.

In conclusion, Mr. Franklin appeared pleased as a result of our visit, was very cooperative, and, in my opinion, should be a good policyholder.

cc: Audit file

Ron Smith—Baltimore Sales

E. W. Williams—Baltimore Audit

Tony Szott—Baltimore Underwriting

copies of claim payment drafts, such as the one shown in Exhibit 3-8. Those drafts indicate the classification of injured employees. A reported claim involving a classification not shown on the policy can alert the auditor to thoroughly investigate the loss exposure. The auditor should also verify the classifications assigned to any particularly large claims so that an error does not distort the ratemaking process.

Finally, loss control and safety engineering reports are excellent sources of information for an auditor, particularly for specific information about an insured's operations. The loss control department routinely sends copies of prospect surveys and periodic service visit reports to the audit department. Safety consultants or loss control representatives can be very helpful to auditors, particularly in situations involving construction operations.

Experience Rating Worksheet

For those policies subject to experience rating, the experience rating worksheet can provide valuable audit information. The workers' compensation experience rating worksheet is especially valuable because of its standardized format. This worksheet shows the classification codes applicable to the insured's operations during the experience period. Because the experience period is three years, the worksheet indicates the types of classifications the auditor might reasonably expect (unless the insured's operations have changed). Also shown are the payrolls (for workers' compensation) for the experience period. An auditor can examine any trends in payroll to verify that the insured's estimates for the policy period are reasonable. Finally, if the modification is an interstate modification, the worksheet alerts the auditor to multistate loss exposures.

Bureau Inspection Records

As a part of the mechanism for supervising and controlling the administration of workers' compensation insurance, most workers' compensation bureaus maintain an inspection procedure that involves visits to the offices and plants of businesses in the state. The bureau inspector, with the assistance of an authorized individual representing the insured, studies the insured's methods of operation and prepares a report. That report describes the operations in detail; for example, it would indicate details about various raw materials received, the production process, and the finished product. The bureau inspector assigns the workers' compensation classification codes that apply.

In most jurisdictions, once the bureau has made an inspection and assigned classifications, no additional codes or changes are allowed without bureau approval. After the bureau has completed the classification inspection, it sends the insurer a summary of the findings and the changes that it requires as a result of the inspection. The bureau then requests the insurer to endorse the policy.

Requests for changes in classifications come from both insureds and insurers. Insureds might request inspections if they believe that the bureau should classify their operations under a different code, one that carries a lower rate.

EXHIBIT 3-8

Claim Payment Draft

Broad and Main	Carpenter	508.	☐ YES ☒ NO	
PLACE OF ACCIDENT	OCCUPATION	WAGES	LOST TIME	EXTRA TERR. STATE

DESCRIPTION OF ACCIDENT	LOCATION CODE
Inj. finger	001-99

DO NOT DETACH THE STUBS

22 250007 – 0

7-5
340

	CO.	B.O.	AGENT	LINE	ISSUED AT	DATE
	2	12	4320	3950	Chicago, IL	9-25-X6
KEY NO.	IMY	EMY	DATE OF ACCIDENT		CAT. NO.	POLICY NUMBER
1200 CS	12-X5	12-X6	9-21-X6			4-10-3890-035825

INSURED XYZ Construction Co.	RISK STATE	CLASS	CAUSE		FIRST PAYMENTS SUPP
INJURED Jack Paterson	12	5403	11	MED.	81 $ $165.00 82 $
TYPED BY KB	P.F.	INST. CODE		EXP.	91 $ 92 $

TO THE ORDER OF

Stratford Medical Center
Outpatient Dept., P.O. Box 4832
Chicago, IL 60860

PAY ONLY
$165.00********

PLEASE PRESENT FOR PAYMENT WITHIN 90 DAYS

CAUTION
START AMOUNT
PAYABLE WITH $
ENDING WITH *

PAYABLE THROUGH THE
BAYWATER NATIONAL BANK
OF MARYLAND
BALTIMORE, MARYLAND

TAX ID # 48-3894751

AUTHORIZED SIGNATURE

NONNEGOTIABLE

COUNTERSIGNATURE

INSURANCE AUDITOR COPY

Insurers might request inspections if they believe the codes are incorrect because of changes or additions to the insured's operations. The bureau generally requires an inspection before an insurer makes any changes in an insured's classifications. However, a letter from an auditor that clearly describes any new operations might be sufficient for the bureau to approve the new or changed classification without another inspection.

The bureau might also require changes if ownership of the insured business changes in any way. The bureaus have a form (ERM—14 for the National Council) on which the insured indicates the exact ownership before and after the change. Based on the information on that form, the bureau reevaluates the classifications and named insured. A change in ownership could require that two policies be issued rather than one, or vice versa. Changes in ownership can also affect the experience rating modification. The workers' compensation experience rating manual has specific rules for the extent of a change in ownership required before the change affects the experience rating modification.

Accurately determining and applying classifications require close cooperation between premium auditors and bureaus. Although bureaus perform essentially the same functions in most states, they vary in their methods. Some bureaus are extremely rigid in administering rules and classifications, while others are relatively liberal. In any event, auditors who become acquainted with personnel in the various bureaus and their individual responsibilities can usually count on them for assistance and additional information.

Producer's Observations

The producer is an important information source for the premium auditor. The auditor must be aware, however, that the producer might reflect a bias in discussing the insured. Nevertheless, if the auditor needs information or general assistance, the producer can be helpful.

For example, producers can help to arrange field audit visits. They might be able to facilitate a field audit appointment when the insured is hard to reach or when the records are maintained at an inconvenient location. Occasionally, producers contribute information relating to the audit itself. For example, they might know which officers are active in the business, or they might be aware of a special job performed by the insured during the year that carries a different classification or is located in a different state. Unlike most insureds, producers are familiar with insurance practices and terminology, so they are often able to help a premium auditor obtain needed information quickly.

Insured's Publications

Auditors can sometimes get information from the insured's own publications. If the organization is large enough to have an annual report, that can be a good information source. Even promotional brochures and advertising can provide important information about an insured's operations or the nature of its business.

Corporations that sell their stock to the public publish annual reports containing audited financial statements as well as news and information about the company. The financial statements include an income statement, a balance sheet, and a statement of changes in financial position with accompanying footnotes. Most annual statements also list corporate officers.

Many other organizations also publish annual reports, even though they are not required to present certified financial statements. These reports might be for the benefit of employees, clients, contributors, members, or anyone else with an interest in the organization. They might include financial statements of some sort, but they do not always conform to generally accepted accounting principles.

An insured might also publish literature to promote the firm's products. That literature helps to identify the firm's products and might offer other clues about the insured's operations, some of which can help an auditor determine a classification or reveal additional loss exposures.

Advertising can also be a useful source of information about an insured's business, its location, and perhaps its officers. When the nature of the business is in question, even a simple listing in the classified telephone directory can reveal the products or services the insured offers.

Financial Rating Service Reports

Many insurers order financial rating service reports on their commercial insurance applicants and insureds. Organizations such as Dun & Bradstreet and Standard and Poor's provide such reports. The reports can provide information about the insured's operations, past financial results, and ownership. The auditor must check, however, that the report being used is current.

Public Records

Various public records contain information useful to a premium auditor. For example, many states require businesses conducted under an assumed name to file the legal names and addresses of the participants with the county clerk. Therefore, a visit to the county clerk's office can clarify confused identities. A premium auditor seeking the officers' names, the incorporation date, or the corporation mission might find such information at the state government level, although it will normally be in the insured's records as well. The corporation commission or secretary of state maintains a record of all corporations chartered within the state.

Federal agencies also have information that can be helpful to premium auditors. Long-haul truckers and other firms under Interstate Commerce Commission jurisdiction must file public records on their operations. The Federal Communications Commission requires similar reports from organizations in the broadcasting industry. And, of course, the Securities and Exchange Commission requires financial reports from all firms selling stock to the public.

Trade magazines are often an excellent source of general information about specific industries and the processes involved. Newspapers carry articles relating to local businesses, reporting such news as plant openings, additional shifts, substantial contract awards, layoffs, and closings. Premium auditors should clip those articles and place them in a file for reference when planning the audit.

Identify Additional Audit Questions

While analyzing the insurance policy and reviewing information about the insured, the premium auditor should note any areas deserving special investigation or unusual arrangements. Those notes should also indicate additional information needed, such as the classifications involved, the basis of premium the auditor uses, and the probable records the auditor needs for the audit. Those notes can then serve as a guide during the actual audit, refreshing the auditor's memory about important concerns.

Classifications Involved

After determining the nature of the insured's operations, the premium auditor should review the classifications that could be involved. The review should include a careful reading of the classification phraseology in the manual and any related classification guides. *The Classification Guide* published by the Premium Audit Advisory Service is available electronically, so many auditors have this guide loaded on their laptop computers. Rating manuals are also being made available electronically.

The auditor should consider alternative classifications that might apply and should determine the criteria for assigning those classifications. The fact that a classification appears in a policy does not necessarily make it applicable. For workers' compensation in some states, the only classifications that insurers can use are those authorized classifications that the bureau has recorded on its records. If the premium auditor believes that the insured's operations justify additional codes, the audit report should contain the relevant information either to justify the assignment of a code used on the audit or to allow the underwriter to obtain the bureau's permission for applying those codes in the future.

Different Basis of Premium

Probably the most common situation in which an auditor uses a premium base different from that specified in the manual occurs when a policy is composite-rated. **Composite-rating** is a rating approach based on a single premium base instead of different premium bases for each type of insurance. It is used when the insurer provides various sub-lines of coverage (normally with different premium bases).

Composite-rating
A rating approach based on a single premium base instead of various premium bases for each type of insurance.

For example, a commercial package policy might provide coverage for general liability, commercial auto, and commercial property. Each of those coverages has a different basis of premium according to the manual. However,

the underwriter can consolidate all of the premium for each type of coverage, relating coverage to a single premium base such as sales, remuneration, gallonage, admissions, kilowatts of electricity, or some other measure. The underwriter then determines the premium by applying a single set of rates to the single premium base indicated.

If the policy establishes a special basis of premium, the auditor should note that fact and become thoroughly familiar with the procedure involved before making the audit. The auditor should also make note of any other special arrangements. In determining the exposure base for the composite rate, the underwriter makes certain assumptions, trying to select an exposure base that fluctuates with the loss exposures assumed under all of the policies. Auditors are often in a position to evaluate the appropriateness of the chosen exposure base because they work closely with exposure bases and because they see the insured's operations firsthand. They should understand why the underwriter chose a certain exposure base and should be willing to examine the underwriter's underlying assumptions in determining the exposure base. They should also be willing to discuss that decision with the underwriter if they believe the exposure base does not reflect the loss exposures assumed under the policies.

The suggested planning procedures for audits might seem far more elaborate than necessary for most premium audits. An auditor might be tempted to dispense with detached planning in order to spend the time on actual audits. That temptation, however, is the biggest single obstacle to efficiency in a premium auditor's work. A single wasted trip to visit an insured whose records are not ready consumes more time than all of the planning activities described in this chapter.

Furthermore, when the auditor habitually performs those planning steps, they become second nature. The advantage of a systematic planning procedure is that it precludes the possibility of overlooking a situation that could result in a great deal of wasted time. When the planning procedure becomes routine, it actually requires very little time.

Premium Audit Preparation

Analyze the policy.

Determine the basis for the premium.

Review information concerning the insured, including the following:

- Audit files
- Other company files
- Experience rating worksheet
- Bureau inspection reports
- Producer's observations
- Insured's publications
- Financial rating service reports
- Public records

Identify additional audit questions.

SUMMARY

The premium audit department is responsible for completing the premium adjustment for policies written on an adjustable basis. Under some circumstances, if the premium is a small amount and the number of exposure units does not fluctuate considerably from year to year, the audit manager might decide to waive the audit and accept the advance premium as the final earned premium. Often, the insurer bases the premium adjustment on the insured's report of the values representing the premium base. The insurer also uses telephone audits and office adjustments.

Many circumstances warrant a field audit to determine the earned premium. In determining whether to conduct a field audit, an auditor might consider such factors as statutory requirements, the potential premium amount, the insured's operations, prior audit experience, and the type of coverage, as well as cost, geography, and available staffing. An auditor's visit to an insured early in the policy term can be beneficial, providing an opportunity to resolve the insured's questions about classifications, recordkeeping requirements, and audit procedures.

Auditors can visit insureds to accomplish other tasks besides the premium audit. The auditor may conduct a pre-audit survey, which can provide useful information not just to the auditing department, but also to the marketing department, the underwriting department, and the claim department, and for accounting/collection/credit and loss control purposes.

After an audit manager decides which policies require an audit and assigns them to individual staff auditors or to independent auditing services, the field auditors must schedule audit visits efficiently. Scheduling involves balancing many factors, such as statutory requirements, premium size, the insured's operations, prior audit experience, type of coverage, direct costs of the audit, geographical factors, and staff workload and skills. The premium auditor then makes appointments with each insured on the schedule so that the insured can prepare for the audit visit and make the necessary records available.

Preparation for each premium audit should begin with analyzing the policy coverage to determine the basis of premium. The premium auditor should also review the available information about the insured. In developing a premium audit schedule, the policy expiration or cancellation date should be considered. Also, the estimated time to perform the audit, the location of the audit, and any extraordinary circumstances should be considered.

Analyzing the policy and reviewing information about the insured as well as recent audits often leads to specific questions the auditor intends to answer during the audit. Questions might also arise after reviewing experience rating worksheets and analyzing bureau inspection reports. Such questions might involve classifications, a special basis of premium, and the appropriate records to use. Producer observations, the insured's publications, financial rating service reports, and public records are valuable to the premium auditor in preparing for the premium audit. As a result of that advance preparation, the premium auditor can be more efficient by performing a better audit in less time.

CHAPTER NOTE

1. Premium Audit Advisory Service, "Net Additional Premium," January 2004. All PAAS surveys are private and are distributed to PAAS members only.

Direct Your Learning 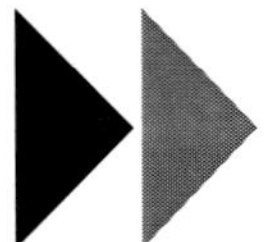

Review of Insured's Operations

Educational Objectives

After learning the content of this chapter and completing the corresponding course guide assignment, you should be able to:

- Describe the advantages and disadvantages to the parties involved of each of the various types of business entities ownership.
- Given a case, explain why an organization might choose a certain form of ownership.
- Describe from the premium auditor's perspective how government entities differ from typical businesses.
- Describe the factors that a premium auditor should include in a complete description of an insured's operations.
- Describe the nature of the typical types of business operations.
- Describe the specific factors a premium auditor might observe that reflect how well the insured operates.
- Describe how a premium auditor can evaluate the insured's financial condition.
- Given appropriate information in a case, interpret the significance of various financial ratios.
- Describe the changes that can occur in the insured's operations and the significance of each change as it applies to an insurer.
- Define or describe each of the Key Words and Phrases for this chapter.

OUTLINE

Develop Your Perspective

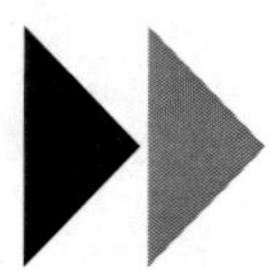

What are the main topics covered in the chapter?

This chapter presents a series of questions the premium auditor should have in mind at the outset of the audit. These questions facilitate the accurate classification of operations and assist the auditor in discovering relevant loss exposures.

Identify questions that an auditor might try to answer about an insured's operations before the audit is conducted.

- Who is the insured?
- What is the nature of the insured's operations?
- What changes occurred in the insured's operations since the inception of the policy or since the last audit?
- What other questions might be relevant to analyzing the insured's operations?

Why is it important to learn about these topics?

Learning about a policyholder's operations will allow the premium auditor to make better judgments about the sources of audit information and to accurately respond to classification questions.

Consider the following questions and determine why they are important to the premium audit and where and how information may be gathered.

- Who are the insured's owners?
- What operations does the policyholder perform?
- What is the insured's financial condition?
- Have any changes to the operations occurred?

How can you use what you will learn?

Evaluate how a premium auditor may be in a better position than any other representative of the insurer to assess the insured's financial condition.

- How can the auditor's opinion of the insured's financial position be of value to the underwriting department?
- How should the auditor balance the insured's need for privacy of financial information with the insurer's need to be kept informed?

Review of Insured's Operations

A preliminary interview in the insured's offices provides much of the background information needed for the audit. Depending on the organizational structure of the insured's business, the auditor might talk to the firm's president, treasurer, controller, accountant, or bookkeeper. Discussion with several individuals might be necessary to obtain answers to all pertinent questions.

A premium auditor familiar with the insured's operation knows which records are necessary for determining the premium. For example, if the premium base is payroll, payroll records alone might not be sufficient. The insured might record payments to drivers or sales representatives in separate accounts. Moreover, the insured might keep separate records for any subsidiary enterprises. By noting and communicating record needs in advance, the auditor gives the insured sufficient time to gather specific information for the applicable insurance coverages.

By taking time to review the operations at the outset of the audit, a premium auditor can perform a more focused and accurate audit. The information gathered can assist the auditor in assigning proper classifications and help the auditor to discover loss exposures that might otherwise be overlooked.

A careful review of the insured's operations should include review and evaluation of the following:

- Form of insured's ownership
- Nature of insured's operations
- Quality of insured's operations
- Insured's financial condition
- Insured's loss exposures

FORM OF INSURED'S OWNERSHIP

Because an insurance policy is a legal contract between an insurer and an insured, the premium auditor must know who is the named insured. To be a named insured under a policy, the person or organization must be indicated in the policy declarations or specified as such by the policy wording or endorsement. Insured persons or organizations have legal identities. The policy declarations page usually identifies the legal form of the named insured as an individual, a partnership, a corporation, or an unincorporated association. The insured can also be two or more entities involved in a joint venture, or a parent company and its subsidiaries; a corporation and its individual stockholders with a controlling interest; or a governmental jurisdiction or authority.

Business Entities

To analyze any business entity, the auditor must first determine its legal form of organization. Business organizations have various legal forms. Knowing the characteristics of those forms is important for understanding the obligations incurred by the business. The three most common forms are sole proprietorships, partnerships, and corporations, so auditors must be familiar with those.

Sole Proprietorships

Sole proprietorship
A business owned by a person who possesses all assets of the business and is personally liable for the business debts.

A **sole proprietorship** is a business owned by a person who possesses all assets of the business and is personally liable for the business debts. The individual who operates a sole proprietorship is the sole proprietor. Any person can create a sole proprietorship business, unless the law prohibits it. A person need have only a minimum amount of capital investment, skill, or property to establish such a business. A sole proprietor has full control of the business and is totally responsible for its operation. Of all forms of business operations, sole proprietorships are subject to the least amount of state and federal control. They pay no federal income taxes, although the owner (proprietor) must include profits from the business on his or her personal tax return. The simplicity and flexibility of the sole proprietorship form of organization explain why sole proprietorships represent about 70 percent of all business units in the United States.

Sole proprietorships, however, can be short-lived. The demands of running a business can be greater than the owner anticipated. Those demands include meeting regular payrolls, obtaining funds to pay creditors, and maintaining premises and equipment to minimize injuries to employees and the public. The need to satisfy customers and remain competitive constantly challenges sole proprietors. Without an intervening contractual obligation, an owner can dissolve a sole proprietorship at will. The business also terminates if the owner dies or becomes disabled. If the business fails financially, the owner has unlimited personal liability for all business debts. Creditors can use both the business assets and the personal assets of the proprietor to satisfy financial obligations.

The amount of property needed to start and operate a business varies by the type of business. The degree of technical skill necessary for success also varies. For instance, a small repair contractor might need only a toolbox and a pickup truck to be in business, but a retailer needs a sizable inventory to attract customers. Purchasing an existing business relieves the new owner of the work of setting up the business, purchasing inventory, and building a clientele, but it usually involves a substantial cash outlay.

Undercapitalization and the lack of a cash reserve for emergencies also create problems for the sole proprietorship. If a proprietor has under-financed the business, funds for property maintenance might not be available. An owner's preoccupation with creditors can adversely affect operations by distracting the owner from what needs to be done to operate the proprietorship.

A sole proprietor owns the insurable interest in the business and is responsible for the acts of employees. The insurance policy usually indicates that insurable interest by showing the owner's legal name, sometimes followed by a word that describes the business, such as "John Smith, Clothier." Often the business trade name follows the owner's name, as in "Mary Johnson d/b/a (doing business as) Mary's Exclusive Clothiers" or "Mary Johnson t/a (trading as) Mary's Exclusive Clothiers." Those descriptive terms do not affect the insurable interests covered by the policies.

Partnerships

A **partnership** is an association of two or more persons entering business to share in profits and losses. Legally, partners are jointly liable for the business's debts, and a creditor attempting to collect amounts owed sues the partners as a group. The law does not require a partnership agreement to be in writing. An oral agreement to share in both the profits and losses binds the partners to the agreement.

Partnership
An business enterprise of two or more people who share in profits and losses.

One advantage of a partnership is that it combines the partners' talents and capital. The partners share the workload. It is a simple organization and is relatively free from government control, much like a sole proprietorship.

A major disadvantage of a partnership is that any one partner can be wholly liable for all of the partnership's debts. If two out of three partners are insolvent, the third is liable for all of the enterprise's obligations to the total extent of all personal assets. Other disadvantages may include divided authority, the possible incompatibility of the partners, and a limited and uncertain duration. A partnership automatically dissolves whenever any one of the partners withdraws or if a partner dies. Furthermore, partners cannot sell their shares to new partners without the consent of all remaining partners.

In addition to general partnership in which all partners have unlimited liability, some states' statutes allow limited partnerships. A **limited partner**, or special partner, invests in the business but takes no other part in its management. Limited partners assume limited liability and receive profits limited proportionately to the size of their investments.

Limited partner
A partner who invests in a business, takes no part in its management, assumes limited liability, and receives a proportionate share of profits.

Like a limited partner, a **silent partner** is someone who invests in a partnership but takes no active part in the business. However, a silent partner's liability is not limited. A silent partner is liable, as is a general partner, for the partnership debts. The advantage of a silent partnership is the ability to spread business profits among several members of the firm, usually family members, to minimize income tax liability.

Silent partner
A partner who invests in a partnership but takes no active role in the business.

A partner has an insurable interest in partnership property and can carry insurance as protection against personal loss. The partnership can also carry insurance, the proceeds of which are payable to the firm. An insurance policy lists all the partners' names and the name of the partnership.

Dissolution of a partnership can occur in several ways, including the following:

- Termination of a particular undertaking as specified in the partnership agreement
- The express will of any partner when the partnership agreement has specified no definite term
- The death of any partner
- The express will of all partners
- Events occurring during the period of the partnership that make the continuance of the partnership impossible or illegal
- Court decree, upon application of one of the partners to a court of equity

Dissolution of a partnership is not immediate. The partnership exists until all the partnership affairs are completed. This process includes liquidating partnership assets to pay creditors and then distributing the remainder to the partners. Dissolution terminates all the authority of any partner to act for the partnership, except as it might be necessary to create liability to complete unfinished transactions or to liquidate the firm's assets. Thus, for insurance purposes, the partnership exists until the insurer has completed the final audit and the partnership has paid or received the final premium adjustment.

Corporations

Corporation
A legal entity created for the purpose of conducting business and limiting stakeholders' liability to their own investments.

A **corporation** is a legal entity created for the purpose of conducting business and limiting stakeholders' liability to their own investments. Creditors cannot attach stockholders' personal property for debts incurred by the corporation, as they can for a business organized as a proprietorship or partnership.

The corporation is the most effective way to manage and control a modern business firm. It permits, to a greater extent than other legal forms, the combination of capital and skill for a vast business enterprise.

Functioning as a legal entity, separate and distinct from its members, a corporation has certain rights and powers, including the following:

- It can sue and be sued in its own name.
- It has the capacity of perpetual succession, although its members could change by withdrawal or death.
- It can own and transfer property, both real and personal, in its own name, separately and distinctly from its stockholders.
- It can enter into contracts with its stockholders.
- It can take property from and convey property to its stockholders.

To form a corporation, a firm must file the appropriate documents within the state in which it wants to incorporate. The corporate charter or articles of incorporation list the corporation name, its purpose, the amount and class of capital stock, the names and addresses of the incorporators, provisions for managing its affairs, and other relevant information. If approved, this

document becomes binding on the corporation because the state has granted it corporate powers and privileges to carry out its stated goals.

Corporate existence can be terminated by the expiration of its charter, through dissolution by the state attorney general, by merger or consolidation, or by the action of the stockholders. When a corporate charter provides that the corporation will exist for a definite period, the corporation automatically terminates at the expiration of that period.

Organizers can form corporations for several legal purposes. Corporations range in size from giant conglomerates to family firms. Some are not-for-profit organizations and government entities, which are described later in this chapter. The following four types of corporations are discussed in this section:

1. Publicly held corporations
2. Privately held corporations
3. Professional corporations
4. Limited liability corporations

A **publicly held corporation** is any profit-making corporation offering more than $500,000 in stocks or bonds for sale to the public. A publicly held corporation is subject to regulation by the Securities and Exchange Commission (SEC). Such corporations must file registration statements with the SEC disclosing pertinent information about the securities offered for sale and must file an annual Form 10-K reporting extensive details about their financial condition. In addition, stockholders receive an annual report containing financial statements attested to by a certified public accountant (CPA). The accounting requirements imposed on the corporation by these regulations and the Internal Revenue Code ensure an abundance of data for a premium audit.

Publicly held corporation
A profit-making corporation offering more than $500,000 in stocks or bonds for sale to the public.

A **privately held corporation** is a corporation that issues stock but does not sell it to the general public. The stockholders tend to be few, and they are usually members of the same family. Privately held corporations, regardless of size, are not subject to the disclosure requirements applicable to publicly held corporations.

Privately held corporation
A corporation that issues stock without selling it to the general public.

Some privately held corporations are **Subchapter S corporations**, so named because they qualify under Section 1371-77 of the Internal Revenue Code to file Form 1120-S for corporate income tax purposes. Other corporations must file Form 1120. Net income of a Subchapter S corporation is not subject to corporation income tax. Instead, stockholders include in their individual gross incomes their distributive portions of the corporation's profits or losses, much like a partnership. In that way, the business owner has the advantages of incorporation without the so-called double taxation of corporate profits.

Subchapter S corporation
A corporation that distributes corporate profits or losses much like a partnership and is not subject to corporation income tax.

To qualify for this election as a Subchapter S corporation, a corporation must meet the following six requirements:

1. Be a domestic corporation

2. Not be a member of an affiliated group of corporations
3. Have only one class of stock
4. Have no more than thirty-five stockholders
5. Have only individuals, estates, or trusts as stockholders
6. Have no nonresident aliens as stockholders

A qualified corporation can make the election at any time within the first seventy-five days of the tax year to which it applies or at any time during the preceding year. Because a corporation can change its election from year to year, investigating the possibility of a change to or from Subchapter S status on each annual premium audit is important.

Professional corporation (PC)
A corporation formed by an individual or a group of individuals who render the same type of professional service to the public.

Another type of corporation is the **professional corporation (PC)**, a corporation formed by an individual or a group of individuals who render the same type of professional service to the public. General business corporation legislation usually prohibits forming a corporation to practice a profession. The reasons for this are (1) that professional activities are usually personal and confidential, requiring privileged communications, and (2) that clients have the right to the uncontrolled opinion of an expert, which in a corporate situation might not exist.

Before the 1960s most professional organizations were partnerships. Starting in about 1960, many states adopted professional corporation acts because of changes in IRS regulations regarding taxes on retirement benefits and some favorable court decisions. Those changes gave professional corporations many advantages over noncorporations, such as partnerships.

Professional corporation acts permit an individual or a group of individuals who render the same type of professional service to the public to incorporate. For example, an individual lawyer or a group of lawyers can form a professional corporation. However, a doctor cannot join that corporation. Many states extend their professional corporation acts to permit corporations in similar fields to merge. For example, some states permit a medical corporation and a dental corporation to merge. Most professional corporation acts contain only the provisions specific to professional corporations and refer to the general corporation act for all other details of incorporation.

One distinctive feature of professional corporations is that their members, unlike stockholders, do not have limited liability regarding their own professional malpractice. General principles, as well as professional ethics, require that professionals be personally responsible for malpractice.

Limited liability corporation (LLC)
A corporation that operates and is taxed like a partnership but provides limited liability for its owners.

A **limited liability corporation (LLC)**, is a relatively new form of corporation that operates and is taxed like a partnership but provides limited liability for its owners. The limited liability corporation has become the fastest-growing form of business, corporate or otherwise, in the U.S. All but a few states have enacted legislation allowing the formation of LLCs; the remaining states have legislation pending. An LLC is formed by filing the necessary papers with the appropriate state agency.

An LLC is a cross between a corporation and a partnership, offering many of the advantages of each. The goal of the LLC is to avoid the tax disadvantages of a corporation while enjoying the limited liability advantages of a corporation. Like a partnership, the LLC is made up of members and managers. The members are taxed individually, but the LLC is not taxed. Therefore, the LLC avoids the double tax at the corporate level. Although the enabling laws for LLCs vary by state, in many states, the LLC dissolves, much like a partnership, when a member dies, when the LLC expels a member, when a member withdraws, or with all members' unanimous consent. As in a corporation, the owners' personal assets are not at risk from business-related lawsuits. Finally, the members and managers of the LLC are granted immunity by statute from any debt, obligation, or liability of the LLC.

Unincorporated Associations

The need for an organization—other than a corporation—that could include large numbers of individuals and continue as a viable organization after one or more of its members died or withdrew gave rise to the unincorporated association. The **unincorporated association** is a voluntary association of several individuals acting together under a common name to accomplish a lawful purpose. The unincorporated association acts without a corporate charter but uses methods and forms similar to those of corporations.

Unincorporated association
A voluntary association of individuals acting together under a common name for a common purpose.

The common law does not recognize an unincorporated association as a legal entity separate from its members. Its members are individually liable for the liabilities of the association, just as in a partnership. Also, the exercise of personal choice and preference in the admission of new members is similar to that of the partnership.

Because it is not a separate legal entity, an association cannot hold title to real property or execute a lease in the association's name. An association can be formed for profit or not for profit. The association is the most common form of organization for not-for-profit institutions. The law treats associations as organizations that might otherwise be classified as partnerships but that have been formed for nonprofit purposes.

The association has formal articles of association or a charter, as well as bylaws. The sharing of expenses and profits, if any, in an association occurs frequently on a basis other than per capita. The organizers usually vest day-to-day management of the association in an elected board of directors or trustees.

The Internal Revenue Code considers an association as a partnership if it has more noncorporate than corporate characteristics. Therefore, each member of an association is considered a partner for income tax purposes.

Few laws are applicable to associations, and associations, not being created by statute, need no special authorization to do business in any state. Associations may be subject to fictitious-name statutes, which require registering the name of the organization and paying a fee. Dissolving an association and winding up its affairs are easier for an association than for a corporation.

Trade associations, such as chambers of commerce, constitute one of the largest and most important groups of associations. More than 10,000 of those associations exchange and compile information, lobby, and foster the particular interests of their members. Another prominent group of associations is labor unions. Certain fraternal and benevolent societies also use the association form.

An association of persons who meet or live together for social purposes or some other common objective is commonly called a club. Most clubs operate as unincorporated associations and generally have the same characteristics as other associations.

A rapidly expanding area of unincorporated associations is condominium owner associations. This is a body formed, according to the condominium enabling acts of most states, by all owners of units within the condominium. The association oversees the condominium's operation and the care and preservation of the common areas, principally the buildings and grounds.

Multiple Organizations

The named insured on a policy can be two or more entities in any of the forms already described. The only restriction is that each entity named as an insured must have an insurable interest. If an owner has pledged property as collateral for a loan, both the owner and the lender have insurable interests and can therefore be named insureds. Cases that require particular scrutiny at audit time are joint ventures and wrap-ups.

Joint Ventures

Joint venture
A temporary association of two or more entities created to carry out a particular business transaction or operation.

A **joint venture** is a temporary association of two or more entities created to carry out a particular business transaction or operation. For example, several contractors might join to build a single building. The completion of the building terminates the association. Members of the venture have unlimited liability in connection with the job, much as partners have unlimited liability in a partnership. A joint venture is considered to be a temporary partnership.

Joint ventures are often informal, without written agreements. Courts use many of the general rules governing partnerships to determine the duties of members of joint ventures. Because of a joint venture's informal structure and temporary nature, determining insurable interests becomes difficult for the insurer. At the joint venture's termination, the members might disagree about who is responsible for what portion of the premium. An auditor should therefore examine the purpose of the joint venture. If a written joint venture agreement exists, the auditor should study it carefully to see whether any parts of the agreement would affect the premium audit.

Wrap-Ups

Multiple construction contractors can be insured under an insurance program called a wrap-up program. A **wrap-up insurance program** is a form of controlled construction insurance plan with which one insurer covers all or most of the contractors working on a given project. The policy might exclude contractors with nominal involvement in the project. The insurer bases such exclusions on a minimum dollar amount of work.

Wrap-up insurance program
A form of controlled construction insurance plan with which one insurer covers all or most of the contractors working on a project.

Contractors and insurers usually confine these insurance plans to large construction projects involving buildings, subways, tunnels, pipelines, bridges, and other similar projects that are self-liquidating as of a definite completion or cut-off date. For some projects, the program provides only general liability coverage. For other projects, the program includes both workers' compensation and general liability coverages. Sometimes the program includes builders risk and marine coverages with workers' compensation and general liability. Rarely, the program combines surety with some or all of the insurance coverages mentioned. Whatever the combination of insurance coverages, one distinguishing characteristic of a wrap-up insurance program is that the insurance covers more than one insured.

An insurer can provide coverage by a master policy or policies. Most states, however, require that separate workers' compensation and employers' liability policies be issued to each employer participating in the project. The primary reason for separate workers' compensation policies is for the benefit of state supervisory authorities who must verify proof of a valid workers' compensation policy for each employer in the state. In either case, the contractor must keep payroll records for the wrap-up program separate from payroll records for other projects.

Wrap-ups offer an insured several advantages over use of separate policies and insurers. Even though the insurer issues separate policies, an owner-controlled wrap-up program permits the owner to enjoy the premium discount based on the size of the standard premium volume of the workers' compensation insurance in the wrap-up program. By paying the premium, the owner also obtains the benefit of any experience credits accruing to the contractors on their payrolls exposed to the wrap-up program. Experience rating is mandatory in virtually all jurisdictions for employers whose average annual workers' compensation premiums at manual rates would equal or exceed $5,000 (some states use a lower amount). Because of that experience rating requirement, a contractor or subcontractor insured by a wrap-up program is highly probable to be subject to experience rating. If the owner selects contractors with good safety records, and if the contractors select subcontractors with good safety records, the owner stands to enjoy substantial benefits through the experience credits.

Construction projects create some of the most difficult insurance problems because work is often dangerous and usually involves hazardous activity such

as blasting or excavation. The construction site offers significant opportunities for loss control activities if handled by one insurer. One insurer with adequate premium can promote job safety more efficiently than the insurers of the general contractor and the many subcontractors who must share the responsibility.

Many of the advantages of the wrap-up program are a result of having the loss exposures of all participants covered by a single insurer. In the event of a claim, therefore, the maze of subrogation actions among insurers of each party is eliminated.

An owner involved in any large project often has difficulty in obtaining or verifying adequate liability protection on behalf of all subcontractors. Unfortunately, however, the size of a loss does not always vary directly with the financial size or responsibility of the contractor. All contractors must have adequate coverage. Asking a small subcontractor for evidence of a comprehensive liability insurance program with a $5 million single limit might be out of the question. Obtaining insurance certificates from all contractors on the job is also an administrative problem. The wrap-up program affords uniform coverage and adequate limits across the board to all parties.

Wrap-ups also have disadvantages in comparison to separate policies. Producers often object to wrap-up programs because they remove the contractor involved from the usual insurer relationship. The producer may continue to advise the contractor on other matters but loses the commission from placing the coverage included in the wrap-up program. That commission is often a substantial amount. Producers also encounter placement difficulties because the bulk of the contractor's insurance premium might be in the wrap-up program rather than in the regular insurance policies.

Contractors may complain that the wrap-up program reduces their safety incentive because the insurance savings go to the owner. Contractors also sometimes complain that the wrap-up program denies them the benefit of superior experience modifications. Conversely, for combined rating such as under a wrap-up program, the program does not hold an unsafe contractor accountable for poor liability experience in terms of premium surcharges.

A contractor involved in one or more wrap-up programs must submit to multiple insurance audits—the audit of the contractor's own insurance and the audit(s) for the wrap-up program(s) as well. In a wrap-up program, an owner's employee is usually responsible for collecting contractor and subcontractor payroll data at the construction site. That employee then checks the data for accuracy and presents them to the premium auditor.

Some wrap-up programs require the owner to appoint an on-site audit project coordinator. That coordinator reviews the payroll forms and withholding payments made to any contractor or subcontractor who has failed to submit in timely fashion the information that the insurer needs to determine the premium. The coordinator also verifies those payroll figures for accuracy. The premium auditor is responsible for ensuring that the owner, general contractor, contractors, and subcontractors all fully understand the auditing requirements.

Government Entities

If the named insured is a government entity, the auditor encounters problems different from those encountered when auditing a business firm. A government entity can be a complex organization with many separate classifications and unique accounting procedures. Despite such complexities, the premium auditor must precisely determine the named insured's identity and the operations it performs. The auditor must also determine whether courts might hold the named insured liable for any other governmental subdivisions.

A government entity might be a state or a municipality, such as a county, city, town, township, village, or borough. The laws of the state define its corporate status and accord it certain governmental powers. Other government entities include **public authorities**, usually organized as separate not-for-profit corporations responsible for public transportation, schools, water, irrigation, fire protection, or similar services. Public colleges and universities are also considered government entities. The named insured can be a single public institution or authority, several in combination, or a municipal government also responsible for several separate institutions or authorities.

Public authorities
Government entities organized as separate not-for-profit corporations responsible for public transportation, schools, water, irrigation, fire protection, or similar services.

Municipal Operations

When auditing a municipality, the auditor must determine what operations are under the named insured's control. The municipality can operate all utilities directly, or each utility may operate as a separate nonprofit corporation. A park, water, sewer, or fire district might also be a division of the municipality and be covered under the municipality's insurance.

The auditor should have a reasonably good idea of how municipalities operate. The annual report shows all operating units within the municipality. If the policy covers several departments, the report can help to organize the audit because individual departments might keep their own sets of books.

The annual report usually provides the following information for each department:

- Budget and actual amounts expended, including payroll and construction costs
- Additions to municipal or county properties, such as miles of streets and sewers, as well as new buildings
- Number of permits issued during the year

Municipal Accounting

Municipal accounting procedures share little uniformity. However, because the municipal accounting system ensures that the municipality is administering its financial affairs legally, most municipalities establish designated funds.

In municipal accounting, a fund is a sum of money or another resource (gross or net) set aside for the purpose of carrying on specific activities or attaining

certain goals according to special regulations, restrictions, or limitations. A fund is an independent fiscal and accounting entity. A later chapter discusses fund accounting procedures and the purposes of specific funds.

NATURE OF INSURED'S OPERATIONS

Before determining the premium base, the auditor should have asked enough questions to understand the insured's operations. If possible, the auditor should tour the premises. The auditor must understand what the insured does to know what premium base information to seek. Otherwise, the auditor might overlook a portion of the premium base. Understanding an insured's operations also facilitates accurate classification of the operations. Finally, such information can be extremely valuable for underwriting decisions.

Description of Operations

A goal of every premium audit should be to develop a complete description of operations. Although a previous inspection report or file audit might provide a description of the policyholder's operations, for a more accurate description, the auditor should first describe the operation independently, compare the description with existing information, and resolve the differences. That procedure ensures that the previous description does not influence the auditor.

Underwriters often classify an entity on the basis of information from the producer or from reports lacking sufficient detail to determine all applicable classifications. Also, operations tend to change over time. A building contractor, for example, might complete a residential housing development during the policy year and begin building an apartment complex involving concrete construction operations that are not part of private residence construction. The auditor should note the addition of that new operation and apply the appropriate classification if advisory organization and legal restrictions permit. The auditor, however, must also avoid the possibly erroneous assumption that operations at the time of the audit applied throughout the policy period.

If the insured produces a product, a systematic approach to the description of operations involves following the insured's product through all the stages of production and handling. Often, this step-by-step analysis reveals additional operations that the auditor might have otherwise overlooked. If a business's operations differ in some regard from those of similar businesses, a more detailed explanation might be needed.

The following discussion examines the part of an audit report that describes the insured's operations. It applies primarily to manufacturers but can also apply to mercantile establishments, many contractors, and some service organizations such as cleaners. It is not generally applicable to organizations offering personal services.

Products or Services

The products or services offered for sale help to identify the nature of the insured's business and source of revenues. The firm's name can indicate its primary products or services. Advertising or promotional material can also be helpful in describing the insured's business.

Raw Materials

If the insured manufactures products, some raw materials must be used. If the insured provides a service, it could involve some treatment of certain goods and the use of other substances in the process. In either case, the description of operations should identify the raw materials that the insured uses as the starting point of its operations.

Processing, Transportation, and Distribution

The description of operations should report each stage involved in transforming raw materials into the product, following the raw materials from the time the business receives them until the product reaches the customer's hands.

Whether the insured performs a particular process on the premises or acquires the material already processed can make a considerable difference in the insured's loss exposure. If the insured performs the processing, the auditor should include the payroll of the employees involved.

To discover all the insured loss exposures, an auditor must know which transportation method the insured uses. The workers' compensation auditor must know whether the business uses its own trucks or employs an independent trucking firm and whether the business includes drivers' payroll in payroll accounts or records them separately as payments to independent trucking companies. Large interstate truckers generally cover their drivers under separate workers' compensation policies, but local truckers might be under the insured's direction and control, so the insured might be responsible for workers' compensation benefits for those drivers. In such cases, the auditor must determine the amount of such payments and include them in the premium base.

The auditor should mention the distribution channels for the insured's products in the description of operations. Not only is such information useful to underwriters, particularly in products liability situations, but it is also another lead to additional loss exposures. If the insured hires sales personnel as regular employees, the auditor can determine the workers' compensation premium base from the payroll records. If, however, the insured markets its products through commissioned sales representatives, the auditor must investigate further to ensure inclusion of the full premium base.

Equipment

In almost all cases, the business's processing and handling of materials require certain equipment, machinery, or tools. An auditor who recognizes the type

of equipment that the insured uses has an advantage when classifying the operation. In fact, the definitions of many classifications specifically refer to particular types of equipment. Noting the equipment in the description of operations also alerts underwriters to the loss exposures involved.

Typical Business Operations

Insurers classify most businesses as manufacturers, contractors, mercantile, services, or professionals. Each type has many common characteristics. A premium auditor must analyze the specific insured's operations in detail before applying manual classifications, but the following general observations can provide a starting point for understanding the insured's operations.

Manufacturers

A manufacturer is a firm that buys raw materials and converts them into finished products. Manufacturers can locate in residential communities, but most locate near means of major commercial transportation such as airports, highways, or rail lines. Although manufacturers are of many types, the two major ones are light manufacturers and heavy manufacturers.

Light manufacturers use hand tools or light automated equipment, such as sanders, bench grinders, saws, files, screwdrivers, soldering irons, and sealing machines. Light manufacturers usually produce small items or components for larger products. An example of a light manufacturer is a small company that makes woven items for a craft shop. This type of business can be a family business, a home operation in which a person makes canvas handbags, or a small furniture shop operating out of a garage. Other examples of light manufacturers include factories employing people to build electrical light fixtures and businesses that assemble component parts for television sets.

Employee loss exposures accompanying these light-manufacturing operations are generally minor, because workers usually use hand tools. Frequently, the types of claims that occur involve cuts, minor burns, bruises, or abrasions.

Possibly the greatest liability loss exposures are in the area of products liability. Because other manufacturers might use the small or light manufacturer's product in a larger, complex product, the failure of the product can damage an item worth many times its own value. Also, the failure of a light manufacturer's product in an airplane, for example, could cause numerous deaths or injuries.

Heavy manufacturers use heavy machines to stamp, grind, or form parts from metal or plastics. They may use completed parts produced by other manufacturers to build their own products, or they can fabricate all of their own parts. The type of products manufactured by heavy manufacturers requires large equipment such as drop forges; milling, grinding, or planing machines; hydraulic presses; shearing machines; and bending machines.

Employees have greatly increased loss exposures to injuries in the heavy manufacturing classification of business, compared to light manufacturing.

Such injuries can include back strains from lifting; broken bones; severe burns; possible loss of limbs, fingers, or toes from metal-cutting and pressing equipment; and eye damage from metal shavings or chemical burns.

The liability loss exposure that manufacturers face arises primarily from the products loss exposure. Manufacturers usually have few members of the public at the manufacturing location, so the premises loss exposure is not great. The extent of the products loss exposure varies by product. Although one might think of heavy manufacturers producing large and therefore more dangerous products than light manufacturers, both can have a significant loss exposure.

Contractors

A contractor is one who agrees to furnish materials or perform a service at a specified price. The term is used because a contract usually states the service that the contractor is to perform and the price to be charged. The construction industry has significant insurance needs because of loss exposures to workers as well as the loss exposure to injury resulting from operations completed by contractors. This industry consists of firms that build or repair residential property or those that build or repair commercial property.

A residential contractor remodels and constructs homes and garages. The stages of the residential construction process are generally as follows:

- The builder clears the land in preparation for a foundation.
- The builder then erects wood or metal forms and pours a cement foundation if a basement is included.
- Either a masonry contractor or a cement contractor constructs basement walls of block or poured cement on the foundation.
- The carpentry contractor then builds the wood floors and walls of a frame house.
- Electrical contractors and plumbing contractors install the electrical wiring and plumbing.
- The insulation contractor installs the insulation.
- The carpentry contractor adds the dry wall.
- A specialty contractor installs the interior trim and kitchen cabinets and performs the finishing touches.

Residential construction employs many different types of contractors doing various types of construction work. Although the contractors' jobs vary, the loss exposures are generally the same. Residential construction is done mostly with hand tools and power hand tools. Power tools expose employees to cuts and serious injuries, and the risk of injury is higher because employees usually work on uneven ground. The possibilities of trips and falls on the job site, a loss exposure affecting both employees and the public, are numerous. The public is also exposed to loss from operations, such as blasting and grading. The law considers building equipment and machinery to be "attractive nuisances" for trespassing children, so those items present a liability loss exposure

for contractors. Residential building contractors also have a completed operations loss exposure if someone is injured or if property is damaged because of the contractor's work.

A residential contractor might build one house at a time or an entire subdivision. So the contractor locates its operations wherever homes exist or residential developments are underway.

Although commercial contractors perform the same general operations as residential contractors, they are generally exposed to greater hazards because of the differences in materials and equipment used and the size of the projects in which they are involved. That greater loss exposure usually results from more employees on the job site (workers' compensation loss exposure) and more persons occupying the completed project (general liability loss exposure). The collapse of a commercial building under construction would likely cause many more injuries than the collapse of a residential building. One positive aspect of the workers' compensation loss exposure is that as the size of the contractor increases, so does the likelihood of some type of safety program. The commercial construction process is as follows:

- The builder clears the land for any type of building.
- The foundation is laid. Unlike a residence with a foundation of poured cement and supporting walls, a commercial structure might have a skeletal steel or reinforced concrete structure. The foundation for a commercial structure is usually wood or steel post pilings driven into bedrock.
- The builder usually attaches forms to this skeletal structure to hold the poured reinforced concrete floors. When the concrete is cured, the builder removes the forms and sets up new ones to pour the next level's floor. That operation continues until the builder has poured all of the floors.
- The exterior walls can be of many different materials, such as glass, concrete, metal, or wood. In a building with a steel skeletal structure, the exterior walls are primarily decorative and do not add any structural strength to the building.
- Finishing the interior and installing plumbing and electrical wiring require the same carpentry, electrical, and plumbing skills needed in residential construction.

Commercial contractors' companies are usually larger than those of residential contractors. One reason for commercial contractors' large size is that, although each employee uses the same hand tools as residential contractors, the commercial construction business must own or rent larger pieces of equipment, such as cranes, generators, and welding equipment. This rental cost or purchase price can be so high that only a large company can afford to do that type of construction.

Mercantile Businesses (Stores and Restaurants)

The great variety of wholesale and retail stores and restaurants can be generally categorized as mercantile establishments, or simply stores. A store

or mercantile operation is an establishment that buys and sells goods and has no manufacturing or construction operations. Mercantile operations employ salespersons to sell their products. The establishment can be as small as a one-room antique shop or as large as a major department store.

Injuries to employees of mercantile operations include strained muscles from lifting items; minor cuts and abrasions from stocking shelves; bruises or bone injuries from tripping; and foot injuries from dropping items.

In mercantile operations, the general liability loss exposures are significant. The premises are open to the public for browsing or window-shopping, leaving the establishment vulnerable to claims from falls, tripping, or damage to customers' clothing from protruding objects or sharp corners.

Service Businesses

Another type of business operation, the service business, involves supplies the public with services for a charge. This transaction constitutes the sale of an intangible product. Examples include the plumber who opens a clogged drain, the laundry or dry cleaner that cleans and presses clothes, the bank that provides financial services, and appliance repair services that restore appliances to working order.

A service business usually employs specialized technicians. Businesses such as television repair, kitchen appliance service, and furnace service/repair require technicians trained for the specific type of equipment. Sometimes municipalities require licenses to provide certain services, such as plumbing or electrical work. Injuries to employees of a service business usually consist of minor burns and cuts. Certain service businesses also have some lifting loss exposures and occupational disease loss exposures. The premises and operations loss exposures are few because this type of business often operates from a truck or van and has no store open to the public. In other cases, such as banks and laundries, however, the premises and operations loss exposures can be substantial. More significant liability loss exposures for many service businesses come from completed operations. Because the service business might repair or clean something belonging to the customer, any damage caused by faulty repairing, cleaning, or renewing can become the service company's responsibility.

Professional Services

A professional service person typically works for one client or patient at a time, performing a personal service for that individual. Examples of professionals are doctors, lawyers, dentists, stockbrokers, and accountants.

Many professionals work alone or in limited partnerships. They usually maintain offices where they offer consultations by appointment. Owners often group such private offices in professional buildings, although professionals can also offer their services in a clinic or similar environment. Because the professional service business deals directly with the public regarding personal matters, the greatest loss exposure is one of professional liability,

or malpractice. Public liability and workers' compensation loss exposures are also associated with maintaining an office, although those are minor in comparison. One concern is the gray area between the general liability and professional liability loss exposures. Whether an injury has arisen from a professional or a nonprofessional act or omission can be difficult to determine. For example, is the failure to put up the railing on a patient's hospital bed a professional or nonprofessional error? If the insurers or limits on the policies covering those two loss exposures are different, adjustment problems could arise about which policy covers the claim, or the limits under one of the policies could be inadequate for the loss.

Some policies classify the staff of a hospital, clinic, school, church, camp, or daycare center as professionals. In those cases, the premium auditor must be careful in determining who is the named insured and whom the policy covers.

QUALITY OF INSURED'S OPERATIONS

Merely observing what goes on in a business does not help the premium auditor determine how well an insured operates. How an insured operates refers not only to how well day-to-day operations function but also to the quality of business relationships. An auditor must be able to recognize how operations affect business relationships as part of compiling an overall portrait of the business.

All of the areas discussed in this section reveal, to some extent, the nature of the insured's operations. Shortcomings in any one area, or even in several areas, may not be particularly meaningful. By evaluating the following five areas, the premium auditor can develop a total picture of the insured's operations:

1. Management competence
2. Employee relations
3. Condition of premises
4. Condition of records
5. Cooperation with insurer

Management Competence

The first area to consider when evaluating the insured's operations is the insured's management competence. The level of management competence influences both operations and business relationships. To measure the management competence of an insured entity, an auditor must consider how the following factors apply to an insured:

- Management ability
- Amount of experience
- Business reputation
- Quality of workmanship
- Prudence of operations
- Caliber of employees

Management ability consists of knowing the administrative methods applicable to a particular business. It involves planning, organizing, motivating, and controlling operations. Knowing how to determine what the business has to do (and when and by whom it must be done) and getting it done indicate management ability. Completing jobs on schedule, keeping jobs within original cost estimates, delivering goods on time, and operating at a profit are all positive management characteristics.

Experience is another factor to consider when evaluating how well the insured operates. The length of time the insured has been in business may often be a good indicator of competence. The insured might have obtained experience and expertise in basic business techniques as an employee or employer, but ownership experience usually indicates managerial ability as well. Generally, the greater the experience, the greater the chance of success.

The audit should also note the level of employees' experience. Having experienced employees may reduce turnover and improve quality of products or services. In contrast, inexperienced employees usually require close supervision, and that increases training costs. If a company can retain employees long enough to develop experience, it may indicate that management is dedicated to continuity of personnel. The effect of employee turnover on costs and production is difficult to measure. The premium auditor can sometimes determine the employee experience level by comparing salaries to those of other similar business concerns.

The business or professional reputation of an insured entity or its management may be an indication of how well the insured operates. Respect or lack thereof is not something an auditor can determine from an audit of the insured's records. The auditor should seek out outside sources, such as other businesses, trade periodicals, newspapers, professional publications, customers, suppliers, and others with whom the insured comes in contact.

Quality of workmanship directly affects the product or service provided and can reflect on management competence. The auditor can gather valuable information by observing the operations while visiting the insured's premises. Shoddy workmanship or careless service can indicate poor supervisory and management attitudes. Evidence of such behavior should alert the auditor that the particular business is probably not a desirable insured. An insured's cutting corners or taking production shortcuts in operations can alert the auditor to the possibility that less than adequate attention has been paid to safety and overall operations throughout the organization.

Prudence of operations indicates the firm's ability to conduct its operations within the limits of its capabilities. That factor is particularly important during periods of rapid expansion when the firm might overextend resources such as capital, personnel, or available talent. A prudent company recognizes its limitations and operates within them. Events such as the following should concern the auditor:

- A small subcontractor suddenly bids on a large construction project.
- A local trial lawyer accepts a large criminal case.

- A manufacturer accepts contracts whose performance taxes its machinery or production capabilities.
- A dealer purchases excessive stocks in anticipation of increased sales.

Caliber of employees is another important aspect of a business's success. Although the owners or management must administer business operations properly, it is the employees who implement employer directives. The caliber of the insured's employees should be equal to or better than average for the industry. Direct employees are those under the insured's immediate supervision. The employer controls performance, productivity, and costs of the direct employees.

When the insured undertakes specialized tasks outside the capabilities of its employees, using independent contractors might be appropriate. However, the employer must provide significant supervision of independent contracts to control results, because the insured is responsible regardless of who has performed the tasks.

Many businesses use manufacturers' representatives or commissioned agents rather than direct sales representatives if sales are insufficient to support a direct employee. One advantage of that method is tax savings. In addition, a business can benefit from the broad customer contacts made by manufacturers' representatives because they usually represent more than one firm. On the other hand, an employer may have less control over sales presentations when using a manufacturer's representative rather than a direct employee, increasing the possibility of legal and insurance problems caused by misrepresentations.

The presence of many part-time employees is another clue to the nature of the business and its operations. Companies use part-time employees to handle peak workloads, seasonal variations, and other temporary needs. However, excessive use of part-time help might indicate cost cutting, management attitude problems, or the beginning of financial problems. In addition, the auditor should consider the possibility of higher risk potential if many of the part-time employees have other full-time jobs. Resulting fatigue can cause accidents or oversights.

The extent to which a business uses union or nonunion employees varies considerably by the territory in which the business is located. Conditions largely outside a firm's control often determine the extent to which union employees are used. If the locale or type of business is unionized, the insured's employees are also probably union members. Some unions have apprentice and training programs; others do not. An employer can encounter difficulty in terminating poorly performing employees if a union is involved.

Nonunion salaries might be lower than union salaries, thereby creating a competitive advantage for nonunion businesses over union shops. That advantage, however, can be at the cost of poor quality workmanship. For coverages and classifications of businesses with payroll as a premium base, higher-salaried union employees should develop higher premium for the same loss exposure as lower-salaried nonunion personnel.

The auditor must consider all operational factors to determine the insured's competence and skill in operating a business. The premium auditor's major concern is whether the insured is comparable to similar businesses in the industry, and if not, why not.

Employee Relations

The second area to consider in evaluating an insured's operations is the insured's employee relations. Among the items to be considered in this regard are the following:

- Wages
- Working conditions
- Prior labor/management problems (including turnover)
- Benefit programs
- Employee opinion
- False claims

The insured's financial ability to pay a wage comparable to what an employee could receive elsewhere—if not higher—is important. Higher-than-average wages reduce turnover. Reduced turnover results in better-trained employees. Well-trained employees are likely to understand safety goals and cooperate in achieving these goals. Below-average wages do not produce those results. An auditor should be able to detect any excessive employee turnover from reviewing payroll records and should investigate it as a sign of more serious problems.

Working conditions include many factors. From an employee morale standpoint, regularly scheduled working hours are preferable to erratic patterns, such as frequent days off followed by heavy overtime requirements. The frequency and amount of overtime in relation to total hours worked are additional considerations. An employee might welcome excessive and continuous overtime from an income-producing viewpoint, but it can have an offsetting negative effect on the employee's social and leisure time.

Adequate and knowledgeable supervision is another gauge of working conditions. Good supervision generally leads to better overall performance. Availability and implementation of employee training programs are other relevant factors. The employer should design training programs not only to improve present job performance but also to improve employees' prospects for promotion and to promote self-development.

The employer should assign work fairly to all employees, and employees should understand their particular roles in the company. Employers should place employees in jobs for which they have been specifically trained or in which they have sufficient experience. Precise work assignments help employees to work toward the company's goals.

Labor/management problems may result from poor wages and working conditions and are often a symptom of problems in other areas. Strikes,

work stoppages, slowdowns, sit-ins, or lockouts are extreme results of such problems, and they all have a direct effect on the ability of the business to operate. Less serious problems can become evident to the auditor during the review of operations and business records.

Benefit programs might not affect how the business operates, but the lack of a benefit program has an indirect effect on employee morale, with a resultant effect on performance. The auditor can compare company vacation policy, medical plans, life insurance, and other such employee benefits to those of equivalent businesses as another measure of how the business operates.

Employee opinion is a grass-roots indicator of the company's operation. During an audit or while reviewing operations, the auditor has many opportunities for discussions with employees. Even without asking, the auditor might overhear comments revealing employee attitudes. Whether or not the comments are favorable, they add to the auditor's information about the business.

Another factor to consider in evaluating employee relations is the frequency of false claims. Employees who are dissatisfied or unhappy with their job, employer, or salary sometimes file false workers' compensation claims. Frequently, a plant closing results in a wave of workers' compensation disability claims because employees are trying to supplement their income after being laid off. Many of those claims involve injuries that are difficult to disprove.

Condition of Premises

The third area to consider when evaluating the insured's operations is the condition of the insured's premises. The premium auditor's observations of the premises' condition should cover more than just the physical quality of the buildings or work space. Of course, a clean, healthy workplace is essential, but other qualities, such as the appropriate equipment to enable the employees to perform their tasks as easily and safely as possible, are also important.

Work space layout is as important as work equipment. The work flow pattern affects production. An inefficient work flow pattern can also cause injuries by unnecessarily exposing employees to workplace hazards.

Condition of Records

The fourth area to consider when evaluating the insured's operations is the condition of the insured's records. All organizations need some system of accounting records. The detail and quality of the accounting and accident records often reflect the quality of management. Unless an organization adheres to generally accepted accounting principles, drawing a conclusion about its financial position is impossible. Government regulations and tax laws also require organized bookkeeping methods.

The insured's specific accident recordkeeping practices should comply with the Occupational Safety and Health Act, particularly Form 100, which is

the basic log for listing all occupational injuries or illnesses. Much of the information posted on Form 100 is derived from the employer's first notice of injury. A system for properly maintaining the employer's first notice can indicate a well-organized recordkeeping approach, and it can also be useful to the insurer's loss control department in structuring a loss control program.

In addition to meeting basic bookkeeping standards, an organization's records should be set up to take full advantage of insurance rules and requirements. The employer should establish payroll records from which the auditor can determine whether the work being performed involves a classification not shown on the original policy. Payroll records should allow easy identification of overtime. In making an accurate premium audit, an auditor might seek the insured's records showing individual salaries, classification identity, certificates of insurance for subcontractors, job cost records, material and labor cost breakdown, segregation of product sales and receipts from services, valuation records, vehicle records, and purchase and disposal records. An employer should keep those records in two forms: a detailed record and a summary format for ease of auditing.

In addition to the quality of the accounting and auditing records, the auditor should be concerned about the availability and accessibility of records.

Cooperation With the Insurer

The fifth area to consider when evaluating the insured's operations is the insured's level of cooperation with the insurer. Willingness to cooperate with the insurer is essential. An insured that fails to provide information requested in a claim investigation, ignores loss control recommendations, or refuses to allow a premium auditor to examine the necessary records is not a desirable account from the insurer's point of view. The auditor's evaluation of the insured's attitude can reveal significant information. Failure to cooperate in one area could signal uncooperative behavior in other areas as well. When the insured is unwilling to cooperate, the auditor should report that experience to the underwriting department so for reconsideration of the account's underwriting desirability.

The following actions indicate cooperation:

- The insured makes all necessary records available for review.
- The insured makes knowledgeable personnel available to answer the auditor's questions.
- The insured or its bookkeeper exhibits a conscious effort to help and to cooperate in the audit.

Occasionally, a policyholder's uncooperative behavior stems from an identifiable cause. For example, a disappointing claim settlement might have left the insured with a negative impression of the insurer or of the premium auditing process. Or the insured may simply not understand the reason for the premium audit. A later chapter explores techniques that an auditor can use to overcome such communication barriers.

INSURED'S FINANCIAL CONDITION

Because the insurance policy states that the auditor has access to confidential financial and accounting records, the auditor is in a unique position to assess the insured's financial condition, which may have changed considerably since the account was initially underwritten. The auditor must respect the confidentiality of the records when using the data extracted during an audit. The insurer must restrict the availability of such information to the auditor, the account underwriter, and those involved in processing the data for accounting or statistical purposes.

In addition to developing specific loss exposure information relevant to the insurance coverages provided, the auditor must be alert to other financial details that could have underwriting value. Insurers do not expect premium auditors to perform a detailed financial audit, but the auditor should know how to evaluate financial information to identify business trends and changes in the organization's financial structure. When a premium auditor discovers declining sales, employee layoffs, sudden business expansion, or other significant changes, an in-depth financial analysis might be necessary. Results of such an analysis can contribute to acceptable or superior underwriting results. The premium auditor's accounting background usually includes the fundamentals of financial statements and techniques of financial analysis. This section reviews those fundamentals to show the benefit of interpreting financial statements as part of a premium audit.

Statement of changes in financial position
A statement that summarizes changes in the assets and liabilities.

Balance sheet, or **statement of financial position**
A financial statement that systematically indicates an organization's assets, liabilities, and owners' equity as of a specific date.

Assets
Things of value, money, or property (tangible or intangible) owned by or owed to a business.

Current assets
Cash and assets that in the normal course of business will be converted into cash within twelve months from the date of the balance sheet.

Financial Statements

The primary financial statements of any business are the balance sheet (statement of financial position), the income statement, and the **statement of changes in financial position**. The balance sheet indicates a business's financial position as of a specified date. The income statement summarizes the results of the business operations over a period of time, usually a fiscal year. The statement of cash flows indicates the sources and uses of funds available during the specified period.

Balance Sheet

The **balance sheet**, or statement of financial position, systematically lists assets, liabilities, and owners' equity as of a specified date. Exhibit 4-1 illustrates a typical company's balance sheet.

Assets represent things of value and money or property (tangible or intangible) owned by the business or owed to the business. Analysts usually categorize assets as follows:

- **Current assets** are cash and those assets that in the normal course of business will be converted into cash within twelve months from the date of the balance sheet. These include such items as accounts receivable, marketable securities, short-term notes receivable, short-term investments, inventory, and accrued interest.

EXHIBIT 4-1

ABC Company Balance Sheet

ABC Company, Inc.
Balance Sheet, as of December 31, 20XX

Assets		
Current assets		
Cash	$ 29,382	
Accounts receivable	171,259	
Notes receivable	20,000	
Inventory	112,538	
Marketable securities	8,870	
Total current assets		$342,049
Fixed assets		
Land	$ 35,000	
Building	70,000	
Machinery and equipment	40,422	
Vehicles	30,400	
Total assets	$175,822	
Less accumulated depreciation	(40,000)	
Total fixed assets		$135,822
Other assets		
Cash value—life insurance	$ 12,000	
Nonmarketable securities	60,069	
Total other assets		$ 72,069
Intangible assets		4,435
Total assets		$554,375
Liabilities and owners' equity		
Current liabilities		
Accounts payable	$ 80,806	
Notes payable	79,963	
Long-term debt—current	22,729	
Accrued expenses	38,806	
Other current liabilities	23,284	
Total current liabilities		$245,588
Long-term liabilities		
Long-term debt—Noncurrent	$ 91,472	
All other liabilities—Noncurrent	14,414	
Total long-term liabilities		$105,886
Owners' equity		
Capital stock	$100,000	
Earned surplus	102,901	
Total owners' equity		$202,901
Total liabilities and owners' equity		$554,375

Fixed assets
Assets that a business cannot readily convert into cash and does not normally intend to sell.

Other assets
Assets with benefits extending into the future.

Intangible assets
Assets with an absence of physical characteristics.

- **Fixed assets** are those assets that a business cannot readily convert into cash and does not intend to sell during the normal course of business. Fixed assets are used regularly in the business' operation, and the benefit derived from them extends beyond one accounting period. Fixed assets include land, buildings, machinery, equipment, and vehicles.
- **Other assets** include assets whose benefits will extend into the future, such as prepaid expenses, deferred charges, unamortized expenses on long-term debt, and other such future values.
- **Intangible assets** are those assets with an absence of physical characteristics. The primary example of an intangible asset is goodwill, which represents the value of the business name and reputation. Businesses also usually show patents and copyrights on balance sheets as intangible assets.

Liabilities
Financial obligations, or debts, owed to another entity.

Current liabilities
Debts that become due within one year.

Long-term liabilities
Debts payable after one year.

Liabilities are financial obligations, or debts, owed to others. The two major types of liabilities are current and long-term:

- **Current liabilities** include those debts that are to become due within one year, such as short-term notes payable, accounts payable, taxes payable, and accruals.
- **Long-term liabilities** include debts payable after one year from the date of the financial report. Those include long-term notes, mortgages, reserves for long-term indebtedness such as debentures, and any other long-term debts.

Owners' equity
The ownership value of a business, which is the difference between assets and liabilities.

Owners' equity is the ownership value of a business, which is the difference between assets and liabilities. It is a balancing figure on the liability side of the balance sheet that represents the residual value of the business to its owners. The specific equity accounts depend on the legal form of the organization. Owners' equity in a sole proprietorship normally consists of a capital account to record investments or withdrawals of capital and a drawing account to record withdrawals such as owners' salaries or personal use of merchandise. In a partnership, the partners can divide owners' equity into separate accounts for each partner. Corporate balance sheets show a capital stock account recording the par value of each class of corporate stock outstanding and a retained earnings account recording the income reinvested in the business.

Income Statement

Although the balance sheet reveals a firm's financial position as of a specified date, the firm's financial strength and potential also depend on its earnings' capacity. The income statement provides specific information about the firm's net earnings experience in a given accounting period by combining the revenue earned during a specified period and the expenses incurred in generating those revenues.

The firm's earnings experience over a particular accounting period typically affects the owners' equity position. Owners' equity increases when revenues exceed expenses and the firm does not entirely pay out the difference—net income—as dividends. To link the firm's earnings experience in a particular accounting period with the owners' equity position shown on the balance

sheet, the income statement must show the retained earnings for the period. Retained earnings are the net income reinvested in the business. If the changes in owners' equity are complicated by additional investments, by partial retirement of owners' interests, or by other nonearnings-based events, the firm usually prepares a separate statement of retained earnings or changes in owners' equity. The income statement shown in Exhibit 4-2 supplements the information provided in the ABC Company's balance sheet.

EXHIBIT 4-2

ABC Company Income Statement

ABC Company, Inc.
Income Statement for Calendar Year Ending
December 31, 20XX

Total sales	$1,269,966
Less discounts and allowances	(2,174)
Net sales	$1,267,792
Less cost of goods sold	(853,225)
Gross margin	$ 414,567
Less operating expenses	(376,534)
Operating profit	$ 38,033
Less miscellaneous expenses	0
Income before taxes	$ 38,033
Less provision for income taxes	(16,751)
Net income	$ 21,282

Net sales, or **operating revenue**
The income received from the sale of merchandise or from services rendered during the income statement period.

Cost of goods sold
The total cost of merchandise delivered to customers as a result of sales.

Gross margin
The net sales or operating revenue minus cost of goods sold, which, on an income statement, covers all other expenses.

The income statement normally lists the total revenues for the period and then shows various adjustments, leaving net income as the remainder. The following describes the typical steps to obtain net income.

- Subtract cash discounts (or cash allowances) and sales returns from the total revenues to show the net amount actually received from customers.
- The remainder equals **net sales**, or **operating revenue**, which represents income received from the sale of merchandise or from services rendered during the income statement period. This amount constitutes normal business income.
- Subtract the **cost of goods sold**, which includes the costs required to produce the income—such as material, labor, rent, maintenance, and repairs. Another cost is depreciation, which accounts for the decline in useful book value of an asset because of wear and tear.
- **Gross margin** is the remaining amount, which covers all other expenses and income.

Operating expenses
The salaries and other expenses necessary for continuing business operation.

Operating profit
The profit derived from continuing business operations.

Other income or expense
The income or expense not directly related to business operations.

Income before taxes
The profit before tax allocation.

Provision for income tax
An accrual account representing tax incurred but not paid for the period.

Net income
The excess of revenues and gains over expenses and losses for a specified period.

Working capital
A firm's current assets minus its current liabilities.

- Deduct **operating expenses**, which include salaries and other expenses necessary for continuing business operation.
- The remainder is **operating profit**, which represents the actual profit derived from continuing business operations but not from discontinued operations or extraordinary events.
- Subtract **other income or expense**, which includes income or expense not directly related to sales or other business operations.
- The remainder is **income before taxes**, which represents profit before tax allocation.
- Deduct a **provision for income tax** as an accrual account representing the tax (based on income during the period) that the business has incurred but has not paid.
- The remainder is **net income**, which is the amount remaining from gross revenues for the period after the firm has paid all the corresponding expenses. Net income is available to the firm to distribute to owners as dividends or withdrawals or for reinvestment in the business through retained earnings

Statement of Cash Flows

To gain insight into the changes in the firm's financial position from one balance sheet date to the next, the premium auditor can examine the statement of cash flows. This statement summarizes changes in the assets and liabilities resulting from operating, investing, and financing activities during the period. It also shows how the firm used its assets during the period, that is, to acquire other assets, to pay debts, or to make distributions to owners. The statement thus reveals the causes of any increases or decreases in **working capital**, which is the excess of current assets over current liabilities. Such information provides additional clues to the firm's future plans. Exhibit 4-3 shows an example of a statement of cash flows.

Financial Statement Analysis

The implications of the information presented in the financial statements are not necessarily obvious. Relationships among various account balances are often more important than the absolute dollar amounts. A person can analyze those relationships by computing ratios. However, neither ratios nor individual account balances are meaningful indicators of success or failure in the absence of benchmarks. Comparing those figures over time as well as against industry averages is necessary.

A person can uncover potentially serious financial problems in an apparently sound business by carefully analyzing financial statements. Many conditions that seem benign can create problems when the economic climate changes. Some of the more prominent conditions are as follows:

- Inadequate working capital
- Excessive investment in fixed assets

- Heavy indebtedness
- Unbalanced inventory values
- Inadequate return on ownership investment
- Excessive credit extensions to customers
- Questionable loans to officers or subsidiary corporations

Premium auditors using fundamental techniques of financial analysis can often identify these conditions in time to save the insurer from becoming entangled in substantial collection problems. Auditors can also glean additional underwriting information through financial statement analysis. For example, underwriters would be interested in a firm's ability to meet its current financial obligations. If a firm is struggling to pay its current bills, it may not be able to pay its insurance premiums.

EXHIBIT 4-3

ABC Company Statement of Cash Flows

ABC Company, Inc.
Statement of Cash Flows
for Calendar Year Ended
December 31, 20XX

Cash flows from operating activities:		
Net income	$21,282	
Add (deduct) items affecting net cash		
Depreciation expense	7,273	
Increase in accounts receivable	(8,576)	
Decrease in inventory	2,657	
Net cash from operating activities		$ 22,636
Cash flows from investing activities:		
Sale of machinery	$ 5,630	
Purchase of building	(36,000)	
Purchase of new machinery	(19,460)	
Purchase of mobile equipment	(5,500)	
Net cash used for investing activities		$(55,330)
Cash flows from financing activities:		
Cash received from bank loan	$50,000	
Payment of dividend on common stock	(12,000)	
Net cash provided by financing activities		$ 38,000
Net increase in cash for the year		$ 5,306
Cash at beginning of year		19,076
Cash at end of year		$24,382

Trend Analysis

Examining trends is important for financial analysis. A steady decline in sales over several years is an obvious cause for concern no matter how strong the firm's financial position. Equally serious is an earnings decline or a decrease in working capital. A combination of trends can also provide significant clues to a firm's financial condition. For example, a 10 percent increase in sales might occur in conjunction with a 20 percent increase in accounts receivable. Those developments warrant a closer look at the firm's credit policies.

Although trend analysis can yield significant information about a particular firm, it also has limitations. The effect of price changes can distort trends, particularly over several years. A change in accounting practices or in the business itself is also possible during the period of comparison. Analysts should consider the general economic climate because the same trends might be characteristic of other firms in the industry to a greater or lesser extent.

Ratio Analysis

Ratio analysis is another powerful tool in evaluating a firm's financial condition. An auditor can compute the relationship of various values in the financial statements as ratios. When a particular ratio is different from previous years' ratios or from the industry average, a problem could be developing. Ratio analysis also uses trend analysis. That is, the trend of a ratio over time can give an analyst a good idea of the direction in which a firm's finances are headed.

Liquidity
A measure of a firm's ability to quickly convert an investment into cash with a minimal loss of principal.

Current ratio
A ratio of current assets to current liabilities that measures a firm's working capital position.

Liquidity measures a firm's ability to quickly convert an investment into cash with a minimal loss of principal. It is therefore a significant consideration in underwriting a sizable account developing large premiums.

The **current ratio**, or ratio of current assets to current liabilities, reveals the firm's working capital position. The higher that ratio, the more working capital the firm has available to meet its current obligations, to expand its volume of business, and to exploit new opportunities. To illustrate, the ABC Company's current ratio is as follows:

$$\text{Current ratio} = \frac{\text{Current assets}}{\text{Current liabilities}} = \frac{\$342{,}049}{\$245{,}588} = 1.39.$$

This ratio means that for every dollar of current liabilities (amounts owed), ABC has $1.39 of current assets to pay those liabilities. By itself, the ratio does not mean much. It becomes significant when compared to ABC's past ratio and to the average ratio for similar firms or the industry as a whole. If ABC's ratio is lower than all of those, then ABC might have difficulty meeting its current obligations relative to the past and to other firms in the same industry. Although stating a universal benchmark current ratio is not possible, a ratio below 1.0 means that current liabilities exceed current assets and indicates likely financial problems.

A firm must also guard against a current ratio that is too high. If that ratio is caused by slow-paying customers, unused cash, or idle inventory, the business is not using its funds wisely.

The **quick ratio** or **acid-test ratio** is a ratio of current assets minus inventory to current liabilities that measures a firm's ability to quickly generate needed cash. Because it excludes inventory from current assets, it is a more stringent test of a firm's liquidity than the current ratio. It is based on the likelihood that a firm cannot sell the inventory at its stated value quickly enough to satisfy a sudden need for cash. The quick ratio considers only quick assets, those resources that are immediately available to meet obligations. Quick assets include cash, temporary investments held in place of cash, and current accounts and notes receivable. The ABC Company's quick ratio is as follows:

Quick ratio, or acid-test ratio
A ratio of current assets minus inventory to current liabilities that measures a firm's ability to quickly generate needed cash.

$$\text{Quick ratio} = \frac{\text{Quick assets}}{\text{Current liabilities}} = \frac{\$229{,}511}{\$245{,}588} = 0.93.$$

As with the current ratio, one must compare this ratio to ABC's ratio in the past or to similar firms in the same industry. The higher the quick ratio, the better able a firm is to pay its bills.

Another indicator of a firm's liquidity, as well as its earnings potential, is the **inventory turnover ratio**, which is calculated by dividing the cost of goods sold by the inventory. Assuming the ABC Company's inventory is at the same level as in the previous year, its inventory turnover ratio is as follows:

Inventory turnover ratio
A ratio of the cost of goods sold divided by the inventory that indicates a firm's liquidity as well as its earning potential.

$$\text{Inventory turnover ratio} = \frac{\text{Costs of goods sold}}{\text{Average inventory}} = \frac{\$853{,}225}{\$112{,}538} = 7.58.$$

ABC turns its inventory over about seven times per year. That is, in theory, it completely sells out its inventory seven times per year. In practice, not all the inventory sells, but this ratio gives a good indicator of sales activity. This ratio must also be compared to ABC's ratio in the past or to similar firms to be relevant. The inventory turnover ratio shows the speed with which the firm can turn inventory into cash. Theoretically, the quicker the firm can turn inventory over, the quicker it can provide cash. Thus, one firm with a higher turnover ratio than that of a second similar firm has less demand on its working capital than the second firm. A firm with slow turnover cannot provide cash quickly. That slow turnover could indicate the possibility of a large amount of goods in inventory that the firm cannot sell. This slow turnover casts doubt on the firm's future earnings.

Solvency indicates a firm's ability to meet the repayment schedules and the interest costs associated with its debt. If a firm does not pay its debits promptly, creditors could force the firm into bankruptcy. So, underwriters must also consider solvency in making judgments about accepting and continuing accounts.

Solvency
A firm's ability to meet the repayment schedules and the interest costs associated with its debt.

Several ratios provide measures of the firm's long-term solvency. For example, if the firm's ratio of current debt to owners' equity exceeds 1.00, the firm could

be experiencing difficulty in meeting its obligations (similar to a current ratio below 1.0). For the ABC Company, this ratio is as follows:

$$\frac{\text{Current debt}}{\text{Owners' equity}} = \frac{\$245,588}{\$202,901} = 1.21.$$

The ratio of fixed assets to owners' equity could indicate a possible disproportionate investment in fixed assets, which could drain expenses and create little income. A general rule of thumb is that the ratio should be below 1.0 for manufacturers and below 0.75 for retailers or wholesalers. For the ABC Company, that ratio is calculated as follows:

$$\frac{\text{Fixed assets}}{\text{Owners' equity}} = \frac{\$135,822}{\$202,901} = 0.67.$$

The ratio of long-term liabilities to net working capital shows the extent to which the firm relies on debt financing. If debt exceeds working capital, the firm is conducting its activities on borrowed capital. If this is the case, the interest and amortization expense might become too great a burden. Financial analysts consider long-term debt to be at a dangerous level when this ratio exceeds 1.0. The ABC Company's ratio is as follows:

$$\frac{\text{Long-term liabilities}}{\text{Net working capital}} = \frac{\$105,886}{\$96,461} = 1.10.$$

If the ratio of total debt to owners' equity exceeds 1.0, then the creditors own more of the business than the owners themselves. A lower ratio generally indicates greater long-term financial stability. In the case of the ABC Company, that ratio is as follows:

$$\frac{\text{Total debt}}{\text{Owners' equity}} = \frac{\$351,474}{\$202,901} = 1.73.$$

Net income ratio
A ratio of net income to sales that measures a firm's rate of profit compared to sales.

Tests of profitability are designed to indicate that in the long run a firm's success depends on its ability to earn a profit. The ratio of net income to sales, the **net income ratio**, shows if a firm is earning a reasonable rate of profit from its business. If not, it could have difficulty weathering a period of rising costs or declining sales. Most financial analysts express this and other profitability ratios as percentages so that they can easily compare the ratios to current interest rates. An adequate rate of return depends on the degree of risk and the prevailing economic climate. An analyst must measure the rate of return against prior financial statements, comparable firms, and alternative investment vehicles. The net income ratio for the ABC Company is as follows:

$$\text{Net income ratio} = \frac{\text{Net income}}{\text{Total sales}} = \frac{\$21,282}{\$1,269,966} = 1.7\%.$$

Another important indicator of profitability is the rate of return on investment. The rate of return also has implications for the firm's long-term solvency. If the

rate of return on investment is too low, the firm might be unable to cover its financing costs from earnings. One measure of return on investment is the ratio of net income to owners' equity (or owners' equity), also expressed as a percentage. The ABC Company's return on equity is as follows:

$$\text{Return on equity} = \frac{\text{Net income}}{\text{Owners' equity}} = \frac{\$21{,}282}{\$202{,}901} = 10.5\%.$$

The preceding ratios help determine the firm's financial position. A premium auditor should become familiar with the *Key Business Ratios* published by Dun & Bradstreet or the similar information published by a number of other organizations. Those publications provide benchmarks of comparison to other firms in the same field. Such benchmarks indicate a desirable range rather than an ideal. Exhibit 4-4 illustrates the business ratios from one publication for furniture and home furnishings stores.

An auditor should use such benchmarks carefully when evaluating an account's financial condition. When changes occur or trends indicate potential problems, the premium auditor should question them. Valid reasons might underlie these changes or trends; therefore, the auditor should not make assumptions without full investigation. Nevertheless, careful use of these benchmarks helps to project future success or failure of a business and the continued desirability of the account. Trends are particularly useful to underwriters who must be alert for financial deterioration indicators, which could increase moral hazard. Financial statement analysis also helps the premium auditor evaluate the reliability of reported financial data.

INSURED'S LOSS EXPOSURE

A premium auditor's review of the insured's operations should note any significant changes since the last audit or since the insurer wrote the policy. Often a change in operations has a significant effect on the premium audit. It could reveal additional covered loss exposures requiring the auditor to assign additional classifications. In any case, the auditor should record the current information so that the underwriter can keep the underwriting file up-to-date. Significant changes in operations include changes in the firm's ownership or management; different locations; and alteration of the operations, products, or services, which frequently lead to additional loss exposures.

Ownership

Changes in the firm's organizational structure can significantly affect both underwriting and the premium audit. A sole proprietor may sell the business to a new owner. Some policies are not transferable, and in such cases, policy provisions terminate coverage automatically. A less apparent change in ownership occurs when the original owner of a business retires from actively running the business but maintains ownership while hiring a new manager.

EXHIBIT 4-4

Business Ratios for Furniture and Home Furnishings Stores

	Assets in Thousands							
	Under $100	$100 to $250	$251 to $500	$501 to $1,000	$1,001 to $5,000	$5,001 to $10,000	$10,001 to $25,000	$25,001 and over
Current Ratio*	1.3	1.8	1.8	2.2	1.9	1.8	1.6	1.9
Quick Ratio*	0.7	0.7	0.7	1.2	0.7	0.8	0.7	0.5
Net Sales to Working Capital*	42.6	13.9	11.1	7.2	7.7	7.3	9.5	5.2
Total Asset Turnover*	7.5	4.9	3.0	2.9	2.8	2.3	2.6	1.3
Inventory Turnover*	14.5	7.2	4.9	5.4	3.9	2.7	4.4	2.1
Receivables Turnover*	57.3	25.2	16.9	13.6	14.6	9.2	10.5	15.9
Total Liabilities to Net Worth*	2.5	1.6	1.9	1.1	1.3	1.1	1.6	1.1
Current Assets to Working Capital*	4.2	2.2	2.2	1.8	2.2	2.2	2.7	2.1
Debt Ratio**	71.3	61.8	65.2	52.3	56.9	52.1	61.0	53.2
Return on Assets**	44.0	20.1	11.6	14.4	11.3	11.3	12.7	12.5
Return on Equity								
Before Income Taxes**	148.2	43.9	25.1	25.7	22.0	20.2	27.9	22.6
Return on Equity								
After Income Taxes**	145.3	42.4	24.1	24.2	20.5	18.3	25.9	15.2
Profit Margin								
Before Income Taxes**	5.6	3.4	2.9	4.2	3.4	4.2	4.2	8.0

*Times to 1

**Percentages

Adapted with permission from Leo Troy, *Almanac of Business and Industrial Financial Ratios*, 2004 ed. (New York, NY: Aspen Publishers, Inc., 2004), p. 206. Based on data for corporations with net income as supplied to the Internal Revenue Service.

Although ownership has not changed, management and control may be in the hands of someone else possibly less qualified than the original owner. The fact that the business name has not changed does not necessarily indicate that no change has occurred in the legal ownership or control. A readily apparent change would involve the sole proprietor's death, with the estate trying to continue the business. Most policies extend coverage while the estate is being settled, but from an insurer's point of view, business operations may have changed considerably in such a case.

From an auditing standpoint, a change in ownership has implications for the payroll that the auditor might include in the premium base. The laws of each state specify whether the workers' compensation law covers sole proprietors or partners. If they are not covered, the laws usually specify whether those persons can elect coverage. The incorporation of a business that was previously a partnership may mean that the workers' compensation auditor must collect payroll information for persons previously excluded. General liability rules also vary by form of organization.

Legally, partnerships become new entities when the original composition of the partnership has changed. A deletion or addition of a partner creates a new partnership entity, with the possibility that the insurance coverage no longer applies. As in sole proprietorships, a change in the active status of a given partner can be of great significance, particularly if the partner assuming an inactive role had been the dominant force behind the partnership.

A corporation continues as an intact legal entity regardless of changes in executive officers. The composition of stockholders owning the corporation is less important than the management abilities of the executive officers. Normally, changes of officers occur gradually, with few of the top executives departing simultaneously. This pattern provides management continuity. However, wholesale changes occasionally occur. At such times, the auditor should ascertain why such a drastic change was necessary. If possible, the auditor should develop background data on the qualifications of the new executive group. Outright purchases of corporate entities by other corporations, mergers, or other acquisitions all change the status of the business. The premium auditor should investigate and report on those changes in detail.

The composition of stockholders is important in closed corporations and family corporations. In such situations, management and control are frequently in the hands of the major stockholder, and other corporate officers are only figureheads. If the dominant stockholder changes, the auditor must conduct the same review of operations as if a sole proprietorship had changed hands.

Locations

Additions, deletions, or changes in locations are other signs of operations different from those originally insured. Acquisition of new sites increases the number and kinds of loss exposures. Deletion of locations eliminates the

need for coverage. Changes in existing locations are less obvious and include an increase or a decrease in building sizes, additional buildings erected on existing sites, and internal rearrangement of wall partitions.

Sometimes changes that appear to be only cosmetic are also signs that the auditor must observe and investigate to determine their effect on premium. A change in where the insured garages a vehicle can mean a significant difference in premium for automobile insurance. Other situations involving changes of location have nothing to do with physical buildings or structures. One is a change in the areas in which the insured sells goods or performs services. A service contractor might expand the territory in which it performs operations to include another state, another city, or even a different neighborhood. Such a change might be significant from an insurance auditing viewpoint. Sales representatives in a new territory are another example. The auditor should thoroughly examine facts pertinent to any significant change in location.

Operations, Products, or Services

Changes in operations, products, or services usually lead to changes in premium because different classifications must be assigned. A premium auditor should also determine why such changes occurred and whether the insured can execute the new venture successfully. Related ventures are less problematic than ventures into new fields. A residential contractor experienced in concrete work and expanding into residential masonry is not making a drastic change. When the same contractor suddenly begins concrete work on large multi-story commercial structures, however, the change is drastic.

Similarly, a manufacturer of certain products might develop additional allied products without causing too much concern. A completely different product, especially one that could be dangerous, should be examined. If a firm that manufactures a product suddenly decides to install it as well, entirely new loss exposures result. For example, addressing or mailing companies might decide to assume an unintentionally more hazardous packaging and delivery function, thus drastically changing the overall loss exposure. Fixed operations, such as warehouses, may have been used to store nonflammable stocks. If they now contain dangerous and flammable materials, the hazard is much greater.

Some changes are obvious, but even subtle changes can be important. The premium auditor should investigate such changes and develop all pertinent information.

Additional Loss Exposures

Investigating existing loss exposures that are not included in a policy is within the auditor's responsibility. In some instances, such as owners' and contractors' protective loss exposures or products and completed operations loss exposures, coverage for previously unidentified loss exposures might be automatic. Some loss exposure might not have existed when the policy was issued, so no charge or estimated exposure base is indicated on the policy declarations page. If

new loss exposures occur during the policy period, the policy covers them automatically, and the auditor must develop the premium charges.

When an audit reveals additional loss exposures, the auditor must obtain sufficient data to amend existing policies, if necessary. New properties might require property or liability coverages that existing policies do not automatically cover. The auditor should bring those loss exposures to the underwriting department's attention so that the insurer can provide coverage. Conversely, by investigating loss exposures not shown on the policies in the auditor's possession, the auditor might discover the existence of other insurance. In such cases, the insurer might require exclusion-type endorsements to prevent possible unwarranted stacking of limits. In either situation, the premium auditor should obtain the information required by the underwriter to make a decision.

SUMMARY

A complete review of an insured's operations involves a great deal of time and effort by the premium auditor, but the information obtained justifies the effort. It facilitates accurate classification of the operations, assists the auditor in discovering all relevant loss exposures, and frequently leads to significant underwriting information.

The auditor should determine the insured's organizational form. Whether a business is a sole proprietorship, a partnership, or a corporation influences the kinds of records it must maintain. The legal form can also affect the extent of coverage provided by a policy. If one policy covers multiple entities, the premium auditor must be careful to include them all. If governmental subdivisions are involved, determining the identity of the named insured and possible additional insureds is important.

The auditor must also determine the nature of the insured's operations. Whether the insured is a manufacturer, contractor, store, service, or professional organization affects the hazards, classifications, and overall account desirability. A premium audit should always include a description of operations. It serves as a starting point for classification assignments as well as a source of information for underwriters. Premium auditors should be familiar with typical operations for various businesses so that they can recognize exceptions.

A premium auditor visiting the insured's premises has an opportunity to assess the character of the business. The auditor might observe various aspects of the insured's competence, such as management ability, experience and reputation, quality of products, prudence of operations, and caliber of employees. Employee relations can affect the success of an enterprise, so premium auditors should explore that area. The physical condition of the premises can indicate the firm's attitude toward safety. Whether the insured maintains proper records is not only important for the premium audit but also essential to managing a business. The insured's willingness to cooperate in the premium audit is also a consideration in determining the continued desirability of the account from an underwriting standpoint.

Because premium auditors have access to the insured's financial records and have experience in interpreting them, they are in a position to assess the insured's financial condition. Although a financial analysis is usually beyond the scope of a premium audit, occasionally the tools of financial analysis can aid a premium auditor in identifying potential problems. Both trend analysis and ratio analysis can be useful in detecting situations out of line with prior years' results or industry benchmarks.

The premium auditor must also be alert for any changes in the insured's operations that could affect premium charges, classifications, coverages provided, and underwriting desirability. If the investigation detects uninsured loss exposures previously unknown to the insured, the auditor should report them to the underwriting or marketing personnel involved.

Generally, the additional premium generated through a careful investigation more than offsets the time spent reviewing the insured's operations. More importantly, investigation can lead to better audit results.

Direct Your Learning 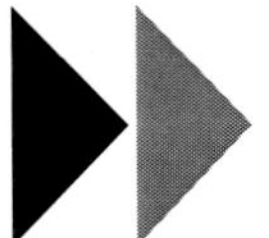

Review of Insured's Employees

Educational Objectives

After learning the content of this chapter and completing the corresponding course guide assignment, you should be able to:

- Describe the duties of the employee and the employer in an employment relationship.
- Given a case, determine whether an employer-employee relationship exists and, if so, identify the type of employment.
  - Summarize the definitions of employees for various purposes.
  - Describe the employee-employer relationship for different types of employers and multiple employers.
  - Describe special situations, including emergency and reciprocal services, illegal employments, gratuitous workers, and illegal aliens, that might create employment relationships.
- Describe the differences among employees, independent contractors, general contractors, and subcontractors.
- Given a case, explain why an organization might want to use independent contractors instead of employees.
- Apply the "right of direction and control" and "relative nature of the work" tests of employment status to various situations.
- Explain how a premium auditor can determine employment status, especially in borderline cases.
- Define or describe each of the Key Words and Phrases for this chapter.

OUTLINE

Develop Your Perspective

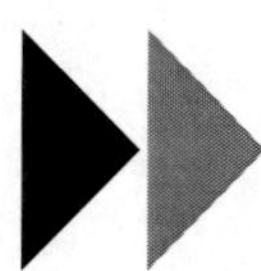

What are the main topics covered in the chapter?

The employment status of the persons performing the work required by an insured's operations and the services they perform affect the classifications and exposure or bases used in determining the insurance premiums the insured pays. A premium auditor determines who contributes to an insured's product or service and how they contribute as part of a premium audit.

Identify the employment relationships necessary for an insured to accomplish work.

- What are the primary ways for an insured to accomplish work?
- What are the tests that can be applied to determine employment status?

Why is it important to learn about these topics?

Employment status is a question of fact, not of law. So, a premium auditor frequently must resolve this question of fact to know whose remuneration to include in the premium base.

Consider the various employment arrangements that can occur.

- What complications may occur if two or more employers are involved.
- What problems may arise with emergency services, reciprocal services, and gratuitous workers?

How can you use what you will learn?

The chapter uses the terms employer-employee and employment relationships in describing the concept of who an employer uses to get the job done: employees or independent contractors.

Examine how work is done in a firm or an organization.

- Why is it important to determine whether employees or independent contractors do work for the organization?
- What are some borderline cases of employment that may require special scrutiny?

Review of Insured's Employees

After developing an understanding of the insured's entire operation, the premium auditor must identify who contributes to an organization's final product or service. The auditor's review of the insured's operation should focus on the people performing the work at each stage of the work process and should ascertain the individual's relationship to the insured.

Generally, a person performing some service for the insured is either an employee or an independent contractor. However, the distinction between those two kinds of workers is not always clear. In addition, in some cases, a person may be employed by more than one entity.

The premium auditor must determine the status of workers to determine whether a particular insurance coverage applies. The insured's liability arising out of an accident could depend on whether the person responsible is an employee or independent contractor. Even if the insured is liable for a loss, the insurer pays for the loss only if the insured has the appropriate coverage.

Analyzing who performs the insured's operations helps a premium auditor better understand the insured's business and is essential for properly computing the basis of premium. It also provides a significant amount of underwriting information. The underwriting significance of such information depends on the coverage provided. For example, for products or completed operations loss exposures, underwriters want to know how much control the insured has over the people doing the work. Unless the insured enforces strict quality control standards, loss can more likely occur when part-time employees or independent contractors perform the work. If the insurer provides workers' compensation coverage, the insured's hiring and training practices are important to the underwriter. In any case, the success of a loss control program can depend on whether the insured has the authority usual to an employer to control the working environment. In every situation, underwriters need to know who performs the work to evaluate the loss exposure's magnitude.

The employment status of those working for the insured can also have an important bearing on the basis of premium. For workers' compensation policies, the question of employment status is crucial. The premium base includes the remuneration (payroll) to every person considered an employee under the workers' compensation laws, which apply a definition of "employee" broader than the definition in other contexts. Other insurance policies can also base the premium on employees' remuneration (including money or substitutes for money). Not everyone considered an employee for workers' compensation purposes necessarily counts as an employee for other kinds of insurance.

Consequently, the question of employment status is both significant and complex. Premium auditors must often investigate the insured's operations and its workers closely to resolve employment status issues. Auditors must know state law and must be aware that, because of variations in state laws, identical situations can lead to different legal outcomes in different states. Therefore, this chapter defines only basic employment relationships and presents some fundamental principles for ascertaining employment status. The latter part of the chapter discusses several ambiguous situations to demonstrate the reasoning involved in determining employment status but not to render definitive conclusions.

EMPLOYMENT

Employee
A person who is hired to perform services for another under the direction and control of an employer.

Employer
A person or an organization who directs and controls the work of an employee.

An **employee** is a person who is hired to perform services for another under the direction and control of that other person, called the **employer**. The relationship is a contractual one, and to be valid, employment contracts must have the essential elements of binding contracts discussed in a previous chapter (agreement, capacity to contract, legal purpose, and consideration).

Contract of Hire

The definition of employment presumes that either an express or an implied contract of hire exists. Although the contract of hire need not be in writing, both parties must agree to the arrangement and must have a reasonable expectation of deriving some benefit from it. One cannot force another to work unwillingly. The element of consideration is particularly significant in employment contracts. The employee provides labor services, and the employer provides consideration in the form of wages, salary, board and lodging, or something else of value. The existence of consideration can be critical in determining whether an individual is an employee. One must examine disputed cases to see whether a valid contract of hire exists.

An employment contract is a written agreement between two or more parties that creates an employment relationship. Unlike some contracts for hire, an employment contract is always written.

Employer-Employee Relationship

The contract of hire defines the relationship between the employer and the employee. The parties are free to agree to any terms of employment as long as they are legal. Some state laws specify some limitations to the employment contract, such as minimum wages, maximum hours, minimum working age, and required safety conditions.

Duties of Employee

The employment contract normally identifies the employee's rights and duties. Additionally, certain duties are implied by law. Employees must perform the services required by the contract of hire. By implication, they agree to serve the employer honestly and faithfully. Employees must obey any reasonable regulations established by employers and must exercise due care when performing their duties.

Duties of Employer

Employers have a duty to provide employees with a reasonably safe place to work. That duty includes providing safe tools and equipment as well as employing a sufficient number of competent workers for the work involved. The employer's duty also includes warning employees of any unusual hazards associated with their work. These duties all stem from the common law. In addition, workers' compensation laws obligate most employers to compensate employees for injuries or occupational disease arising out of the course of employment. Further, the Federal Occupational Safety and Health Administration Act of 1970 authorizes the Secretary of Labor to set safety standards for employers.

The law also obligates employers to compensate their employees for the services they perform. Generally, an employer discharging an employee must pay wages through the expiration of the last pay period. Many contracts for hire even provide compensation for an additional period or severance pay. Either party can terminate a contract for hire by giving notice to the other, although some limitations apply. Some state laws and most union contracts specify the period of notice an employer must give to an employee. Some employees, such as public school teachers or civil service workers, cannot be discharged without a hearing. Employees who believe that they were wrongfully discharged can bring action against the employer under federal or state labor relations laws.

Definitions of Employees

Little disagreement exists about the definition of employment and the surrounding legal principles just presented. Applying the definition to particular situations, however, can be more difficult. The issue is the subject of frequent litigation relating to vicarious liability, employers' liability, workers' compensation, labor legislation, unemployment compensation, Social Security, and other laws relating to employees.

Therefore, premium auditors cannot rely exclusively on the insured's reports to the Internal Revenue Service (IRS), for example, to determine who the insured's employees are for insurance purposes. Whether a particular person is an employee depends on the context in which questions about employment

arise. The question of employment status has particular significance, and sometimes produces varied answers, in the following areas:

- Taxes
- Labor laws
- Legal liability and insurance

Taxes

An employer must pay a variety of payroll taxes based on remuneration to employees. Additionally, an employer must usually withhold a portion of its employees' pay to meet their anticipated tax liabilities. Therefore, an employer has an advantage if a person renders services as an independent contractor rather than as an employee. Although the employer must still report the remuneration, many of the payroll taxes that apply to employees do not apply to independent contractors, and in most cases the law does not require withholding taxes. Consequently, an employer saves tax expense and reduces some of the recordkeeping burden by using independent contractors. Insureds' reluctance to agree that certain workers are employees sometimes stems from those tax consequences.

Federal tax liability of employers include income tax, Social Security taxes, and unemployment taxes. The Internal Revenue Code (IRC) requires employers to withhold federal income taxes from the earnings of individual employees. The amount withheld reflects the number of exemptions the employee claims on a W-4 Form. Within forty-five days of the end of each calendar quarter, the employer must file an Employer's Quarterly Tax Return (Form 941) showing the earnings records of all employees and the federal income and Social Security taxes withheld. The employer must pay those taxes at that time. By January 31 of each year, the employer must furnish the employee with a W-2 Form showing the total earnings and taxes withheld for the preceding year.

Employers must report payments to individuals other than employees on Form 1099. No withholding requirement exists for such individuals. Whether a person is an employee for income tax withholding purposes depends on whether that person performs services under the employer's direction and control regarding both what will be done and how it will be done.[1] An employer who is unsure of a particular individual's status can obtain an IRS determination by submitting Form SS-8 to the district director. The appendix at the end of this chapter shows a copy of IRS Form SS-8 although the answers to the questions on that form can offer useful information, an auditor must remember that an IRS determination is not binding for insurance purposes.

The IRC considers an employer a person or an organization that controls wage payments and therefore has the duty to withhold taxes and to remit the taxes withheld.[2] However, premium auditors are likely to encounter many cases in which an insured might be liable to third parties or liable for workers' compensation even though someone else actually controls the wage payments.

The Federal Insurance Contributions Act (FICA) requires employers to pay Social Security and Medicare taxes based on each employee's compensation and to withhold an equal amount paid by the employee. The Social Security taxes paid by both employers and employees fund retirement and Medicare benefits to retired workers as well as family benefits for deceased or disabled workers. The employer reports those taxes on the same 941 and W-2 Forms that show the federal income taxes withheld.

An employer could be liable for Social Security taxes but not for federal income tax withholding. Social Security covers certain occupations even though they might otherwise have the status of independent contractors. Those occupations include the following:

- Full-time life insurance salespersons
- Drivers delivering laundry, dry cleaning, food, or beverages (except milk)
- Full-time salespersons soliciting orders from retail merchants, hotels, or restaurants
- Home workers (a worker who performs services according to the specifications provided by the person for whom the work is performed)[3]

Employers also must pay a payroll tax to fund unemployment compensation benefits for unemployed workers. As the federal government does with Social Security, the state defines the term "employee" broadly for unemployment tax purposes so that benefits are available to those who need them. Specific provisions, however, vary by state. Nonfarm employers must pay both federal and state unemployment taxes. So, an auditor must check state requirements because an employee for purposes of one payroll tax law is not necessarily an employee for purposes of another payroll tax law.

Labor Laws

A variety of state and federal laws protect workers from employment abuses. In some cases, a court might first need to decide whether an individual is an employee to determine whether a particular law applies.

Both federal and state laws regulate the minimum hourly wage and maximum workweek. Generally, an employer must pay an employee who works more than forty hours in one week one and one-half times the regular hourly wage for the excess hours. However, that requirement does not apply to certain types of employees, such as executives and outside salespersons, and to certain employees of airlines, motor carriers, hospitals, hotels, radio and television stations, and seasonal establishments, such as camps or amusement parks. The law's provisions, however, are complex and contain numerous other exceptions.

Federal law also stipulates the minimum age of employees. For most nonfarm jobs, the minimum age is sixteen, but news carriers can be fourteen. Federal and state laws further restrict employing minors to operate dangerous equipment and limit the number of hours per day that children can work.

Legal Liability and Insurance

An auditor must determine which persons are considered to be employees both under policies covering the employer's liability to third parties and under policies covering the employer's liability for workers' compensation.

An employee is a special class of agent. Consequently, the employer's liability to third parties for wrongs committed by employees falls within the laws of agency described in the chapter on insurance law. The employer is generally liable for all acts committed by employees within the scope of employment. The employer is liable, for example, if a nightclub bouncer inflicts an injury when ejecting a rowdy patron.

Naturally, liability also exists when the employer has expressly directed the act. However, the employer can still be liable if the harm has resulted from some unauthorized action of the employee. Liability might be based on the employer's failure to hire competent employees, to give sufficient instructions, or to properly supervise employees. For example, the employer might be liable if an employee overcharges a customer, even if the employee pockets the overcharges without the employer's knowledge. An employer can also be liable for an employee's unauthorized act by virtue of a subsequent ratification of the act. That is, the employer learns of the unauthorized act but does nothing to object to it.

However, an organization is not usually liable for wrongs committed by an independent contractor while working for the organization. That absence of liability stems from the assumption that an employer has less control over the independent contractor's actions than over employees' actions. If the person or organization retains control in some material manner over the project and how it is performed, then the person performing the work is an employee, not an independent contractor. Most jurisdictions, however, define certain situations in which a person or an organization cannot evade liability, even by retaining an independent contractor. Those situations involve inherently dangerous operations, such as the wrecking of buildings, or ultra hazardous operations, such as blasting. The employer could be held liable for negligence for selecting an incompetent independent contractor.

Because the distinction between employees and independent contractors is not clear, the premium auditor should report to the liability underwriter any persons who are serving the insured's business and who conceivably could cause a third-party claim against the insured. In that case, the insured's control over the individuals' acts becomes key.

Similar issues arise in workers' compensation. All states have workers' compensation laws requiring employers to compensate employees for injuries and occupational disease arising out of, and in the course of, employment. The courts have broadly interpreted the definition of an employee in workers' compensation cases to afford legal protection to those who need it.

A premium auditor must carefully analyze the work relationship between an employer and any alleged independent contractors. Because the broad approach to determining the existence of an employer-employee relationship also applies to providing benefits, an auditor should use the same broad definition for workers' compensation purposes.

The Workers Compensation and Employers Liability policy covers the employer for all workers' compensation benefits paid to workers who qualify as employees under the law. The policy also obligates the insurer to pay the cost of defending a claim for workers' compensation benefits, even if the court ultimately finds the claim groundless. The law, therefore, entitles an insurer to a premium based on the earnings of all individuals with an apparent right to claim benefits.

Again, it is important to remember that the determination of employee versus independent contractor depends on the context. Consider, for example, the case of a nurse who assists a surgeon in a hospital operating room. The nurse must follow the surgeon's directions and must also use considerable independent professional discretion. The nurse cannot really be subject to the hospital's control during the operation. In a professional liability case, therefore, a court could reasonably hold that the nurse is not the hospital's employee, and the hospital might escape liability for the nurse's error. Suppose, however, that the nurse sustains an injury in the operating room. If a workers' compensation claim results, then a court could find an employer-employee relationship between the hospital and the nurse.

Similarly, a person might be considered an employee under one law and still legitimately be considered an independent contractor under another law with a different purpose. For example, an injured person might not be an employee entitled to the protection of the National Labor Relations Act but might be an employee under the workers' compensation law.

Employers

An auditor investigating employer-employee relationships must clearly establish the identity and status of the employer. For instance, an employer cannot also be an employee. In some states, however, business owners can be eligible for workers' compensation coverage under certain conditions. A premium auditor must know such state regulations to determine whether to include such individuals in the basis of premium.

Sole Proprietors

A sole proprietor cannot be an employee because the individual and the business are one and the same. The insured entity is the individual. The sole proprietor can have employees, but the owner is not one of them regardless of the duties performed. The courts consider such individuals self-employed for

Social Security purposes. Sole proprietors must pay self-employment taxes at one and one-half times the Social Security tax rate for employees. However, the law does not require withholding of federal income tax.

A sole proprietor injured while working probably cannot hold anyone else liable for the injury. Approximately thirty-seven states, however, allow a workers' compensation insurance policy to cover sole proprietors. The auditor should include a sole proprietor electing such coverage in the basis of premium.

In some jurisdictions, one spouse cannot be an employee of the other for workers' compensation purposes. The rationale behind that restriction stems from the common law, which holds that married persons cannot make personal contracts with one another. However, that provision of the common law does not always apply. Courts may consider the circumstances of the employment arrangement to make a final determination. For example, one court upheld a husband's claim to workers' compensation benefits when his wife, as an employer, paid insurance premiums based on a payroll including the employed spouse's name. Further, some states' workers' compensation rules explicitly provide that when a spouse appears on an insured's payroll, the insurer must include that compensation in the basis of premium computation.

Partners

Similar rules apply to partnerships. A partner is an owner of the business and cannot be an employee. Therefore, partners are exempt from withholding and wage and hour law requirements. As with sole proprietors, the law does not entitle partners to workers' compensation benefits, but in the majority of states they can elect to be included under a policy. Consequently, the policy must name the partners who have elected coverage.

Working partner
A partner who performs regular duties and draws a salary independent of profits.

A partner who performs regular duties and draws a salary independent of profits is sometimes called a **working partner**. Some states' workers' compensation laws cover such working partners unless they elect not to be covered. One state has no provision for the coverage of partners but does treat certain limited partnership associations as corporations. In such cases, the association's active managers have the status of corporate officers and, hence, employees.

Corporations

If the insured is a corporation, it is a legal entity that can enter employer-employee relationships with others. Even the president of an organization is an employee if the organization is incorporated. So, too, is the vice president, secretary, treasurer, or any other officer the stockholders appoint or elect. An auditor can obtain the identities of corporate officers from the insured or from the insured's federal income tax return or articles of incorporation.

The common law considers corporate officers employees and, therefore, the workers' compensation acts of most states cover them. However, some states exclude corporate officers for closed corporations. In many states, executive officers can elect not to be subject to the law. The names of officers who have made such an election must be listed on the insurance policy.

If an executive officer elects not to be covered under a particular state law, the exclusion applies only to that state and only to Part One of the workers' compensation policy. A premium charge might still be appropriate for coverage in a different state or under the U.S. Longshore and Harbor Workers Compensation Act if the insured has such coverage. The act covers maritime workers but not masters or members of the crew.

Premium auditors must identify all the executive officers, because they might not appear on the regular payroll. The corporation might compensate them with a share of the profits, particularly if the corporation qualifies as a Subchapter S Corporation under the Internal Revenue Code. Even though executive officers are employees, the auditor must treat them separately because limitations usually apply when including their remuneration in the premium base. However, the limitation does not generally apply to a shareholder-employee who is not an executive officer.

Not-for-Profit Organizations

Although religious, educational, and charitable organizations are usually exempt from federal income taxes under Section 501(c) of the Internal Revenue Code, they must still comply with the various payroll laws. The same is true of federal, state, and local government agencies, which are also tax-exempt. For general liability and workers' compensation insurance purposes, the law treats employees of not-for-profit organizations differently, depending on the applicable state law.

When the insured is a religious organization, the auditor normally considers all persons compensated for their services to be employees. If remuneration for clergy includes meals, housing, or other benefits in addition to, or instead of, a regular salary, the auditor needs to include at least a portion of the value of those benefits as remuneration.

Members of religious orders are not considered employees because the order is an association of individual members. Generally, the members of a religious order (nuns and brothers, for example) receive no individual income but share in communal living arrangements. Presumably, the order as a whole would take care of an injured member's needs. In addition to its own members, the order might have employees who are not order members, who should be included in the premium base if the order has a workers' compensation policy.

Members of religious orders also work in parishes, hospitals, schools, or other organizations separate from the order. Customarily, in such situations, the institution involved reimburses the order for the services provided. No salary goes to an individual nun or brother; the institution usually pays it directly to the order instead. An employment relationship exists even though the institution pays compensation to the order. When auditing a separate institution employing members of religious orders, the auditor should include those payments as remuneration to employees.

Some states have enacted exceptions to those general rules, specifically listing certain persons, such as priests, whom the law considers *not* to be employees. Thus, insurers should not collect premiums based on any gifts, cost-of-living expenses, or other monies passing to the persons listed.

In the majority of states, the law considers elected and appointed public officials of a state, county, or municipal corporation or political subdivision to be employees, provided that they receive remuneration for their services. In some states, public officials are employees whether or not they receive remuneration. In many states, public officials are not considered employees unless the legislative body of the employing subdivision has declared its intention to provide coverage for those people.

Certain volunteer activities, such as those for civil defense or volunteer fire departments, have been brought under the workers' compensation laws of some states by specific reference in the statutes.

Multiple Employers

Loaned employee
A person assigned by an employer to work temporarily for another employer.

Sometimes an individual can have multiple employers. An individual assigned by an employer to work temporarily for another employer is called a **loaned employee**. Other cases of multiple employers arise when an individual holds two different jobs simultaneously or when two or more organizations share the services of an individual. In those cases, the question is not *whether* an employer-employee relationship exists, but rather *with whom*. For both general liability and workers' compensation insurance purposes, that question can determine which insurer must pay a claim.

General Employers and Special Employers

General employer
The employer for whom an employee normally works.

Special employer
A person or an organization for which a general employer allows an employee to perform services.

The employer for whom an employee normally works, the general employer, might occasionally allow an employee to perform services for another person or organization, termed the special employer. When a **general employer** lends an employee to a **special employer**, the special employer also becomes liable for workers' compensation, but only if the following three conditions apply:

1. The employee has a contract of hire, express or implied, with the special employer.
2. The work done is essentially that of the special employer.
3. The special employer has the right to and is, at time of injury, controlling the details of work of the lent employee.

In most states, the determining factor for responsibility for workers' compensation is whether the general employer or special employer controls the lent employee's actions at the time of injury. An injury to a lent employee often creates a conflict between the respective insurers of the two employers. When the lent employee is on the general employer's payroll and is lent to the special employer, a premium auditor might have to analyze the relationship to determine whether to include the lent employee's remuneration in the basis of premium.

An example of such a relationship occurs when one town (the general employer) contracts with another town (the special employer) to allow an employee to act as a town sanitation worker for two days each week. That lent employee is under the direction and control of the second town, even though on the first town's payroll. If the three conditions previously mentioned are met, a premium auditor determining the special employer's premium base would have to include the lent employee's remuneration, even though it appears on the general employer's payroll.

A common example of a general employer is a temporary employment agency that provides temporary clerical workers to replace office workers who are sick or on vacation or to handle other short-handed situations. The general employer is the temporary employment agency. The special employer is the company using the services of the agency.

One of the advantages of such an arrangement is that it simplifies bookkeeping for the special employer. Because the special employer pays the agency for the services of the temporary employees, the special employer does not have to compute and deduct payroll taxes. Normally, the temporary employees are not eligible for the fringe benefits available to the company's regular employees. If the duration of service is uncertain, the company avoids the possibility of a future unemployment claim, for instance, that would result if it instead hired a regular employee and subsequently dismissed that employee when the need for extra help subsided.

Because the special employer directs and controls the temporary employee's work, the special employer is liable for any harm caused by the temporary employee in the course of that work. The special employer might also be liable for workers' compensation if the temporary employee is injured. A temporary agency can change that result by adding an Alternate Employer Endorsement (WC 00 03 01) to its workers' compensation policy. A policy so endorsed enables the temporary agency to either pay the benefits directly or reimburse the special employer for any claims paid based on the determination that an employer-employee relationship existed between the special employer and the loaned employee. That endorsement also stipulates that the temporary agency's basis of premium will include the remuneration of employees engaged in temporary employment by a special employer.

Another example of a lent employee is a person assigned by one organization to work with another organization to ensure compliance with the contract specifications. For example, for a highly technical defense project, the U. S. government (the general employer) might assign an employee to work for the defense contractor (the special employer) to assist in executing the contract. Although in that case the special employer exercises little direction and control, if any, over the loaned employee, the question of who is the employer for workers' compensation or third-party liability purposes exists.

For example, New York hires construction advisers and assigns them to housing contractors within the state. Those contractors pay salaries to the

construction advisers assigned to them at the rate stipulated by the state, although such payments are actually drawn against funds contributed by all contractors based on a percentage of the mortgages on all projects subject to inspection. Because construction advisers are hired and directed by the New York Division of Housing and Community Renewal but are paid by the housing contractor, the question arises of who the employer is. A court held in one such case that an injured construction adviser was an employee of the state, not the construction company.[4] Thus, the state was responsible for workers' compensation.

A different interpretation, however, is possible in a case involving liability to third parties. If a construction adviser's actions harms a passerby, that person might sue the construction company for liability. If a court upholds such a claim, the construction company's general liability insurer would have reason to include the construction adviser in the basis of premium.

Joint Employment and Dual Employment

When an employee works for two or more employers, a dual or joint employment relationship exists. The concepts of joint employment and dual employment are similar and often used interchangeably. However, joint employment and dual employment impose liability on the employers in different ways.

Joint employment is a job in which the essential terms and conditions of the employee's work are controlled by two or more entities. For example, in a rural area a school superintendent might provide the superintendency services for two or more separate boards of education. The boards of education are then joint employers of the superintendent.

Another example occurs when the business of different firms is closely related. A worker hired by a stevedoring corporation at a particular pier might be selected by another corporation, which is in charge of the pier's general operation, to act as harbor master under the general control of its dock's boss. The two corporations then become joint employers.

Most courts hold joint employers both jointly and individually liable in workers' compensation cases. Thus, there should be no doubt about including the remuneration of joint employees in the basis of premium. If the joint employers each pay a part of the employee's compensation, the auditor should include the full amount paid by an employer when computing insurance premium for the employer with the workers' compensation policy.

Dual employment is similar to joint employment in that the employee is under a contract of hire with two or more different employers. Dual employment differs from joint employment in that the employment contract, method of payment, and activities on behalf of each employer are separable and can be readily identified with one employer or the other. Employers do not agree to share the worker's time. When the work can be clearly separated, the particular employer whose work was being done at the time of the injury is

liable. If the employee's activities cannot be separated, then both employers are liable, and a court would allocate any award between them.

An example of dual employment is a manufacturer's representative who buys or sells for more than one company. A representative who sells different product lines travels a given route and sells whichever products the customers want at the time. In that case, each manufacturer is liable because the representative's efforts for the benefit of one do not cease when selling for another. A workers' compensation award might allocate each manufacturer's share in proportion to the amount each had compensated the representative before injury.

Another example of dual employment is a driver hired to deliver prescriptions for two different pharmacies. If the driver delivers for one pharmacy in the morning and the other in the afternoon, then the store whose errand the driver was on at the time of an accident would be totally liable. In all of those situations, the premium auditor would have to uncover the existence of the employment relationship and determine the method of compensation.

Employee Leasing

A relatively new arrangement is that of employee leasing. Under an **employee leasing** arrangement, a business entity (the client or original employer) uses the services of a third party (labor contractor or leasing firm) to provide the client with employees for a fee. In many cases, the employees are the client's former employees, whom the client transferred to the labor contractor and then leased back. The arrangements are usually long term, so auditors should not confuse leased employee arrangements with temporary labor service contractors. The labor contractor or leasing firm handles all of the personnel and administrative matters, including payroll and benefits and workers' compensation. The client, or original employer, has the same work force in many cases but, technically, has no employees.

Employee leasing
An arrangement in which a third party provides a firm with employees for a fee.

Small employers became interested in employee leasing as a way to reduce their administrative overhead costs. Some leasing firms can offer better benefits to the employees as a result of having a large number of employees from many different employers.

Some leasing firms and employers, however, began using the employee leasing concept to avoid experience rating debits under their insurance policies. The debit of the client or original employer did not follow the employees. As a result, the National Council on Compensation Insurance amended its rules to make clear that an employer could not use leasing, at least in workers' compensation, to avoid the experience rating debits. In fact, the National Council took legal action against some employers to recover monies owed. Other employee leasing firms also described all employees as clerical, despite their actual duties.

Employee leasing also affects general liability insurance. An employer normally has coverage for the acts of its employees, and employees have coverage under the employer's general liability policy for liability to third parties

while performing duties of the employer. But, if the "workers" are technically employees of another organization (the labor contractor or leasing firm), coverage is jeopardized. Consequently, Insurance Services Office (ISO) filed an amendment to its liability policies to recognize the existence of leased employees and to provide coverage similar to that provided for employees.

Employee leasing arrangements may cause problems in the insurance market, such as the understatement of payrolls, improper classifications or experience modifications, and the relaxing of safety rules by the client company. State variations in the regulations further complicate matters.

Laws and regulations designating who is the employer of leased workers for workers' compensation vary. To determine which of a leased worker's employers is required to furnish workers' compensation coverage, the premium auditor must review the controlling jurisdiction's laws and regulations. The majority view under a traditional common-law analysis holds that the leased workers are the employees of the client entity absent contrary statutory or regulatory actions.

The statutory obligation of employers to retain workers' compensation coverage for their leased employees is automatically insured by the Standard Policy. Endorsements attached to the policy determine whether the employer is the client or the leasing contractor.

Policy issuance regarding leased workers requirements varies greatly among states. Some states have different requirements for the voluntary and residual markets while other states use the same requirement for both. Within the insurance business, the following three types of policies provide coverage for leased employees:

1. Client Policy—The client secures coverage by obtaining a standard workers' compensation policy in its own name to cover workers obtained from the labor contractor.
2. Multiple Coordinated Policy (MCP)—Each client of the labor contractor is issued a policy in its own name to cover the employees leased from the labor contractor. The policy does not cover a client's nonleased workers or workers leased from another labor contractor. Appropriate endorsements are attached to restrict the coverage to specific employees and to coordinate coverages between the client company and the labor contractor. All policies are issued by the same insurer with common renewal dates. Billing is issued on a master invoice to the labor contractor.
3. Master policy—A workers' compensation policy is issued in the labor contractor's name. It covers the workers leased to all of the client companies as well as the nonleased employees of the labor contractor and is usually endorsed to exclude nonleased workers of the client companies. Client companies are responsible for obtaining coverage for all excluded workers. Master policies are typically used in the voluntary market and are not usually available in the residual market.

Special Situations

Although in special situations statutes have altered the principle that for an employee-employer relationship to exist there must be an express or implied contract of hire, courts often cite that principle to resolve the following ambiguous situations.

Emergency Services

If an employee asks a person for help in an emergency that threatens the employer's interest, that person becomes an employee of the person asking for help under an implied contract of hire. An example is a bystander whom an employed trucker asks to help move a truck out of a ditch. The trucker, although ordinarily without power to make contracts binding on the employer, has implied authority to employ an assistant. Courts presume that the trucker's employer intends that someone take the necessary measures to set the business (truck) in motion again.

Courts have applied that emergency doctrine to cases in which a duly constituted law enforcement official asks a private citizen to assist in making an arrest or to help quell a disturbance. The appropriate governmental body would have to compensate the citizen for injuries suffered.

A Wisconsin court, for example, held that a volunteer posse member injured while pursuing a fugitive was a county employee. Generally, all emergency cases are subject to the rule that, if persons acting to assist in an emergency advance the interest of their own employer to any degree, then the act remains within the course of their regular employment. Their regular employer would be responsible for the workers' compensation liability.

Reciprocal Services

An employer does not have to pay an employee in money. A court might hold payment as anything of value to establish an employer-employee relationship subject to a workers' compensation act. Courts have held reciprocal services to be payment for that purpose. For example, the state might grant workers' compensation for a case in which a florist and an undertaker agreed to work with each other whenever they had time. To grant workers' compensation, the reviewing authority must find a valid employment contract in which the consideration was mutual services. The state could deny workers' compensation in that situation, however, if the reviewing authority found that the relationship was a joint venture instead of an employer-employee relationship.

Illegal Employments

Like all other contracts, a valid contract of hire must be for a legal purpose. An illegal employment contract is one that requires performance of an illegal act. States usually deny workers' compensation benefits to persons hired

under such contracts. For example, states denied benefits to bartenders and beer delivery persons during the prohibition era because their duties involved illegal acts.

On the other hand, when the contract of hire itself is illegal, as in the hiring of minors, but the act to be performed is not illegal, an injured employee is entitled to benefits under the workers' compensation laws.

Gratuitous Workers

Because a contract of hire requires mutual assent, a person cannot become an employee without the employer's agreement. Similarly, if a person works without expecting compensation, no contract of hire exists.

For example, courts usually do not consider volunteers to be employees because a volunteer neither receives nor expects to receive any kind of payment for services rendered. Some state laws, however, give employee status to certain individuals rendering service without pay.

Payment of any kind changes a person's status from volunteer to employee. A court might find that payment is anything of value, such as board or lodging. A court might find an implied agreement to pay when the parties have failed to make an express agreement on payment. Therefore, a person's motivation becomes an important factor in determining whether the person is a volunteer or an employee. Consequently, courts have usually held that when a person's acts are reasonably construed as stemming from patriotism, civic-mindedness, or religious or charitable purposes, the person is a volunteer and, therefore, is not entitled to workers' compensation benefits.

Relatives who occasionally help in a family business are not necessarily employees if they do not expect to be paid. If they are minor children, it might be illegal to employ them. The workers' compensation laws of several states either exclude resident relatives or, though considering them employees, allow an insurer to exclude relatives from workers' compensation coverage. Often when the workers' compensation policy insures an individual or a husband and wife as individuals or as a partnership, the standard workers' compensation policy does not apply to resident relatives, as defined. In that situation, some insurers exclude all resident relatives on the basic workers' compensation policy form but extend coverage to relatives named in an endorsement.

Illegal Aliens

The Census Bureau estimates that one in every seven persons in cities such as Los Angeles and Houston is an illegal alien resident of the United States. Across the nation, illegal aliens hold jobs in almost every sector of the economy. Many are agricultural workers. Federal law prohibits an employer from hiring an illegal alien. Consequently, employers that do hire illegal aliens often pay them in cash. An illegal alien injured on the job may choose not to file for workers' compensation benefits to avoid being exposed. However, aliens who do file for benefits are likely to receive them because they are

the insured's employees. If an auditor discovers payments to an illegal alien, they should be included as remuneration. The auditor should also report that practice to the underwriter because it reflects on the employer's desirability as an insured.

INDEPENDENT CONTRACTORS

Generally, a business can accomplish a particular task in only two ways. It can either hire an employee to perform the task or contract with an independent contractor. An independent contractor is someone who makes a business of providing a certain service to different customers. Not all independent contractors work for more than one customer, however.

Characteristics

Often, an independent contractor receives compensation in a lump sum, sometimes after submitting a bill for services. The bill may itemize the cost of labor and materials, but it need not segregate those costs if the contract simply set a price for completing the job. Although the parties can agree on any terms for payment and specifications for the project, an independent contractor works under an ordinary contract in which one party promises a certain sum of money in return for the other party's performing a certain kind of work.

One major distinguishing factor between employees and independent contractors is that independent contractors are not subject to direction and control regarding the details of their work. They agree to perform a task meeting the specifications stipulated in the contract, but they use their own judgment and methods in performing the task. Independent contractors may also employ others (subcontractors) to perform the task, but the general contractors remain responsible for the contract's completion.

An employer can discharge an employee whose work is unsatisfactory. When an independent contractor's work is unsatisfactory, however, the usual recourse is to sue for breach of contract. Unless breach is proven, the other party must pay the independent contractor the sum specified in the contract.

Independent contractors usually offer their services to the public. Large firms can be readily identified as independent contractors, but small ones often cannot. For example, large firms possess such things as a commercial telephone listing, printed invoices, incorporation, commercial insurance coverage, and a separate place of business, suggesting an independent status. However, the auditor must carefully investigate the actual working relationship between an insured and any alleged independent contractor.

Because of the importance that independent contractor status assumes in workers' compensation cases, the California workers' compensation manual states that for premium determination purposes, "Whether a person is an employee or independent contractor shall be determined in accordance

with the relevant Labor Code provisions, common law, and Workers' Compensation Appeals Board (WCAB) decisions."[5] The manual lists, in order of importance, the following eleven factors to be considered in making that determination:

1. The right to control the manner and means of accomplishing the results desired
2. The right to terminate the relationship at will
3. Whether the person performing the service is engaged in a distinct occupation or business
4. Whether the work usually is done under the employer's direction or by a specialist without supervision
5. The skill required in the particular occupation
6. Whether the employer or the person performing the service supplies the instrumentalities, tools, and the place of work
7. Whether the person performing the services has the right to hire and terminate others
8. The length of time for which the person is to perform the services
9. The method of payment, whether by time, a piece rate, or the job
10. Whether the services are a part of the employer's regular business
11. Whether the parties believe they are creating the relationship of employer-employee or employer-independent contractor[6]

Although similar principles apply in most situations and in most states, state laws do not always define independent contractor status so explicitly. Therefore, a premium auditor needs to know the particular state's law as well as the general characteristics of independent contractors.

Reasons for Using Independent Contractors

Employers might prefer independent contractors over employees for three reasons. First is cost. This chapter previously described the tax and wage and hour laws applicable to employers/employees. Those laws impose a cost on employers for their employees that is not imposed when independent contractors are used.

A second reason is that using independent contractors allows an employer more flexibility to meet fluctuating staffing requirements. As the economy fluctuates, so does an employer's need for labor. Employers do not want to hire employees knowing that within a short time they will no longer be needed. The hiring and subsequent firing can create morale problems as well as increase an employer's unemployment taxes. By using independent contractors for an "overload" or unusual fluctuation, an employer avoids such problems.

The third reason for using independent contractors is that they can provide specialized services, often requiring a high degree of knowledge and skill. Some independent contractors are licensed professionals with specialized

training. Public accountants, for example, often keep the books for small businesses because the owners do not have the necessary knowledge of accounting principles and cannot afford to hire a full-time person who does. Similarly, attorneys, architects, or other professionals may offer their services to handle a particular case or project.

In other situations, independent contractors possess specialized equipment or facilities enabling them to perform particular tasks in a cost-effective manner. For example, a small business might prefer to contract with a trash removal firm than to assign an employee to haul the trash in the same van the company uses for deliveries. If a company wants to apply insecticide to the trees surrounding its office, it could send its employees out with ladders and spray cans. It probably makes more sense, however, to hire a landscaping firm with a power sprayer to do the job.

Infrequent occurrences can often be better handled by a specialist. For example, if a business holds an annual banquet to honor its top salespeople, a caterer may provide the food.

Auditors must remember that it is not the occupation that makes a person an independent contractor; it is the work that is performed and how it is performed. An attorney can represent a client as an independent contractor or can represent an employer as a full-time employee. In another example, if a homeowner contracts with a plumber to build an extra bathroom, the courts would probably consider the plumber an independent contractor. If, however, a home builder were to engage the same plumber to build bathrooms of the same type in new homes, the courts would probably consider the plumber an employee, particularly if the builder pays the plumber by the hour, supervises the work, and can discharge the plumber at any time during the construction.

General Contractors and Subcontractors

Independent contractor relationships become more confusing when there is a hierarchy of such relationships. One person can contract a project to another person, who can contract a portion of the work to a third person, and so on. In such cases, the terms "general contractor" and "subcontractor" are commonly used to distinguish the parties. Such distinctions can clarify the hierarchy on a particular job, but both general contractors and subcontractors are independent contractors.

A **general contractor** is an independent contractor who obtains the primary contract for a project and who either completes all work or subcontracts certain portions, or all, of the work to other specialized independent contractors. Although the use of general contractors and subcontractors occurs most frequently in the construction industry, it is also common in manufacturing and can occur anywhere.

Subcontractors, or **specialty contractors**, are independent contractors who specialize in a particular type of work. A general contractor engages them

General contractor
An independent contractor who obtains the primary contract for a project.

Subcontractor, or **specialty contractor**
An independent contractor who specializes in a particular type of work and who performs work for a general contractor.

to perform a particular portion of the contract. Plumbers and electricians, for example, might be subcontractors on a building construction project. Subcontractors may also contract directly with an individual or a company instead of using a general contractor as an intermediary.

Workers' Compensation Obligation

Most states have adopted "statutory employer" laws, which impose workers' compensation liability on principal employers (usually general contractors) for their subcontractors' injured employees. In most states, the general contractor's liability is secondary. However, some states' laws impose joint liability on the general contractor and the subcontractor. Other states make the general contractor primarily responsible. In practice, that means that when the subcontractor does not have insurance, the general contractor's insurer must pay the claims of the subcontractor's injured employees. The U.S. Longshore and Harbor Workers Compensation Act also imposes a secondary obligation on general contractors for injuries to subcontractors' employees.

The purpose of such legislation is to protect employees of uninsured contractors by imposing ultimate liability on the responsible principal employers or general contractors who have it within their power to choose subcontractors and to insist that they provide appropriate insurance coverage for their own employees. Usually, the statutory obligation applies only when the work done by the subcontractor is a part of the principal employer's trade or business. In many states, however, the obligation extends to the building's owner who engages specialty contractors directly rather than through a general contractor. When the law imposes a workers' compensation obligation on such an employer, it also gives the statutory employer immunity from suits by injured employees of the uninsured subcontractor.

Certificates of Insurance

When premium auditors discover that insureds have contracted work to someone else, their concern is whether the insured might have any resulting additional workers' compensation loss exposures. If the person receiving the contract has employees, the premium auditor must either verify workers' compensation insurance coverage or include those employees in the basis of premium chargeable to the insured. Normally in such cases, the insured should have certificates of insurance from the subcontractors involved. Those certificates prove that the subcontractor can satisfy the workers' compensation obligation and that it will not revert to the principal employer or general contractor.

However, the auditor must take care when verifying a subcontractor's insurance coverage. Suppose, for example, that an insured with operations subject to the U.S. Longshore and Harbor Workers Compensation Act subcontracts a portion of those operations. The subcontractor provides the insured with a certificate of insurance. Unless that certificate of insurance indicates coverage for the loss exposure under the act, the subcontractor would be uninsured, and the insurer must charge a premium for its employees.

The auditor must also verify that the coverage dates on the certificates of insurance cover the period the work was conducted. Any payroll during periods not covered by the certificates should be included in the premium base.

The auditor should also be alert to potential fraud through the use of bogus certificates. If anything unusual appears on the certificate (for example, consecutive policy numbers for two different policy periods), auditors should check with the issuing producers or their managers.

Subcontractors With No Employees

The protection afforded by statutory employer laws applies only to subcontractors' employees. A subcontractor with no employees has no workers' compensation obligation. A premium auditor should not look for a certificate of insurance in that case and should not become confused if, by some chance, one exists. The existence of such an unnecessary certificate of insurance has no bearing on the real question facing the auditor. That question is whether the subcontractor is an employee of the general contractor or an independent contractor. The tests of an employer-employee relationship determine the subcontractor's status.

Using independent contractor labor rather than employees is a common method of avoiding payroll taxes and fringe benefits. Premium auditors often encounter situations in which individuals are called subcontractors but are actually employees under the workers' compensation law.

Premium Audit Procedure

A premium auditor must consider the following two separate and distinct possibilities when the insured subcontracts work:

1. That the insured can be liable for workers' compensation to injured employees of uninsured subcontractors
2. That the insured can be liable for compensation to injured individuals who perform work as alleged independent contractors but who are found to have an employer-employee relationship with the insured

Many questions arise about the auditing procedures an auditor should follow for possible subcontracted work. Manual rules expressly cover some of the procedures, but legal complexities obscure others. Those complexities require considerable review and evaluation for an auditor to establish an equitable premium charge for an insured.

If, in examining an insured's records, an auditor notices that the insured has subcontracted work, the auditor must investigate the insured's relationship with each subcontractor. The minimum amount of information needed includes the following:

- Each subcontractor's name
- Dates worked
- Type of work performed

- Whether a subcontractor worked alone or used employees for the job performed
- Whether materials and equipment used on the job were furnished by the subcontractor or the insured
- Name of any insurer and the period of coverage
- Amount paid to each subcontractor

EMPLOYMENT STATUS

Employment status is a question of fact, not of law. If an issue arises about whether a particular individual is an employee or an independent contractor, a court or an administrative body decides the issue on the basis of the facts of the case. A court normally analyzes the relationship using the common-law tests of an employer-employee relationship. That analysis does not require that a court give each factor equal weight. Courts usually base their decisions on the predominance of evidence presented by each party.

Tests of Employer-Employee Relationships

Although the courts or administrative bodies with jurisdiction decide whether an employer-employee relationship exists on a case-by-case basis, certain factors are significant in making that determination. Traditionally, court decisions hinge on whether the alleged employer has the right to direct and control the work. An auditor can consider many factors to determine the extent of the employer's direction and control. Courts have based many recent decisions on the work's relative nature. Premium auditors should understand the reasoning involved in each of these employment status tests, even though only the appropriate judicial body can ultimately resolve the question.

Direction and Control

The common-law test of an employer-employee relationship is the extent of the employer's direction and control of the employee. Some indications of the employer's direction and control can be that the employee does the following:

- Receives a regular salary, usually based on an hourly, daily, weekly, or monthly rate
- Works during hours set by the employer
- Performs duties assigned by the employer
- Uses materials, tools, and equipment furnished by the employer
- Has federal income, FICA, and other taxes deducted by the employer
- Performs ongoing service for the employer
- Is subject to dismissal by the employer

- Is subject to supervision and instructions about the details of the work
- Works at a place set by the employer

Those signs provide guidelines for a premium auditor who is determining whether an individual is an employee.

Relative Nature of the Work

The element of control emphasized in the common-law test of employment status relates to the employer's liability to third parties. It is less relevant in other contexts. In applying social and labor legislation, courts tend to define employee status in a way that provides the protection of those laws to the people who need it. Because the direction and control test leaves considerable leeway, courts also examine the economic reality of the alleged employer-employee relationship. This "relative nature of the work" test assumes particular importance in workers' compensation cases. In such cases, injured workers can qualify for benefits because they depend economically on the alleged employer, even though they are not subject to direction and control. Because of their economic dependence, such individuals would have no protection unless they were eligible for the benefits of the workers' compensation law.

For example, if A hires B, a janitor, to provide cleaning service and pays the amount B stipulates for the services provided, then B is probably an independent contractor. However, if A, the owner of a large industrial building, hires B on the same basis but provides continuous employment to B assuming that the building's maintenance is part of the business, then B would be considered A's employee according to the relative nature of the work test.

The relative nature of the work test considers the following two factors:

1. The nature of the alleged employee's work, including level of skill and credentials required
2. The relationship of the alleged employee's work to the employer's business

For the first factor, if a license is necessary to perform the work, a court is more likely to consider it an enterprise separate from the employer's business. The court, therefore, is more likely to say the person is an independent contractor. The extent to which the trade or enterprise might be expected to carry its own insurance is also important.

The relative nature of the work test also considers the relationship of the alleged employee's work to the employer's business. Only considering the nature of the employee's work would lead to standard classification of some occupations always performed by employees and others always performed by independent contractors. Because such classifications would not hold, the auditor must also consider the relation of the work to the employer's business. If the work is an integral part of the business, then a court is likely to find

that an employer-employee relationship exists. The same is true if the person performs the work continuously rather than intermittently or if the work lasts long enough to be deemed continuous service rather than project work. Even if control appears lacking, the court might determine that an employer-employee relationship exists if the employer appears to accomplish its regular business through the individual's regular services.

For example, consider the case of a dump truck operator killed while working on a construction project. The court found an employer-employee relationship existed despite several indications of independent contractor status. The truck operator owned his own truck and was paid for each load of dirt he removed from the construction site. He obtained his own liability and workers' compensation insurance and signed a form stating that he would be responsible for his own income tax. He worked at other places as well. However, at the time of his death, he had been devoting 81 percent of his workdays to the construction project. The court based its finding of employee status on the relative nature of the work test. The contractor relied on the truck operator's efforts, which represented "a substantial cog" in the project's completion, and the truck operator relied on that construction project for a substantial portion of his livelihood.[7]

The fact that the two parties agree that one of them has the status of an independent contractor relative to the other does not make it so. A court might consider the parties' intent, but it will also be suspicious of attempts to avoid an employment relationship. Similarly, the fact that an individual carries workers' compensation insurance has little value as evidence of independent contractor status.

Borderline Cases

Premium auditors often encounter situations in which insureds insist that certain regular workers are independent contractors rather than employees. Frequently, a policyholder not required by IRS regulations to withhold income taxes does not understand that the court might consider the individual as an employee for insurance purposes. Occasionally, insureds go to great lengths to create independent contractor status for some of their workers to save payroll taxes, fringe benefits, and insurance premiums. A contract's existence stipulating that a person is an independent contractor has no significance. Employees cannot normally waive their rights under the workers' compensation law, nor can they waive their survivors' rights. Courts determine employee status by the facts, not by a contract's wording.

Premium auditors must examine the relationship and judge for themselves whether each individual is an employee within the policy's context. Examining the employment relationship includes studying any regulations or legislation governing the business's practice. Knowing the business's usual practices also helps. Additionally, a premium auditor might have to ask many questions about the employment arrangement's specific terms.

An additional source the auditor might consider consulting is any contract signed by the independent contractor. Because such contracts often state the relationship as one of independent contractor, policyholders may use them as evidence that an employer-employee relationship does not exist. However, by reading the contract closely, the auditor might learn that specific clauses indicate the existence of an employer-employee relationship. For example, the contract might state the employment relationship is terminable at the will of either party, a common condition of an employer-employee relationship. Other examples indicating an employer-employee relationship might be if the employer establishes specific work hours or if the worker uses supplied equipment.

No distinct method can be used to distinguish employees from independent contractors. The following section describes some borderline cases to illustrate the principles used in resolving questions of employment status. A premium auditor, however, must always check the applicable state law as well as the facts of the particular case.

Commission Sales

Perhaps the most common borderline case involves individuals who are compensated by commission rather than by wages or salaries. Unless they run their own businesses, those individuals might receive commissions from someone whom courts construe to be an employer. Such workers do not appear on the regular payroll, however, because their incomes depend on the sales volume, not on the time worked. Common-law rules usually apply in determining whether such individuals are considered employees for tax purposes. However, the Internal Revenue Code expressly defines commission salespeople who meet certain conditions (specified in the code) as employees for Social Security purposes.[8] If there is no statutory definition for insurance purposes, premium auditors must consider the degree of direction and control and the relative nature of the work, not the manner of compensation. Items sold on a commission basis range from million-dollar real estate to fifty-cent newspapers, but the nature of the work and the degree of control involved vary considerably depending on the item being sold.

Distinguishing between a retailer, wholesaler, broker, manufacturer, and manufacturer's representative is difficult because the customary activities of one can overlap with any of the others. Generally, a manufacturer's representative is just that—an individual or a company representing one or more manufacturers in the sale of products. The representatives never own the product sold, although they might stock a small supply of samples used for display or demonstration.

Most manufacturers' representatives work strictly on a commission basis. They might employ additional salespeople and pay them a salary or commission without affecting their relationship with the manufacturer. Manufacturers' representatives might demonstrate the product and, sometimes, supervise its installation. They might also train customers' employees in using the product.

Frequently, however, they do not actually deliver the product, and they might never see it. They do not repackage or rebuild the product. Therefore, they do not maintain or use warehouse or storage facilities from which they distribute products.

When the manufacturer's representative is a corporate entity, the question of employment relationship should not arise because the corporation should be providing the necessary workers' compensation coverage. For those situations in which the manufacturer's representative is an individual, the question of employment relationship arises.

The safest approach to determining the status of a manufacturer's representative is to ask whether the person is acting as an agent or a principal. If salespeople are selling on their own accounts, extending their own credit, and purchasing in the market at the lowest competitive figure, then they are independent contractors. If they are selling for the account of a principal who extends credit, makes collections, and ships the order, then they are employees, regardless of the fact that they handle other noncompetitive lines or the fact that they are not permitted drawing or expense accounts. Using a questionnaire similar to the sample provided by Exhibit 5-1 can help resolve the employment status of a commission salesperson.

Another kind of commission sale comes from route sales. Certain businesses (such as laundries, milk dealers, ice cream manufacturers, soft drink bottlers, and bakeries) commonly set up route salespeople as independent contractors. Normally, the business and the driver make a contract that assigns a specific route or territory to the driver. The contract might require the driver to distribute that business's products exclusively and to use a vehicle marked with the business's name. The business might furnish the vehicle and transfer ownership to the driver. If so, the firm often holds a chattel mortgage on the vehicle so that it can reclaim the vehicle if the driver has not met the contract's conditions. Route salespeople are usually responsible for their own Social Security, unemployment, and other taxes. The business might pay drivers on a commission basis, or drivers might buy the products wholesale and sell retail. In the latter case, the price differential covers the driver's compensation and expenses. A variation is for the business to bill the route salesperson for the product at its retail price less commission, expenses, and perhaps delivery cost.

For such businesses, courts would consider the route salespersons, in the majority of cases, to be employees. Denying a workers' compensation claim to such persons on the grounds that they are independent contractors would be difficult. Evidence is usually sufficient to show that the insured provides direction and control by prescribing the route, rendering the bills, and providing the exclusive product. Even without that degree of control, a court would normally consider a person delivering a product to be an employee under the relative nature of the work test. Distributing the product is an inherent part of almost any business. A deliverer rarely delivers or distributes products on a given route as an independent contractor.

EXHIBIT 5-1

Questionnaire on Commission Salespeople

1. Is there a written contract between the insured and the commission salesperson? ____________
   If so, attach a copy of the contract.
2. If there is no written contract, what oral agreement exists between the parties about the rights and obligations of each?
   ____
   ____
3. Does the insured have the right (whether or not it is exercised) under the written contract or the oral agreement to control the commission salesperson regarding:
   a. Hours of work? ____________
   b. Methods of travel? ____________
   c. Routing of calls? ____________
   d. Persons on whom calls are to be made? ____________
   e. Work reports about the salesperson's activities? ____________
   f. Sales quotas? ____________
   g. Territories worked in? ____________
4. How is the commission salesperson remunerated? (Insert the amounts earned for each during the audit period)
   a. Commissions ____________ $____________
   b. Drawings ____________ $____________
   c. Travel expenses or allowances ____________ $____________
   d. Salaries or wages ____________ $____________
   e. Bonuses ____________ $____________
5. Does the commission salesperson also represent other concerns? ____________ If so, name such concerns, and state whether they handle lines in competition with the insured. ____________
   ____
6. Does the insured report the commission salesperson for Social Security, unemployment, or withholding taxes?
   ____
7. How are the following transactions handled?
   a. Are sales made in the name of insured or commission salesperson? ____________
   b. Does the insured reserve the right to accept or reject sales orders? ____________
   c. Who ships the goods to the customer? ____________
   d. In what shipper's name are the goods shipped? ____________
   e. Does the insured or the commission salesperson bill the customer? ____________
   f. Is the insured or the commission salesperson responsible to the customer in case of error or dissatisfaction with the goods? ____________
   g. Who ultimately sustains losses, if any, on uncollectible accounts? ____________
8. Does the commission salesperson operate as a separate organization? ____________
   a. Is an office or salesroom maintained? ____________ Location: ____________
      If so, state ____________
   b. Under what trading name is the business conducted? ____________
   c. Is the telephone listed in this trading name? ____________
   d. Does this trading name appear on the stationery, order blanks, advertising matter, etc.? Does the insured's name also appear? ____________
   e. Does the commission salesperson employ others? ____________ How many? ____________
   f. Is workers' compensation insurance carried by the commission salesperson? ____________
   g. Are such employees reported for Social Security, unemployment, and withholding taxes by the commission salesperson?
      ____
   h. Is the commission salesperson reimbursed by the insured for rent, telephone, salaries, workers' compensation premiums, Social Security, unemployment taxes, or other expenses? ____________
      ____

Products Installation

The sale of products such as carpeting, roofing, aluminum siding, and storm doors frequently includes installation. The firm selling the product receives an order from the customer. When necessary, its representative takes measurements or obtains other needed information. The price contracted for the product includes the installation and is paid entirely to the seller. The sales agreement may include an installation warranty and may provide for any necessary service for a stipulated time.

In such cases, the seller often employs installers to perform the installation work on a per-job basis. The seller does not withhold Social Security or income taxes from the payments made to the installers. For each job, the installers receive work orders that specify just what work is to be performed. If the job requires additional work or the customer requests additional work, the installers do not have the authority to proceed until first obtaining the seller's authorization. The seller requires the installers to perform the work correctly. If a customer submits a complaint during the warranty service period, the seller would require the installer to return to the job and correct any problems. If the installer is not available, the seller would employ another installer to perform the necessary work.

Answers to questions such as those in Exhibit 5-2 help establish the degree of control and the relative nature of the work in cases involving installation subcontractors.

Sellers often contend that installers are independent contractors to whom they have subcontracted the installation work. The degree of direction and control can be difficult to ascertain. The relative nature of the work test can help determine the installer's status. In most cases, installation is not an independent business. Installers depend on work orders from the product's seller. When that dependence is substantial and the installation is an integral part of the product's sale, a court might hold the installer to be the seller's employee.

Owner-Operators

Perhaps the most perplexing case of ambiguous relationships involves truckers who own their own equipment and operate it for the benefit of others. The same set of circumstances can lead to entirely different legal conclusions in different states. It is not unusual for an insurer to pay workers' compensation claims of owner-drivers at the same time the insured refuses to pay premiums on those same owner-drivers on the grounds that they are independent contractors.

The owner-operator owns a truck and drives it, carrying shipments assigned by a trucking company. In some cases, a driver might lease a truck from a trucking company and operate independently. In other cases, the trucking company might finance the operator's purchase of a truck. Owner-operators do not have Interstate Commerce Commission (ICC) licenses, so they must operate under the rights of an ICC-licensed carrier if they transport goods between states.

EXHIBIT 5-2

Questionnaire on Installation Subcontractors

	Yes	No
1. Is the subcontractor free to solicit business from other companies?		
2. Is the subcontractor free to substitute one employee for another?		
3. Is the subcontractor free to choose own working hours?		
4. Is the subcontractor free to reject assignments?		
5. Does the subcontractor furnish own tools and equipment?		
6. Does the subcontractor furnish all materials?		
7. Does the subcontractor pay for own repairs and maintenance costs?		
8. Does the subcontractor have, and pay for, own: A. Workers' compensation insurance?		
B. Liability insurance?		
9. Is the subcontractor licensed?		
10. Does the subcontractor pay license fees?		
11. Are Social Security and income taxes deducted from contract price?		
12. Does the subcontractor keep own records?		
13. Does the subcontractor do the same type of job for anyone?		
14. Does the subcontractor have own place of business?		
15. Does the subcontractor make a profit on materials as well as on labor?		
16. Is the subcontractor paid on a distinctly different basis than the regular employee?		
17. Is there a written contract? (Obtain a copy if possible.)		
18. Does the subcontractor choose own methods and frequency in serving customers?		
19. Can the subcontractor terminate the contract without a penalty?		
20. Does the insured specify a completion date?		

21. What is the description of subcontractor's operations?

22. If no written contract exists, what is the nature of the oral agreement? (What is to be done, how it is to be done, rights and obligations of each party, etc.)

23. What is the extent of direction and supervision exercised by the insured over the subcontractor's operations?

24. What is the method of payment—flat amount for job or hourly, daily, or weekly rate, and amounts paid during audit period and who determines amount of payment?

Owner-operators contract with a trucking company to haul a load to a designated location. When that run is completed, the owner-operator can either contract with the same carrier or with a different one for the return trip.

The carrier usually pays either a percentage of the gross revenue or pays on a mileage or per-trip basis. On a percentage, the drivers might get about 75 percent of the gross revenue. The rate received per mile or per trip varies by cargo, region, and company. Out of that amount, the driver must pay for the vehicle, depreciation, loan interest, license fees, insurance, maintenance, tolls, tires, fuel, wages, living costs on the road, profit, and miscellaneous overhead such as bookkeeping.

Regardless of the number of trips involved, ICC regulations require a written lease agreement to cover each trip. Exhibit 5-3 is an example of such a lease agreement. The fact that a lease agreement exists between a trucking company and owner-operator does not make the owner-operator an independent contractor. Often the lease agreement imposes many of the controls expected in an employer-employee relationship. In Exhibit 5-3, for example, Clause 1 states that during the lease's term the vehicle is for the trucking company's exclusive use. Clause 4 gives the trucking company the right to reject equipment if it is defective. Clause 9 requires the driver to report any delays during the trip's progress.

Unless the trucking company has an established route between points, the owner-operator can usually choose any route as long as the delivery occurs at the time specified. Despite that freedom, a trucking company can impose other controls. To monitor progress, the trucking company might require a driver to call in each day by a certain time. Even though the owner-operator might be responsible for maintaining the equipment, the trucking company can require copies of all repair orders or bills to help determine the equipment's condition. In some cases, the trucking company might conduct spot-checks done on the road to determine whether the owner-operator is operating the equipment according to company regulations.

The question of whether an owner-operator is an employee or an independent contractor for purposes of workers' compensation insurance has frequently come before the courts. The answer depends on the facts in each case, regardless of what the parties might include in any contract.

Courts have cited various conditions to determine the degree of direction and control that a trucking company employer must have over an owner-operator to result in an employer-employee relationship. Those conditions include the following:

- Designation and control of the route
- Appearance of the carrier's name on truck panels
- Requirement of carrier's prior approval for owner-operator to engage in other jobs
- Provision by the carrier of operating and shipping licenses as well as truck and cargo liability insurance

- Payment of operating expenses by the trucker
- Safety standards set and maintained by the trucking company
- Owner-operator lease of the equipment to the trucking company
- Owner-operator payment in same manner as employee, that is, withholding deductions taken from pay or W-2 and W-4 Forms prepared by the trucking company
- Furnishing of tractor by trucking company for the use of the owner-operator
- Termination of relationship at will

Federal and state regulations require many trucking company controls over owner-operators. The ICC regulates issuance and enforcement of operating rights, setting of rates, cargoes, and insurance requirements for trucking companies operating in interstate or foreign transportation.

The regulations for leasing and interchanging equipment by regulated trucking companies show how much control trucking companies must exercise over leased vehicles and their operators. For example, the regulations state that during the lease period, the vehicle must be in the trucking company's service. The regulations also require that the lease provide that the trucking company has exclusive control for the lease period.[9]

In addition to the Interstate Commerce Commission, the Department of Transportation also issues regulations concerning the safe operation of equipment and the safety of drivers and the public. Those regulations apply to all trucking companies involved in interstate commerce.

According to the regulations, drivers must be subject to the control, direction, and supervision of the trucking company—not a truck lessor. The trucking company must direct driver activities regarding loading, unloading, routes, breakdowns, safety, refueling, rests, eating periods, and company rules and must retain the right to dismiss drivers. The trucking company must maintain a personnel record for each driver. Those mandated federal and state regulations that require the trucking company to exercise strict, direct controls over any vehicle's operation operated on the trucking company's behalf (whether by employees or owner-operators) create an employment relationship, regardless of any contracted agreement to the contrary.

Should an owner-operator hire a helper during the course of employment, a court might hold the owner-operator to be acting as the trucking company's agent in employing such helpers. The court then might consider such helpers the trucking company's employees even if the owner-operator obtained workers' compensation insurance to provide protection for the helper.

The relative nature of the work test essentially involves the extent to which the owner-operator is an integral part of the trucking company's business and the extent to which the independent contractor depends economically on the trucking company. Applying that test has resulted in a determination of employee status when an owner-operator worked exclusively or continuously

EXHIBIT 5-3

Sample Trucker's Trip Lease

FREIGHT LINES, INC.
2000 W. 12th Street
Anytown, Anystate 00000
Phone 1-000-000-0000

THIS AGREEMENT by and between ______________________________

of ______________________________ (LESSOR)

and ______________________________

of ______________________________ (LESSEE)

WITNESSETH

The LESSOR hereby leases to the LESSEE the following vehicle equipment:

Tractor ______________________________
(Make) (Year) (Serial No.) (State and License No.)

Trailer ______________________________
(Make) (Year) (Serial No.) (State and License No.)

Semitrailer ______________________________
(Make) (Year) (Serial No.) (State and License No.)

Wherever it (or they) may be, for a period of ______________________________

from ______________________________ to ______________________________

1. It is understood that the leased equipment under this agreement is in the exclusive possession, control, and use of the authorized carrier LESSEE and that the LESSEE assumes full responsibility for the equipment it is operating, to the public, the shippers, and the ICC.
2. During the term of this agreement, the LESSOR will pay all the maintenance and operating expenses, including the compensation coverage and all taxes, state or federal based on payroll, for one or more drivers, as may be required, of the motor vehicle(s) and/or equipment herein described.
3. During the term of this agreement, the LESSEE will be responsible for the loss or damage to cargo transported in such vehicle(s) and/or equipment and will be responsible for any property damage and/or public liability resulting from the operation of said motor vehicle(s) and/or equipment. The LESSEE will hold the LESSOR responsible for any loss or damage resulting from the negligence, incompetence, or dishonesty of any driver, also for disobeying rules and regulations of any company and all state and government regulatory bodies as the case may be.
4. In the event that equipment referred to herein is not in proper mechanical condition or for any other reason is deemed inadequate to the LESSEE, then the LESSEE will have the authority to transfer any shipment from this equipment and to handle same according to the best judgment of the LESSEE. All charges such as delivery and storage incident to the rehandling of such shipment will be deducted from the amount paid to the LESSOR for the use of the equipment under this agreement.

5. LESSEE will be responsible to shippers for any loss, damage, or happening giving rise to claims and will withhold payment of any and all sums then or thereafter due the LESSOR, to the extent of such expenses and claims until the determination of such expense and valid claims, which amounts will then be deducted to the satisfaction thereof.
6. LESSEE will not be liable for the loss of, or damage to, the aforesaid equipment, however caused, while in use under the terms of this lease.
7. LESSOR agrees, on termination of this lease, to remove and to return all identification signs owned by the LESSEE to the LESSEE or be deducted the cost thereof.
8. In consideration of the foregoing, LESSEE agrees to pay the LESSOR, and the LESSOR agrees to accept as hire of the said equipment and reimbursement for the service of any driver or drivers the following compensation, on receipt of clear signed delivery receipts and driver's log sheets.

____

9. NOTE: If driver is delayed en route, the driver is to PHONE ____________. Failure to report delay will result in a $50 fine to be deducted from settlement.

This duly signed form shall constitute a receipt for the possession of the above motor vehicle equipment by the LESSEE.

____________________ (LESSOR) FREIGHT LINES, INC.

By ____________________ By ____________________

DATED AT ________________ A.M. P.M. DATED AT ________________ A.M. P.M.

Physical ____________________

RECEIPT FOR POSSESSION OF MOTOR VEHICLE EQUIPMENT

10.
Received of ________________ FREIGHT LINES, INC. ON ________________

____

____ 20____, at ____ (A). (P). M.	MAKE	YEAR	MOTOR NUMBER	SERIAL NUMBER	LICENSE NUMBER
A. Tractor					
B. Trailer					
C. Semitrailer					

BY ____________________ BY ____________________

OWNER AND LESSOR AGENT OR EMPLOYEE

for one trucking company. Whether an owner-operator is a trucking company's employee or an independent contractor depends on the facts of the case and the laws of the specific state involved. Therefore, a premium auditor faced with such a situation must know both the law and the facts. A questionnaire such as the one shown in Exhibit 5-4 can help determine the facts in each case involving owner-operators.

Personal Services

Similar complications arise when individuals provide a personal service to the public but use others' equipment or facilities in the process. Sometimes the facilities such individuals use are so substantial that it becomes inconceivable that they could operate as independent businesses without those facilities. A barber or beautician, for example, normally uses the space and equipment of an established shop. Similarly, taxicab drivers often use a cab and perhaps a dispatching service provided by a taxicab company. Both the elements of control and the nature of the work might indicate an employment relationship in such cases.

Often barbers and beauticians are on the direct payroll of the shop in which they work. However, some of those professionals with a large clientele have an entirely different basis for remuneration. Instead of being on the payroll, they will rent a chair or space from the barbershop or beauty salon. That rent is usually a percentage of the take for the chair. The shop collects the fees from the customers, keeps the rental charge, and pays the balance to the barber or beautician. The shop also sets the barbers' and beauticians' hours. The shop's owner often contends that such beauticians and barbers are independent contractors.

For example, three registered barbers operated a barbershop as a partnership. The state might try to require them to pay unemployment taxes for a fourth barber added as an apprentice as the business expanded. Each of the four barbers, however, serves a separate clientele and independently sets prices, purchases materials, collects receipts, and fixes working hours. The arrangement among the four barbers is merely a space-sharing plan, and the parties do not have an employment relationship.

However, for workers' compensation purposes, the arrangement might be considered an employment relationship. A premium auditor should be prepared to treat barbers and beauticians as employees unless clear evidence to the contrary exists.

A similar situation can arise when a taxicab company contends that the taxicab drivers are not employees within the provisions of the workers' compensation laws. Taxicab companies often make lease agreements with their drivers in an attempt to establish an independent contractor relationship. With one arrangement, the company leases the cab to the operator, often under a short lease of twenty-four hours. Under that leasing arrangement, the taxicab operator pays the company a daily rental charge. The operator then collects the fares, and any excess over the rental charge belongs to the driver.

EXHIBIT 5-4

Questionnaire on Owner-Operators

	Yes	No
A. Is the owner-operator		
1. Free to solicit business from other companies?		
2. Free to substitute one driver or helper for another?		
3. Free to choose:		
a. Routes?		
b. Loads?		
c. Working hours?		
4. Free to reject assignments?		
5. Free to choose the method and frequency of serving customers?		
6. Paid on a distinctly different basis than regular employees?		
7. Excluded from:		
a. Carrier contributions for unemployment compensation?		
b. Company pension and welfare plans?		
8. An employee for collective bargaining purposes (a member of a union that bargains with the trucking company over conditions of employment, etc., for the owner-operator)?		
B. Does the owner-operator		
1. Pay for all vehicle repairs?		
2. Have and pay for general liability insurance (other than bobtail)?		
3. Pay license fees?		
4. Keep records?		
5. Pay for the vehicle?		
6. Own the vehicle?		
7. Perform tasks different from those of regular employees?		
8. Have to meet different employment requirements than regular employees?		

Obtain a copy of the written contract, if any.
What was the basis of remuneration?
Per Hour, Day, Week, Weight, Unit, Load,
Other—Explain.

Comments. (Include reason why insured believes that the owner-operator should not be included.)

The driver might have to pay for gasoline out of the receipts, but the company assumes the other maintenance expenses, including the cost of insurance and major repairs.

Under a similar arrangement, the taxicab driver pays a fee based on the mileage driven. A third kind of arrangement is based on meter readings. The operator retains a percentage of the total fares shown on the meter for the day, and the balance goes to the company. Under that arrangement, the company ordinarily pays all expenses, including gasoline, maintenance, and routine operating expenses.

Even though the parties might draw up the lease in an attempt to eliminate all elements of an employer-employee relationship, a court might still find a taxicab driver to be an employee for workers' compensation purposes. For example, a lease agreement provides for a daily rental fee and allows the driver to keep all fares and tips. The driver is not subject to the owner's control and direction. The lease provides that the driver is solely liable for income tax, Social Security, and unemployment insurance payments. The owner assumes responsibility only for repairs, replacements, and public liability insurance. Despite the independence given the driver in that lease, some courts might find that an employer-employee relationship exists. Other courts, however, might rule that the lease agreement does establish an independent contractor status.

Professional Services

Professionals who provide services can also depend on another organization even though they provide the service directly to the public. For example, a hospital might contract with a group of physicians who agree to provide emergency room services. If the doctors cannot provide complete emergency room service, they then would subcontract with other doctors to provide the balance of the needed emergency room coverage.

In an arrangement of that sort, the physician's association agrees to provide adequate physician's coverage for the emergency room. The association hires, at its own expense, additional physicians as necessary. One of the association's members may act as director of emergency services, on approval of the hospital credentials committee, and is responsible for supervising association members.

In a contract for services, the fee schedule stipulates a set amount per hour for each hour a physician of a certain category is on duty. The hospital bases association compensation for providing emergency room services on fees billed, less professional discounts. The hospital approves the fee schedule, and the physician or association cannot change the schedule without the hospital's consent. Also, a minimum income might be guaranteed to the association.

The personnel furnished by the hospital to staff the emergency room are hospital employees that are administratively responsible to the hospital. However, the physician on duty, who is an association employee, assumes the full responsibility for the medical direction and control of the hospital employees.

Despite the contractual arrangement, most courts consider the physicians providing the emergency room care to be hospital employees for workers' compensation purposes. In such cases, rather than considering control of professional discretion, courts consider whether the professional worker is regularly at the disposal of the employer to perform the employer's work, as opposed to being available to provide professional services to the public on his or her own terms.

For professional liability purposes, however, the employment status revolves around an entirely different issue than in workers' compensation cases. The extent of direction and control becomes paramount in determining professional liability. The auditor must look to the policy to determine the coverage's intent and then examine the facts of the employment relationship.

Casual Labor

In addition to its regular employees, a business or another organization may occasionally hire individuals to perform temporary odd jobs. If those individuals are not likely to earn enough to require income tax withholding, their names probably do not appear on the payroll. Even so, workers' compensation laws might cover them, depending on the state and the nature of the work.

The workers' compensation laws of many states exclude casual labor. The rationale for excluding casual labor from workers' compensation coverage stems from the possible moral hazard involved. The brief and irregular nature of casual employment can encourage unwarranted claims and malingering recoveries among casual employees trying to stretch their income. The exclusion removes an obstacle that might otherwise prevent an employer from hiring casual labor.

Some statutes provide a definition of casual labor. Although the precise definition varies by state, courts generally hold casual labor to be irregular, unpredictable, sporadic, and brief in nature. For example, a sixteen-year-old boy allowed to work for brief periods, whenever he pleased, would probably be considered a casual employee and not covered by workers' compensation. Many state statutes, however, require that the labor be outside the employer's regular business to be considered casual. So, a laborer hired for one day to help at a construction site is a contractor's temporary employee. In most states, workers' compensation coverage does not exclude such a day laborer because it is a part of the employer's regular business and, therefore, not casual labor. Washing dishes in a restaurant, washing store windows, mowing lawns, or cleaning the premises might all be occasional, part-time jobs. However, the need for all of those services can be anticipated as part of the regular business. Therefore, those jobs are not casual labor.

A few state laws also add a time or monetary limitation to the definition of casual labor. For example, casual labor must be completed within ten days and must cost less than $100.

Because relatively few cases meet the conditions of casual labor, premium auditors must be alert for occasional or temporary employees working for the insured even though they do not appear on the payroll.

Domestic Workers

Domestic workers are employees engaged exclusively in household or domestic work, such as cooks, housekeepers, laundry workers, maids, butlers, companions, nurses, babysitters, chauffeurs, and gardeners. Only individuals or couples can employ domestic workers. Businesses or organizations cannot. Courts consider persons performing domestic services, such as those previously mentioned, who are employed by an organization to be miscellaneous employees.

In many ways, domestic workers are treated differently from other employees. In most cases, the employer does not have to withhold federal income tax. If domestic workers receive more than $50 in a calendar quarter, however, they are covered for Social Security and minimum wage purposes. In that case, overtime regulations also apply, except for sleep-in domestics. In many states, the workers' compensation statutes specifically exclude domestics. Other states consider domestics to be employees only if they are hired to work a certain minimum number of hours per week. Some states exclude coverage for certain types of domestics by excluding part-time babysitters and cleaning persons. Some states now allow homeowner policies to include workers' compensation coverage for domestic workers.

Normally, a premium auditor need not worry about household employees. When an agency provides babysitters, housekeepers, or other domestic workers, however, the possibility exists of an employer-employee relationship between the agency and the domestic worker. An agency that supplies babysitters, for example, might be a source of regular employment. The agency might send a person on the agency's list of babysitters to several different homes in the course of a month. Each client pays the standard agency rate directly to the babysitter. The babysitter then gives the agency a designated proportion of the rate as a service fee. Under that arrangement, the agency is not an employer for FICA, unemployment, or income tax withholding purposes.[10] A court considers the babysitter self-employed and subject to self-employment taxes.

For workers' compensation and liability insurance purposes, however, a court might consider the babysitter an agency employee. A liability policy defines who is covered. For a workers' compensation policy, however, the premium auditor might have to judge whether the agency provides substantial employment to domestic workers as an integral part of its business. If so, a court could consider a domestic worker an agency employee by the relative nature of the work test. One would more reasonably expect the agency making a business of providing babysitting services to incur a workers' compensation obligation, rather than the private individuals who are its clients.

Agricultural Employees

Another group of workers that sometimes raises questions to premium auditors is farm workers. The main question is not whether they are employees but whether they qualify under the law as agricultural employees. The workers' compensation laws of most states either exclude or limit coverage for agricultural employees. For example, a workers' compensation law might cover agricultural employees only if they use machinery or power equipment. Other states exempt employers with less than a specific number of employees from the requirements of the law.

Whether individuals are exempt as agricultural employees might depend on whether the employer is an agricultural or a commercial enterprise. Agriculture means growing food by tilling the soil, cultivating orchards, or raising livestock. Sometimes, however, agricultural activities might involve only one stage in a food-processing operation. In that case, the enterprise uses the work methods and accounting procedures of an industrial operation, and exempting agricultural employees is inappropriate.

Even an enterprise that merely produces food can become more of a factory than a farm by intensive specialization. For example, when chickens are hatched, nurtured, and butchered within a single building, the operation does not meet the conventional definition of agriculture.

A farmer can also lose the agricultural exemption by engaging in other businesses besides farming. For example, a farmer who furnishes ground grain for others as well as for himself would be required to provide workers' compensation for the helper operating the grinder. The helper would not be considered an agricultural employee. If a farmer hires workers to help clear the land of trees, the work is agricultural even when the farmer sells the timber. The same activities on land not used for farming, however, constitute a lumbering business, and the agricultural employment exemption does not apply. When farm workers engage in other activities, such as repairing farm machinery or fixing a fence, they are still agricultural employees as long as the other jobs are a routine part of operating a farm. In the same way, workers covered by the workers' compensation law, such as carpenters repairing a barn, do not lose that status merely by working temporarily on a farm. As in other cases, the premium auditor must examine the nature of the work and the employer-employee relationship.

SUMMARY

In an employment relationship, the employees must perform the services for which they were hired, and, by implication, they agree to do so honestly and faithfully. Employers must provide employees with a reasonably safe environment, safe tools, and competent coworkers. In addition, employers must warn employees of dangers associated with the job and compensate them for their services. Whether individuals are employees depends on the context

of employment, which might be determined by examining (1) the report of their remuneration through payroll taxes, (2) the application of labor laws to the individuals, and (3) the definition of an employee under the employers' liability and workers' compensation policies.

A premium auditor investigating employer-employee relationships must clearly establish the identity and status of each relationship. Varying state regulations determine the roles and definition of an employee based on the status of an employer as a sole proprietor, partner, corporation, or not-for-profit organization. An individual working for multiple employers, such as an employee loaned by a general employer to a special employer, is included in the workers' compensation of the special employer when the following three conditions apply:

1. The employee has a contract of hire, express or implied, with the special employer.
2. The work done is essentially that of the special employer.
3. The special employer has the right to and is, at time of injury, controlling the details of work of the lent employee.

In a joint employment situation, most courts hold joint employers jointly and individually liable for workers' compensation, while in a dual employment situation the employer whose work was being done at the time of the injury is liable if the work can be clearly separated. Leased employees are covered for workers' compensation by their labor contractors; however, the client employer's general liability policy provides coverage for leased employees similar to that provided for employees.

In the following ambiguous employment situations, courts require proof of an expressor implied contract to determine an employer-employee relationship:

- Emergency services—An employee asking a person for help in an emergency becomes an employer of the person who provides the help under an implied contract.
- Reciprocal services—An employer may pay an employee in reciprocal services rather than money.
- Illegal employments—Contracts must be for a legal purpose. Workers' compensation benefits are denied for performance of an illegal act.
- Gratuitous workers—Volunteers are generally not considered to be employees, because they receive no payment.
- Illegal aliens—Payments made to illegal aliens should be included as remuneration because they are considered employees and are likely to receive workers' compensation benefits.

The distinction between employees and various types of contractors is important in determining the appropriate workers' compensation remuneration. Independent contractors are not subject to direction and control regarding the

details of their work. Independent contractors (general contractors) may hire subcontractors for the completion of tasks. Independent contractors usually offer their services to the public. An organization might use independent contractors instead of employees for a variety of reasons, including cost, flexibility in meeting fluctuating staffing requirements, and to obtain specialized services.

A premium auditor can determined employment status by applying the following tests to various employment situations:

- The right of direction and control test is the examination of the extent of an employer's direction and control of an employee's work, duties, remuneration, and continued employment.
- The relative nature of the work test examines the nature of the work, skills and credentials required to perform the work, as well as the relationship of the work to the employer's business.

In borderline cases of determining employment status, a premium auditor must use judgment in examining the relationship, the policy's context, any applicable regulations or legislation governing business practices, and knowledge of usual business practices. In addition, the auditor might examine any contract signed by an independent contractor for evidence that an employer-employee relationship exists.

CHAPTER NOTES

1. Internal Revenue Code, §3401.
2. Internal Revenue Code, §3401 (d).
3. Internal Revenue Code, §3121 (d).
4. *Salvatore De Stefano v. State of New York Division of Housing*, et al., 341 N.Y.S. 2d 707, 41 A.D. 2d 801 (1973).
5. *California Workers Compensation Insurance Manual*, General Rules, Underwriting and Auditing Procedures, "21. Employment Status," p. 12 (effective 1 January 1993).
6. *California Workers Compensation Insurance Manual*, General Rules, Underwriting and Auditing Procedures, "21. Employment Status," pp. 12–13 (effective 1 January 1993).
7. *Caicco v. Toto Bros. Inc.*, 62 N.J. 305 (1973).
8. Internal Revenue Code, §3121 (d).
9. *Federal Register* (Vol. 44, Nr. 16), §1057:11–12.
10. Internal Revenue Code, §3506.

Appendix

Internal Revenue Form SS-8

Form **SS-8**
(Rev. June 2003)
Department of the Treasury
Internal Revenue Service

Determination of Worker Status for Purposes of Federal Employment Taxes and Income Tax Withholding

OMB No. 1545-0004

Name of firm (or person) for whom the worker performed services		Worker's name	
Firm's address (include street address, apt. or suite no., city, state, and ZIP code)		Worker's address (include street address, apt. or suite no., city, state, and ZIP code)	
Trade name		Telephone number (include area code) ( )	Worker's social security number
Telephone number (include area code) ( )	Firm's employer identification number	Worker's employer identification number (if any)	

If the worker is paid by a firm other than the one listed on this form for these services, enter the name, address, and employer identification number of the payer.

Important Information Needed To Process Your Request

We must have your permission to disclose your name and the information on this form and any attachments to other parties involved with this request. **Do we have your permission to disclose this information?** . . . . ☐ **Yes** ☐ **No**
If you answered "No" or did not mark a box, we will not process your request and will not issue a determination.

You must answer ALL items OR mark them "Unknown" or "Does not apply." If you need more space, attach another sheet.

A This form is being completed by: ☐ Firm ☐ Worker; for services performed ____________ (beginning date) to ____________ (ending date).

B Explain your reason(s) for filing this form (e.g., you received a bill from the IRS, you believe you received a Form 1099 or Form W-2 erroneously, you are unable to get worker's compensation benefits, you were audited or are being audited by the IRS).

C Total number of workers who performed or are performing the same or similar services ____________.

D How did the worker obtain the job? ☐ Application ☐ Bid ☐ Employment Agency ☐ Other (specify) ____________.

E Attach copies of all supporting documentation (contracts, invoices, memos, Forms W-2, Forms 1099, IRS closing agreements, IRS rulings, etc.). In addition, please inform us of any current or past litigation concerning the worker's status. If no income reporting forms (Form 1099-MISC or W-2) were furnished to the worker, enter the amount of income earned for the year(s) at issue $ ____________.

F Describe the firm's business.

G Describe the work done by the worker and provide the worker's job title.

H Explain why you believe the worker is an employee or an independent contractor.

I Did the worker perform services for the firm before getting this position? . . . . ☐ **Yes** ☐ **No** ☐ **N/A**
If "Yes," what were the dates of the prior service?
If "Yes," explain the differences, if any, between the current and prior service.

J If the work is done under a written agreement between the firm and the worker, attach a copy (preferably signed by both parties). Describe the terms and conditions of the work arrangement.

For Privacy Act and Paperwork Reduction Act Notice, see page 5. Cat. No. 16106T Form **SS-8** (Rev. 6-2003)

Form SS-8 (Rev. 6-2003) Page **2**

Behavioral Control

1 What specific training and/or instruction is the worker given by the firm? ______

2 How does the worker receive work assignments? ______

3 Who determines the methods by which the assignments are performed? ______

4 Who is the worker required to contact if problems or complaints arise and who is responsible for their resolution? ______

5 What types of reports are required from the worker? Attach examples. ______

6 Describe the worker's daily routine (i.e., schedule, hours, etc.). ______

7 At what location(s) does the worker perform services (e.g., firm's premises, own shop or office, home, customer's location, etc.)? ______

8 Describe any meetings the worker is required to attend and any penalties for not attending (e.g., sales meetings, monthly meetings, staff meetings, etc.). ______

9 Is the worker required to provide the services personally? ☐ **Yes** ☐ **No**

10 If substitutes or helpers are needed, who hires them? ______

11 If the worker hires the substitutes or helpers, is approval required? ☐ **Yes** ☐ **No**
If "Yes," by whom? ______

12 Who pays the substitutes or helpers? ______

13 Is the worker reimbursed if the worker pays the substitutes or helpers? ☐ **Yes** ☐ **No**
If "Yes," by whom?

Financial Control

1 List the supplies, equipment, materials, and property provided by each party:
The firm ______
The worker ______
Other party ______

2 Does the worker lease equipment? ☐ **Yes** ☐ **No**
If "Yes," what are the terms of the lease? (Attach a copy or explanatory statement.) ______

3 What expenses are incurred by the worker in the performance of services for the firm? ______

4 Specify which, if any, expenses are reimbursed by:
The firm ______
Other party ______

5 Type of pay the worker receives: ☐ Salary ☐ Commission ☐ Hourly Wage ☐ Piece Work
☐ Lump Sum ☐ Other (specify) ______
If type of pay is commission, and the firm guarantees a minimum amount of pay, specify amount $ ______.

6 Is the worker allowed a drawing account for advances? ☐ **Yes** ☐ **No**
If "Yes," how often? ______
Specify any restrictions. ______

7 Whom does the customer pay? ☐ Firm ☐ Worker
If worker, does the worker pay the total amount to the firm? ☐ **Yes** ☐ **No** If "No," explain. ______

8 Does the firm carry worker's compensation insurance on the worker? ☐ **Yes** ☐ **No**

9 What economic loss or financial risk, if any, can the worker incur beyond the normal loss of salary (e.g., loss or damage of equipment, material, etc.)? ______

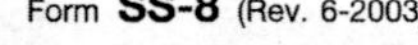
Form **SS-8** (Rev. 6-2003)

Form SS-8 (Rev. 6-2003) Page 3

Relationship of the Worker and Firm

1 List the benefits available to the worker (e.g., paid vacations, sick pay, pensions, bonuses).

2 Can the relationship be terminated by either party without incurring liability or penalty? ☐ Yes ☐ No
If "No," explain your answer.

3 Does the worker perform similar services for others? ☐ Yes ☐ No
If "Yes," is the worker required to get approval from the firm? ☐ Yes ☐ No

4 Describe any agreements prohibiting competition between the worker and the firm while the worker is performing services or during any later period. Attach any available documentation.

5 Is the worker a member of a union? ☐ Yes ☐ No

6 What type of advertising, if any, does the worker do (e.g., a business listing in a directory, business cards, etc.)? Provide copies, if applicable.

7 If the worker assembles or processes a product at home, who provides the materials and instructions or pattern?

8 What does the worker do with the finished product (e.g., return it to the firm, provide it to another party, or sell it)?

9 How does the firm represent the worker to its customers (e.g., employee, partner, representative, or contractor)?

10 If the worker no longer performs services for the firm, how did the relationship end?

For Service Providers or Salespersons—Complete this part if the worker provided a service directly to customers or is a salesperson.

1 What are the worker's responsibilities in soliciting new customers?

2 Who provides the worker with leads to prospective customers?

3 Describe any reporting requirements pertaining to the leads.

4 What terms and conditions of sale, if any, are required by the firm?

5 Are orders submitted to and subject to approval by the firm? ☐ Yes ☐ No

6 Who determines the worker's territory?

7 Did the worker pay for the privilege of serving customers on the route or in the territory? ☐ Yes ☐ No
If "Yes," whom did the worker pay?
If "Yes," how much did the worker pay? $ ______

8 Where does the worker sell the product (e.g., in a home, retail establishment, etc.)?

9 List the product and/or services distributed by the worker (e.g., meat, vegetables, fruit, bakery products, beverages, or laundry or dry cleaning services). If more than one type of product and/or service is distributed, specify the principal one.

10 Does the worker sell life insurance full time? ☐ Yes ☐ No

11 Does the worker sell other types of insurance for the firm? ☐ Yes ☐ No
If "Yes," enter the percentage of the worker's total working time spent in selling other types of insurance. ______%

12 If the worker solicits orders from wholesalers, retailers, contractors, or operators of hotels, restaurants, or other similar establishments, enter the percentage of the worker's time spent in the solicitation. ______%

13 Is the merchandise purchased by the customers for resale or use in their business operations? ☐ Yes ☐ No
Describe the merchandise and state whether it is equipment installed on the customers' premises.

Signature (see page 4)

Under penalties of perjury, I declare that I have examined this request, including accompanying documents, and to the best of my knowledge and belief, the facts presented are true, correct, and complete.

Signature ▶ ______ (Type or print name below) Title ▶ ______ Date ▶ ______

Form **SS-8** (Rev. 6-2003)

General Instructions

Section references are to the Internal Revenue Code unless otherwise noted.

Purpose

Firms and workers file Form SS-8 to request a determination of the status of a worker for purposes of Federal employment taxes and income tax withholding.

A Form SS-8 determination may be requested only in order to resolve Federal tax matters. If Form SS-8 is submitted for a tax year for which the statute of limitations on the tax return has expired, a determination letter will not be issued. The statute of limitations expires 3 years from the due date of the tax return or the date filed, whichever is later.

The IRS does not issue a determination letter for proposed transactions or on hypothetical situations. We may, however, issue an information letter when it is considered appropriate.

Definition

Firm. For the purposes of this form, the term "firm" means any individual, business enterprise, organization, state, or other entity for which a worker has performed services. The firm may or may not have paid the worker directly for these services. **If the firm was not responsible for payment for services, be sure to enter the name, address, and employer identification number of the payer on the first page of Form SS-8 below the identifying information for the firm and the worker.**

The SS-8 Determination Process

The IRS will acknowledge the receipt of your Form SS-8. Because there are usually two (or more) parties who could be affected by a determination of employment status, the IRS attempts to get information from all parties involved by sending those parties blank Forms SS-8 for completion. The case will be assigned to a technician who will review the facts, apply the law, and render a decision. The technician may ask for additional information from the requestor, from other involved parties, or from third parties that could help clarify the work relationship before rendering a decision. The IRS will generally issue a formal determination to the firm or payer (if that is a different entity), and will send a copy to the worker. A determination letter applies only to a worker (or a class of workers) requesting it, and the decision is binding on the IRS. In certain cases, a formal determination will not be issued. Instead, an information letter may be issued. Although an information letter is advisory only and is not binding on the IRS, it may be used to assist the worker to fulfill his or her Federal tax obligations.

Neither the SS-8 determination process nor the review of any records in connection with the determination constitutes an examination (audit) of any Federal tax return. If the periods under consideration have previously been examined, the SS-8 determination process will not constitute a reexamination under IRS reopening procedures. Because this is not an examination of any Federal tax return, the appeal rights available in connection with an examination do not apply to an SS-8 determination. However, if you disagree with a determination and you have additional information concerning the work relationship that you believe was not previously considered, you may request that the determining office reconsider the determination.

Completing Form SS-8

Answer all questions as completely as possible. Attach additional sheets if you need more space. Provide information for all years the worker provided services for the firm. Determinations are based on the entire relationship between the firm and the worker.

Additional copies of this form may be obtained by calling 1-800-829-4933 or from the IRS website at **www.irs.gov.**

Fee

There is no fee for requesting an SS-8 determination letter.

Signature

Form SS-8 must be signed and dated by the taxpayer. A stamped signature will not be accepted.

The person who signs for a corporation must be an officer of the corporation who has personal knowledge of the facts. If the corporation is a member of an affiliated group filing a consolidated return, it must be signed by an officer of the common parent of the group.

The person signing for a trust, partnership, or limited liability company must be, respectively, a trustee, general partner, or member-manager who has personal knowledge of the facts.

Where To File

Send the completed Form SS-8 to the address listed below for the firm's location. However, for cases involving Federal agencies, send Form SS-8 to the Internal Revenue Service, Attn: CC:CORP:T:C, Ben Franklin Station, P.O. Box 7604, Washington, DC 20044.

Firm's location:	Send to:
Alaska, Arizona, Arkansas, California, Colorado, Hawaii, Idaho, Illinois, Iowa, Kansas, Minnesota, Missouri, Montana, Nebraska, Nevada, New Mexico, North Dakota, Oklahoma, Oregon, South Dakota, Texas, Utah, Washington, Wisconsin, Wyoming, American Samoa, Guam, Puerto Rico, U.S. Virgin Islands	Internal Revenue Service SS-8 Determinations P.O. Box 630 Stop 631 Holtsville, NY 11742-0630
Alabama, Connecticut, Delaware, District of Columbia, Florida, Georgia, Indiana, Kentucky, Louisiana, Maine, Maryland, Massachusetts, Michigan, Mississippi, New Hampshire, New Jersey, New York, North Carolina, Ohio, Pennsylvania, Rhode Island, South Carolina, Tennessee, Vermont, Virginia, West Virginia, all other locations not listed	Internal Revenue Service SS-8 Determinations 40 Lakemont Road Newport, VT 05855-1555

Instructions for Workers

If you are requesting a determination for more than one firm, complete a separate Form SS-8 for each firm.

Form SS-8 is not a claim for refund of social security and Medicare taxes or Federal income tax withholding.

If the IRS determines that you are an employee, you are responsible for filing an amended return for any corrections related to this decision. A determination that a worker is an employee does not necessarily reduce any current or prior tax liability. For more information, call 1-800-829-1040.

Time for filing a claim for refund. Generally, you must file your claim for a credit or refund within 3 years from the date your original return was filed or within 2 years from the date the tax was paid, whichever is later.

Filing Form SS-8 does not prevent the expiration of the time in which a claim for a refund must be filed. If you are concerned about a refund, and the statute of limitations for filing a claim for refund for the year(s) at issue has not yet expired, you should file **Form 1040X,** Amended U.S. Individual Income Tax Return, to protect your statute of limitations. File a separate Form 1040X for each year.

On the Form 1040X you file, do not complete lines 1 through 24 on the form. Write "Protective Claim" at the top of the form, sign and date it. In addition, you should enter the following statement in Part II, Explanation of Changes to Income, Deductions, and Credits: "Filed Form SS-8 with the Internal Revenue Service Office in (Holtsville, NY; Newport, VT; or Washington, DC; as appropriate). By filing this protective claim, I reserve the right to file a claim for any refund that may be due after a determination of my employment tax status has been completed."

Filing Form SS-8 does not alter the requirement to timely file an income tax return. Do not delay filing your tax return in anticipation of an answer to your SS-8 request. In addition, if applicable, do not delay in responding to a request for payment while waiting for a determination of your worker status.

Instructions for Firms

If a **worker** has requested a determination of his or her status while working for you, you will receive a request from the IRS to complete a Form SS-8. In cases of this type, the IRS usually gives each party an opportunity to present a statement of the facts because any decision will affect the employment tax status of the parties. Failure to respond to this request will not prevent the IRS from issuing a determination letter based on the information he or she has made available so that the worker may fulfill his or her Federal tax obligations. However, the information that you provide is extremely valuable in determining the status of the worker.

If **you** are requesting a determination for a particular class of worker, complete the form for **one** individual who is representative of the class of workers whose status is in question. If you want a written determination for more than one class of workers, complete a separate Form SS-8 for one worker from each class whose status is typical of that class. A written determination for any worker will apply to other workers of the same class if the facts are not materially different for these workers. Please provide a list of names and addresses of all workers potentially affected by this determination.

If you have a reasonable basis for not treating a worker as an employee, you may be relieved from having to pay employment taxes for that worker under section 530 of the 1978 Revenue Act. However, this relief provision cannot be considered in conjunction with a Form SS-8 determination because the determination does not constitute an examination of any tax return. For more information regarding section 530 of the 1978 Revenue Act and to determine if you qualify for relief under this section, you may visit the IRS website at **www.irs.gov.**

Privacy Act and Paperwork Reduction Act Notice. We ask for the information on this form to carry out the Internal Revenue laws of the United States. This information will be used to determine the employment status of the worker(s) described on the form. Subtitle C, Employment Taxes, of the Internal Revenue Code imposes employment taxes on wages. Sections 3121(d), 3306(a), and 3401(c) and (d) and the related regulations define employee and employer for purposes of employment taxes imposed under Subtitle C. Section 6001 authorizes the IRS to request information needed to determine if a worker(s) or firm is subject to these taxes. Section 6109 requires you to provide your taxpayer identification number. Neither workers nor firms are required to request a status determination, but if you choose to do so, you must provide the information requested on this form. Failure to provide the requested information may prevent us from making a status determination. If any worker or the firm has requested a status determination and you are being asked to provide information for use in that determination, you are not required to provide the requested information. However, failure to provide such information will prevent the IRS from considering it in making the status determination. Providing false or fraudulent information may subject you to penalties. Routine uses of this information include providing it to the Department of Justice for use in civil and criminal litigation, to the Social Security Administration for the administration of social security programs, and to cities, states, and the District of Columbia for the administration of their tax laws. We may also disclose this information to Federal and state agencies to enforce Federal nontax criminal laws and to combat terrorism. We may provide this information to the affected worker(s) or the firm as part of the status determination process.

You are not required to provide the information requested on a form that is subject to the Paperwork Reduction Act unless the form displays a valid OMB control number. Books or records relating to a form or its instructions must be retained as long as their contents may become material in the administration of any Internal Revenue law. Generally, tax returns and return information are confidential, as required by section 6103.

The time needed to complete and file this form will vary depending on individual circumstances. The estimated average time is: **Recordkeeping,** 22 hrs.; **Learning about the law or the form,** 47 min.; and **Preparing and sending the form to the IRS,** 1 hr., 11 min. If you have comments concerning the accuracy of these time estimates or suggestions for making this form simpler, we would be happy to hear from you. You can write to the Tax Products Coordinating Committee, Western Area Distribution Center, Rancho Cordova, CA 95743-0001. **Do not** send the tax form to this address. Instead, see **Where To File** on page 4.

Direct Your Learning 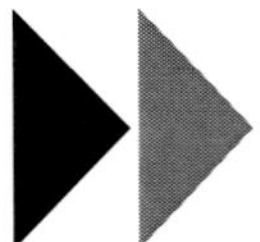

Accounting System Evaluation

Educational Objectives

After learning the content of this chapter and completing the corresponding course guide assignment, you should be able to:

- Describe the following aspects of accounting systems used by government and private entities:
  - Purpose and function
  - Users of accounting information
  - Accounting procedures
  - Performers of the accounting function
- Given a case, evaluate the adequacy of internal control procedures.
  - Describe the elements of an organization's internal control structure.
  - Describe an organization's principal accounts that require internal control.
- Given a case, evaluate the reliability of specific accounting records for use by the premium auditor.
  - Describe the kinds of records and reports produced by an accounting system, and evaluate each as a source of information for a premium auditor.
  - Describe the tax returns and other reports filed by employers, and evaluate each as a source of information for a premium auditor.
- Define or describe each of the Key Words and Phrases for this chapter.

OUTLINE

Develop Your Perspective

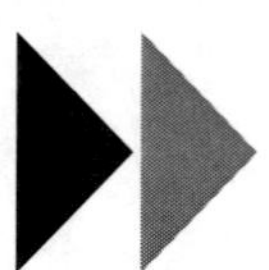

What are the main topics covered in the chapter?

Auditors rely on an insured's accounting system and records for information necessary to evaluate their operations and exposures. The chapter summarizes the kinds of records that may be available for a premium audit and the information that can be determined from those records.

Identify the types of accounting records available for a premium audit.

- How can the adequacy of internal financial controls be evaluated?
- What are the areas of concern for internal financial controls?

Why is it important to learn about these topics?

Accounting systems can vary significantly, so premium auditors must evaluate the system before extracting data.

Consider why it is important for a premium auditor to assess the accuracy and reliability of accounting records.

- How might a premium auditor assess the accuracy of accounting records?
- What should premium auditors do if records do not appear to be reliable?

How can you use what you will learn?

Evaluate the accounting records for a policyholder.

- Determine the reliability of these records for premium audit purposes.
- Describe the tax reports filed by employees and how these reports are used for premium audit purposes.

Accounting System Evaluation

Although reviewing the insured's operations and analyzing employment relationships provide essential audit information, premium auditors also depend on the insured's accounting system for much of the data they require to complete the audit. Therefore, premium auditors must understand the accounting requirements of all types of organizations. Auditors must also be able to communicate with the personnel responsible for the insured's accounting system and be able to interpret accounting records. Because not all insureds keep their books in exactly the same way, premium auditors must be prepared to follow different paths to find the information they need.

Ultimately, the information premium auditors must determine is the number of exposure units covered by the insurance policy. Underwriters choose exposure units that not only reflect the actual loss exposure but that also are difficult to fraudulently manipulate. If the insured's accounting system follows good legal and business practices, it should provide reliable information needed as the basis for the premium.

Although the total employees' remuneration is the basis of premium for workers' compensation insurance, insurers may base the premium for other insurance coverages on gross sales, tons of coal mined, pounds of carrots harvested, or any other agreed-upon basis. The specific premium basis consists of data systematically recorded by the insured. The premium auditor must examine the insured's accounting records to obtain and then verify those data.

ACCOUNTING SYSTEMS

Accounting is the process of identifying, measuring, and communicating economic information to permit informed judgments and decisions by users of the information. Accounting includes all methods and records that identify, assemble, analyze, classify, record, and report an organization's financial transactions. Although those methods might vary by organization, establishing them creates an accounting system for the organization. When the system meets the standards of full disclosure, materiality, transparency, consistency, conservatism, and fairness, the information is considered reliable.

Generally accepted accounting principles (GAAP)
The common set of standards and procedures by which audited financial statements are prepared.

The standards for accounting systems are the **generally accepted accounting principles (GAAP)**, which include the pronouncements of the Securities and Exchange Commission, the Financial Accounting Standards Board, and the American Institute of Certified Public Accountants (AICPA). When certified public accountants (CPAs) perform an independent audit of an organization's financial statements, they issue an opinion attesting whether those statements present information in accordance with GAAP. That independent review and the self-regulation of the accounting profession enforce accounting standards.

Purpose and Function

An accounting system's purpose is to present information in an organized form to the people who need it. The information reflects a multitude of economic events affecting the organization and appears in a format understood by a variety of users, allowing them to make rational decisions about the organization.

An accounting system performs the following three separate functions:

1. Accumulation
2. Measurement
3. Communication

For an accounting system to provide information about economic events, it must accumulate and process large amounts of data. Each transaction must be recorded consistently and classified.

Accounting information is measured by dollar values. Sometimes the transaction itself establishes the dollar values. At other times, applied values are assigned according to specified guidelines as part of the accounting process. Because all the information consists of precise values, it is useful as a basis for insurance premiums.

Because a random listing of every transaction would be too unwieldy to be useful, accounting systems use certain conventions that organize, summarize, and report information in an easily comprehended format. Some of those conventions relate to reports. **Management reports** present operational information that enables managers to monitor and control organizational efforts. **Financial reports** indicate the organization's financial position. Examples of financial reports include the balance sheet (or the statement of financial position), the income statement, the statement of owners' equity, and the statement of changes in financial position. Depending on the type of organization, the accounting system can also produce **regulatory reports**, required by regulatory authorities. Finally, the accounting system must include all the information required for tax returns to federal, state, and local governments.

Management report
A report that presents operational information, enabling managers to monitor and control organizational efforts.

Financial report
A report that presents an organization's financial position.

Regulatory report
A report that presents data required by regulatory authorities.

Users of Accounting Information

When an accounting system conforms to GAAP, it conveys significant information to many users both inside and outside the organization. Those users include the following groups:

- *Management*. To oversee an organization, management needs detailed records of the organization's performance. Managers must be able to compare the expenses and revenues generated by certain activities. They need performance indicators for individual operating units. They must also evaluate the returns from specific ventures so that they can accurately allocate resources.
- *Investors and creditors*. Most of the capital for business enterprises comes from banks, pension funds, insurance companies, and other institutions and individuals with funds to lend or invest. Because businesses can select from many loan and investment opportunities, they need detailed information about the sources of the capital to choose the best one. Business decisions depend on assessing an enterprise's solvency and earnings potential. Even not-for-profit organizations make financial accountings to their contributors to show that they have used funds efficiently and legitimately.
- *Suppliers, customers, and employees*. Anyone doing business with an organization has an interest in its financial condition. Interested parties might examine the business's financial statements for clues to its stability and practices, as well as for insights into business conditions. Also, specific contractual arrangements between entities occasionally require a precise accounting of the business covered by applicable contracts.
- *Tax and regulatory authorities*. The Internal Revenue Service (IRS) uses, and often audits, accounting information to collect tax revenue. State and local tax authorities also require organizations to file tax returns. In addition, the Securities and Exchange Commission, the Federal Trade Commission, the Interstate Commerce Commission, and many other regulatory agencies might require reports to ensure compliance with their regulations.

Accounting Procedures

All organizations build their accounting systems around the following fundamental accounting equation:

Assets = Liabilities + Owners' equity.

An asset is the dollar value of anything owned by the entity; a liability is a debt owed by the entity; and owners' equity is the residual value (assets minus liabilities) to the owners. The system used to document accounting transactions can range from one small account book to an enormous computer program, but the procedures are essentially the same. Every transaction affects the assets and either the liabilities or the owner's equity. The accounting system analyzes each transaction and records its effect on assets and on liabilities or equity.

Double-entry bookkeeping
A method of recording financial transactions in which each transaction is entered into two or more accounts to provide a two-way, self-balancing posting.

The recording system used to document accounting transactions, each of which affects assets and liability or equity, is called **double-entry bookkeeping**. In that system, each transaction must have a minimum of two entries, one debit and one credit, and the total dollar value of debits and credits must be equal. Each transaction must be assigned to a particular account. That is, if an organization

receives cash for merchandise, the "cash account" would be affected. The number of accounts is almost limitless, although all organizations use many of the same types of accounts, including cash, accounts receivable, accounts payable, and equipment. The number of accounts depends on the organization's information needs. If a company needs information about equipment at each owned location, the equipment in each location should be a separate account.

T-account
A form of account, which resembles the letter T, used to analyze financial transactions.

One way to illustrate how those accounts operate and to analyze transactions is through a **T-account**, so called because the form on which it is recorded resembles a capital "T." Exhibit 6-1 is an example of a T-account.

EXHIBIT 6-1

An Example of a T-Account

Cash	
$1,000	$600

Debit
A dollar value that appears on the left side of a double-entry accounting statement.

Credit
A dollar value that appears on the right side of a double-entry accounting statement.

A **debit** is a value that appears on the left-hand side of the T-account. A **credit** is a value that appears on the right-hand side of the T-account. For some types of accounts, an increase is a debit. For others, an increase is a credit. The following T-account illustrates the rules about debit and credit for the major types of accounts.

Debits	**Credits**
Increase assets	Decrease assets
Decrease liabilities	Increase liabilities
Decrease stockholders' equity	Increase stockholders' equity
Decrease revenues	Increase revenues
Increase expenses	Decrease expenses

Following are the six essential accounting procedures involving T-accounts:

1. Journalizing source documents in a journal
2. Posting those journal entries in the general ledger
3. Preparing a trial balance
4. Preparing a worksheet
5. Preparing financial statements
6. Closing the ledger

Journalizing

The **journal** is commonly called the **book of original entry** because it is the first book in which an organization records a business transaction. The organization journalizes (records) all transactions in a journal from source documents, which are the documents created by financial transactions. Sales slips, checkbooks, sales and purchase invoices, and deposit slips are examples of source documents for a typical business. Transactions are recorded in chronological order with a separate entry for each transaction. Exhibit 6-2 shows a journal page with all transactions for the first five days of January.

Journal, or **book of original entry**
The first accounting record in which an organization records daily financial transactions.

EXHIBIT 6-2

Bob Smith Company—General Journal

Date	Account Title	Debit	Credit
Jan 20X6			
1	Cash	$10,000	
	Bob Smith, Capital		$10,000
	(To record initial investment)		
3	Accounts Receivable	$ 500	
	Income		$ 500
	(To record work done on account)		
3	Equipment	$ 1,000	
	Accounts payable		$ 1,000
	(To record purchase of equipment on account)		
5	Expenses	$ 225	
	Cash		$ 225
	(To record rent for month)		

Posting

Posting is the procedure of transferring the journal entry totals, usually on a monthly basis, to the appropriate general ledger account. Exhibit 6-3 is an example of informal T-Accounts for a small business, with posting.

Posting
The procedure of transferring journal entry totals to the appropriate general ledger account.

Preparing a Trial Balance

A **trial balance** is an interim financial statement that the organization prepares at the end of the accounting period, and at any other time on request of management. The trial balance proves the equality of the debits and credits posted to the general ledger accounts from the journal but does not prove that the organization made the postings to the correct accounts. The trial balance helps determine errors before the organization prepares the official financial statements. Exhibit 6-4 is a simple trial balance prepared from the general ledger accounts in Exhibit 6-3. In addition to the standard accounting procedures, management might request that a trial balance or other interim reports be periodically prepared.

Trial balance
An interim financial statement prepared at the end of the accounting period to prove the equality of debits and credits posted to the ledger accounts from the journal.

EXHIBIT 6-3

Informal T-Accounts

Cash	
$10,000	$225

Equipment	
$1,000	

Accounts Receivable	
$500	

Accounts Payable	
	$1,000

Bob Smith, Capital	
	$10,000

Income	
	$500

Expenses	
$225	

Preparing a Worksheet

An accountant prepares a worksheet on a pad containing several columns. This text uses a six-column worksheet that contains a trial balance, income statement, and balance sheet. Each section has a debit and credit column. Accountants prepare a worksheet at the end of the fiscal period, which can be a month, six months, or a year. Once the worksheet is completed, the

EXHIBIT 6-4

Bob Smith Company—Trial Balance

Date		Debit	Credit
January 31, 20X6			
1.	Cash	$ 9,775	
2.	Equipment	1,000	
3.	Accounts Receivable	500	
4.	Accounts Payable		$ 1,000
5.	B. Smith, Capital		10,000
6.	Income		500
7.	Expense	225	
		$11,500	$11,500

accountant uses it to prepare the official financial reports of a business. Exhibit 6-5 is a sample worksheet. The figures on the worksheet can be traced back to the general ledger accounts, the trial balance, and the journal entries in Exhibits 6-2, 6-3, and 6-4. Following is a step-by-step description of how to prepare a worksheet:

- *Establish columnar headings*. Enter headings at the top of each column. For a six-column worksheet, the columns from left to right are as follows: Trial Balance (Debit and Credit), Income Statement (Debit and Credit), and Balance Sheet (Debit and Credit).
- *Prepare the trial balance*. Enter the account titles and numbers in the appropriate columns, and enter their balances in the worksheet's trial balance section. Obtain the account balances from the general ledger accounts (Exhibit 6-3). Then total the debits and credits. If debit and credit totals are equal (they should be) and if all the figures are correct, draw a double line below the totals.
- *Transfer balance sheet items*. Transfer the account balances (assets, liabilities, and equity) from the trial balance section of the balance sheet to the worksheet's balance sheet section. Extend the debits to the debit column and the credits to the credit column. Then total the debit and credit columns.
- *Transfer income and expense items*. Transfer the income and expense items from the trial balance section to the income statement section; transfer the debits to the debit column and credits to the credit column. Then total the debits and credits.
- *Calculate net income (or loss)*. Determine the net income by subtracting the smaller total on the income statement from the larger total. If the credit column (income) is larger than the debit column, the difference is

net income; if the debit column (expenses) is larger, the difference is a net loss. Write the amount of net income (or loss) below the smaller of the two totals on the income statement section. On the same line, write the words "net income" (or "net loss") in the account titles column. Total the columns. They must be equal. If they are not equal, determine where the error occurred.

- *Transfer net income*. Transfer the net income from the income statement section to the credit column of the balance sheet section. (If a loss has occurred, it would be transferred to the debit column.) That amount shows the increase in capital because of net income earned for the fiscal period reported. Now total the balance sheet columns.
- *Double-rule final totals*. Draw a double line under the totals of the income statement and balance sheet sections. The double line indicates that the accountant has correctly completed the necessary work.

Preparing Financial Statements

Businesses prepare the following four financial statements from the information on the worksheet (Exhibit 6-5):

1. Income statement
2. Statement of changes in owners' equity
3. Balance sheet
4. Statement of cash flows

The information used to prepare the sample financial statements in Exhibits 6-6 through 6-9 was obtained from the worksheet in Exhibit 6-5.

Income statement
A financial statement that summarizes an entity's revenues and expenses incurred over a period of time.

The **income statement** summarizes the revenues earned and the expenses incurred by an entity over a period of time. It is the first financial statement prepared. The accountant finds the information required for the statement in the worksheet's heading, account titles, and income statement sections. Exhibit 6-6 is an example of an income statement.

Statement of changes in owners' equity
A financial statement that presents the changes in owners' equity (assets minus liabilities) over a period of time.

The next financial statement prepared is the **statement of changes in owners' equity**, which shows the changes in owners' equity over a period of time. The accountant finds the information required to prepare this statement in the worksheet's balance sheet section. Exhibit 6-7 is an example of a statement of changes in owners' equity.

The balance sheet is prepared after the income and owners' equity statements. The balance sheet is a statement that shows the financial position of an entity's assets, liabilities, and owners' equity on a specific date, usually the end of the month or year. The accountant obtains the information for the balance sheet from the worksheet's balance sheet section and the owner's equity statement. Exhibit 6-8 is an example of a balance sheet.

EXHIBIT 6-5

Bob Smith Company—Work Sheet for Month Ended 31 January 20X6

	Trial Balance		Income Statement		Balance Sheet	
Account Titles	**Debit**	**Credit**	**Debit**	**Credit**	**Assets**	**Liabilities**
Cash	$ 9,775.00				$ 9,775.00	
Equipment	1,000.00				1,000.00	
Accounts Receivable	500.00				500.00	
Accounts Payable		$ 1,000.00				$ 1,000.00
J. Jones Capital		10,000.00				10,000.00
Income		500.00		$500.00		
Expense	225.00		$225.00			
Totals	$11,500.00	$11,500.00	225.00	500.00	11,275.00	11,000.00
Net Income			275.00			275.00
Balances	$11,500.00	$11,500.00	$500.00	$500.00	$11,275.00	$11,275.00

EXHIBIT 6-6

Bob Smith Company—Income Statement for the Month Ending 31 January 20X6

Income	$500
Expenses	225
Net income	$275

EXHIBIT 6-7

Bob Smith Company—Statement of Owners' Equity for the Month Ending 31 January 20X6

Owners' equity, 1 January 20X6		$10,000
Net income for month	$275	
Less withdrawals	0	
Increase in capital		275
Owners' equity, 31 January 20X6		$10,275

EXHIBIT 6-8

Bob Smith Company—Balance Sheet, 31 January 20X6

Cash	$ 9,775	Accounts payable	$ 1,000
Equipment	1,000		
Accounts receivable	500	B. Smith equity	10,275
Total assets	$11,275	Total liabilities and owners' equity	$11,275

Statement of cash flows
A financial statement that shows the change in cash reported on the balance sheet from one accounting period to the next.

The **statement of cash flows** shows the change in cash reported on the balance sheet from one accounting period to the next. That statement shows the sources and uses of funds during the period divided, into three primary categories: operating, investing, and financing activities. The information comes from the income and equity statements shown in the sample statement of cash flows in Exhibit 6-9.

EXHIBIT 6-9

Bob Smith Company—Statement of Cash Flows for the Month Ending 31 January 20X6

Cash flows from operating activities:		
Net income	$275	
Increase in accounts receivable	(500)	
Increase in accounts payable	1,000	
Net cash flow provided (used) by operating activities		$ 775
Cash flows from investing activities:		
Purchase of equipment	(1,000)	
Net cash flow provided (used) by investing activities		(1,000)
Cash flow from financing activities:		
Capital investment		
Net cash flow provided (used) by financing activities		10,000
Net change in cash		9,775
Cash at beginning of month		0
Cash at end of month		$9,775

Closing the Ledger

Once the accountant has prepared the financial statements, the next step is to close the income and expense accounts and transfer the net income (loss) to the owners' equity account. Closing the ledger serves two purposes. First, the income and expense accounts are not permanent accounts because they reflect transactions for a specific fiscal period. When that period is over, their function has been fulfilled. Then the accountant must close those accounts so that they are ready for the next fiscal period. Second, the accountant must transfer the net income (loss) to the equity account so that account reflects the true residual value of the business.

To close the ledger, the accountant uses a new account called the "income and expense summary." Using the income statement as a source document, the accountant records closing entries in the journal and posts them to the income and expense summary account. The accountant follows the same procedure to close the income and expense summary account to the owners' equity. Exhibit 6-10 is an example of the closing journal entries. Exhibit 6-11 shows the posting to the general ledger accounts affected and the closing of those accounts. (The "J.E." number refers to the journal entries as shown in Exhibit 6-10.) After posting the closing entries to the general ledger accounts, the accountant must total the debit and credit sides of the income, the expense, and the income and expense summary accounts. Those totals must be equal. Then the accountant draws a double line to show that the accounts are closed.

EXHIBIT 6-10

Bob Smith Company—Ledger Closing Entries, General Ledger

		Debit	Credit
Jan 31	Income	$500	
	Income and expense summary (to close income account)		$500
Jan 31	Income and expense summary	225	
	Expense (to close expense account)		225
Jan 31	Income and expense summary	275	
	B. Smith capital (to transfer net income to capital account)		275

EXHIBIT 6-11

Bob Smith Company—Posting and Closing of General Ledger Accounts

Bob Smith, Capital

Posting Reference	Date	Debit	Credit	Balance
	Jan 1		$10,000	$10,000
J.E. 3	Jan 31		275	10,275

Income and Expense Summary

	Date	Debit	Credit	Balance
J.E. 1	Jan 31		$500	($500)
J.E. 2	Jan 31	$225		(275)
J.E. 3	Jan 31	275		0

Income

	Date	Debit	Credit	Balance
	Jan 31		$500	($500)
J.E. 1	Jan 31	$500		0

Expenses

	Date	Debit	Credit	Balance
	Jan 31	$225		$225
J.E. 2	Jan 31		$225	0

Government Accounting Procedures

When compared to the accounting procedures for private profit-making organizations, the accounting procedures for government bodies are not as specific because of the variety of activities that governments perform. Services are usually provided without a profit motive, and the entities are often subject to various legal and contractual requirements. The term "government accounting" applies to state and local government units but commonly includes other not-for-profit institutions such as hospitals, churches, schools, professional associations, and health and welfare organizations. For state and local governments, the Governmental Accounting Standards Board has developed accounting principles, and other not-for-profit organizations have published standards for their particular groups.

Fund Accounting

A **fund** is a financial account or other resources set aside for a specific purpose. Fund accounting is a way of separating certain government goals or activities in accordance with special regulations or requirements. A school might have an education fund for all activities relating to children's education and a transportation fund for all transportation needs. Each fund is a separate fiscal and accounting entity with a self-balancing set of accounts.

The Governmental Accounting Standards Board specifies the types of funds that state and federal governments should use to operate. Those funds can be grouped into the following three categories:

1. Government funds
2. Proprietary funds
3. Fiduciary funds

There are five types of government funds. Accounting for all five should be done on the modified accrual basis. The **modified accrual basis** recognizes revenues when they become available and measurable, while recognizing expenditures when the liabilities are incurred if measurable.

The five types of government funds are as follows:

1. The **general fund** accounts for all financial resources except those required to be accounted for in another fund. leftover
2. **Special revenue funds** account for the proceeds of specific revenue sources or for major capital projects that are legally restricted to expenditures for specified purposes.
3. **Capital projects funds** account for financial resources used to acquire or construct major capital facilities.
4. **Debt service funds** account for accumulating resources for and the payment of general long-term debt principal and interest.
5. **Permanent funds** account for resources that are legally restricted to the extent that only earnings and net principal may be used.

Fund
In government accounting, a financial account or other resources set aside for a specific purpose.

Modified accrual basis
An accounting system that recognizes revenues when they become available and measurable and recognizes expenditures when the liabilities are incurred.

General fund
A financial account for all of an entity's resources except those required to be accounted for in another fund.

Special revenue fund
A financial account used by a governmental entity for the proceeds of specific revenue sources or for major capital projects that are legally restricted to expenditures for specified purposes.

Capital projects fund
A financial account used by a governmental entity for resources to acquire or develop land or buildings.

Debt service fund
A financial account used by a governmental entity for accumulating cash to retire long-term debt, principal, and interest.

Permanent fund
A financial account used by a governmental entity for resources that are legally restricted to the extent that only earnings and net principal may be used.

Proprietary fund
A financial account, consisting of enterprise and internal service funds, used to account for a government's ongoing organizations and activities that are similar to those found in the private sector.

Enterprise fund
A financial account for government operations financed and operated similarly to private business enterprise.

Internal service fund
A financial account for financing goods or services provided by one governmental department or agency to other departments.

Fiduciary fund
A financial account set aside by a fiduciary entrusted with the duty of caring for the assets of another based on trust and confidence.

Trust and agency funds
Financial accounts for assets held by a governmental entity in a trustee capacity or as an agent for individuals, private organizations, other government units, or funds.

Another category of government accounting funds, **proprietary funds**, are used to account for a government's ongoing organizations and activities that are similar to those found in the private sector. Accounting for the two proprietary funds should be done only on the accrual basis. Following are the two types of proprietary funds:

1. **Enterprise funds** account for operations financed and operated similarly to private business enterprises. The intent is to finance or recover the ongoing expenses, including depreciation, of providing goods or services to the general public primarily through user charges.
2. **Internal service funds** account for financing goods or services provided by one department or agency to other departments or agencies of the government unit.

Governments use a third type of fund, the fiduciary fund. A **fiduciary fund** is entrusted with the duty of caring for the assets of another based on trust and confidence. Accounting for fiduciary funds should be done on an accrual basis. **Trust and agency funds** account for assets held by a governmental unit in a trustee capacity or as an agent for individuals, private organizations, other government units, and/or other funds.

Budgeting and Budgetary Reporting Requirements

Financial reporting for an ongoing business concern requires the comparison of revenues and expenditures. In contrast, government entities must compare actual amounts to the budget. The Governmental Accounting Standards Board states the following:

- Every government unit should adopt an annual budget.
- The accounting system should provide the basis for appropriate budgetary control.
- Budgetary comparisons must be included in the appropriate financial statements and in schedules for government funds for which an annual budget has been adopted.

General Purpose Financial Statements

GAAP requires that the following general purpose financial statements be prepared:[1]

- A combined balance sheet for all fund types and account groups
- A combined statement of revenues, expenditures, and changes in fund balances for all government fund types (see Exhibit 6-12)
- A combined statement of revenues, expenditures, and changes in fund balance—budgeted and actual—for general and special revenue fund types
- A combined statement of revenues, expenses, and changes in retained earnings for all proprietary fund types
- A combined statement of cash flows for all proprietary fund types

EXHIBIT 6-12

Sample Government Fund Statement

Nottoway Borough Revenues, Expenditures, and Changes in Fund Balance

Budget and actual fiscal year ending 31 December 20X5

	Budget	Actual	Variance
Revenues			
Real estate tax	$2,357,000	$2,364,000	$ 7,000
Mercantile tax	1,290,000	1,285,000	(5,000)
Building permits and fees	400,000	403,000	3,000
Business privilege tax	517,000	515,000	(2,000)
Other revenues	609,000	585,000	(24,000)
Total revenues	$5,173,000	$5,152,000	$(21,000)
Expenditures			
General government	$ 729,000	$ 728,000	$ (1,000)
Police	2,097,000	2,105,000	8,000
Public services	1,271,000	1,275,000	4,000
Park and recreation	239,000	236,000	(3,000)
Library	465,000	464,000	(1,000)
Other expenditures	549,000	535,000	(14,000)
Total expenditures	$5,350,000	$5,343,000	$ (7,000)
Excess of revenues over expenditures	$ (177,000)	$ (191,000)	$(14,000)
Other financing sources			
Operating transfers—in	$ 583,000	$ 511,000	$(72,000)
Operating transfers—out	(200,000)	(200,000)	0
Total other financing sources	$ 383,000	$ 311,000	$(72,000)
Excess of revenues and other sources over expenditures and other uses	206,000	120,000	(86,000)
Fund balance—beginning of fiscal year	252,000	252,000	0
Fund balance—end of fiscal year	$ 458,000	$ 372,000	$(86,000)

Because of the variations in government accounting practices, premium auditors should interpret governmental financial statements cautiously. When appropriated funds are not entirely spent within one year, for example, some municipalities do not include the remaining expenditures on the following year's budget statement because that statement compares expenditures to the funds appropriated for that year. Thus, auditors must examine all the financial statements to ensure that the information for the audit is complete.[2]

Persons Responsible for the Accounting Function

Although businesses of all sizes follow essentially the same accounting procedures, the person who performs the accounting function varies. Some small businesses employ an accountant's services a few hours a week to keep the payroll records and to prepare the financial statements and tax returns. Slightly larger firms might have a full-time bookkeeper to maintain the payroll records as well as to bill customers and prepare checks to suppliers. Large corporations normally have an entire accounting department as well as an elaborate electronic data processing system to perform accounting tasks.

Corporate Accountants

The budgeting, billing, payroll processing, cost accounting, statement preparation, and tax reporting requirements of corporations are all tasks of an accounting department. Responsibility for those tasks normally belongs to the corporate controller. Small firms might combine the controller's responsibilities with those of the treasurer, who is responsible for the flow of funds. In a large corporation, both of these positions probably report to a vice president of finance.

When premium auditors have questions about responsibility for accounting matters, an organizational chart, a company telephone directory, or an annual report might help to resolve them. Premium auditors should be aware that accounting personnel might hesitate to furnish information without authorization. Therefore, the auditor should try to make the initial audit appointment with the highest level person possible. That person, who is usually the corporate accountant, might also be better able to explain the overall accounting procedures.

Public Accountants

Public accountants are independent professional accountants who offer their services for a fee. They might represent a large national accounting firm or work independently. Small businesses primarily use that type of independent accounting service because they lack the time or the expertise to do the accounting themselves.

The level of service rendered by a public accountant depends on the client's needs. A small firm might hire a public accountant to do all of the accounting. The public accountant would probably receive all the time reports, invoices, check stubs, deposit slips, and other source documents on a weekly basis. The accountant then processes the information through the entire accounting cycle. Most accounting services are computerized.

If the firm has a full-time bookkeeper, the public accountant's services might be limited to such tasks as preparing the financial statements and the tax returns from the ledger maintained by the bookkeeper. The public accountant might also provide advice on bookkeeping procedures and other financial matters.

Because public accountants are professionals, premium auditors can expect to find the records they maintain in good order. However, accountants may be less familiar with the details of the insured's business than with its finances. So a premium auditor might have to visit both the accountant's office and the insured's premises to obtain the total premium base and to classify it. Advance communication about needed information, made to both the insured and the accountant, can often eliminate the need for more than one visit.

Planning can eliminate many other pitfalls as well. A public accountant needs the client's authorization before giving the premium auditor access to confidential records. To prevent a delay of the audit, the auditor should ask the accountant to obtain that authorization in advance. The auditor can also arrange for the accountant present at the insured's office to assist in the premium audit.

Independent Auditors

Independent accounting firms can act as independent auditors to attest that a firm's financial statements present its financial position fairly in accordance with GAAP. The person who issues this opinion must be licensed by the state as a certified public accountant (CPA). The law requires an annual independent audit for all firms that publicly trade their stock. In addition, banks often require an audit before they approve a loan to the firm.

Besides performing independent audits, CPA firms frequently provide management with advice and tax preparation services. They usually work closely with the firm's own accounting personnel and become knowledgeable about the firm's business.

INTERNAL CONTROL EVALUATION

Evaluating internal control is a fundamental and essential step for an outside auditor in reviewing accounting systems and financial statements. The AICPA has defined internal control as "policies and procedures established to provide reasonable assurance that specific entity objectives will be achieved."[2]

That broad definition extends the evaluation of internal control beyond the traditional accounting and financial areas into the areas of budgetary control, standard costs, and other management controls. However, for financial statement audits, the relevant records generally include the policies and procedures relating only to recording, processing, summarizing, and reporting financial data.

The insured's internal control influences audit data quality, reliability, and accuracy. Premium auditors must also recognize that the quality of internal control varies enormously by the insured. Both the time involved and the insured's possible reluctance may limit the depth of an internal control review. Premium auditors must be alert for significant departures from sound internal control that could threaten the reliability of the audit data.

Internal Control Elements

An organization's internal control structure consists of the following three elements:[3]

1. Control environment
2. Accounting system
3. Control procedures

In addition to understanding all three of these elements, an auditor must consider factors such as the organization's size, type of ownership, nature of operations (including the diversity and complexity of operations), data processing method, and the legal and regulatory environments within which the organization operates. Each of those factors affects the degree of control and the formality of controls that the auditor can reasonably expect.

Control Environment

The organization's control environment consists of the operations and practices that the organization uses to establish or enhance the effectiveness of specific policies and procedures. The control environment includes anything management does to show concern for control and for the degree of emphasis that control receives within the organization. Those operations and practices include the following:[4]

- The philosophy and operating style of the organization's management
- The organizational structure
- The functioning of the organization's board of directors and its committees, including the audit committee
- How the organization assigns responsibility and authority
- The control methods management established to monitor performance, including the internal auditing responsibility

- Personnel practices and policies
- Other external influences that affect the organization's operations and practices, such as regulatory examinations

Accounting System

An accounting system "consists of the methods and records established to identify, assemble, analyze, classify, record, and report an entity's transactions and to maintain accountability for the related assets and liabilities."[5] An effective accounting system should do the following:[6]

- Identify and record all the organization's valid transactions
- Describe those transactions in a timely manner and in enough detail to permit someone to classify the transaction for financial reporting purposes
- Measure the transaction's value so that it can be recorded at its proper monetary value in the financial statements
- Determine the time period within which the transaction occurred so that it can be recorded in the proper accounting period
- Present the transactions in the organization's financial statements

Control Procedures

Control procedures are the additional policies and procedures that management establishes to safeguard its assets and to provide a reasonable assurance that the organization's financial information is accurate and reliable. Control procedures relate to the following:[7]

- Requiring authorization for all transactions and activities
- Segregating or separating duties so that employees cannot both commit and conceal errors or irregularities in the normal course of their duties
- Designing and using the appropriate records and documents to ensure that transactions and events are properly recorded
- Establishing adequate safeguards over access to and use of assets and records
- Using independent checks on performance and valuation of the amounts recorded (bank reconciliations, clerical checks, management review of reports, and so on)

Principal Accounts Requiring Internal Control

Several accounts within an organization require greater internal control because of their size or importance. The accounts that typically require internal control are the following:

- Cash receipts and disbursements
- Accounts receivable

- Inventories
- Property, plant, and equipment
- Current liabilities
- Revenues
- Costs and expenses

Following is a summary of the problems unique to each account.

Cash Receipts and Disbursements

Cash includes items such as amounts on deposit in banks, undeposited receipts, and cash funds. Cash is different from most company assets in that it requires no further conversion, is generally acceptable in trade, and loses its identity easily. Internal control varies by organization, depending on the organization's size and the points at which employees handle cash in the business.

An auditor should evaluate how cash receipts are handled in the context of proper authority and segregation of duties. The type of receipt is also important because the organization's concerns about handling cash sales receipts are different from its concerns about handling receipts from customers on account. Generally, handling receipts should be separate from controlling the merchandise or accounting records involving the receipts. Reviewing the timeliness of the deposits is also important to internal control.

Generally, an organization authorizes certain individuals to make disbursements within prescribed limits. The auditor should review cash disbursements to determine that payments were authorized. All disbursements should have adequate supporting documents authorized by persons other than the disbursing agent.

The auditor can evaluate the accuracy of cash balances by reviewing who handled each transaction. Someone other than the person handling cash receipts or cash disbursements should do the bank reconciliation.

The auditor can evaluate the adequacy of the internal control for cash by using a questionnaire such as the one in Exhibit 6-13. The questionnaire shown is general. An organization can modify it to evaluate its own internal control system. Auditors can use similar questionnaires for each area of internal control evaluation.

Accounts Receivable

The key internal control consideration involved in receivables is the organizational independence among the operating, custodial, and accounting functions. The charges to receivables should originate from a different department than the accounts receivable, as should the credits for cash receipts. An employee from outside the accounts receivable department should approve noncash credits or adjustments. The employee responsible for credit should report to a financial officer rather than to a sales or production manager. The credit manager should also approve credit and withhold credit when a customer has not met the credit terms.

EXHIBIT 6-13

Internal Control Questionnaire—Cash

1. Does the board of directors properly authorize bank accounts?
2. Is the mail opened by an employee who does not prepare the bank deposit?
3. Is the mail opened by an employee who does not have access to accounts receivable or the general ledger?
4. Is a list of the receipts made? By whom?
5. Does someone else periodically compare this list to the accounting records?
6. Does corporate management authorize lists of check signers?
7. Are cash receipts deposited daily?
8. Are receipts from cash sales supported by invoices, cash register tapes, sales tickets, or other pre-numbered tickets?
9. Does someone other than the person who has access to the cash approve cash sales?
10. Are employees who handle the cash bonded?
11. Does someone other than the person who prepares the deposit make the deposit?
12. Are returned checks delivered to someone other than the cashier?
13. Can employees redeem dishonored customer checks?
14. Does proper documentation support all cash disbursements?
15. Are disbursements made by check whenever possible?
16. Are all checks pre-numbered?
17. Are spoiled or voided checks retained?
18. Are unused checks controlled?
19. Is a check protector used?
20. Are all checks made payable to a person or a company?
21. Are employees who sign the checks authorized to do so?
22. Are employees who sign the checks prohibited from
    a. Having access to petty cash funds?
    b. Approving cash disbursements?
    c. Recording cash receipts?
    d. Posting to the ledger accounts?
23. Have bankers been instructed not to cash checks made payable to the company?
24. Is signing blank checks prohibited?
25. Are transfers between banks properly approved and promptly recorded?
26. Are long-outstanding checks researched and controlled?
27. Is presenting an invoice for payment twice impossible?
28. Do two different employees prepare checks and approve invoices?

Continued on next page.

29. Are bank accounts reconciled at least once a month?
30. Are bank statements and canceled checks delivered directly to the person who prepares the reconciliation?
31. Does the person preparing the reconciliation
    a. Sign checks?
    b. Handle cash?
    c. Record cash transactions?
32. Does the person handling the reconciliation
    a. Account for all check numbers?
    b. Examine signatures?
    c. Examine endorsements?
    d. Examine the payee's name?
    e. Follow up on long-outstanding checks?
    f. Examine bank transfers?
33. Are improperly endorsed checks returned to the bank for correction?
34. Are petty cash funds
    a. Operated on an imprest* basis?
    b. Limited to a specific amount covering requirements for a short time?
35. Do correctly completed petty cash slips support disbursements from petty cash funds?
36. Are petty cash funds intermingled with other funds?

* A petty cash fund in which all expenditures are documented by vouchers or vendors' receipts or invoices; the total of the vouchers and cash in the fund should equal the established balance.

Creating receivables begins with credit approval of a sales order by authorized personnel. When a receivable is created, separating the following duties among different individuals or departments is recommended:

- Approving credit
- Issuing inventory from stock
- Shipping inventory
- Preparing the invoice for the shipped goods
- Verifying invoices
- Posting control accounts
- Posting customer accounts
- Receiving payment from customers

As an organization divides those duties, it has more control over its accounts receivable.

Settling the receivables balances might result from cash receipt, return of merchandise, adjustment for allowances, pricing errors, or write-off of bad debts. A cash receipt is part of the cash process previously discussed. For other adjustments, authorized personnel other than the person handling receivables should provide the documentation prescribed by company procedures to support the adjustment.

The auditor verifies receivable balances by examining transaction documents and independently confirming the amounts with debtors. Separating duties in connection with receivables includes having different persons posting subsidiary ledgers and general ledgers. Internal controls should have someone other than the regular accounts receivable staff independently confirm receivables. Independent auditors or the internal audit department can make those confirmations.

Exhibit 6-14 shows a sample questionnaire to evaluate sales and accounts receivable internal control.

EXHIBIT 6-14

Internal Control Questionnaire—Sales and Accounts Receivable

1. Are monthly statements mailed to customers?
2. Does someone other than the bookkeeper review them before mailing?
3. Is the customer's subsidiary ledger reconciled monthly to the general ledger control?
4. Is an aged listing of accounts receivable prepared monthly for review by an officer or owner?
5. Does an officer or owner approve all returns, allowances, and write-offs?
6. Does an officer or owner approve customer orders and credit before acceptance?
7. Are shipments made only on controlled shipping invoices?
8. Are those shipping invoices used as the basis for billing?
9. Is there a prescribed follow-up procedure on collections?
10. Are pricings, extensions, and footings on sales invoices independently checked?

Inventories

Inventories are of special interest to auditors because a company's inventory often represents a major portion of its current assets. The auditor should verify the physical existence, valuation, and clerical accuracy of inventory records. Internal control of inventories requires maintenance of appropriate inventory levels and orderly flow of inventory from suppliers to customers.

The first step in inventory control—obtaining the right product at the right time and at the best possible price—occurs at the time of purchasing. All employees should make purchases in accordance with prescribed company procedures. Companies should use written purchase orders and have copies for the receiving department, accounting department, and the department that originated the purchase request (usually a production or other operating department).

After the appropriate department has issued the purchase order, the next step is to receive the merchandise from the supplier. The receiving department should be separate from the purchase department to make an independent count of goods received. The receiving department then sends the independently prepared receiving reports to the departments that received copies of the purchase order.

Companies should use centralized storerooms for inventory, if possible, and access should be available only to authorized storeroom personnel. Employees should check all inventories and place them in designated areas. Storeroom personnel should retain perpetual inventory records, and they should use a physical inventory to check the perpetual inventory records periodically. The company should develop a follow-up procedure to use when physical inventories and perpetual inventory records differ.

Employees should make inventory withdrawals only by following prescribed approval procedures. The storeroom personnel should provide the accounting department with a copy of all withdrawal requisitions. The organization must also control scrap and broken or damaged materials from manufacturing operations. The company should prescribe accounting procedures for controlling such unused materials.

After the company manufactures the goods, employees should return the finished goods to the storeroom or to the shipping department. Shipping personnel should make shipments only on a properly authorized shipping order. All shipping documents should be pre-numbered and accounted for to determine that all billings are made.

Each task should be accounted for by an employee from a department other than any of those involved in the process. Matching the various invoices is an important control procedure. The company should have a written policy and procedures for inventory valuations.

Property, Plant, and Equipment

The investment in property, plant, and equipment (capital expenditures) can make up a large part of a company's total assets. Those assets have a service life longer than one year. They normally require different control procedures because of the relatively high cost of each asset and the low turnover during an accounting cycle. Because of the high initial cost of those items, many companies emphasize controlling expenditures before the commitments are made rather than after. A properly planned program of capital expenditures encompasses all the basic elements of internal control, namely, organization, policies, procedures, standards of performance, reports and records, and internal auditing.

The first step in controlling capital expenditures is developing capital budgets. Capital expenditures, just as in any budgeting process, are limited. Therefore, planning how to use funds is important to obtain maximum results or to meet the organization's most crucial needs. In a small company, allocating capital

expenditures might not be a major problem because management can directly observe the company's capital goods needs. However, in large organizations with many departments and divisions, the demands for capital funds often exceed the available supply. The company must set priorities by considering need, employee safety and morale, return on investment, and, of course, the total amount of funds available.

After investment decisions are made, the appropriate employee should issue approval for the expenditure and should also issue a work order authorizing the expenditure. Supporting documents with the work order should indicate the reasons for the expenditure, including the cost/benefit to the company.

Between the expenditure authorization and the capital goods delivery, employees involved should submit progress reports to ensure that the expenditure is being controlled within the authorized amount. If the asset is being constructed, the involved employees should submit a progress report to management indicating the amount of expenditure authorized, actual cost to date, percentage of construction completed, additional commitments, estimated cost to complete, and any estimated overrun.

After the expenditures are made and the asset is in use, management should conduct a post-completion analysis of the expenditure. That analysis should compare the actual cost with the estimated cost—particularly important for a constructed asset (such as a building or machinery)—and should determine the value of the asset's operation.

Current Liabilities

From an internal control standpoint, the problems with assets are primarily in valuing the assets, but the main problem with liabilities is determining their existence. Asset overstatement is normally the result of a mistaken entry or valuation determination—an act of commission. In liabilities, most understatements result from the lack of recognition of the liability, which is an act of omission. The internal control should ensure that liabilities are recorded correctly and that the company has recorded all actual liabilities.

Various types of liabilities are subject to internal control procedures. For example, companies should designate certain employees to review notes payable for proper authorization. Companies should also have written guidelines for loans regarding amounts, length of time, sources, and interest rates and proper management authority for each. The authorized manager should review and control interest payments to ensure that the company pays the correct amounts.

Accounts payable normally represent the organization's largest volume of current liabilities. Someone should verify the existence of liabilities before the company pays them. The procedures described in purchasing, receiving, and storing inventory should provide documentation necessary for payment authorization.

Companies generally use a voucher system to authorize payment. The appropriate department issues pre-numbered vouchers for each payable item. The person requesting the voucher attaches the supporting documents and proper approvals. Dividing the labor among the approving parties, voucher preparers, and check writers is wise. Also, the open accounts payable items should be reconciled to the general ledger account at the end of each month.

Companies generally control miscellaneous liabilities, such as accrued wages, commissions, taxes, deferred credits, and withheld payroll taxes, by comparing the accrual to the actual expense item. A company should periodically clear those items and verify that it does so. The disbursements are subject to the regular procedure that employees, other than those handling the accruals or reconciliation of the accrued accounts, should make disbursements.

Because premium auditors rely heavily on payroll records, that area of internal control deserves careful study. Exhibit 6-15 provides an example of a questionnaire to evaluate internal control of payroll processing.

Revenues

Determining revenues is different from valuing and verifying assets and liabilities. The assets and liabilities are balance accounts at one point in time, but revenues relate to a period of time and represent a total for that period. Also, in most businesses, revenues represent an accumulation of many transactions that the organization must properly record in terms of time and value.

The AICPA defines "revenues" in Accounting Terminology Bulletin No. 2 as follows:

> Revenue results from the sale of goods and the rendering of services and is measured by the charge made to customers, clients, or tenants for goods and services furnished to them. It also includes gains from the sale or exchange of assets (other than stock in trade), interest and dividends earned on investments, and other increases in the owners' equity except those arising from capital contributions and capital adjustments.[8]

In most companies, revenues are a result of credit sales. In some, such as retail stores, revenues are a result of cash transactions. Each type of transaction presents unique internal control considerations.

The receipt of the customer's order initiates the credit sale. That order can come from contact with the customer in the field or office, by mail, or from a company sales representative or the Internet. Authorized personnel should check the order for accuracy and approve the order. The credit department should then approve the order's credit terms. The company might use copies of the sales order for the following:

- Authorization to release the goods from inventory
- Authorization for shipping by the shipping department
- Basis for the billing by the billing department
- Recording of the transaction by the accounting department

EXHIBIT 6-15

Internal Control Questionnaire—Payroll

1. Do different persons perform the following tasks?
   a. Approve hours worked
   b. Prepare payrolls
   c. Distribute paychecks
   d. Maintain custody of unclaimed wages
   e. Hire and terminate employees
2. Does someone outside of the payroll department check payroll totals against independently compiled labor distribution totals?
3. Are clerical operations in preparation of payrolls double-checked before payment?
4. Are appropriate payroll-related records maintained for accumulated employee benefits (vacations, pension data, and so on)?
5. Is the general ledger distribution of labor periodically reconciled to the payroll register?
6. Are responsibilities for payroll segregated from those for the general ledger?
7. Are payroll disbursements made from an imprest bank account?
8. If a separate payroll bank account is maintained,
   a. Are all checks pre-numbered and accounted for?
   b. Is the supply of unused checks adequately safeguarded and in the custody of persons who do not sign checks manually, control the use of facsimile signature plates, or operate the facsimile signature machine?
   c. Are spoiled checks mutilated to prevent reuse and kept on file for subsequent inspection?
   d. Are controls over the use of the facsimile signature plates adequate where a check-signing machine is used?
   e. Does the board of directors designate the check signers?
   f. Is the signing of checks before they are prepared prohibited?
   g. Is the amount for which checks can be drawn limited, or is a check protector used?
9. Is the payroll bank account reconciled by someone who has no other function with respect to the payroll?
10. If payment is made by cash,
    a. Do employees who do not prepare payrolls or approve hours worked prepare pay envelopes?
    b. Are receipts obtained?
11. Are completed payrolls adequately reviewed and approved before disbursements? (For example—compared with previous periods?)
12. Are confidential executive payrolls adequately controlled? (For example—approved by an executive other than the preparer of the payroll?)
13. What control is exercised over back pay and unclaimed wages?
14. Are advances to sales personnel periodically evaluated on the basis of current sales performance?

Once the company has processed the sales order, an invoice for the goods can be prepared based on data received regarding the goods ordered and the goods shipped. The appropriate personnel should make comparisons between the invoice and the amounts ordered and shipped. The employees who record the invoice for the sales register and the accounts receivable ledger should be different from the employees who prepare the sales orders, shipping orders, and invoices. That general procedure for receiving and recording sales orders varies by company, depending on the special circumstances involved in the creation of sales. Auditors should look for a properly coordinated division of responsibilities to ensure checks and balances among the various steps in the sales process.

Cash sales are handled differently. In the normal cash sale in a retail store, the same person who accepts the cash also gives the merchandise to the customer. The control of cash sales is closely related to inventory control. If a company properly controls and accounts for inventory, an automatic check of the cash sales should result. If obtaining inventory control over cash sales is impractical, the company must use other measures to maintain cash flow. Many retail stores use the retail inventory method, which, in effect, charges the goods into inventory at retail prices. A company obtains aggregate control under that method by comparing total beginning and ending inventory with the actual cash sales. That method makes the salespeople accountable for any differences in the value of stock on hand. A second effective control is having the employee making the sale issue a sales invoice and then having central cashiers receive the money.

Costs and Expenses

Another basic audit goal is matching expense to revenue. To ensure that costs and expenses are properly handled, budget procedures, cost-accounting procedures, and general expense control must be implemented.

The company accomplishes budget control by comparing actual expenses with budgeted amounts and following up on variances to identify waste and to improve performance. The company can also identify nonbudgeted or unauthorized expenditures.

The system of cost accounting can help monitor costs and expenses by distributing expenditures among inventory, capital items, and cost of sales. Costs can be distributed by product, operation, department, process, or organizational unit. A company might even distribute direct and indirect costs. Whatever cost system a company uses, it should periodically review the accuracy and timeliness of the results to ensure that the system provides the information needed for expense analysis.

General expense control should ensure that expenses are legitimate and authorized. It should also provide accurately recorded and classified expenses for reporting purposes. The accounting system should have clear, written procedures for classifying expenses and for determining expense items as compared to expenditures for assets. Those procedures ensure that the system

accurately presents the organization's expenditures or amounts owed on the financial statements.

A sound understanding of an organization's internal control system is valuable to premium auditors who collect and evaluate information from within the accounting system. By understanding the duties of the insured's personnel, premium auditors can obtain information most efficiently. By using a system's strengths and avoiding or adjusting for the system's weaknesses, auditors can design appropriate audit programs for each audit situation. No two systems are identical; therefore, independent verification of data in the systems cannot be performed by identical methods.

ACCOUNTING RECORDS

The records maintained by most businesses can be diverse and voluminous. Unless premium auditors know which records exist and which ones have the information they need, they can spend an inordinate amount of time searching for the basis of premium. Fortunately, however, GAAP and legal and tax requirements impose some consistency on accounting systems. Although the form records take can vary enormously by firm, the purposes of the records are essentially the same. The accounting records of most businesses include the following in some form:

- Source documents
- Books of entry
- General ledger
- Financial reports
- Tax returns

Exhibit 6-16 illustrates the steps in payroll accounting, moving from the source document to the income statement.

Source Documents

Every transaction produces a document of some sort. The document provides the information for the accounting system and is the legal evidence for the transaction. For employees' wages, the source documents might be timecards. For sales, the source documents might be customers' orders or invoices. Once a company has processed those documents, it usually preserves them for future reference.

Time Records

Companies use a wide variety of methods to record the hours worked by each employee. The result of this recording process is an hours-worked report that lists each employee by name or number and the number of hours worked each day. When separate job cost records are maintained, the report also indicates the hours each employee worked on each job. Each operation or each job may be identified by a code number.

EXHIBIT 6-16

Payroll Accounting

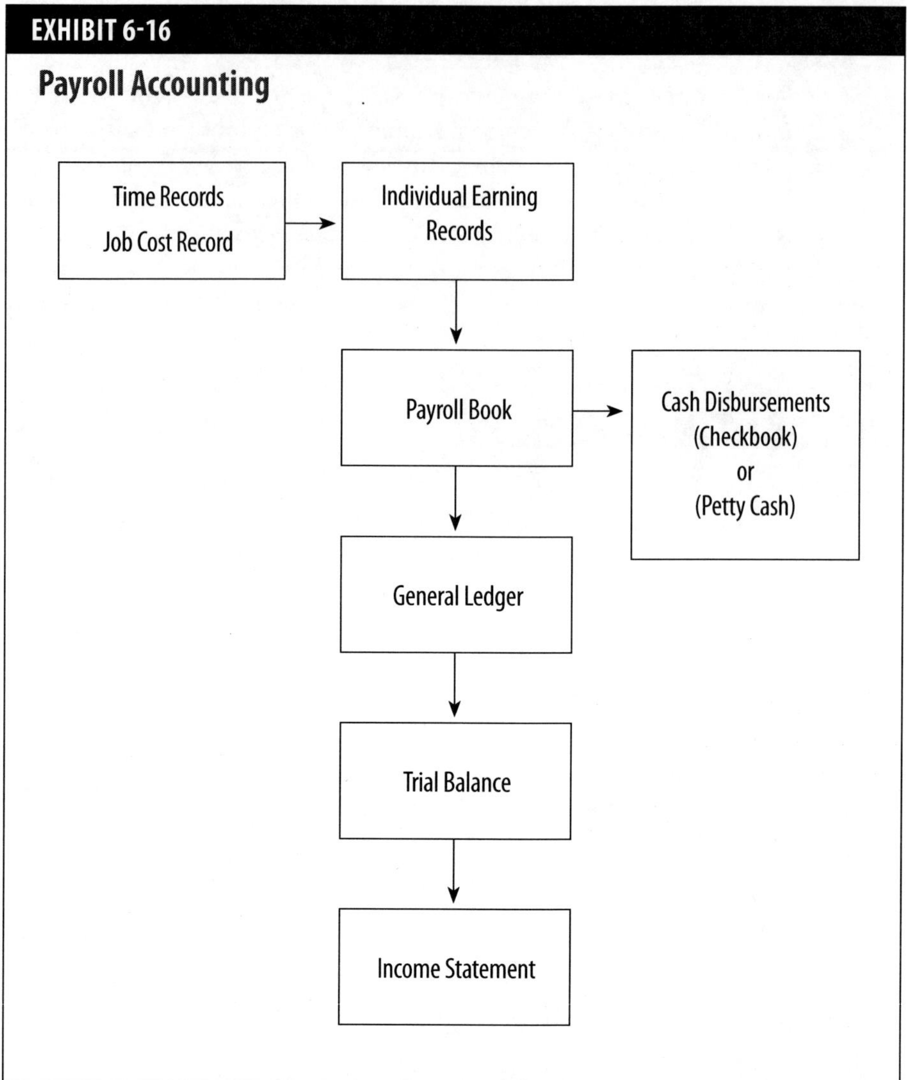

If the basis of an employee's wages is something other than time, the original source documents might be job tickets showing the job completed and the employee's name. In stores and restaurants, the sales check usually includes the employee's name or number so that the store or restaurant can allocate commissions or tips accordingly. Whatever the basis of compensation, some evidence of the work performed must exist so that the accounting system can process the payroll.

Sales Records

When a firm sells goods to customers, at least one document is needed to complete the transaction. Customers might place orders by letter, by telephone, by e-mail or internet, by printed form, or through company sales agents. In any case, the firm must record the quantity, description, and price of the goods on a sales order. If the company ships the goods, it must prepare

a bill of lading or another shipping document describing the goods and destination. Along with the merchandise, the customer receives a sales invoice indicating the quantity and description of the goods, the price (including freight and insurance), and the payment terms.

Books of Original Entry

Processing transactions begins with a journal entry. Journals have different names and appearances, but they perform the same task in the accounting system. Every system has a starting point, conventionally called a journal or book of original entry. It may well be a computer file rather than a book, but the first place the accounting system records the transaction. Small firms might enter all transactions in a single journal, but large firms maintain separate specialized journals for cash receipts, sales, purchases, cash disbursements, and payroll.

Cash Receipts Journal

A company normally enters cash payments received (either in a computer or manually) from customers in a cash receipts book. Cash receipts and cash disbursements might be in one book with receipts on one side and disbursements on the other. A review of the receipts could produce information on rental of equipment or property to others and reveal the sale of equipment, land, or buildings. Receipts for any or all such items might appear in other records but probably not in as much detail as in the cash receipts book.

The cash receipts for a contractor usually record for whom the work was done. That information can be important in determining the proper classification for some operations. Receipts from a city, county, state, or land development company could indicate street paving rather than paving driveways or parking lots. Receipts from utility companies usually indicate installation of gas, sewer, or water mains rather than installation of house connections.

Sales Journal

Companies might enter sales on account in the sales journal, either manually or by a computer. The information for each transaction comes from the sales invoices. Cash sales do not appear in the sales journal because the company enters such transactions in the cash receipts journal. The sales journal indicates the customer account to be debited along with the date, the invoice number, and the transaction amount.

Purchase Journal

The purchase journal is the record of purchases made on account. The number and purposes of the special columns provided in the journal depend on the nature of the business and the frequency of purchases. Each entry is recorded in the purchase journal as a credit in the accounts payable column. Remaining columns are used to post debits to the particular accounts most

frequently affected. The names of firms from which the insured purchases materials can provide clues for classification purposes.

Cash Disbursements Journal

Cash disbursements journal
An accounting record that records all payments.

A company might use a **cash disbursements journal** to record all payments. Some firms, however, keep separate books for payroll, checks, or petty cash expenditures. In either case, premium auditors should carefully review all cash disbursements, not just payroll or salary columns.

From the cash disbursements journal, the auditor can identify payments to subcontractors or independent contractors and payments for equipment and commission. Payments to subcontractors, if any, might necessitate examining several sources. A company might enter all payments made by check in the cash disbursement book but may not indicate clearly which payments include labor and which are for materials only. Also, an entry might be for only a portion of the work actually performed, or for work performed several months before the payment. If so, the auditor might have to combine that information with information from the cash book, purchase book, or accounts payable ledger.

Assume, for example, that the insured has a column headed "subcontractors" in the cash disbursements journal. That column includes individual payments to subcontractors as well as payments for building, trucks, and other equipment. An auditor taking only the figures from that column in the cash disbursements journal would ignore a sizable amount of exposure units. The insured might also maintain a purchase journal that has a column headed "subcontractors." When the company pays for the items in the purchase journal, it posts them in the cash disbursements journal under the column headed "accounts payable" and not in the "subcontractors" column. To establish the total exposure unit entries, the auditor must analyze both the cash disbursements and the purchase journal.

The cash disbursements journal also provides clues about purchasing or renting land, buildings, and equipment. Generally, the cash disbursements journal contains a "miscellaneous" column because there are rarely enough columns to accommodate all payments. Companies normally break down each type of payment at the end of each month. Premium auditors should always review the contents of the "miscellaneous" column.

A check register is a modified form of the cash disbursements journal that records all payments made by check. The check register lists checks, including voided ones, in sequence along with the date, amount, payee, and usually the purpose. That information enables the firm to reconcile its bank statements. It also provides premium auditors with the same information revealed in other forms of cash disbursements journals.

Petty cash book
A cash disbursements journal used to pay for minor items from a petty cash fund.

Another cash disbursements journal used for minor items is the **petty cash book** in which payments from the petty cash fund are recorded. Most companies, regardless of size, use a petty cash fund. Payments made from petty cash are

usually supported by petty cash vouchers, which show to whom the company made payment and briefly explain the purpose. Good accounting practices require that someone analyze petty cash payments and post the monthly totals to the proper general ledger accounts.

In some industries, paying part-time help out of petty cash is common. That practice occurs regularly with car washes, service stations, laundries, and some retail stores. In the trucking industry, truck drivers commonly secure the service of others to load and unload their trucks. The truck driver submits a voucher for such payments, as well as the bills or other expenses. Because petty cash payments do not normally show up in the general ledger labor accounts, premium auditors should review the petty cash book carefully in those cases. Companies often do not record cash payments to casual labor on the unemployment or Social Security records.

Payroll Journal

The **payroll journal** summarizes employee earnings. A payroll journal is also called a payroll register, weekly payroll, or payroll book.

Payroll journal
An accounting record that summarizes employee earnings.

Companies usually compute payrolls for each individual from the hours-worked report and at the same time enter payrolls in the payroll journal. The journal generally follows a standard format showing the following information:

- Employee name and employee number
- Number of hours worked
- Rate of pay
- Overtime
- Gross pay
- Payroll deductions
- Net pay

The journal shows a total for each column, that is, a total of regular pay, overtime pay, gross pay, various deductions, and net pay. Some journals also indicate payroll distribution by department.

Companies use different methods to compute overtime pay. If the column headed "regular time" indicates wages for the total hours worked at a straight rate, then the column headed "overtime" indicates only the premium pay for overtime. Exhibit 6-17 shows a payroll journal entry illustrating that situation and assuming a forty-hour workweek. The employee worked forty-four hours, and the "regular time" column includes forty-four hours of pay at the straight rate ($10 per hour). The "overtime" column shows only the four hours of work over the regular work week multiplied by the additional $5 per hour. In that example, $20 is premium pay for overtime. In most, but not all, states the basis of premium for workers' compensation insurance does not include the premium pay for overtime.

EXHIBIT 6-17

Sample Payroll Journal Entry

	Rate	Hours	Straight Time	Overtime	Gross
M. Bullock	$10.00	44	$440.00	$20.00	$460.00

Other companies may use the "regular time" column to record the wages for the standard workweek only and the "overtime" column to record the wages for overtime hours at the overtime rate. Exhibit 6-18 illustrates that method, using the same example as previously provided. The "regular time" column includes only the wages for forty hours of work at the straight rate of $10 per hour. The "overtime" column includes four hours of wages at the overtime rate of $15 per hour. In that situation, the premium auditor must calculate the premium pay portion in those states in which the overtime rule applies. In that example, one-third of the $60, or $20, is deductible as premium pay.

EXHIBIT 6-18

Alternative Payroll Journal Entry

	Rate	Hours	Straight Time	Overtime	Gross
M. Bullock	$10.00	44	$400.00	$60.00	$460.00

Auditors should spot-check entries to determine how the company computes the payroll. Occasionally, errors occur in audits because someone misunderstood the rating manual definition of overtime.

Companies often use the overtime column as a catchall for miscellaneous payments. Frequently, companies enter the pay for holiday and vacations not worked in the overtime column. Auditors should spot-check weeks in which holidays occur to be certain that the company records holiday pay with regular wages. A company might also enter shift differential or jury duty pay under overtime. The auditor must analyze the overtime column to determine whether any of those items appears in the overtime column. If the company has incorrectly inserted such items in the overtime column, the premium auditor must make adjustments to obtain the correct amount for the premium base.

Many insureds group entries in the payroll book by department with a subtotal for each department. The auditor should encourage all insureds to keep records showing payrolls by classification because that grouping helps auditors properly classify payrolls. Auditors should encourage insureds in the construction or erection business to subdivide payrolls by job or location.

Payroll processing also requires recording each employee's total yearly earnings. The individual earnings record might consist of a separate page for each employee in the payroll book or on a computer printout. That record shows when the employee's wages have reached the Social Security wage base so that the employer knows when to stop FICA deductions. That record usually indicates regular earnings, overtime pay, gross pay, deductions, and net pay. The records might show that information for each pay period and then add it to the cumulative total. For insureds with only a few employees, using the individual earnings records is probably the quickest and best method of developing the payroll.

Payroll records do not show payments to subcontractors and independent contractors, nor do they show payments for hired trucks and other equipment. To secure that information, the auditor must use other records. Companies make most of those payments by check and then enter the record of payments in a cash disbursement journal.

General Ledger

The **general ledger** summarizes the information from the books of original entry. Journals organize transactions chronologically, but the general ledger organizes transactions according to separate accounts. Each necessary classification of assets, liabilities, equity, income, and expenses has a separate general ledger account. Because organizing accounting data that way is necessary both to produce the financial statements and to monitor an entity's financial position, the general ledger is the heart of the accounting system.

General ledger
An accounting record that summarizes the information from the books of original entry.

The general ledger is also an important document for premium auditors. Although it contains the same information as the journals, the general ledger provides a more convenient overview. It can be a quick way to spot payments for contract labor, casual labor, rental equipment, additional structures or equipment, and other unusual items. If auditors need more detail about such payments, they can find it in the journals more easily.

Financial Statements

As part of the accounting cycle, a business prepares financial statements from the general ledger. As mentioned, the conventional financial statements prepared are the income statement, the statement of owners' equity, the statement of financial position, and the statement of changes in financial position. Those statements summarize the organization's financial transactions and provide an overview of an organization's financial strength and direction. Because the statements are only summaries, however, they rarely categorize data in enough detail for premium audit purposes. Also, the period covered by the financial statements rarely coincide with the insurance policy term. For a premium auditor, the major advantage of financial statements is that they are usually readily available. Although they normally lack sufficient information for a premium audit, they can offer some insight into the insured's finances and the reasonableness of data obtained from other sources.

Tax Returns

An important accounting task is to file the organization's required tax returns. Although tax returns are an additional source of information, premium auditors should use them cautiously. For example, the tax return the insured furnishes to the premium auditor might subsequently be corrected before the insured files the official copy. Also, the company might not have to include various items, such as intercompany sales, in tax returns. Accordingly, information obtained from tax returns might be incomplete. Used carefully, however, tax returns help verify information from other sources.

Federal Tax Returns

An employer must file a quarterly report of total and taxable earnings for all employees. In January of each year, employers must furnish employees with a record of taxes withheld and must relay that information to the IRS. Companies must report payments to corporations or individuals other than employees on an information return. Finally, businesses and other organizations subject to federal income tax must file an annual income tax return.

All employers required to withhold income taxes or liable for Social Security taxes must file a quarterly return. Usually, companies file that return on Form 941, which can be a valuable source of payroll information. It is not necessarily a complete record, however. Employers use additional quarterly tax returns for certain purposes and make payments to certain employees that do not have to be included in the report.

Exhibit 6-19 depicts a sample Form 941, combining Social Security taxes and income-tax withholding. An auditor can quickly check the validity of a particular copy of the return by multiplying the taxable payroll by the FICA tax rate. The result should equal the FICA taxes paid for the quarter.

Employees receiving remuneration or other payments not reported on Form 941 include the following:[9]

- Domestic servants in college clubs, fraternities, and sororities
- House workers of industrial firms who are statutory employees
- Household workers in private homes who are paid less than $50 per quarter
- Ministers of churches performing duties as such
- Newspaper carriers under age eighteen
- Real estate agents and direct sellers if treated as self-employed
- Salespersons of life or casualty insurers who are not common-law employees
- A son or daughter under twenty-one employed by a parent for domestic work
- Employees receiving tips under $20 per month
- Meals and lodging furnished for the employer's convenience and on the employer's premises

EXHIBIT 6-19

Sample Form 941

Form **941** (Rev. January 2004) Department of the Treasury Internal Revenue Service (99)

Employer's Quarterly Federal Tax Return

▶ See separate instructions revised January 2004 for information on completing this return.

Please type or print.

Enter state code for state in which deposits were made **only** if different from state in address to the right ▶ ☐ (see page 2 of separate instructions).

Name (as distinguished from trade name) | Date quarter ended

Trade name, if any | Employer identification number

Address (number and street) | City, state, and ZIP code

OMB No. 1545-0029

T
FF
FD
FP
I
T

If address is different from prior return, check here ▶ ☐ IRS Use

1 1 1 1 1 1 1 1 1 1 2 3 3 3 3 3 3 3 3 4 4 4 5 5 5

6 7 8 8 8 8 8 8 8 8 9 9 9 9 9 10 10 10 10 10 10 10 10 10 10

A If you **do not have to file** returns in the future, check here ▶ ☐ and enter date final wages paid ▶

B If you are a seasonal employer, see **Seasonal employers** on page 1 of the instructions and check here ▶ ☐

1	Number of employees in the pay period that includes March 12th . ▶ 1		
2	Total wages and tips, plus other compensation (see separate instructions)	2	
3	Total income tax withheld from wages, tips, and sick pay	3	
4	Adjustment of withheld income tax for preceding quarters of **this calendar year**	4	
5	Adjusted total of income tax withheld (line 3 as adjusted by line 4)	5	
6	Taxable social security wages . . . . . 6a ___ × 12.4% (.124) =	6b	
	Taxable social security tips . . . . . . 6c ___ × 12.4% (.124) =	6d	
7	Taxable Medicare wages and tips . . . 7a ___ × 2.9% (.029) =	7b	
8	Total social security and Medicare taxes (add lines 6b, 6d, and 7b). **Check here if wages are not subject to social security and/or Medicare tax** ▶ ☐	8	
9	Adjustment of social security and Medicare taxes (see instructions for required explanation) Sick Pay $ ___ ± Fractions of Cents $ ___ ± Other $ ___ =	9	
10	Adjusted total of social security and Medicare taxes (line 8 as adjusted by line 9)	10	
11	**Total taxes** (add lines 5 and 10)	11	
12	Advance earned income credit (EIC) payments made to employees (see instructions)	12	
13	Net taxes (subtract line 12 from line 11). **If $2,500 or more, this must equal line 17, column (d) below (or line D of Schedule B (Form 941))**	13	
14	Total deposits for quarter, including overpayment applied from a prior quarter	14	
15	**Balance due** (subtract line 14 from line 13). See instructions	15	
16	**Overpayment.** If line 14 is more than line 13, enter excess here ▶ $ ___ and check if to be: ☐ Applied to next return **or** ☐ Refunded.		

- **All filers:** If line 13 is less than $2,500, **do not** complete line 17 **or** Schedule B (Form 941).
- **Semiweekly schedule depositors:** Complete Schedule B (Form 941) and check here ▶ ☐
- **Monthly schedule depositors:** Complete line 17, columns (a) through (d), and check here. ▶ ☐

17 Monthly Summary of Federal Tax Liability. (Complete **Schedule B (Form 941)** instead, if you were a semiweekly schedule depositor.)

(a) First month liability	**(b)** Second month liability	**(c)** Third month liability	**(d)** Total liability for quarter

Third Party Designee

Do you want to allow another person to discuss this return with the IRS (see separate instructions)? ☐ **Yes.** Complete the following. ☐ **No**

Designee's name ▶ **Phone no.** ▶ ( ) **Personal identification number (PIN)** ▶

Sign Here

Under penalties of perjury, I declare that I have examined this return, including accompanying schedules and statements, and to the best of my knowledge and belief, it is true, correct, and complete.

Signature ▶ **Print Your Name and Title** ▶ **Date** ▶

For Privacy Act and Paperwork Reduction Act Notice, see back of Payment Voucher. Cat. No. 17001Z Form **941** (Rev. 1-2004)

- Moving expense reimbursements for qualified expenses
- Public official fees
- Service not in the course of the employer's trade or business if the employee is paid less than $50 per quarter

Because an employer need not include all remuneration to employees on Form 941, the auditor should not use it as a primary source of gross payroll information. However, Form 941 can be an extremely helpful secondary source for verifying information.

Certain tax-exempt organizations and other employers not liable for Social Security taxes file Form 941E, Quarterly Return of Withheld Federal Income Tax. That form reports income tax withheld from wages, tips, annuities, supplemental unemployment compensation benefits, and certain gambling winnings when the law does not require FICA coverage. The due dates and other filing requirements are the same as for Form 941.

Employers of household employees earning more than $50 per quarter must file Form 942, Employer's Quarterly Tax Return for Household Employees. A sole proprietor who files Form 941 for business employees can include household employees on that return.

Employers who report taxes on agricultural employees' wages use Form 943, Employer's Annual Tax Return for Agricultural Employees. Form 943 is also used to report taxes on wages of household employees in a private home on a farm operated for profit. Although Form 943 serves the same purpose as Form 941, it is filed only annually.

In addition to income taxes withheld and Social Security taxes, employers might also be subject to Federal Unemployment Tax Act (FUTA). If so, they must file Form 940, Employer's Annual Federal Unemployment Tax Return. Except for employers of domestic servants or agricultural labor, employers are liable for FUTA taxes if, during the current or preceding calendar year, they paid wages of $1,500 in any calendar quarter or if they had one or more employees for any part of a day in twenty different calendar weeks. The law includes all regular, temporary, and part-time employees, but a partnership should not count its partners. Employers of domestic servants are liable for FUTA taxes if they paid $1,000 in cash wages during any calendar quarter. Farmers are liable only if they paid $20,000 in cash wages during any calendar quarter, or if they had ten or more agricultural employees for any part of a day in twenty different calendar weeks.

Form 940 requires the employer to record all remuneration paid during the calendar year for the services of employees. That total can help verify payroll information obtained elsewhere in the insured's records.

An individual can be an employee for insurance purposes but not for income tax withholding, FICA, or FUTA purposes. Forms 940 and 941 do not show compensation paid to such individuals, but the employer should report it on Form 1099. Copies of those forms have limited usefulness for premium audits.

They are individual reports only on a calendar-year basis, so they can be unwieldy and might be incomplete. A Form 1099 might help resolve a question about the amount paid a particular individual, but such information normally comes from the general ledger or other sources.

In addition to withholding and employee-related tax records, businesses must file an appropriate federal income tax return. Sole proprietors must attach Schedule C, Profit or (Loss) From Business or Profession, to their personal income tax returns. Partnerships file Form 1065, U.S. Partnership Return of Income. Corporations file Form 1120, U.S. Corporation Income Tax Return. Those returns show annual totals for receipts, rents, salaries and wages, and similar items of interest to premium auditors. By themselves, however, those totals do little more than give a premium auditor an idea of the overall size of the insured's operations. The tax year probably does not coincide with the policy period, and a premium audit requires more detail than provided in those returns.

State and Local Tax Returns

A premium auditor should also check state and local tax returns, although they are generally less useful than the federal returns. Auditors can use state payroll tax returns in the same way as they use Forms 940 and 941. Because of the differences among states about who is considered an employee and what income is taxable, listing all variations is not possible. However, on a multistate operation, state payroll tax returns are not even a good secondary source for gross payrolls. Auditors could easily miss the payroll for an entire state if they examined only state tax returns.

Many states and municipalities levy sales tax on retail sales. The retailer can file the tax returns on either a monthly or quarterly basis, depending on the taxing body. Those returns can help verify gross receipts because they usually require gross sales to be recorded. Although such tax returns can be an ultimate source for reconciliation, they alone do not provide sufficient information for a premium audit. The sales journal, cash disbursements journal, and general ledger must be the primary sources when the premium is subject to adjustment on the basis of sales.

Regulatory and Other Records

Accounting systems also generate many additional reports and records. Depending on the premium base, premium auditors might find the information they need in those miscellaneous reports and records, including reports to regulatory agencies.

For example, motor carriers must file an Interstate Commerce Commission Annual Report by March 31 each year. Those reports can help verify truckers' revenues. Summaries of those reports appear in Central Analysis Bureau reports. Auditors can use Federal and State Excise Tax Reports to verify admissions and number of gallons sold if they are the premium base for the policy.

Nonregulatory reports can include financial information filed with franchises parent companies, or other similarly interested parties. Examples include fast-food restaurants that must provide information to the franchise holder and automobile dealers that must report information to the manufacturer. Each industry or company usually has a prescribed format and chart of accounts. The reports generally segment the business into cost categories, giving details about the receipts and related expenses for different activities within the business. Auditors should be familiar with the accounting requirements and the industries in which they exist. That familiarity not only enables auditors to identify additional sources of audit information but also allows them to determine whether the insured follows the prescribed accounting requirements.

The insured might be required to make other reports useful to the auditor. For example, Bureau of Labor Statistics reports contain information on the number of employees, sometimes by categories, and the average number of hours worked. Union reports from trade unions can help classify payroll. The Central Records Bureau of the Shipping Association reports hours worked and vacation time accrued. School attendance reports show the number of students in a school. Membership or dues records indicate the number of members in an organization. An auditor might find the number of vehicles or boats in depreciation schedules. Usually, production reports indicate the number of units produced.

Some internal management reports assist management in guiding and controlling the organization. Others are reports for specific parties with a need for certain information about the organization. Many such reports can provide information about the basis of premium.

SUMMARY

To determine the correct basis of premium, premium auditors obtain much necessary information from the insured's accounting system. The accounting system accumulates, measures, and communicates information about an organization's financial transactions for use by managers, investors, creditors, suppliers, customers, employees, and tax and regulatory authorities. Accounting systems must consistently follow standard procedures to satisfy those needs. Although systems vary to suit the needs of the particular organization, both generally accepted accounting principles (GAAP) and government accounting procedures have common features. Familiarity with those common features enables premium auditors to find appropriate sources of information more readily. Even so, auditors should review the particular insured's entire accounting system before collecting data to ensure that they can identify the most efficient sources for premium data and evaluate the reliability of those sources.

When reviewing an accounting system, auditors should follow a particular transaction through the steps in the accounting cycle. Regardless of the mechanics for processing transactions, the accounting cycle begins with a

source document for the transaction. When the firm journalizes the necessary information about the transaction, it records it in a book of original entry. Posting the information to the general ledger involves organizing it by account. The trial balance prepared at the end of the accounting period gives totals for each account and can help detect errors if debits and credits are not equal. After the firm completes the necessary adjustments, it prepares financial statements for the entire accounting period. The final step involves closing the ledger to transfer net income or loss for the period to the owner's equity account and to return the income and expense accounts to zero for the beginning of the next accounting period. Some small organizations might use public accountants rather than their own accounting staff to perform many tasks.

An essential consideration for any accounting system is the strength of its internal control. The elements of internal control include organization, policies and procedures, standards of performance, reports and records, and internal auditing. An evaluation of internal control should precede any decision about an appropriate audit program. If the accounting system has a high degree of internal control, a premium auditor can have more confidence in the system's final output and may choose to use summaries and reports normally generated by the system. If internal control is weak, however, the premium auditor is less able to rely on the system's output and must work more from source documents. Areas in which internal control is of greatest concern to premium auditors include cash receipts and disbursements, accounts receivable, inventories, property, plant, equipment, current liabilities, revenues, and costs and expenses.

Depending on the strength of internal control, a premium auditor might be able to select from several accounting records to obtain premium data. Most reliable, but also most cumbersome, are the original source documents. Books of original entry usually provide a more convenient record. Those books include cash receipts journals, sales journals, purchase journals, cash disbursements journals, and payroll journals. Usually, the journals or their equivalents furnish the detailed information required for a premium audit in a reasonably convenient form. However, some nonroutine transactions relating to the premium base do not appear in a particular journal. The general ledger provides the best overview of all the insured's transactions and helps to uncover the unusual ones that the auditor should include in the basis of premium. The insured's financial statements indicate the organization's financial position more readily than other sources, but they generally lack sufficient detail to determine the basis of premium. Because failure to comply with tax laws involves severe penalties, tax returns offer a highly reliable source of information. The insured usually does not classify that information, however, the same way the manual defines the basis of premium.

Other accounting records that might be helpful to premium auditors include various reports to management, regulatory agencies, unions, and other interested parties. Although premium auditors might find disadvantages to each of those sources of information, examining a combination of sources can

overcome most disadvantages. A premium auditor well-versed in accounting systems can select the records that provide the necessary premium information in both the most convenient and most reliable form. Choosing an audit program to accomplish that goal is the subject of the next chapter.

CHAPTER NOTES

1. Douglas R. Carmichael and William W. Holder, *Guide to Audits of Local Governments* (Fort Worth, Tex.: Practitioners Publishing Company, 1994), p. 110.04.
2. AICPA *Professional Standards*, "Consideration of Internal Control Structure in a Financial Statement Audit," §319.06, (New York: American Institute of Certified Public Accountants, 2004), p. 322.
3. AICPA *Professional Standards*, § 319.07, p. 322.
4. AICPA *Professional Standards*, § 319.09, p. 323.
5. AICPA *Professional Standards*, § 319.10, p. 323.
6. AICPA *Professional Standards*, § 319.11, pp. 323–324.
7. AICPA *Professional Standards*, § 319.12, p. 324.
8. Project Updates, "Revenue Recognition," Financial Accounting Standards Board, December 7, 2004.
9. Circular E, Employer's Tax Guide, Internal Revenue Service, January 2005.

Direct Your Learning 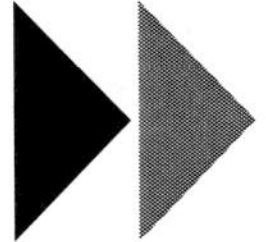

Audit Program Design

Educational Objectives

After learning the content of this chapter and completing the corresponding course guide assignment, you should be able to:

- Explain how to organize an efficient audit.
- Given a case, evaluate audit information that would be appropriate for a premium auditor to use.
- Explain how a premium auditor verifies the quality and accuracy of evidence gathered for a premium audit.
- Describe the uses of the general ledgers as part of a premium audit.
- Describe the purpose of an audit trail in the premium audit process.
- Summarize the uses of the payroll and sales cycles and records in a premium audit.
- Explain how a premium auditor measures owned auto loss exposures, inventory, and fixed assets.
- Define or describe each of the Key Words and Phrases for this chapter.

OUTLINE

Develop Your Perspective

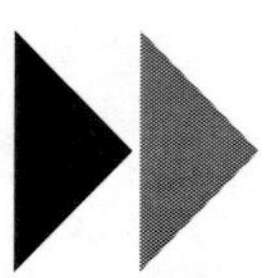

What are the main topics covered in the chapter?

A well designed audit program is a mark of a professional auditor. An effective design allows the auditor to reliably and efficiently select the records of the insured that will provide the necessary audit data.

Identify the reasons for designing an audit program properly.

- What considerations must be made in determining objectives, selecting procedures, collecting data, and establishing work papers?
- What determines the amount of evidence or records that an auditor needs in performing a successful audit?

Why is it important to learn about these topics?

To conduct an audit, a premium auditor must understand how an accounting system operates and when to make adjustments in the data provided by the insured.

Describe how an accounting system operates.

- What are the steps a premium auditor might use to extract the premium base from the general ledger?
- When necessary, how are adjustments made to the general ledger accounts?

How can you use what you will learn?

Consider how a premium auditor answers questions concerning the information included in a particular account by following the transaction forward or backward along the audit trail.

- What are the techniques involved for auditing payroll records in the payroll accounting cycle?
- How can a premium auditor determine what should be included and what should be excluded in the premium base of the insured?

Audit Program Design

In public accounting, the term audit program describes a variety of procedures that an auditor must perform during an audit to evaluate a firm's financial statements. The same is true of premium audits. Designing a comprehensive audit program is a significant part of the audit process. An auditor who plans and organizes before beginning an audit eliminates needless delays, increases the audit's quality, and projects a professional image to the insured. A properly designed audit program can eliminate questions about the types and amount of information to gather, the records to use, and the sequence in which to conduct the audit.

As part of audit procedures, many pages of details about internal control, confirmation of accounts receivable, observation of inventory, and reconciliation of bank statements can accumulate. Because an audit might require several weeks or months and can include several auditors, detailed procedures are necessary to ensure that all the steps in the audit are completed. A sound audit program provides a sequence of steps for the auditor to follow and a checklist to record which auditor completed each step.

Although the appropriate audit program varies in each case, the procedures (shown in the box) remain the same. This chapter explains these procedures and presents some guidelines for the design of a sound premium audit program.

Premium Audit Program Design

1. Organize the premium audit program
2. Identify appropriate audit information
3. Verify audit information
4. Review the general ledger
5. Create the audit trail
6. Review the payroll cycle
7. Review the sales cycle
8. Measure owned automobile loss exposures, inventory, and fixed assets

ORGANIZE THE PREMIUM AUDIT PROGRAM

The initial procedure of an audit program is to organize the audit. Proper organization and preparation not only reduce the audit time but also can minimize future problems that might arise.

The auditor must understand the audit goals thoroughly and, during the planning stage, should listen to, and work closely with the policyholder. For example, an insured might question the need for an audit early in the communication process. The auditor should be prepared to explain why the audit is necessary, what the auditor will be doing, and what the auditor and insurer will do when the audit is completed, and to answer any questions the insured might have. Establishing a positive relationship with the insured at the outset of the process can save time and promote the insured's cooperation.

Throughout the audit, the auditor should try to minimize the disruption to the insured's business by coordinating meetings and contacts around the schedules of all concerned. The auditor should also organize the audit to avoid interruptions to his or her own schedule. Having to stop in the middle of an involved audit to attend to other business or personal issues consumes additional time of both the auditor and policyholder.

Generally, an auditor should plan to complete the audit at the insured's office. Leaving the office when the audit is incomplete with plans to finish it later means having to become reacquainted with the facts. The best time to finish the job is when the insured's records and personnel are available to answer questions and all the details are fresh in the auditor's mind.

The audit should also be organized to protect the insured's records. Payroll information is highly confidential and records should not be left unattended, for example, over a lunch break. The auditor should always ask the insured which records should not be left unattended. Before leaving the insured's office, the auditor should look through work papers to make sure none of the insured's records have been mixed among them. Finally, the auditor should return records to the same person who provided them.

In organizing the audit, the auditor must do the following:

- Determine and consider the audit's goals
- Select the proper audit procedures
- Collect and record the data in a logical, systematic manner
- Prepare proper work papers

Determine Goals

A premium audit differs from an independent audit in several ways. The scope of the premium audit is not as broad, and the premium auditor does not express an opinion on the firm's financial statements. Although the audit of a corporation with records in many locations might require several auditors, typically only one auditor performs the premium audit. The extent of planning needed for a premium audit can depend on the size of the insured. An auditor might need a detailed list of questions to audit a multidivisional conglomerate but not a neighborhood barbershop. Most premium audits involve smaller companies. Determining the goals of the audit, based on the size and complexity of the organization, lays the foundation for the audit plan.

Primary Goal

Because of the differences in organizations' size and recordkeeping systems, no one audit program applies in every case. However, one goal is always primary: to determine the exposure amounts and classifications for the coverages provided by the applicable insurance policy within a reasonable time period. One of the decisions that the auditor must make in designing the audit program is to choose the most suitable procedures to accomplish this primary goal. For example, for a workers' compensation audit, the auditor will seek records needed to assign payrolls by state and by classification and to determine overtime and weekly wage limitations.

The condition of the insured's records sometimes limits or dictates the procedures that can be used. Many insureds keep less than ideal records, some consisting of little more than check stubs and bank deposit receipts. Few insureds keep books that conform exactly to generally accepted accounting principles. Business analysts often cite poor bookkeeping practices as the most common reason for business failures. Therefore, the audit program's design should consider the condition of the insured's records, allowing additional time, if necessary, to verify and summarize the information.

Secondary Goal

A secondary goal of a premium audit is to provide information for use by others. For example, a description of the insured's operations assures underwriters, sales representatives, and anyone reviewing the audit that the auditor used the correct classifications. The description of operations also helps justify any changes the auditor might have made in classification of exposure units. Although an audit might not involve prior years, the auditor should also report any changes in the organization's operations, size, location, ownership, or officers. Such changes can have underwriting significance.

Select Audit Method

The auditor should spend a few minutes reviewing alternative methods to conduct an audit before beginning the audit. The two audit methods are:

1. Auditing by exception
2. Auditing individual earnings

The auditor should first determine gross exposure amounts and assign them to the classifications required by the manual. Once the gross amounts are verified,

the auditor can total each classification using the two different methods. For example, when the accounts show earnings by departments, the auditor can use departmental totals if all the employees in a department belong in the same classification. If most employees share the same classification, then the auditor should determine the gross and individual payroll of the exceptions.

Auditing by exception
An auditing method for determining the appropriate payroll-based exposure amounts and classifications (gross payroll minus payroll of exceptions); used when most employees are in the same classification.

Auditing by exception is an auditing method for determining the appropriate payroll-based exposure amounts and classifications (gross payroll minus payroll of exceptions); used when most employees are in the same classification. Using this method the auditor takes the gross payroll, or the gross payroll by department, and deducts the payroll relating to standard exceptions and other employees who must be classified separately. The advantage of auditing by exception is speed. However, before using this method, the auditor should determine how many employees are exceptions. It works best when the number of exceptions is small.

Individual earnings method
An auditing method for determining the appropriate payroll-based exposure amounts that requires listing every employee's name and wages.

The **individual earnings method** is an auditing method for determining the appropriate payroll-based exposure amounts that requires listing every employee's name and wages. This method is more cumbersome because it requires listing every employee's name and wages. The auditor should use it only as a last resort or only if the insured has few employees and several applicable classifications.

To select the most efficient audit method, the premium auditor should analyze the insured's accounting system by following the audit trail. Businesses usually modify accounting practices to suit their own needs, so premium auditors should not hesitate to ask questions about a particular accounting system. By discussing the needs of the audit, the auditor can usually find the person best able to help answer questions about the insured's system.

Insurance policies grant the insurer, and hence the premium auditor, a broad right to examine all records applicable to the policy. Usually, the size and type of organization guide the auditor in choosing the most useful records. The auditor should select the records that will provide the most complete information in the shortest amount of time. If records are needed beyond those that the insured has voluntarily provided, the auditor should ask for them. The auditor can usually gain the insured's cooperation by explaining why specific records are needed.

Most auditors have probably had the experience of starting an audit with one type of records and then discovering that a better set exists. In such cases, starting over with the better records is probably more efficient than using the original set.

Determine Audit Period and Obtain Data

An important decision the auditor must make in organizing the audit is to determine the cutoff dates of the audit period. Because the procedures of individual insureds vary, the auditor cannot indiscriminately select a convenient period to audit. The auditor should discuss the audit period with the insured, particularly when the exposure amounts at the beginning and end of the audit period are significantly different.

To avoid juggling odd periods in each audit, the auditor should identify the cutoff date at the audit's start. Including a complete month or quarter in the audit period greatly simplifies verification and makes the next auditor's task much easier. When policies expire at the end of a calendar year or the end of a calendar quarter, the cutoff date should be the end of the last week in that period. For policies expiring near the end of a month, the auditor should include the last week's payroll in that month's posting. The auditor can examine the cash disbursements journal, the payroll summary, or the general ledger to determine which week is the final one in that month's posting.

When possible, the audit period should match the policy period as closely as possible to avoid distorting the premium base. When auditing a period that does not coincide with the policy period, the auditor must judge the flow of operations. The audit period is not too important for operations that occur evenly throughout the year. However, when the level of operations during the beginning and ending weeks varies significantly, the audit period becomes extremely important. That can happen when a business is growing or declining rapidly, when the business makes bonus payments, or when a strike occurs.

Avoiding and detecting errors are easier when the auditor has a complete set of accounting records for the entire audit period. For example, the auditor should consecutively record the entire fifty-two weeks from a payroll journal. Reviewing the books systematically also provides a better perspective on the entire audit period.

Occasionally, the auditor cannot obtain a complete set of data from one source because the business has not yet prepared the last report. When that occurs, the auditor should subtotal the data from the original source and then individually label and add to the subtotal the data from the additional source, such as a quarterly payroll summary. When the insured has not yet posted one or two months' data to the general ledger, the auditor can usually identify those data from the regular posting source and add them separately.

Prepare Work Papers

Work papers are an auditor's records of audit procedures, including tests performed, information obtained, and conclusions reached in developing the premium base. Whether paper or electronic, work papers are the physical evidence of an audit. Although not all audits lend themselves to a standardized approach to developing work papers, a logical, detailed approach is necessary. Audit work papers enable audit managers and supervisors to evaluate the quality of auditors' work, detect errors, and recommend improvements. The audit manager should prohibit the use of shortcuts and procedures that are familiar only to the individual auditor. An insured reading the work papers should be able to start from the premium base and work backward by tracing the details to the books and records. If both the insured and the auditor have copies of the work papers after an audit, the auditor can answer most questions that arise over the telephone.

Work papers
An auditor's records of audit procedures, including tests performed, information obtained, and conclusions reached in developing the premium base.

The auditor should clearly identify sources of information and present them in a consistent, logical manner, avoiding abbreviations. For example, when a payroll journal is the source for gross wages, the auditor should title other work papers according to the source: "Per Payroll Journal." The auditor should title the payrolls recorded as "Gross Wages." The time period would normally list fifty-two or fifty-three weeks of gross wages in consecutive, chronological order.

Auditors should not mix or combine sources of data. They should separately label and record data from the weekly payroll journal and the biweekly journal. The data on the work papers should be an actual transcript of the figures on the books and records. Combining amounts and presenting totals on the work papers make determining the source of an error almost impossible.

Each page of the work papers should contain the policyholder's name, the policy number, and the policy period. Pages should be numbered consecutively. When new information is combined from several pages, the auditor should identify each source by page number. Auditors should also write the total number of work paper pages on each page, such as 1 of 12 or 1/12. Auditors should not use a system such as 2-A, 2-B, for example, to identify any pages added after page 2 but should instead identify the new pages as 3 and 4 and then renumber all pages thereafter.

The overall appearance of work papers creates an impression of the auditor's professionalism. The papers should be clear, legible, accurately typed, and logically presented. Finally, data that later prove to be irrelevant can be omitted from the audit work papers.

IDENTIFY APPROPRIATE AUDIT INFORMATION

After organizing the audit program, a premium auditor will identify appropriate audit information. Information for a premium audit comes from many different sources, including the following:

- Physical observation
- Accounting records
- Documents other than accounting records
- Oral communication
- Ratios and comparisons

Physical Observation

The more information the auditor obtains about the operations, the greater the basis for judging whether policy classifications are correct. If the classifications are not correct, observations help determine the necessary changes. Once the auditor arrives at the policyholder's premises, many sources of information about the type of work performed are available. A count of autos in the employee parking area might yield the approximate number of persons

on the payroll. Sales brochures, product advertisements, or annual reports may be displayed in the lobby or reception room. The auditor should ask for copies of those publications and append them to the audit report or place them in the underwriting file. Even when the accounting office is located away from the manufacturing operations, such observations can reveal much about the physical operations. For example, a variety of sample products might be on display in the lobby, or pictures on the wall might depict factory operations or retail activities.

Nothing can compare to a tour of the plant to observe operations and count employees. The auditor can also observe other significant activities or hazards that should be reported or that might require loss control inspections. Sometimes the controller or accountant will offer to show the auditor around. If no tour is offered, the auditor may have other opportunities to observe operations, for example, when passing through the shop to get a cup of coffee or to reach a restroom.

Auditors should not limit observations to what they see. For example, a firm that had been baking crackers for many years was classified as a baker. While working in the office, the auditor noticed the lack of the usual bakery aromas and consequently learned that the firm had begun buying baked crackers and was now just packaging and distributing them. In another example, a company was supposed to be doing only light assembly work, but the auditor could hear heavy forging hammers.

If an insured tells the auditor that ten people belong in the clerical classification, a glance around the office provides verification. If the auditor sees only three people and if the size of the office accommodates only three desks, the auditor should investigate. If the number of clerical employees is not too large, the auditor can make a list of names and note what each person is doing. Similarly, each delivery truck should have approximately one driver, and each company car should have one salesperson.

The officers are usually the most difficult to classify because they may be involved in many tasks. A classic case cited to audit trainees involves an officer who appeared wearing dirty work clothing but who told the auditor that his duties were strictly clerical. A firm's officers' duties might have changed because of a change in the business or because of an increase or decrease in sales. A rapidly growing business might require an officer to move from the plant to the office. In a business with decreasing sales, an officer might spend most of the day in the plant rather than in the office. Termination of one of the officers usually means a reassignment of duties among other officers.

Accounting Records

Auditors rely heavily on accounting records, so it is important to select the right ones. A simple comparison of the company name on the accounting records with the name of the company being audited is a good precaution. Errors are possible if a corporation has several entities and only one is to be audited. An

auditor reviewing the insured's records at the office of a public accounting firm should make sure that the correct company's records are presented.

Whenever the policy year being audited involves two fiscal years, the auditor should look closely at the period the records cover. If the two fiscal years require using two general ledgers, they must correspond to the time period being audited. It is easy to mix quarterly tax reports, especially if the policyholder does not clearly write the time period on each one. An auditor can waste substantial time trying to balance incorrect totals that can never balance because the insured has provided the wrong year's records.

With the multitude of diverse records available, auditors understandably tend to concentrate on certain standard sources. Because each organization must file various government payroll reports, all auditors at times use tax forms such as the federal Form W-2, state and federal unemployment reports, and state and federal tax reports. But each report has its exceptions and potential pitfalls for an auditor. Some W-2s do not include bonuses covered separately by a Form 1099. School districts usually do not report tax-sheltered annuities as salaries. Some states do not require restaurants to report tips as wages. In other states, farm labor might not be subject to state unemployment tax requirements. Additional inconsistencies include the federal requirement that some company-provided cars be included as employee income and the lack of a federal requirement that employers report wages of household employees earning less than $50 per quarter.

The federal tax reports (Form 941) are a common source of information. However, auditors may need to adjust the data they provide, noting the many deductions that are now exempt from income tax or are tax deferred or the payments that are not wages but are subject to tax. Making these adjustments can be time-consuming.

Just as the nature of the accounting records varies by organization, so does the terminology. To be understood by the insured's personnel, the auditor should use the same terms for accounting records that the organization uses. If they call a cash disbursements and receipts journal a general ledger, then the auditor should also. The auditor should note any significant variations in terminology in the audit report.

To avoid misunderstandings, the auditor should explain the insurance definition of payroll because insureds might have their own interpretations. Some insureds might record some payments as bonuses or commissions when the insurance policy considers them to be payroll.

Although not actually accounting records, some informal records can also be helpful to the auditor. Distributing holiday pay, vacation pay, overtime, or bonuses among several classifications is difficult. However, the controller or accounting manager might be able to produce several pages of detailed calculations showing an actual distribution. Although the insured usually intends those informal records only for internal expense allocations, an auditor can often save time by asking whether the insured has such records.

Documents Other Than Accounting Records

Documents are usually divided into two groups—internal and external. For purposes of the audit, internal documents are those within the organization being audited, and external documents are those the insured sends to someone outside the firm and that are subject to an independent confirmation. The minutes of the board of directors' meeting are one type of internal document. In those minutes, the auditor would find a list of the names and titles of the corporate officers.

The annual report of a corporation whose stock is publicly traded, an external document, is usually free and can provide useful information. The report normally contains such information as the type of products manufactured, a list of divisions or subsidiaries, the location of major plants, the names of corporate officers, and the total number of employees. It also contains audited financial statements comparing the current and previous years.

When a family-owned business is incorporated during the policy year, the auditor must know the exact incorporation date to determine when to include the officers' payroll. If the insured has not divided payroll records to show the incorporation date, the articles of incorporation in some states may provide it.

When the insurance policy provides contractual liability coverage, the date on the contract will usually state when the loss exposure began. For the purchase of a subsidiary, the contract date can resolve any confusion over the effective date.

Other types of documents the auditor can use include the following:

- Other insurance policies
- Insurance records
- Automobile titles
- Specific contracts

Oral Communication

For parts of every audit, oral communication is the only practical source of needed information. When obtaining information by that method, the auditor must have confidence in that person's credibility and should explain the purpose of the questions.

The auditor should remember that most people have a limited knowledge of insurance. The average accounting department allocates its expenses using categories for office, shop, supervisors, and administration, an allocation different from that needed for insurance purposes. Therefore, auditors must clearly communicate their needs. Because the insurance policy usually provides only brief descriptions of classifications, explaining the meaning of various classifications can help considerably. To avoid using confusing explanations, the auditor can use the workers' compensation *Basic Manual*, the *Scopes Manual*, or the PAAS *Classification Guides* to clarify different

classifications. For example, because insureds often misunderstand the clerical category, the auditor can be more precise by quoting the Standard Exceptions portion of the *Basic Manual*.

Occasionally, the accounting manager or controller might not know the duties of certain employees. Sometimes the auditor can ask the specific employee, either in person or by phone, to describe his or her duties. That direct information is reliable because it is not being channeled through another person. The next best alternative is to ask the department supervisor what a particular employee does.

Particularly in small businesses, a casual remark to the auditor might reveal a change of entity or ownership. Auditors should always record those changes. Many businesses overlook notifying an insurer because they do not realize the effect of those changes on coverages and premiums.

One inherent danger of gathering information orally is that no tangible record of what was said exists. A conversation might be recorded only in the memories of the people involved, and people may be unable to recall parts of conversations. When an invoice arrives indicating an increased premium, the insured may not recall the details of the conversation that led to that increase.

Whenever oral information might result in a large additional premium, the auditor should carefully repeat what the other party said to make sure both parties understand the conversation and to reinforce both of their memories. The auditor should also make notes or write a memo as soon as possible while the facts are fresh. Another technique is to include more people in the conversation. Having several people participate increases the odds that the information will be correct. When reviewing the audit with the insured before leaving, the auditor can summarize any oral statements from other employees.

Ratios and Comparisons

A complete audit program includes the use of ratios and other comparative data to verify and analyze the information gathered. The amount of analysis and verification that is necessary is unique to each audit, and the auditor must determine this amount on a case-by-case basis.

Some simple ratios and comparisons that are useful in audits include the following:

- Audit results to insurance policy estimates
- Audit results to previous audits (including many of the ratios that follow)
- Ratio of gross wages to sales
- Ratios of various payrolls classes to each other (for example, clerical payroll to manufacturing payroll)
- Overtime versus gross wages
- Ratio of clerical to other employees
- Trends

VERIFY AUDIT INFORMATION

Another procedure in an audit program, to verify information, can occur along with any of the other procedures throughout the audit process. **Verification** is a comparison of alternative sources of information to confirm data's accuracy. Every audit program must verify the quality and accuracy of the information. Although one of the goals of an audit is to obtain all the audited loss exposure information in the least amount of time, auditors should try to use information sources that can also be used as cross-checks. When an auditor cannot balance the data between two independent sources and a material difference exists, a third source might be necessary to determine accuracy. If the auditor still cannot balance the data from three sources, the alternatives include seeking a fourth source or billing at the highest total.

Verification
A comparison of alternative sources of information to confirm data's accuracy.

Time is a major constraint in finding the cause of a discrepancy. In any audit, the auditor must determine at what point the variations no longer justify more time. Even though differences relating to individual items can be small, the auditor should consider their cumulative effect on the totals. A small variation on a small premium does not justify much time. However, as the difference or the size of the premium increases, so does the amount of time necessary to verify information.

Because the policyholder's records could be wrong, the auditor should notify the accounting manager whenever the auditor might require additional time to resolve a discrepancy. Sometimes the amount of the difference triggers an immediate explanation.

Independent Auditing Standards

The generally accepted auditing standards developed by the American Institute of Certified Public Accountants (AICPA) provide a useful guideline in forming a judgment on time expenditures. The third Standard of Field Work states: "Sufficient competent evidential matter is to be obtained through inspection, observation, inquiries, and confirmations to afford a reasonable basis for an opinion regarding the financial statements under examination."[1] The third General Standard states: "Due professional care is to be exercised in the performance of the examination and the preparation of the report."[2] Although those standards apply to an independent auditor's opinion on a firm's financial statements, premium auditors can apply the principle to premium audits.

The concepts of sufficient evidential matter and due professional care are relevant to premium auditing, especially when measuring the quality of a premium audit and the competence of the premium auditor who performed it. If an insurer evaluates an auditor's job performance on those bases, then the amount of detail needed directly relates to the level of assurance or accuracy that the insurer expects the auditor to have. Although absolute confidence in evidence is not practical, the degree of confidence required is a matter that auditing management must determine and then communicate to its auditors.

In exercising due professional care, the auditor must keep an open mind until the facts are presented. That sometimes requires asking the same questions asked previously, even if the auditor is 99 percent sure of the answers.

Relative Size of the Discrepancy (Materiality)

Materiality
In accounting, the importance of a variation in affecting the total.

Materiality is a common term in public accounting. **Materiality** is the importance of a variation in affecting the total.

To determine their degree of confidence in the information, auditors consider the connection between the amount of information and the size of the discrepancy in information. Is the discrepancy large enough to make resolving it worthwhile? In that regard, there are no right or wrong answers. However, the relative size of the discrepancy, the size of the organization, and the degree of internal control provide some general guidelines about whether further investigation is warranted.

As a percentage of payroll, the discrepancy's relative size decreases as the size of the payroll increases. A 5 percent variation on a $1,000 payroll, or $50, is not material, but a 5 percent variation on a $10,000,000 payroll, or $500,000, is. Given the controls that should exist over payroll, the dollar amount of variation must be reasonable. Obviously, the inability to locate a $500,000 portion of the payroll is a significant problem.

The amount of premium involved is the most important criterion for judging how much time to spend collecting information. Other than the amount of payroll, the insurance rate is a major determinant of the premium involved. Although a variation entirely in clerical payroll would mean a nominal premium variation, a difference in payroll involving steel erection would be material. Similarly, a $5,000 difference in payroll might mean a difference of $500 in workers' compensation premium, whereas a $5,000 difference in gross sales might mean a difference of only a few dollars in general liability premium.

Accuracy of Information

Examining actual records or directly communicating with the employees involved results in the highest level of confidence about information accuracy. Information gained through direct personal knowledge has a higher level of credibility than information gained indirectly. There is no substitute for examining journals and ledgers and being able to trace them to the original source documents.

If the insured maintains internal control at a consistently high level, then the accounting records should be complete and accurate. In large organizations, the existence and proficiency of an internal audit staff are directly related to the level of internal control. An annual independent audit also indicates good internal control.

However, manually maintained accounting information systems can also be efficient, particularly for small or medium-sized firms. Because of the uniqueness of

handwriting, the insured can refer an auditor to the specific person who posted the account. Talking to the person who made the entry is the simplest and fastest way to answer a question. In addition, those people usually remember the reasons why they handled a transaction in any unusual manner.

Insufficient records should raise justifiable suspicions, prompting an auditor to consider spending more time than normal on verification. Also raising suspicions are records with numerous corrections, records entered in pencil, columns that show incorrect totals, and records with missing information. The auditor cannot apply the normal auditing standards to organizations with those types of records and should make every effort to obtain accurate information.

Amount of Detail

The information shown on the audit work papers should be an exact recording of the information on the insured's records. The insured should be able to take the audit work papers and trace each figure back to the record shown. Including sufficient detail permits both the auditor and the policyholder to understand an audit from the work papers. Ideally, if the original auditor is not available, the work papers should have enough detail to answer any other auditor's questions. Occasionally, a question arises about a previous audit. By that time, the auditor may have little memory of the audit other than what was written. A reference to a "Journal Entry" would not mean much to an insured or to the auditor unless the work papers also show that it was, for example, Journal Entry #8 dated 7-31-X6. If the journal entry was actually the sum of three journal entries and only the total is shown on the work papers, reconstructing what the auditor did would become even more difficult.

Sufficiently detailed work papers are helpful when audits undergo judicial scrutiny, even though this happens infrequently. Well-documented work papers should therefore contain adequate detail to justify the collection of premium. Because the auditor cannot know in advance which audits might be the subject of legal action, all work papers for every audit should be prepared as if they might eventually become a court exhibit.

REVIEW THE GENERAL LEDGER

Another procedure in an audit program, reviewing the general ledger, is often where the audit itself begins. Insureds sometimes misuse the term "general ledger" to mean a combined cash receipts and disbursements journal. Occasionally, auditors need to explain to insureds that a general ledger is the record containing all the categories of assets, liabilities, owners' equity, income, and expense accounts and into which all subsidiary ledgers, journals, and registers ultimately flow.

Also, the titles of individual accounts can be misleading. An auditor should ask what the insured has included in each account category even though the insured might think the answer is obvious. Occasionally, the ledger accounts for payroll correspond exactly to insurance definitions. More often, the auditor

must analyze and transfer into several classifications such accounts as "executive salaries" or "administrative salaries."

A policyholder may question the auditor's need for the general ledger and may be reluctant to release it. That concern usually stems from the desire to keep the organization's profitability confidential. Rather than insisting on the right to review the ledger as a policy condition, the auditor should consider whether records available other than the ledger are adequate to follow good audit procedures.

General Ledger Configurations

Generally, insureds enter payroll accounts on a "gross" basis, that is the amounts posted reflect wages before the insured has made any deductions. But some organizations consider payroll to be the "net" amount, which is the actual cash the firm paid to the employees after deductions. Adding back federal withholding taxes, state withholding taxes, and the employee's portion of Social Security taxes to arrive at gross wages is time-consuming. Instead of adjusting records posted on a net basis, auditors should seek a different source. However, the auditor can still use payroll accounts to trace the postings from the ledger back to the source showing the development of both net and gross wages.

Sometimes an insured includes the employer's portion of Social Security taxes, state unemployment taxes, and hospitalization insurance costs in the gross wages and posts these total expenses to the payroll accounts. Because of the amount of detailed analysis involved in arriving at actual gross wages, auditors should consider such general ledgers as impractical for premium auditing.

Some manufacturing firms use a standard cost accounting system, so using such general ledgers might also be impractical. Unless actual costs are readily available, adjusting standard costs for variances or for under- or over-absorbed overhead is complicated. Contractors might use a "work in progress" account, which contains labor expenses, overhead, materials, subcontract costs, and other items. Adjusting that account to reflect labor can also take considerable time.

Source of Discovering Premium

The general ledger can be a convenient source for locating additional loss exposures that might be scattered throughout other records. In reviewing expense account titles, the auditor should investigate such terms as "casual labor," "outside labor," "day labor," or "extra help" for workers' compensation loss exposures not found in the regular payroll records. An asset account titled "aircraft" should trigger a question about the pilot's payroll and the aircraft seat surcharge. Likewise, an asset account for "trucks" should trigger a review of drivers' payrolls. If the insured has removed any of those accounts from the ledger, the account for accumulated depreciation for each asset should be an additional alert to the auditor to investigate further.

The account "rental income" should immediately raise the question, "What is being rented?" If a building or contractor's equipment is being rented,

then a premises/operations loss exposure exists. The account "subcontractors" leads an auditor to find an independent contractor's loss exposure and possibly workers' compensation and premises/operations loss exposures for uninsured subcontractors. Although this list of different accounts is not exhaustive, it should indicate the variety of ledger accounts that indicates insurance loss exposures.

Skimming the chart of accounts to determine which accounts to examine more closely makes reviewing the general ledger faster. If the ledger is bulky or is needed by someone else, using the chart of accounts as a screening device saves time.

Reading the Accounts

When using the payroll accounts, the auditor should scan the ledger folio column for consistent debit postings. The simplest system involves monthly debit postings from the same source, such as payroll register (see Exhibit 7-1). The next simplest system posts beginning and ending accruals in addition to the twelve monthly entries (see Exhibit 7-2). When the insured posts accruals monthly, the auditor can scan the next month's credit entries and follow the pattern of the same amounts neutralizing themselves regularly (see Exhibit 7-3). However, when the insured makes separate credit entries, the auditor should trace the entry backward to determine the account to which the insured transferred this expense (see Exhibit 7-4).

EXHIBIT 7-1

Payroll Register—Monthly Postings

Account 400

Direct Labor

Date	Description	Folio	Debit	Credit	Balance
20X6					
1-31	January Payroll	PR-4	7,249.52		7,249.52
2-28	February Payroll	PR-8	7,621.41		14,870.93
3-31	March Payroll	PR-13	9,499.21		24,370.14
4-30	April Payroll	PR-17	6,837.82		31,207.96
5-31	May Payroll	PR-21	7,106.85		38,314.81
6-30	June Payroll	PR-26	8,920.70		47,235.51
7-31	July Payroll	PR-30	7,619.90		54,855.41
8-31	August Payroll	PR-34	7,900.24		62,755.65
9-30	September Payroll	PR-39	10,021.50		72,777.15
10-31	October Payroll	PR-43	7,714.20		80,491.35
11-30	November Payroll	PR-47	8,004.73		88,496.08
12-31	December Payroll	PR-52	9,814.26		98,310.34

Credit entries to payroll accounts can indicate that payroll is being charged to nonpayroll accounts such as inventory or that it is being capitalized into machinery asset accounts. Whenever a general ledger payroll total is less than the total from another source, scanning the accounts for credits might reveal that payroll is being transferred to nonpayroll accounts. A transfer of payroll between two plant accounts, such as from indirect labor to inspection, does not affect the insurance premium because the auditor assigns both accounts to the manufacturing classification.

EXHIBIT 7-2

Payroll Register—Monthly Posting Plus Annual Accruals

Account 400

Direct Labor

Date	Description	Folio	Debit	Credit	Balance
20X6					
1-1	Reverse 12-31-X5 ACCRUAL	JE-1		1,812.38	
1-31	January Payroll	PR-4	7,249.52		5,437.14
2-28	February Payroll	PR-8	7,621.41		13,058.55
3-31	March Payroll	PR-13	9,499.21		22,557.76
4-30	April Payroll	PR-17	6,837.82		29,395.58
5-31	May Payroll	PR-21	7,106.85		36,502.43
6-30	June Payroll	PR-26	8,920.70		45,423.13
7-31	July Payroll	PR-30	7,619.90		53,043.03
8-31	August Payroll	PR-34	7,900.24		60,943.27
9-30	September Payroll	PR-39	10,021.50		70,964.77
10-31	October Payroll	PR-43	7,714.20		78,678.97
11-30	November Payroll	PR-47	8,004.73		86,683.70
12-31	December Payroll	PR-52	9,814.26		96,497.96
12-31	ACCRUED Payroll to 12-31-X6	JE-26	2,944.28		99,442.24

Policy Year Is the Same as the Fiscal Year

If the policy year is the same as the insured's fiscal year, the auditor can use the payroll ledger account balances directly. The auditor should carefully label work sheets showing the fiscal year totals and the fiscal year dates. When the audit is on an earned basis and the accounts have been posted for accruals, adjusting the account balances is unnecessary. However, if ledger totals must be verified against a source on a paid basis, then the auditor must adjust the paid source to an earned basis. That adjustment involves subtracting the beginning entry in the accrued payroll account and adding the ending entry to the total paid wages.

If the audit is on a paid basis, the auditor must adjust the ledger payroll accounts. The auditor can accomplish that task by adding back the beginning accrual in each account and subtracting the ending accrual. Scanning the postings should reveal the system used because insureds usually post accruals from a journal source. The beginning accrual is commonly the first posting in each account as a credit entry. Accordingly, the ending accrual is most often the last entry in the debit column.

EXHIBIT 7-3

Payroll Register—Monthly Posting Plus Monthly Accruals

Account 400

Direct Labor

Date	Description	Folio	Debit	Credit	Balance
20X6					
1-1	Reverse 12-31-X5 ACCRUAL	JE-1		1,812.38	
1-31	January Payroll	PR-4	7,249.52		
1-31	ACCRUED Payroll to 1-31-X6	JE-2	1,143.21		6,580.35
2-28	Reverse 1-31-X6 ACCRUAL	JE-3		1,143.21	
2-28	February Payroll	PR-8	7,621.41		
2-28	ACCRUED Payroll to 2-28-X6	JE-4	1,139.91		14,198.46
3-31	Reverse 2-28-X6 ACCRUAL	JE-5		1,139.91	
3-31	March Payroll	PR-13	9,499.21		
3-31	ACCRUED Payroll to 4-30-X6	JE-6	1,709.46		24,267.22
4-30	Reverse 3-31-X6 ACCRUAL	JE-7		1,709.46	
4-30	April Payroll	PR-17	6,837.82		
4-30	ACCRUED Payroll to 4-30-X6	JE-8	2,132.06		31,527.64
12-31	Reverse 11-30-X6 ACCRUAL	JE-25		2,453.57	
12-31	December Payroll	PR-52	9,814.26		
12-31	ACCRUED Payroll to 12-31-X6	JE-26	2,944.28		99,442.24

Policy Year Is Different From the Fiscal Year

If a policy year differs from a fiscal year, then the auditor must use two fiscal years to complete the audit. In that case, placing the same accounts for both fiscal years side-by-side allows the auditor to see the activity throughout the audit period. The auditor then can trace the old year's ending accrual to the new year's beginning accrual. Because those accruals offset each other, the auditor is concerned only with the accruals affecting the accounts' beginning

and ending balances. The beginning accrual on the old ledger has reduced the account balance for the first month, but the other months' figures reflect the actual amount paid. Subtracting one balance from the other eliminates the beginning accrual's effect, leaving the remainder on a paid basis.

For audits on a paid basis and for accruals posted only annually, the auditor can use the payroll ledger balances. No adjustments are needed to verify those totals against a source on a paid basis.

EXHIBIT 7-4

Payroll Register—Monthly Posting Plus Separate Credit Entries

Account 400

Direct Labor

Date	Description	Folio	Debit	Credit	Balance
20X6					
1-31	January Payroll	PR-4	7,249.52		7,249.52
2-28	February Payroll	PR-8	7,621.41		14,870.93
3-31	March Payroll	PR-13	9,499.21		24,370.14
4-30	April Payroll	PR-17	6,837.82		
4-30	Transfer—Machinery A/C 170	JE-9		2,500.00	28,707.96
5-31	May Payroll	PR-21	7,106.85		35,814.81
6-30	June Payroll	PR-26	8,920.70		44,735.51
7-31	July Payroll	PR-30	7,619.90		
7-31	Transfer—Inspection A/C 470	JE-16		831.22	51,524.19
8-31	August Payroll	PR-34	7,900.24		59,424.43
9-30	September Payroll	PR-39	10,021.50		69,445.93
10-31	October Payroll	PR-43	7,714.20		77,160.13
11-30	November Payroll	PR-47	8,004.73		85,164.86
12-31	December Payroll	PR-52	9,814.26		
12-31	Transfer—Inventory A/C 150	JE-27		1,017.79	93,961.33

When insureds post accruals annually, an audit on an earned basis requires a manual calculation of the accruals to the policy date. In that case, the auditor should work backward to the posting source to obtain the information necessary. The auditor should use the actual payroll as much as possible so that any adjustment involves the minimum amount of payroll. For example, assume that an auditor needs to add sixteen days' payroll. The auditor can use the amounts for the two complete weeks involved from the weekly payroll journal. Assuming a five-day workweek, and that the two remaining days are workdays, the auditor should then add two-fifths of another week's payroll.

That method records actual payroll for two weeks and an adjustment involving only two days. So, it is a more accurate method than using 12/20 of a four-week payroll or 16/30 of a month's payroll. In verifying against a source on a paid basis, however, the auditor must use ledger account balances before making those manual adjustments for accruals.

Many insurers avoid the need for such adjustments by using only full weekly payrolls as a basis of premium. These insurers treat payrolls for the fifty-two weeks falling closest to the policy year as the annual payroll. For example, if the policy term runs from 1 July 20X6 to 1 July 20X7, and the insured's pay periods end on Fridays, the auditor might record fifty-two consecutive weekly totals starting with the pay period ending on Friday, 5 July 20X6 and continuing through the period ending on Friday, 27 June 20X7. The next year's audit, even if the insurer has changed, would then include weekly totals from the period ending Friday, 4 July 20X7 through the period ending 26 June 20X8. Auditors can also apply the same procedure to policies canceled before expiration. That procedure eliminates the need for a percentage allocation of loss exposure, which can be subject to controversy.

The examples in Exhibits 7-1, 7-2, 7-3, and 7-4 demonstrate the most commonly required adjustments of payroll accounts for premium purposes.

An auditor working on a paid basis should have no difficulty with payroll adjustment. In Exhibits 7-1 through 7-4, the account title "Direct Labor" clearly indicates a payroll account: all postings are identified as payroll; the posting reference is consistently the payroll register; and there are no credit entries. The auditor can record the exact balance directly without any adjustments.

Exhibit 7-2 differs from Exhibit 7-1 because it includes beginning and ending accruals that adjust payroll to an earned basis. The one credit entry, the first entry in the account, is identified as an accrual. Its posting reference is the following journal entry:

1-1-X6		**Journal Entry No. 1**		
	222	Accrued Payroll	$1,812.38	
	400	Direct Labor		$1,812.38
		(To reverse 12-31-X5 accrual)		

The final entry, a debit, is also an accrual with a journal entry as the source:

12-31-X6		**Journal Entry No. 26**		
	400	Direct Labor	$2,944.28	
	400	Accrued Payroll		$2,944.28
		(To accrue December payroll)		

Adjusting that account to a paid basis is simply a matter of adding the final balance and the beginning accrual and then subtracting the ending accrual from that total.

Final accrued balance	$ 99,442.24
Add: Beginning accrual	1,812.38
	$101,254.62
Less: Ending accrual	2,944.28
Final paid balance 20X6	$ 98,310.34

The account in Exhibit 7-3 appears to have much more activity because of the posting of monthly accruals. However, the accruals are clearly identified, and the posting reference is a journal entry in every case. The journal entry for the January accrual, for example, is as follows:

1-31-X6		Journal Entry No. 2		
	400	Direct Labor	$1,143.21	
	400	Accrued Payroll		$1,143.21
		(To accrue January payroll)		

Scanning the debits and credits in the account reveals a consistent neutralizing effect. Converting that account to a paid basis involves exactly the same procedure as in Exhibit 7-2.

If the audit is on a paid basis as of a date different from the end of the fiscal year, the auditor needs only to adjust the accruals on the audited period. If the policy expires on 28 February 20X6, then the adjustment is as follows:

Accrued balance 2-28-X6	$ 14,198.46	
Less: 2-28-X6	(1,139.91)	
		$13,058.55
Final balance 12-31-X5	$ 93,821.63	
Less: balance 2-28-X5	(12,707.37)	
	81,114.26	
Add: 2-28-X5 accrual	968.17	
		$82,082.43
Total payroll 3-1-X5 to 2-28-X6		$95,140.98

The 1-1-X6 accrual credit would offset a 12-31-X5 debit, and all other monthly accruals would offset themselves.

Exhibit 7-4 is different because no accruals are posted to this account, but three credit entries have been made. The corresponding journal entries are as follows:

4-30-X6		**Journal Entry No. 9**		
	170	Machinery	$2,500.00	
	400	Direct Labor		$2,500.00
		(To transfer machinery rebuilding labor)		
7-31-X6		**Journal Entry No. 16**		
	470	Inspection Labor	$ 831.22	
	400	Direct Labor		$ 831.22
		(To transfer labor of new inspector)		
12-31-X6		**Journal Entry No. 27**		
	150	Inventory—Finished Goods	$1,017.79	
	400	Direct Labor		$1,017.79
		(To transfer inventory expense)		

To determine the total payroll, the credit entries to Account 170 "Machinery" and Account 150 "Inventory—Finished Goods" must be added to the direct labor account. The transfer to Account 470 "Inspection Labor" needs no adjustment because Inspection Labor is a payroll account falling under the same classification as Direct Labor. Thus, the adjustment is as follows:

Final balance shown in Direct Labor Account 400	$93,961.33
Add:	
Payroll expense transferred to Machinery Account 170	2,500.00
Payroll expense transferred to Inventory Account 150	1,017.79
Adjusted final balance for Direct Labor Account 400	$97,479.12

Note: Additional payroll expense shown in Inspection Labor Account # 470.

These accounts are simplified, and many policyholders do not use such easy systems. Auditors must identify all payroll accounts, but insureds might not always label them with such terms as "labor," "wages," and "salaries." Examining the posting source will show the distribution of the total and can help the auditor find all the payroll accounts.

In practice, many organizations do not describe the postings, and they sometimes post out of chronological sequence or make errors and corrections. Because organizations also commonly add or combine accounts during the year, looking at the January posting source does not reveal accounts created in July. Of course, transfers to new payroll accounts do not require adjustments unless the new accounts involve different classifications. Auditors must carefully examine the accounting records at the beginning of the audit so that they thoroughly understand those records before recording data.

CREATE THE AUDIT TRAIL

Audit trail
The documentation of the flow of information from the original source to the general ledger; is used to validate or invalidate accounting entries.

An important procedure in an audit program is to create the audit trail. The **audit trail** documents the flow of information from the original source to the general ledger and is used to validate or invalidate accounting entries. It spans all accounting records, beginning with the source documents and records that serve as the physical evidence for each transaction. The audit trail allows the auditor to trace entries from the original source documents to the intermediate summarization and recording in journals. Classifying and recording information from journals into ledger accounts end the recording sequence. Corporate management, stockholders, and government authorities depend on the financial statements and reports that are based on that information. Those reports must be traceable to the ledger accounts. From a premium audit viewpoint, however, the audit trail begins with the original source documents and ends with the general ledger (see Exhibit 7-5).

The normal accounting process records, summarizes, and classifies many individual transactions. Payroll processing uses hourly time records to prepare payroll checks, and the insured usually summarizes the paychecks in a payroll journal. The insured then classifies and records that summarized information in various ledger accounts. The audit trail for sales transactions starts with sales orders as the original source, which are recorded and summarized in sales journals and subsequently classified and posted in various ledger accounts.

Once information enters the accounting system, it is usually accurate. An effective independent verification of original source documents comes from employees reviewing their paychecks and from customers reviewing their sales invoices. However, this verification is one-sided. Employees are more likely to point out paycheck errors that are for less than the agreed-on amount than they are to point out incorrectly issued paychecks for a higher amount.

Within the accounting system, balancing journal columns usually detects and eliminates most errors. Using control accounts and cross-checking gives the ledger accounts a high level of accuracy, which the auditor can verify by a trial balance.

EXHIBIT 7-5

The Direction of the Audit Trail

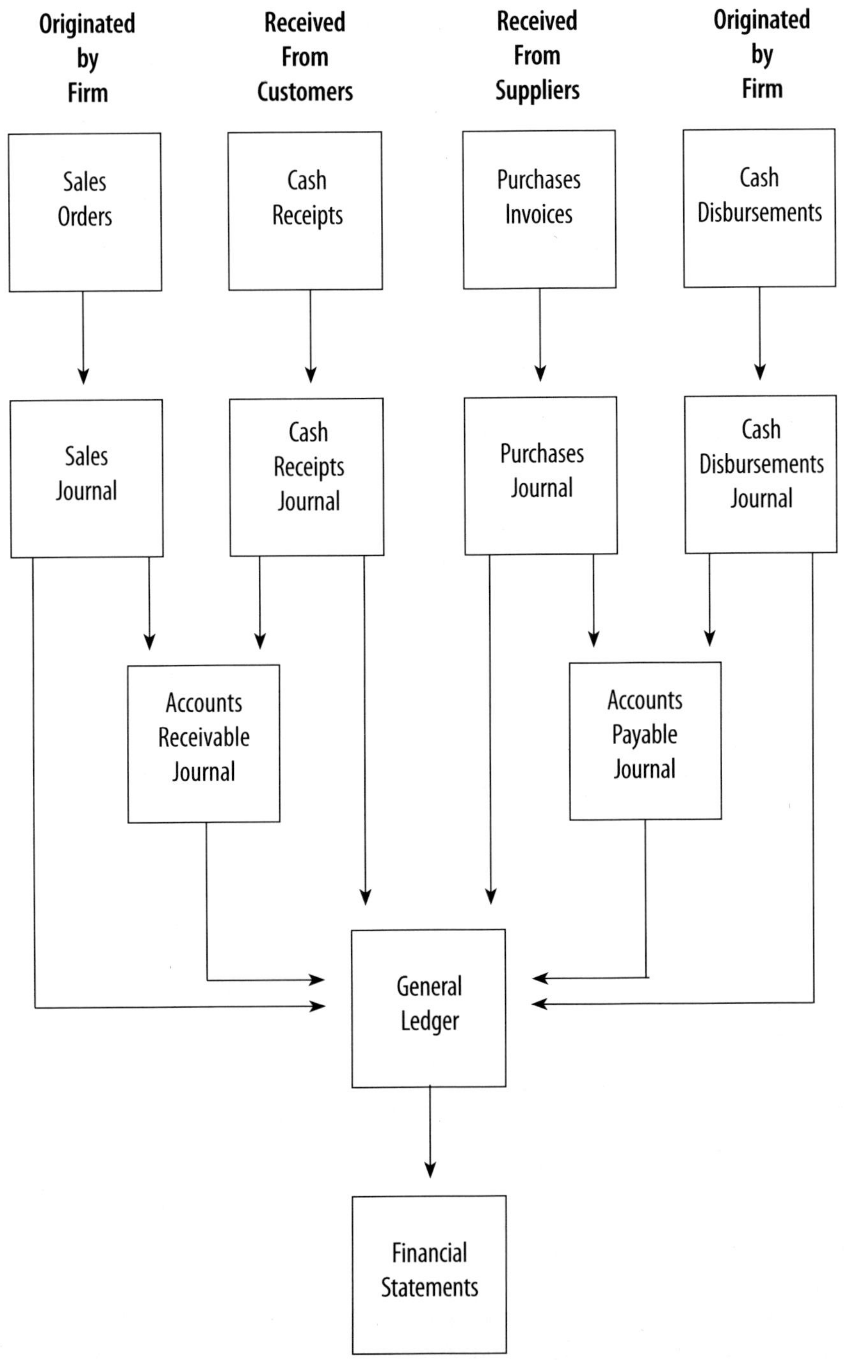

Although the insured regards the audit trail to be one-way, from source to general ledger, an auditor can also use it to trace from the general ledger to the source. Whenever a question or a problem arises, an auditor can look in either direction to seek an answer.

The order and chronological sequence of accounting entries can also provide important clues for unusual events. Reviewing the historical recording of entries reveals the annual fluctuations in business activity. Any exceptions to that normal seasonal rhythm should be a reason for further investigation.

REVIEW THE PAYROLL CYCLE

Payroll cycle
An entity's functions for recording, processing, and reporting employee payrolls and payroll taxes.

Another procedure of an audit program is to review the payroll cycle. The **payroll cycle** encompasses all functions related to recording and processing employee payrolls and payroll taxes, including the following:

- Human resources and employment
- Timekeeping and payroll administration
- Payment of payroll
- Preparation of payroll tax returns and payment of taxes
- Payroll for non-regular employees
- Payroll records and reports
- Record balances

Human Resources and Employment

The human resources department generally controls both the beginning and ending of employment, although an immediate supervisor might make the final decision. For a new employee, the time, place, duties, and rate of pay are established at the time of hire. In large organizations, hiring procedures become standardized, and auditors rarely need to question whether most people are considered employees.

However, certain types of employment are different. Workers' compensation laws can cover many workers whom the policyholder does not usually consider regular employees. Although the IRS does not require employers to deduct income taxes from their pay, workers, like casual laborers, can still be considered regular employees under workers' compensation laws. An auditor must determine whether the law might consider certain people employees if a workers' compensation claim occurs.

For large organizations operating in a wide area, the human resources department can be the best source of classification information for the auditor. By using standard job descriptions and titles, the auditor can satisfactorily classify employees at remote locations.

Timekeeping and Payroll Administration

Although auditors do not often become involved in the mechanics of preparing payrolls, they should know how the system operates. If an employer uses a time clock, the timekeeper or supervisor should approve the hours of each employee. When an employer does not use a time clock, a supervisor usually makes sure each employee starts and ends the day on time. Once approved, the time information goes to the payroll department, which uses the hourly rate to calculate gross wages and various deductions. The payroll department also prepares quarterly tax reports and the annual W-2 forms. The treasurer's office signs the checks, and the payroll department reports the total expenses to the accounting department. Someone not otherwise involved in payroll preparation usually distributes the checks to individual employees.

Normally, hourly employees receive their paychecks several days to a week after the end of the workweek. That delay permits the payroll department to calculate the gross and net wages and to prepare the paychecks.

The auditor must sometimes calculate employee advances, which are a partial prepayment of wages, in addition to the regular payroll. If a check is incorrect or lost, the employer usually voids it or stops payment and issues a new check. As long as the employer makes those adjustments within the next pay period, the auditor can usually ignore them. When the employer treats the adjustments individually, however, each becomes easy to overlook and frustrating to find. Because the individual amounts are generally small, the total gross wages will be very close to balancing.

Federal quarterly payroll tax returns are due by the last day of the next month after the end of the quarter. So the returns for the first quarter ending March 31 are due by April 30, the returns for the second quarter ending June 30 are due by July 31, and third and fourth quarters by October 31 and January 31.[3]

Most state income tax and unemployment taxes use the same due dates as the federal government. Employers must furnish the federal W-2 forms to the employee by January 31 or within thirty days after employment ends. Knowing when the insured must prepare those forms help the auditor to schedule appointments.

Payroll for Non-Regular Employees

An employer-employee relationship can include a variety of individuals not on the regular payroll. Part of the auditor's task is to determine the earnings of any such individuals. For workers' compensation loss exposures, the auditor should include payments for people who have the right to claim benefits even though they are not on the regular payroll. Those workers typically are casual labor, independent contractors, and hired truckers.

Casual Labor

Occasionally, an organization might need to hire workers as casual labor to perform temporary odd jobs. Casual labor is generally irregular, unpredictable, sporadic, and brief. Payments for casual labor are usually small amounts made to a variety of people. If all payments in a particular ledger account are not included in the premium base, then the cash disbursements journal, the petty cash book, 1099s, the general ledger, or the check register usually provides the best means for analyzing this loss exposure. Some of those sources list individual names, making reviewing specific payments easier.

As long as the work is performed in the regular course of business and is not casual, it constitutes covered employment in most states. The auditor should include 100 percent of payments to such workers as payroll for premium purposes. Because some states have individual interpretations, the auditor must know the specific law of the state(s) involved. To be excluded from coverage and not included for premium determination purposes, the payments must be irregular, unpredictable, sporadic, and brief. The work cannot be a part of the employer's regular business. If only one of those conditions exists, then the auditor must determine the specific rules for that state.

Occasionally, insureds make cash payments for casual labor that they do not record on their books. The auditor can discover that loss exposure only by discussing it with the insured. Although this method might lead to inaccuracies, such discussions may be the only way to obtain that information.

Independent Contractors

The term "independent contractor" can be misleading in a premium audit. Sometimes a contractor lists payments to regular employees as subcontractors' costs when they do additional work outside their normal duties, such as cleanup work on Saturdays. An employer might separate payments to the same person into different categories depending on the type of work. Regardless of what terms insureds use, the auditor should add to the payroll base all payments to employees, excluding only reimbursements for expenses.

In auditing that loss exposure, probably the most practical way to identify individual subcontractors and the amounts paid to them is through the cash disbursements journal and purchases journal. Mistakes occur when the "Subcontractors" account also includes suppliers of materials. Often the same column includes fees paid to attorneys or architects or for building permits. The auditor must analyze each entry in this column carefully to be certain it is not remuneration to an employee under the workers' compensation laws.

Determining who actually performed work on the job site is essential to understanding the subcontractor loss exposure. Even though an organization's name appears to reveal what it does, the name might not be a reliable clue because the organization might have changed its focus of operations while preserving its original name, or the same organization might use several different names.

When the insured cannot furnish satisfactory evidence of workers' compensation and general liability coverage for subcontractors and the auditor cannot determine the exact payrolls, the auditor should add a percentage of the payments to the payroll base according to the rules of the workers' compensation *Basic Manual*. The percentage of payment to use is the following:

- No less than 33⅓ percent if the work performed by the subcontractor involved required the use of mobile equipment
- No less than 50 percent if the subcontractor furnished materials
- No less than 90 percent if the contract was for labor only

Although the *Basic Manual* does not distinguish among specific types of work, an auditor can develop the appropriate percentage to apply for different types of construction. For example, when auditing a plumbing contractor, the auditor need note only the total sales and construction wages to determine the relative wage percentage. That information, which the auditor can gather over time for various types of construction, serves as a reasonable basis in deciding the percentage of payments to add as payroll for uninsured subcontractors.

Hired Truckers

If trucks are under the insured's direction or control, the auditor must verify workers' compensation coverage. If coverage cannot be verified , then the auditor must add the actual drivers' payroll to the payroll base. When the actual payroll is not available, the *Basic Manual* states that the auditor should use one-third of the payments as payroll. However, a few states have exceptions to the one-third rule, so auditors should review the rule for each state.

As with independent contractors, the cash disbursements journal is the best source to use to identify individual truckers and payments. To simplify that part of the audit, the auditor should separate the common carriers from other carriers or methods of transporting goods. A **common carrier** is a transportation provider that offers its services to the public and that is licensed by federal or state agencies. For example, trucking companies offer their services to the public and are licensed by federal or state agencies. They normally pick up goods at the insured's shipping dock and deliver them at their convenience. For distant shipments, the goods might be transferred between one or more common carriers. Verifying workers' compensation coverage is unnecessary because the insured has no control over that loss exposure.

Common carrier
A transportation provider that offers its services to the public and that is licensed by federal or state agencies.

The best way to verify common carrier status is to review the source documents. Interstate Commerce Commission regulations require common carriers to give bills of lading. A **bill of lading** is a contract between a shipper and a carrier for transporting goods and a receipt for those goods. The bills of lading prove that the shipper is paying for the goods' transportation, not for hiring the vehicles.

Bill of lading
A contract between a shipper and a carrier for transporting goods and a receipt for those goods.

Hired vehicles are evidenced by invoices showing that the trucks were furnished, usually with a charge by the day, week, hour, or mile. No bill of lading is given if the vehicles are hired.

Payroll Records and Reports

Internal Revenue Service (IRS) standards and the resulting formalization of payroll reporting have helped to develop consistent accounting procedures throughout the United States. Employers classify and report almost all wages with a very high degree of accuracy. In addition, IRS audits have facilitated access to payroll information. All those developments have benefited premium auditors.

The standardization of accounting records and reports also benefits premium auditors. Although large corporations can develop complicated and unique accounting procedures, IRS requirements enforce a minimum level of compliance with certain standards for even the smallest organization. The IRS requires an organization to select one accounting method, obtain permission before changing it, receive approval to change the accounting period, and retain records for specified times. In addition, the IRS recommends that accounts be classified in groups following regular accounting procedures; that all disbursements be made by check to provide expense documentation; and that checks, invoices, duplicate deposits, and other records be retained to substantiate entries.

To a lesser degree, auditors have also benefited from the Wage and Hour Division of the Labor Department and various state agencies. Because government regulation extends to overtime payments, auditors can usually rely on consistent overtime payment procedures for each class of employee. Union contract provisions have also led to uniform overtime rules for every union employee.

Individual Earnings

Using individual earnings records as original source documents is usually time-consuming because the auditor must list each person's name. For a small firm, however, it can be the most practical approach.

Auditors who use that method must be sure to obtain all payroll cards. To facilitate the processing of current employee records, many payroll clerks separate the earnings cards of terminated employees from those of active employees. A bookkeeper commonly gives an auditor only active employee records, forgetting that the terminated employees were active during the period being audited. The insured might also run out of forms near year end and purchase different forms or prepare them from plain paper. When the new cards are not the same size as the others, they can be easy to overlook. Also, the auditor must remember that the employer usually uses the earnings cards only for employees. Those cards will not show casual labor and independent contractor exposure amounts.

Depending on the type of card, some firms with high turnover might list several employees on one card. The auditor should scan both the front and back of each card to be sure that the insured has not added names.

Columnar headings can also be misleading. For example, the "Overtime" column might include overtime plus other payments. The column titled "Gross Wages" usually contains gross wages, but the auditor should ensure that its entry is the largest number in each row. Gross wages should be the sum of regular wages, overtime, and any other deductions. Auditors have lost much audit time by trying to balance net wages, regular earnings, or wages after 401(k) deductions against gross wage totals.

Reports to Unions

Although reports to unions constitute another source of payroll information, union requirements can actually complicate the auditor's job. The auditor must ascertain whether the records show all employees or just union employees.

If an employer must pay a fixed amount per hour for a union vacation or holiday fund, the employer might show those payments separately from regular wages. Employers commonly credit the amount paid to the fund against each individual employee in the payroll record and on the same line show this amount in the payroll deduction columns. The policyholder's report to the union includes the sum of all such amounts. Generally, the auditor should include those amounts in the payroll base. The auditor should include any wages reported as payments to individuals for tax purposes. However, if the employer pays the union vacation fund a flat percentage of the total weekly payroll, the auditor should exclude such payments from the premium base because the payments cannot be credited to specific individual employees. The auditor must ensure that the union descriptions for the work performed are the same as the class description shown in the records.

Other union provisions might specify payments for travel expenses to distant jobs or allowances for special clothing or safety shoes. Although the employer might consider those payments a part of payroll costs, such expenses are not part of the wage base. However, the auditor should include payments for the time spent traveling as wages.

Also, the employer might record payments made by the employer to union pension funds as payroll. Normally, the employer shows those payments as deductions from the employee's gross pay. The auditor should not use those payments to determine payroll.

An auditor cannot automatically classify a union employee based on the particular union's name or work rules. Some unions' work rules help the auditor classify an individual when, for example, a union positively forbids a union member from doing anything outside the union's trade. In other cases, the union definition of a "trade" might involve several different insurance classifications, and the auditor must analyze the work to determine the proper class.

Payroll Journal

The payroll journal can be a valuable source of information for the auditor. However, no standard requirements exist for what information should be included, so company journals can vary. The auditor must make certain that all of the following are shown in the journal:

- Remuneration for all employees
- Overtime, if applicable
- Executive officers
- Department descriptions that match the actual functions performed

A common problem with department descriptions occurs when the journal shows "office personnel" and includes officers, salespeople, counter clerks, and others who might not fit the exact insurance manual definition of office personnel.

The payroll journal usually records each employee's earnings for every pay period, whether it is on a weekly, biweekly, or semimonthly basis. The listing of employees shows the details of gross wages, overtime, net wages, and various deductions for taxes and benefit plans. The payroll journal might distribute payroll by department on a weekly basis or on a monthly basis. More often, the employer enters payroll in the cash disbursements journal and posts the amount each month to the payroll accounts in the general ledger. No single uniform method for recording payroll is used, so auditors should be alert for differences. Determining how the insured shows payroll includes analyzing each department's payroll to be sure it corresponds to insurance classification definitions.

Although most payroll journals have normal column headings on each page, a few do not. On some, employers might title columns simply "A," "B," and so forth. Although the people using the payroll journals are familiar with the layout, before starting the audit, the auditor must understand which columns relate to the audit. An auditor should not assume that an employer uses a particular column for overtime merely because it follows the column for regular wages or seems to contain overtime wages.

When using a payroll journal, an auditor should turn over each page individually. If the employer normally uses four pages for each week's payroll, an auditor might just count four pages and turn them over as a group. By doing so, however, the auditor might overlook special payrolls for vacations, retroactive pay, or bonuses, particularly if they are on just one page.

Payroll Tax Returns

Because many policies end on the calendar year or at the end of a quarter, quarterly tax reports provide a convenient means of verifying gross wages. When the tax period does not coincide with the policy period, an auditor can use tax returns as a secondary verification source but not as the primary source. However, auditors must remember that tax reports do not necessarily list total gross wages. They list only those wages subject to a particular tax. Although

the Employer's Quarterly Federal Tax Return, Form 941, has separate lines for total gross wages and wages subject to Social Security tax, employers often state the Social Security taxable wages in both places. As long as no employee's earnings exceed the annual Social Security payroll limitation, then the two totals are the same. If an employee's payroll exceeds the annual limitation, however, those totals (total gross wages and wages subject to Social Security tax) should differ. If they consistently agree, then they do not show total gross wages, and the auditor should not use them.

Another possible pitfall of relying on tax returns is that certain family employees are exempt from Social Security taxes. For example, children under the age of eighteen who are employed by their parents, a husband who is employed by his wife, and a wife who is employed by her husband are all employees who are exempt from Social Security taxes.[4] Also, the tax returns do not show payments to independent contractors or casual labor workers.

Because tax regulations are complicated and are revised regularly, employers do not necessarily have up-to-date knowledge of them. Therefore, tax reports are not always correct. Mistakes in tax reports can occur in any size organization.

Federal Form 941 is the tax form that auditors most commonly use, but auditors often overlook two additional information sources. For a policy on a calendar year, the auditor can obtain gross wages from the Federal Unemployment Tax Report (Form 940) and the Transmittal of Income and Tax Statements (Form W-3). Form W-3 also contains a count of the number of W-2s filed.

If Federal Form 941 has higher total wages than other sources, the employer probably pays someone outside the regular system. The auditor should ask whether a "private payroll," a "confidential payroll," or a "special payroll" exists. If the response is negative, the auditor should determine by how much the tax return for one quarter exceeds the other source. Often the employer has paid one person the amount in question, which the auditor can identify by scanning the tax return details. Corporation officers and salespeople are generally paid outside the regular payroll.

Comparing Form 941 with the state unemployment return can reveal out-of-state payroll exposure amounts. If the payroll on the 941 is larger than the state return total, the insured might have operations in another state, and the employer might have separately filed the return for the other state.

Payroll Summaries

If the insured prepares a payroll summary intended for classification purposes, the auditor should test the classification assignments and amounts. That test usually involves working backward to trace the accumulation and source of the summarized information. Those summaries are usually unacceptable for audit purposes unless the insured can document their preparation.

Because the office classification has the lowest rate, it is the most important one to confirm. The auditor should list the names, duties, and payroll for each employee in the office category on a schedule. The auditor should add those

individual payrolls for a sample period of a week or a month and balance that amount to the total amount included in the summary. By analyzing the specific duties of the listed employees, the auditor should be able to judge the accuracy of the insured's allocation to a particular classification.

Independent Auditors' Work Papers

At times, the work papers of independent auditors can be a helpful source of information. Although their goal is different from a premium auditor's goal, the independent auditors' efforts in reconciling payroll can reveal accounts or balances that the premium auditor might have overlooked. Although the time period of the independent audit, which is for a fiscal year, might not coincide with the policy year, any copies of independent auditors' work papers and schedules left with the insured can be useful for premium auditing.

Record Balances

Auditors are often faced with records that do not balance. The first step in reconciling the difference should be looking for payments outside the routine procedure. Although the insured might systematically handle regular weekly payroll, payments for vacations, bonuses, holidays, sick pay, and retroactive wage adjustments may be treated differently. The auditor should ask whether any wages receive special treatment. Often the answer to that question reveals separate records for confidential, private, or special payrolls.

Another approach to locating payroll differences involves determining which total is correct. By using another source that does balance, the auditor can determine whether the primary source is too high or too low. If the auditor uses additional sources, they should be easy to record, such as a comparison of a year-to-date summary to quarterly tax reports. Once an accurate total is determined, the auditor should determine the difference between the primary source and the verifying source. Often that difference explains the problem—for example, one source omitted one week's payroll; an error in addition occurred; or one source failed to include the president's salary.

If the auditor still cannot determine the cause of the difference, an alternative is to try balancing a smaller period such as a month or a quarter. When those records do not balance, the difference is usually detected easily. Once the auditor has balanced a smaller period, then balancing the totals is just a matter of adding to the time period until the yearly totals are equal.

REVIEW THE SALES CYCLE

Sales cycle
An entity's functions for documenting and processing transactions with customers.

In addition to the payroll cycle, the sales cycle is also reviewed as part of an audit program. The **sales cycle** encompasses the functions required to document and process transactions with customers, including the flow of information, classifications, deductible items, and nondeductible categories.

Flow of Information

The sales cycle begins when the customer agrees to buy a product either by sending in an order or by contacting a sales representative directly. Once an organization receives an order, it verifies the customer's credit. Next the organization determines the cost of each product, totals the sales invoice, and enters the amount as a debit to the accounts receivable ledger and a credit in the sales journal. At the same time, someone takes the products from inventory and packages and ships them. Invoices are mailed separately. Firms usually total the sales journal monthly and post it to various sales accounts in the general ledger. Presumably when the customer pays the bill, the organization credits accounts receivable and debits cash.

In auditing for products loss exposures, the auditor should always use the sales accounts from the general ledger, not from accounts receivable, which omit cash sales and require recording each month's amount.

Classifications

Products loss exposures allow more flexibility in classifications than do workers' compensation loss exposures. Because the rating manual has fewer classifications for products loss exposures, the products classifications are broader. Determining when to classify a loss exposure separately depends on its importance to the insured's overall operations, whether the insured (as well as the auditor) expects the loss exposure to continue, and on the amount of premium.

If a manufacturer of pens begins selling stationery, two specific classifications are involved. But when stationery sales are only $10,000 out of a total sales volume of $1 million and the insured does not expect to continue selling stationery, the difference in premium does not justify adding a new category.

If an organization uses only one sales account but more than one products classification applies, then the auditor must divide the sales within that one account by classification. The insured's operations or the way in which the insured records transactions might help the auditor make that division. For example, all sales in one classification might involve only one or two customers. State sales tax returns can be helpful because they indicate those sales subject to a retail tax. However, the sales tax return omits both nontaxable sales and out-of-state sales. Another method for determining classifications is to analyze specific purchases and adjust the purchases' amounts by their individual markup. If a restaurant has only one sales account and the auditor must determine liquor sales for a liquor liability policy, the auditor can calculate the liquor sales by reviewing liquor purchases and multiplying by the normal markup.

Deductible Items

Although the audit should always start with gross sales, several items are deductible from the sales base. When the insured collects a specific tax on the sales and remits it directly to a governmental department, the auditor subtracts

the amount of the tax. In that way, an auditor can deduct a state retail sales tax but not the federal income tax.

If a customer returns goods as unwanted or if the goods have arrived damaged, an organization normally debits a sales return and allowances account and credits either cash or accounts receivable. If sales returns and allowances occur infrequently, an organization might directly debit the sales account rather than create a separate returns account. If the insured uses a separate returns account, the auditor should deduct both returns and allowances for damaged goods from the sales base. The reasoning for making the deduction is that in either case, the products exposure amount is reduced.

Returns and allowances should normally be a low percentage of gross sales. If not, the auditor should investigate. The insured might have included consignment sales as regular sales. Because the manufacturer holds title even though the goods are in the retailer's custody, the auditor should not include their value in the sales base until the manufacturer transfers ownership.

When the insured shows freight charges in the insured's records as a separate expense and separately bills the customer, the auditor should subtract freight charges from the sales base. Because freight is posted as an individual item, its cost is separate from the product's cost and is not part of the products exposure base. If all customers picked up their orders themselves or if the insured provides free delivery, no freight would be charged, but the loss exposure would be the same. When the insured makes a freight allowance to customers, the auditor should include that allowance in the premium base.

If the insured's records separate finance and interest charges from sales, the auditor should not include those charges. The auditor must identify them as such, however, and not combine them under cost of sales.

Nondeductible Items

Auditors should not deduct certain items. When the insured gives a cash discount for prompt payment, such as a 2 percent discount for payment within ten days, the auditor should not subtract those discounts from sales. The purpose of that discount is to improve cash flow, not to reduce the product's price. Although the number of products outstanding remains the same, the discounts depend more on the overall level of interest rates and the liquidity position of customers.

Even though every organization has some uncollectible accounts receivable that are written off, auditors do not deduct those amounts from the sales base. The sales cycle becomes blurred for sales that are uncollectible. For example, a customer who purchased a product from a retailer does not know whether the retailer paid the manufacturer. So, a customer injured by a defective product might have a legitimate claim against the manufacturer even though the retailer never paid the manufacturer. Because the loss exposure exists, the auditor must include the sales of merchandise in the premium base even if the customer does not pay for it.

When insurance provides coverage for specified vendors, the auditor should point out that fact to the accounting manager early in the audit. That situation usually requires someone to tabulate the specific sales manually. Because that can take a considerable amount of time, starting early is important. Also, auditors should not deduct **intercompany sales** between two or more commonly owned companies. The common practice is to include those sales unless specifically excluded by policy endorsement (for the products loss exposure only). The main reason for the inclusion is that each organization has the right to sue the other even if the same policy insures them. If there are any doubts about whether to include intercompany sales, the auditor should discuss them with the underwriter before completing the audit.

Intercompany sales
Sales between two or more commonly owned companies.

MEASURE OWNED AUTOMOBILE LOSS EXPOSURES, INVENTORY, AND FIXED ASSETS

As another procedure on a premium audit, the auditor may measure owned automobile loss exposures, inventory, and fixed assets. Payroll and sales are the most important factors in most premium audits, but for specific insureds, determining loss exposures for owned automobiles, inventory, and fixed assets may be required.

Owned Automobile Loss Exposures

Auditing owned automobile loss exposures is similar to auditing fixed assets. Because the audit's goal is to ensure that the auditor schedules all owned autos on the policy, the procedure is to reconcile the asset account and the insurance policy schedule of units. Most insurers treat vehicles leased for twelve months or more the same as owned units.

As with the first step in the audit, the auditor should thoroughly study and understand the insured's system of internal control regarding automobiles. If an organization has many distant locations, the auditor must learn whether local personnel have authority to purchase or sell vehicles, and if so, how the insured controls those sales. The automobile asset account's accuracy depends on the efficiency of internal control. If those controls operate satisfactorily, then the auditor can trace the vehicles from the individual asset accounts to the insurance policy schedule.

The premium auditor must adequately document the organization's vehicles. Therefore, the audit should include examining evidence of ownership such as invoices, certificates of title, and vehicle and license registrations. The auditor should trace both the purchase dates and sales along with the garaging locations. As an overall verification, the auditor should also review the depreciation schedule to ensure that the depreciation expense is proportional to the value of the vehicles listed.

For commercial vehicles, the auditor must classify trucks correctly, and by correct territory. Classification includes verifying the year, make, type, garaging,

location, gross vehicle or gross combination weight (GVW or GCW), use, radius of operations, and original cost as new.

Inventory

As previously mentioned, the needs of independent auditors differ from the needs of premium auditors. The independent auditor's concern is that the insured values inventory on a consistent basis, which can be either on original cost, the lower of original cost or market, the retail method, or a quoted market price for standard commodities. When the insured uses original cost to value inventory, methods such as FIFO (first in, first out), LIFO (last in, first out), a weighted average, and standard costs are all available.

When property insurance covers inventory, the auditor must determine an inventory's current value to the policyholder. That value might be the replacement cost or the actual cash value at the time of the loss, which is the replacement cost minus depreciation. So determining the original cost, unless the insured has recently purchased or manufactured the goods, is not necessary for insurance purposes. Although a premium auditor can use the physical count of an inventory as a starting point, the valuation of various items can differ considerably.

Although an insurer might ask a premium auditor to review the appropriateness of an insured's method for reporting inventory values, the auditor usually applies the results of the method used.

Fixed Assets

An organization's financial statements always start with original cost plus improvements for fixed assets such as buildings or machinery. By using an estimated useful life, the insured accumulates regular depreciation, resulting in a book value for each asset. However, in inflationary times, the book value often is meaningless compared to current replacement costs.

An auditor can be of considerable help to property insurance underwriters and claim adjusters in explaining accounting concepts of valuing assets. Although some of the policyholder's records are useful for insurance purposes, insureds design them for noninsurance purposes. Auditors must recognize their limitations and be willing to explain valuation discrepancies to other insurer staff.

SUMMARY

A thorough and accurate premium audit program requires careful organization. By formulating a plan and following it through, premium auditors can avoid missing crucial items or being slowed down by irrelevant detail. Auditors must first determine the goals of the audit, which include the primary goal, to determine the exposure amounts and classifications under the policy in the minimum amount of time. A secondary goal is to provide

information for use by others, such as the insurer's marketing, sales, and underwriting departments.

Designing an appropriate audit program involves several additional decisions. Premium auditors must decide which audit procedures to use, which cutoff dates to apply, and what format to use for work papers. Auditors must also determine the type and amount of information they need. The potential sources of evidence for an audit are extensive.

Audit information can include physical observations, accounting records, documents other than accounting records, oral communications, and ratios and comparisons. Once the information is gathered, auditors must verify its quality and accuracy, using other information as cross-checks. Determining the degree of verification required depends on the time involved, the accepted professional standards, the materiality of the information, the condition and reliability of the insured's accounting records, and the detail required for an adequate audit report.

Generally, an audit program should begin with an examination of the general ledger. That examination acquaints the premium auditor with the policyholder's accounts and the overall business. The general ledger can provide adequate payroll information, but if not, it should reveal which posting sources contain the necessary detail. The general ledger is also a convenient means of discovering additional exposures in other accounts. Premium auditors should take special care in reading general ledger accounts to be certain that they understand the insured's accounting procedure. Throughout the audit process, the auditor must create an audit trail, allowing anyone reviewing the audit to trace an item in the audit back to its source. An auditor can follow an audit trail in either direction to answer questions.

Payroll processing is one of the most involved and one of the most standardized accounting functions. The auditor can obtain both classification information and information concerning employees not on the regular payroll from personnel records. Although regular payroll records are normally reliable, individual earnings records, payroll journals, payroll tax returns, and payroll summaries have certain limitations that the auditor must consider during the audit.

If the premium base is gross sales, the premium auditor should trace the sales cycle of the insured's accounting system in the same manner. As with the payroll cycle, that step should reveal which records might provide the premium base and classification information in the most convenient form. The auditor must also see how the accounting systems handle sales to determine whether the totals include deductible items such as sales taxes or returns.

When the premium base is a fixed asset category such as owned automobiles, the auditor must study the insured's system of internal control thoroughly. Occasionally insurers ask premium auditors to verify the values of inventories or fixed assets. In those situations the premium auditor must study the insured's accounts and assign values relevant for insurance purposes.

Of course, the success of any audit program depends on how well the auditor interacts with the insured's personnel and whether the auditor uses the most efficient techniques. Following the guidelines in this chapter should help an auditor to produce thorough, efficient audits.

CHAPTER NOTES

1. Committee on Auditing Procedure, *AICPA Professional Standards* (New York: American Institute of Certified Public Accountants, 1 June 1993), p. 81.
2. *AICPA Professional Standards*, p. 81.
3. Internal Revenue Service, *Employer's Tax Guide*, Circular E, Publication 15, January 2005, p. 8.
4. *Employer's Tax Guide*, p. 16.

Direct Your Learning

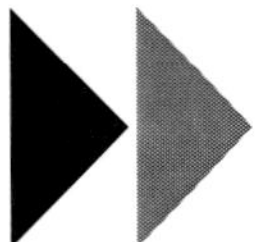

Data Verification and Analysis

Educational Objectives

After learning the content of this chapter and completing the corresponding course guide assignment, you should be able to:

- Explain how premium auditors verify data sufficiency.
- Explain how premium auditors use different data sources to verify data accuracy.
- Describe the problems that premium auditors encounter with data reconciliation.
- Explain how reviewing the following can help premium auditors to analyze data reasonableness:
    - Policy coverages and changes
    - Audit findings
        - Comparison to prior audit findings
        - Comparison to industry averages
        - Relationship analysis
        - Sampling techniques
    - Classification review
        - Insured's operations
        - Insured's employees
        - Insured's exposure bases
- Define or describe each of the Key Words and Phrases for this chapter.

OUTLINE

Develop Your Perspective

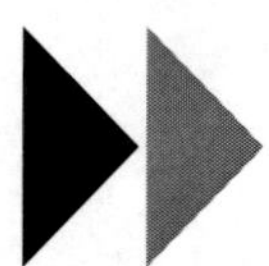

What are the main topics covered in the chapter?

An auditor is responsible for ensuring that data collected in an audit is accurate and adequate. The auditor is in a unique position to access an insured's premises and records. This chapter will aid premium auditors in judging whether the information contained in the audit is sufficient to establish confidence in its reliability.

Identify judgments a premium auditor must make to ensure that audit data is adequate.

- How can an auditor know if audit data are sufficient?
- How can an auditor know if audit data are accurate?
- How can an auditor know if audit data are reasonable?

Why is it important to learn about these topics?

Because the purpose of a premium audit is to obtain sufficient, accurate, and reasonable data to determine the premium, an essential step in the audit process is for the premium auditor to double-check the audit findings.

Consider what an auditor must do if the audit findings do not conform to expectations.

- What should an auditor do if financial data do not appear realistic?
- What should an auditor do if classifications do not appear realistic?

How can you use what you will learn?

Analyze how your organization verifies and analyzes data.

- How does the process assist in reconciling data obtained from different sources?
- What techniques are used to assess the reasonableness of data that determine classifications?

Data Verification and Analysis

A premium auditor has two obvious responsibilities. One is to perform a thorough audit that develops the appropriate premium for the loss exposures covered by a policy. The other is to complete a reasonable number of audits in a given time period. Those two responsibilities seem to conflict because, as the number of audits performed increases, the time available for each decreases. However, verifying and analyzing the data obtained during the audit and reconciling any discrepancies often enable an auditor to improve the audit's quality and save time simultaneously.

As part of establishing the appropriate premiums, auditors check to ensure that data are sufficient and accurate. As part of analysis, premium auditors determine the reasonableness of data to ensure that the correct loss exposures have been identified and the correct classifications applied.

To perform an audit as thoroughly and efficiently as possible, premium auditors must ask the following questions, which help them to verify and analyze data:

- Are *sufficient* data available to complete the audit? Are enough records available to develop all pertinent loss exposures?
- Are the data *accurate*? Are the records free from deliberate or unintentional error?
- Are the data *reasonable* and *complete*? Are the facts consistent with what is expected for the particular business?

Those questions are interrelated.

During the audit's planning stage, the premium auditor must decide which records are needed. Of course, an auditor should not hesitate to ask for any records that might improve the audit's accuracy. Computers can produce many management reports that summarize data. Auditors might need only original entry records to spot-check and verify reports.

While conducting the audit, the premium auditor should be alert for clues to additional loss exposures or unexpected operations. Facts discovered during an audit can confirm such situations or reveal a previously unknown area that requires further investigation. Therefore, premium auditors must always be prepared to redirect their investigation in the light of new facts.

VERIFICATION OF DATA SUFFICIENCY

Because the insurance policy obligates the insurer to pay claims resulting from any losses covered by the policy, the premium auditor must determine the appropriate premium for the coverages provided. Often, the insured might be completely unaware that the policy covers a particular loss exposure until a loss occurs. An essential part of a premium audit, therefore, is to examine the insured's operation in sufficient depth to discover all facts pertaining to the correct premium for the policy. Such an in-depth examination requires sufficient data.

Premium auditors must verify that the data they have assembled for a premium audit are sufficient. They should be confident that they have not overlooked any data concerning material facts (facts that would have a significant effect on the premium determination). The fundamental test of materiality is the amount of premium at stake. In some cases, that test might be easy to apply, but in other cases the auditor might have to completely analyze the insured's operations before discovering any substantial premium charges. The auditor must judge the materiality of particular information in each individual case. The more data a premium auditor examines, however, the more time the audit consumes. Locating one additional record could consume hours that could be devoted to another audit instead. So achieving relative certainty can become very costly to the insurer. Auditors must balance the importance of additional information against the cost of obtaining it.

Audit risk
The probability of generating inaccurate audit reports because of the failure to detect or properly interpret properly material factors in the premium base.

For premium auditors, having insufficient data can increase **audit risk**, which is the probability of submitting inaccurate audit reports because material factors in the premium base were not detected or were measured improperly. Although the insufficient data is always a risk in a premium audit, the auditor must make every reasonable effort to minimize it by verifying the sufficiency of data. Such verification involves determining whether data may have been intentionally withheld and analyzing particular industries that produce most data-gathering problems.

Premium Evasion

Premium evasion
The insured's intentional fraudulent act resulting in underreporting or misclassifying loss exposures.

Premium evasion, also called premium fraud, is a significant problem in the insurance industry. **Premium evasion** is the insured's intentional fraudulent act resulting in underreporting or misclassifying loss exposures. It results in increased premium rates and an unfair burden on insureds who do pay the correct premium for their loss exposures.

In other words, premium evasion is the withholding or distortion of facts with intent to deceive. Because most insureds are honest, fraudulent evasion is uncommon. However, those cases in which insurers have discovered fraud involve substantial premiums.

Most forms of fraud are not obvious. They are discovered through inconsistencies in the information the insured provides. If an auditor discovers or suspects fraud, the auditor should consider the possibility of error and thoroughly

document all inconsistencies. Because of the potential legal implications, the auditor should not challenge the insured or otherwise alert the insured to suspicions. The premium auditor should complete the audit as usual and separately document the irregularities supporting the suspicions of premium evasion.

Because instances of fraud have escalated in recent years, most insurers and many states have formalized programs to deal with it. Audit management and auditors should be aware of such programs and know how to take advantage of them when fraud is suspected. In any event, auditors should be prepared to verify that data are sufficient to develop the proper premium for the loss exposures covered by the policy.

Data-Gathering Problem Industries

Premium auditors may encounter particular problems in gathering and verifying sufficient data in certain industries. The construction and transportation industries produce most of the data-gathering and verification problems encountered by premium auditors. In construction, the validity of contractors' and subcontractors' certificates of insurance continues to be a major source of problems. In the transportation industry, significant problems relate to verifying insureds' assertions that truckers are independent contractors instead of employees, and verifying garaging locations.

Premium auditors should be alert to the idiosyncrasies of each industry and each insured. Competition, deregulation, and technological advances are changing the operations of many businesses. At the same time, many older accounting systems leave a poor trail for audit verification and analysis. The following points illustrate potential problems that might warrant additional investigation for some insureds:

- Workers' compensation payroll summaries that are distributed on a cost center basis or after journal adjustments often reveal inconsistencies. A corporation might assign managerial and professional employees to different cost centers at different locations, resulting in substantial undercharges and misclassifications. The insured might allocate wages and salaries partly to corporate payroll expense and partly to a subsidiary's expense. Payroll summaries might also distribute net payrolls to the payroll account and charge amounts withheld to other accounts, such as taxes withheld to taxes payable or employee purchases to accounts receivable.
- Multiple location stores and restaurants frequently have separate records for each location. For example, a restaurant's workers' compensation policy indicated one location. However, when recording the data supplied by the insured's accountant, the auditor noticed the label "Vol. I" on the ledger cover and asked for Vol. II. The auditor discovered five insured but unreported locations.
- Many companies maintain several bank accounts. A common practice is to assign payrolls to one bank account and operating expenses to another.

Some companies charge salaries and wages to the payroll bank account and charge commissions and bonuses to the operating expense account.

- Casual or temporary labor omitted from payroll records might appear in several accounts. Mercantile firms might charge temporary labor to special sales promotions or to advertising to keep the charge from the payroll records. Some companies might charge payrolls for repair or remodeling work to maintenance or to capital accounts for additions and improvements.

Construction

The construction industry presents a unique challenge to the premium auditor, especially for workers' compensation audits. The auditor must be familiar with common industry work practices for the various trades as well as the accounting practices and the special manual rules that apply to contracting.

Insurers can lose substantial premium dollars if the auditor fails to properly identify all employees. Uninsured subcontractors and misclassification of operations also can cause large premium losses. Contracting audits frequently require detailed analysis of records and a thorough evaluation of the insured's accounting controls.

Attempts to circumvent the rules that establish employee/employer relationships occur in many industries but are most common in the construction industry because of the nature of the business. A rule of thumb is that a contractor can save one dollar of tax, employee benefit, and insurance costs for each dollar moved from payroll to independent contractor expense. Current tax laws and the structure of many benefit programs have eliminated that temptation by providing incentives for many employees to declare themselves "independent" until severely injured.

It is not unusual for a carpenter or concrete worker to also have a contractor's license. The ability to be a legitimate contractor on one job and an employee on the next tends to blur the status of the employee relationship in the minds of both the employer and the employee.

Problems that are common when auditing construction risks include the following practices of insureds:

- Lack of records or improper records.
- Improper assignment of people to the executive supervisors classification because the insured does not understand the manual requirements for a "buffer" level of management between the executive supervisors and the actual on-site supervisors.
- Assignment of employees to more than one classification. For example, if a contractor has a crew only to install cabinetry at a jobsite, class 5437 would apply because they are specialty contractors. However, if that contractor is building a residential development with the same crew doing the same work, but additional employees are doing other carpentry work, class 5645 would apply for all of the employees on the site. There are

other classes for which the class description specifically states "all work to completion." Classification notes supersede general manual rules.

- Use of uninsured subcontractors who say they are insured.

In addition, auditors face the following problems or challenges because of the nature of the construction business.

- Verification of insurance for subcontractors who say they are insured.
- Travel to a contractor's multiple locations to complete the audit.
- Inability to observe every location at which the contractor or its employees perform work.

The auditor should support classification and distribution of payrolls with time records or other appropriate records. Auditors should examine individual jobs to determine whether total payrolls are reasonable and whether the governing class is appropriately using job cost records. However, the insured frequently does not post payrolls by the time of audit. Alternate sources of verification include contract bid specifications, change orders, and project blueprints to obtain an indication of the extent of the work or payroll.

Auditors should review check registers and cash disbursements journals for additional payments made to workers designated as independent contractors, but who are really employees. Auditors should examine payments made for materials to be sure they are not for "labor and material" or "labor only" subcontracts.

Large construction projects frequently have records separate from the insured's main records. By incorporating the records of those projects into the insured's main records, an auditor may lose some important details. Additionally, auditors must separately account for operations in other states, requiring reference to additional records.

Auditors should verify certificates of insurance for subcontractors with the insuring company to verify coverage during the exposure period, especially those certificates furnished after an audit. In many cases, auditors have discovered that several large subcontractors had no insurance during the actual exposure period. In other cases, auditors have discovered that the insured or someone else has falsified certificates. If all copies of certificates are in an identical format and typeface, regardless of the insurer providing coverage, the auditor should investigate further. Auditors should also check that the period of coverage shown on the certificates coincides with the dates of the projects involved. Otherwise, coverage might not exist.

Wrap-up insurance programs or separately insured projects can cause confusion, and the auditor should thoroughly investigate them. Auditors might need proof of insurance and copies of policy exclusions for verification of what is actually included in the insurance coverage.

Insurance rates vary substantially among adjacent states. The auditor should thoroughly analyze operations of contractors with projects in two or more states for correct assignment of loss exposures. Many contractors charge their

"permanent" supervisory employees to a home state even though they might be working and residing in another state.

Transportation

Transportation, particularly trucking, like contracting, is a highly mobile industry and presents similar data-gathering and verifying problems to premium auditors. Frequently, the status of a sub-hauler either as an "independent trucker" or as an employee can be difficult to ascertain. The terminal or garage location can be critical to accurately assign loss exposures for both workers' compensation payrolls and vehicles rated on a per unit basis. It is not unusual to have a terminal located in one state or rating territory and the corporate office in another. The insured tends to assign as much of the loss exposure as possible to the lower-rated territory. The auditor should include the street address and ZIP code of each terminal and the number of drivers and vehicles assigned in the audit documentation for transportation firms.

VERIFICATION OF DATA

A fundamental rule for premium audits is that the auditor must use at least one independent source to verify the accuracy of the exposure base data. Naturally, independent sources do not necessarily report the same information or cover the same accounting periods. Therefore, verification is essential. In that context, verification means comparing alternative sources of information to confirm or improve the original data's accuracy. Auditors must use considerable judgment and carefully choose sources for verification purposes while keeping the audit's goals in mind. Discrepancies must be resolved quickly and satisfactorily.

Premium auditors should ask questions whenever they do not understand something in the insured's records. Often, the answers give insight into the insured's operations. Oral information can also influence an auditor's confidence in the audit data.

Data Verification Sources

A previous chapter describes various accounting records that are useful in a premium audit. Although many of those records lack sufficient detail for determining the premium base, they might have enough information for verification purposes. Verification sources do not have to duplicate the original audit data, but they must provide additional ensurance of the audit data's accuracy. Again, the auditor must evaluate what type of verification is warranted in each situation.

Several sources are available to verify data accuracy:

- Accounting records
- Tax returns
- Regulatory reports

- Financial statements
- Other information

Accounting Records

Because the original audit data come from the insured's accounting records, the auditor should be sure those records are accurate and consistent. Computer printouts can simplify the task of accumulating the audit data but do not eliminate the need for verification.

Often the initial accounting record is a payroll record. An auditor should spot-check to determine that the insured properly figured the gross amounts from the number of hours worked at the prescribed rate. At the same time, the auditor should verify the method of calculating overtime.

Companies often group persons in the payroll record by departments, with a subtotal for each department. That grouping helps in classifying payrolls properly. However, the grouping might be vastly different from what the auditor needs for insurance purposes. Therefore, the auditor must also ensure that the insured has grouped employees in the proper categories for insurance purposes.

Entries to the payroll record should agree with the cash disbursement records and the general ledger's expense section. An essential verification step, then, is to determine that all records (general ledger, disbursement, and payroll records) are consistent with one another. Auditors can use individual earnings records to determine remuneration for employees in standard exception classifications, which include occupations or operations so common to many businesses that they are separate classifications; for example, clerical office workers. In that case, checking that the individual earnings records agree with the entries in the payroll record is necessary. Auditors often use payroll summaries for the initial determination of the premium base. However, verifying the accuracy of the total payrolls and the distribution by classification or operation is still important and is done by reviewing the records from which the insured prepared the payroll summary.

Auditors should carefully check several items when reviewing the insured's records. Frequently, titles need clarification. For example, under the heading "administrative," the insured might list salaried employees including supervisors and job superintendents. Also, setting up one heading for employees paid on an hourly basis and another heading for employees paid on a salaried basis is not unusual. In a small office, the auditor can observe the number of clerical employees to determine if it corresponds to the records. In a large office, however, reviewing the functions of the individuals listed and, perhaps, observing the actual operation and location of the individuals is necessary to classify them properly.

For example, one insured's payroll record listed ten employees under "office." The auditor observed only eight employees in the office. The insured told the auditor the other two were in an office on a lower floor. The auditor asked to see the other office. The two employees were indeed performing a clerical function, but they were in the shipping room and were not physically separated as

required to be included in the clerical classification. As in this example, most cases of misclassification result from a lack of understanding and a failure on the part of the auditor to verify and analyze the information presented.

Generally, the cash disbursements book provides payment information. The auditor should verify the book's various accounts against the general ledger accounts. However, auditors cannot rely on account headings alone. They must analyze each account to see what it contains. The cash disbursements book also provides information about the purchase or rental of land, buildings, and equipment. In addition, auditors can develop classification information from names of firms from which the insured has purchased material.

The cash receipts for a contractor usually show for whom the contractor performed the work. That information helps to determine the classification for some operations. A paving contractor's receipts from a city, county, state, or land development company might indicate street paving rather than driveways or parking lots. Receipts from utility companies often indicate installation of gas, sewer, or water mains rather than installation of house connections. Generally, companies enter each individual payment in the cash receipts book as received. In determining such things as total receipts or contract price, or total sales to a particular vendor, the auditor would have to refer to the accounts receivable or the sales register. In going from record to record, the auditor must verify the figures compared against one another.

Tax Returns

Tax returns can be a valuable verification source. Much of that value stems from the enforcement powers of tax authorities. Stiff penalties for failure to comply with tax laws provide a strong incentive for insureds to prepare their tax returns accurately. Although tax return figures rarely directly match the information needed for a premium audit, they provide benchmarks for judging the accuracy of audit data. However, tax reports are not always correct.

Because of the changing tax laws, the insured might have amended the return, and the auditor might not have a copy of the most recent return. Auditors must check to ensure that they are using the most current returns and that the period for which the insured files the tax return is the same as the policy period.

Insureds usually prepare payroll tax returns from a payroll summary or directly from the payroll journal, making it impossible for an auditor to determine whether the employer has charged any employee's remuneration to a nonpayroll account. Payroll tax returns include only the remuneration subject to the particular tax law. The definitions of what constitutes an employee under the tax laws and the workers' compensation laws often differ. For example, sales representatives paid on a commission basis might be employees under the workers' compensation law but might not be included on the payroll tax return.

Likewise, payroll tax records do not show payments to independent contractors for hired trucks or other equipment. Most often, companies make those

payments by check and enter them in the cash disbursements book. For a corporation, the auditor can verify those items with the corporate income tax return (Form 1120), or with the individual tax return (Schedule C) or partnership return (Form 1065).

For commission sales representatives or other persons providing services, the insured might have issued separate information returns (Form 1099). The income tax return should include such payments to commissioned sales representatives. Although all of those items should appear on the tax return, the insured's records might have combined items or included them in different categories. A careful and detailed analysis of tax returns might be necessary to verify the premium base.

In states and localities that have sales taxes, the auditor can use sales tax returns to verify an exposure based on sales. Auditors must be aware, however, that some sales may be exempt from the particular sales tax. Generally, verification with income tax returns is preferable in those instances. In addition to verifying payroll and cash disbursements in payroll tax reports and expense items in the income tax return, the auditor should verify receipts or sales by the income shown on the income tax return or sales tax return when applicable.

Regulatory Reports

Regulatory and accounting authorities require many industries to follow prescribed accounting methods and file periodic reports. Those industries include insurance, utilities, trucking, and airlines, along with many others—in general, any business whose rates or revenues are either established or approved by a federal or state regulatory authority. Auditors can review reports of those authorities to determine the various sources of income as well as the prescribed categories of payroll and expenses. The auditor should analyze those items and verify them with other records and with the audit.

Most regulated industries usually have a prescribed chart of accounts, which clearly defines what each account should include. The chart of accounts can help the auditor locate where the insured has included various items within the records. Verifying payroll with regulatory reports might be difficult because the insured might have allocated payroll to several different accounts. Nevertheless, regulatory reports are valuable because they provide information about the types of activities creating revenues and the expenditures and activities represented by those expenditures. The reports also often indicate payments for services not reflected in payroll accounts.

Financial Statements

An organization's annual statement provides financial information in a summarized format. The statements of publicly held corporations offer the additional assurance of certification by independent auditors. The financial information shows the organization's financial condition and profitability and generally includes sales by product lines. However, expenses are usually recorded in such broad categories that they are not very helpful to a premium

auditor. The annual report's narrative can be helpful in determining the insured's products or businesses, locations, and future plans and products. Auditors can detect many misclassifications by reviewing the annual report.

Internal financial statements generally provide much more detailed financial information than the annual report, and often much greater detail than the company books, if they allocate income and expenses to smaller units or departments. Some internal financial statements just summarize the information included in the company books. In any case, internal financial statements can help the auditor reconcile information already developed from other sources. Such statements also help the auditor determine ratios of sales to expenses, sales to payrolls, and ratios of one classification of payroll to another.

The auditor should review the chart of accounts to determine just what each account includes and should test some transactions to ensure that the accounts contain the correct information. The auditor should verify that the audit information obtained from the financial statement is consistent with other company records in both dollar amounts and allocation of payrolls and operations performed.

Other Information

Accounting records, tax returns, regulatory reports, and financial statements are not the only sources an auditor can use to verify audit information. Union health and welfare reports, which show the number of regular and overtime hours by individual employee for each trade, can also be valuable sources of verification. A company's organizational chart or telephone directory can help clarify an employee's occupation. Usually the departmental breakdown lists the employee name, job title, site location, and telephone extension. For example, checking the telephone listing for the Shipping and Receiving Department might reveal that John Smith, Receiving Supervisor, ext. 441, works on the loading docks and not in the main office complex.

The auditor should also review product or sales brochures to verify that classifications are correct for what the insured is actually doing. The auditor can usually find that material in the reception area. If not, the auditor should ask for it. Sources within the insurance company, such as claim history and loss control reports, can also be valuable verification tools.

Data Reconciliation

To verify audit data using different services, the premium auditor must often reconcile data differences. The attempt to locate causes of discrepancies can be frustrating, but the auditor must make every attempt to resolve differences quickly.

Although there may be a sense of satisfaction in balancing totals from different sources, auditors must consider how large the difference is in relation to the total amount of dollars involved. How much premium does the difference involve? How much time has the auditor spent in looking for the difference,

and how much more time might be required? Is the controller agreeable to accepting the audit using the higher amount of payroll or sales?

To reach agreement about a difference, the auditor should conduct a review with the insured's controller and then determine whether the time required to find the difference is justified. The review would include the dollar difference, the percentage difference, and the amount of premium involved and the methods needed to determine the difference. For example, $100,000 difference in sales would be a minimal difference for a company with $1 billion annual sales. However, it is a substantial difference if annual sales are $1 million. If the auditor has spent a reasonable time investigating the difference, and the premium difference is not large, then most controllers will accept the larger amount.

When the difference is large, a controller who previously has not been involved in the audit might now become interested. Gaining the cooperation of the key individual is vital because this might be the only person who knows about unusual or exceptional circumstances.

Problems that can cause differences among data sources that must then be reconciled, include the following:

- Communication failures
- Mathematical errors
- Record variations

Communication Failures

When totals from different sources fail to agree, the first area to examine is probably communication. Has the audit's purpose been clearly communicated? Even if the controller knows the audit's purpose, another person assigned to assist the premium auditor might not. Explaining the purpose each time can be repetitious, but the auditor must remember the conflicting requests made of accounting personnel. Bookkeepers tend to furnish only the individual earnings records of current employees, not realizing that a premium auditor also needs records of terminated employees. Explaining the reasons for the audit can eliminate many of the frustrations arising later if the sources do not balance.

Mathematical Errors

Another problem that can create the need for data reconciliation is mathematical errors. Mathematical errors can occur when someone misreads data, transposes numbers, or copies or enters numbers incorrectly. Computers have reduced the likelihood of many types of mathematical errors, but have not reduced the likelihood of no errors in the data entry.

The first step in reconciling differences is to subtract one amount from the other to find the exact variation. Often this difference quickly identifies the source of the problem. A round amount of $300 or $1,000 is usually an error in addition. The accounting "rule of nines" is useful to reconcile differences.

According to that rule, if the difference between two numbers is divisible by nine, there is a good chance that someone transposed two numbers.

Handwritten numbers can be difficult to read, requiring testing of the totals. One test involves adding a column to compare with the total listed. In the ledger, the auditor can add a posting to the previous balance to confirm the new balance.

Picking up the final total for each period is essential. A handwritten cash disbursements journal often has check marks indicating that someone has posted the totals to the general ledger, and manually prepared records usually have a double-ruled line under the totals. Some people use a different color pen to highlight a total. Knowing how each system works helps the auditor avoid picking up a subtotal and overlooking a single additional entry at the top of the next page.

When a discrepancy in totals is equal to about one week's payroll, the auditor should look at the beginning and ending amounts. Often the problem can be a case of starting or ending the audit a week too early or too late. A quick way to search for that error is to trace the beginning and ending week to a monthly summary. Sometimes the insured might enter a monthly summary every four or five weeks in a payroll journal but might enter a summary at the end of the month in a cash disbursements journal, a monthly journal voucher, or a payroll control account in the general ledger. Another way to detect that problem is to do a simple recapitulation on a worksheet so that the auditor can be sure that the monthly postings to the general ledger balance with the gross payroll. Once the auditor determines how each week flows into the other records, adjusting for the beginning and ending weekly periods becomes easy. The auditor can add the twelve monthly amounts to verify an annual total.

If a large difference still exists, the auditor should review the dates to see if a week was omitted. If not, the auditor might have omitted vacation pay or a bonus. The quickest way to check that possibility is to ask the person assisting in the audit if all vacation and bonus payments were included in the regular payroll. If so, the auditor should ask the approximate time the payments were made. Those payments should be conspicuous because they are rarely close to the regular payment amounts. If this process does not resolve the problem, the auditor should ask if the insured has made any payments apart from the regular payroll. The answer might reveal special payments, for example, to the president, to members of the president's family, or to other officers, as well as incentive bonuses, sales commissions, or retirement pay.

Record Variations

Another problem that can create the need for data reconciliation is record variations. Monthly totals are a useful and convenient test of quarterly totals. The sum of three months should agree with a quarterly payroll tax

report for the same period. When the three-month total is higher, the quarterly report might be listing only payrolls subject to Social Security tax or unemployment tax. Often, a quarterly worksheet listing gross wages before the insured has deducted any amount over the tax limitation is more helpful in a premium audit.

A recapitulation of the monthly postings to the general ledger is also a good summary of the various accounts. The auditor should compare the listed accounts to ensure that one was not overlooked when picking up accounts from the general ledger. Scanning all twelve monthly recaps might show that the insured has posted payroll to a new account for only a month or two.

When a tax report is significantly higher than the amounts the auditor has arrived at, the auditor should determine if the policyholder is using net amounts in payroll records. An insured might title a columnar heading in a journal as "gross wages," but an auditor might find it is actually the net amount.

The auditor should watch for differences between earned and paid amounts. Payroll tax reports use the actual paid amounts, but the insured often adjusts the general ledger for earned or accrued amounts. Usually, adjusting the beginning and ending periods to bring the earned and paid amounts in balance is necessary. To determine if accruals will affect a premium audit, the auditor should scan the account posting references, check for regular credits washing out a previous month's debit, and review the accrued liability accounts.

When an audit involves only one division or a subsidiary of a multicompany corporation, an auditor should check for inconsistencies. A division president might be on either the division or corporate payroll registers, general ledgers, or payroll tax reports. It is confusing to find that the insured has included an individual on a division level payroll register but not on the corporate level general ledger and tax report, or any other combination. Although those differences offset each other on a corporate consolidation, a premium auditor should review anyone who is subject to different handling. Usually, those inconsistencies involve only a few people. Such inconsistent treatment might appear only for a single month or over many years.

For a closely held corporation, similar inconsistencies can exist. For example, the insured might include the housekeeper at the president's home in some, but not all, of the corporate payroll records.

A variety of other payments might be in only part of the records. Payments such as profit-sharing distributions, corporation directors' fees, expense allowances, dividends, annuity payments, and per diem payments might all be found in some but not all of the payroll records. Relying on experience and asking questions help the auditor to locate those types of payments.

ANALYSIS OF DATA REASONABLENESS

The auditor should not only verify data sufficiency and accuracy but should also analyze the reasonableness of data. Auditors analyze data reasonableness by reviewing the following:

- Policy coverages and changes
- Audit findings
- Classification review

Policy Coverages and Changes

The auditor must carefully analyze the audit information in light of any policy endorsements to determine any potential changes that would affect the audit and must be sure that all businesses named on the policy are included in the audit. If a named insured business has not been audited, the auditor must include an explanation in the audit report explaining why not. The audit report must "clear" all named entities, loss exposures, and states either by showing an estimated premium basis or by explaining its absence.

It is not uncommon for large corporations to have subsidiaries within their corporate structure for which the insured would not expect to have a loss exposure under a particular policy. For example, a manufacturing corporation might have a subsidiary company that doesn't currently perform any function but might serve a purpose in the future. The insurer might still name that subsidiary on the policy because the insurer previously provided coverage for it. Some organizations consist of several different companies, but all employees are on the payroll of only one company. Any number of valid reasons can exist for that type of corporate structure. However, companies that appear inactive for years might develop an insured exposure during the policy period. The auditor must investigate and comment on each in the audit report.

Conversely, if the auditor discovers a loss exposure for an entity not shown on the policy, the auditor must note this and also notify the underwriter. Possibly, the insurer intentionally did not provide coverage in the policy for that entity with the underwriter's and the insured's agreement and knowledge.

Audit Findings

After analyzing the policy and making the necessary comments and adjustments, the auditor should analyze the audit findings by comparing them with prior audit findings and industry averages. The overall loss exposures and the assignment to each classification should be aligned with the loss exposures and assignments of the prior period as well as with the normal pattern for the industry. If a variance from what the auditor would expect is found (either up or down), the auditor should investigate and explain it.

Comparison to Prior Audit Findings

Correct audit findings normally correspond to the previous audit's findings. However, expenses might have increased, for example, because of a large rush order that necessitated substantial overtime or the addition of a second shift. The auditor should add a written comment on those events to the audit report, indicating whether they are a temporary condition or are expected to be permanent. Such comments not only explain the audit as submitted but also allow the underwriter to evaluate any adjustments necessary to the current policies.

Auditors should do the same for decreases in loss exposures. The auditor should determine, substantiate, and note the reason for the decrease. Some obvious reasons for an overall decrease include lower incoming orders or sales, the completion of old contracts with no replacement contracts, or a phasing out of a particular operation.

If no prior audit report is available, the auditor should check total payrolls, sales, or other relevant data for the prior year in the insured's records. In addition, workers' compensation exposures reported to the bureau might be available from the underwriter.

Equally important to the comparison of the overall results is the comparison of each of the individual loss exposures to those developed for the prior period. Again, the first check is to determine whether the auditor has omitted a loss exposure for a prior period from the current audit. For example, if the prior audit included payrolls for a subsidiary company that is not shown on the current audit, the auditor should determine if the current policy names that subsidiary. If so, the auditor either has failed to pick up loss exposures from that subsidiary or the subsidiary has had no payroll or sales. If the latter has happened, the auditor should explain so in the audit report. If the policy does not show the subsidiary, the auditor should determine why. Perhaps the insured has closed the subsidiary, sold it, or transferred the employees to one of the other named companies, or perhaps an oversight occurred in producing the current policy.

Another example of a discrepancy might be the omission of a special limits endorsement on a liability policy for a specific job although loss exposures exist during the current policy period. Inclusion of the endorsement on the previous audit might indicate that the underwriter had expected the insured to complete the job or possibly that the insurer erroneously omitted the endorsement. The previous policy and audit might have included a vendor's loss exposure, but the policy being audited includes no such coverage. If the insured still sells to the vendor, the auditor should ask whether the underwriter intended to provide coverage.

If the overall audit results are aligned with information from the prior audit, the auditor should determine whether classifications within the audit are aligned with prior years' audits. If not, the auditor should ask if the insured's operation changed during the year. For example, the sales classification

exposure might have decreased because the insured is now selling through independent manufacturers' representatives. If so, a loss exposure for those representatives might exist under the insured's workers' compensation policy. Similarly, the insured might have used an outside contractor rather than regular employees for building maintenance. The insured might have curtailed a part of its production operation by eliminating a product or might have decided to purchase components previously produced internally. A contractor might subcontract parts of jobs previously performed by direct employees. The auditor should ensure that the audit includes any loss exposure for additional subcontractors and that the affected classifications reflect the change.

Comparison to Industry Averages

Personal knowledge of similar businesses within the auditor's territory aids in judging whether audit figures are reasonable. A business not only competes to sell its products and services, but it also competes within an area to obtain its personnel. Consequently, both prices and wages are generally competitive in similar businesses within a territory. The wage rate might be slightly higher in the metropolitan area than in the suburbs. The auditor should consider that difference when making the comparison. Likewise, a union worker might receive slightly higher pay than the nonunion worker, who might receive slightly different benefits. Although allowing for such minor variations is necessary, comparisons of this sort can still be useful. Knowing the average or "going" wage rate in an industry helps the auditor to approximate the payroll and compare it to the audit results.

The Bureau of Labor Statistics of the U.S. Department of Labor compiles average wage rates as well as average hours worked for hundreds of industries and job classifications. Average hours worked usually indicate which industries are experiencing an increase or decrease in the volume of business. Those trends can explain a particular insured's change in volume of business. Numerous industry groups also publish similar data for their industries. Often the insured has those data from an industry association and can provide them directly.

For example, assume that the average hourly rate for an industry is $16. An insured has ten employees working a forty-hour week. The total payroll would be approximately $332,800 ($16 per hour × 40 hours × 10 employees × 52 weeks = $332,800). If the audit shows a substantially different amount, the auditor should determine and note the reason. Substantial deviations from expected wage levels and abnormal increases or decreases in business are also important underwriting factors.

The auditor can ask the following questions if the insured's wages do not correspond to industry averages:

- Is the actual wage rate approximately the indicated average rate?
- Did the insured maintain the average number of employees throughout the policy period?
- Did the insured pay employees for the entire policy period, or was there a shutdown or partial layoff for a period of time?

- Did a strike occur during the policy period?
- Did employees work full time for the entire period, or was there a period of reduced hours or substantial overtime?

While references are available to determine average wages and hours, auditors usually become familiar with such data with experience. In addition to the knowledge acquired through experience, auditors can obtain information from business magazines and daily newspapers. When making industry comparisons, auditors should be certain they are comparing similar entities. For example, the plastics industry has businesses doing many things. Producing sheet plastic might not be comparable to extruding plastic jugs and bottles. A printing operation is not the same as a bookbinder. Within printing, a shop doing all offset printing might not compare with a typeset printing operation. Auditors cannot compare a newspaper publisher to a print shop even though both involve printing. Comparisons must be made within the same industry group and ensure that the operations within the industry group are similar.

Relationship Analysis

Another way to analyze the audit findings is to use certain fundamental ratios or percentages. Relationships among different categories of financial data "may reasonably be expected by the auditor to exist and continue in the absence of known conditions to the contrary."[1] Auditors can presume, therefore, that specific ratios will fall within a certain numerical range. If not, further investigation might be necessary.

Auditors should learn what relationships to expect in various businesses. One valuable way of determining "normal" or "average" ratios is to ask the insured about the expectations for the insured's type of business. Most insureds can probably explain what is typical for their business, how their specific operations compare to similar businesses, and why their particular business might differ from others within the industry. Auditors can then confirm those expectations during the audit.

A public accountant can also provide insights about expected ratios for an industry. One accountant might not be an expert on all industries, but the accountant for several firms in one line of business should be well qualified to provide such information. In addition, Robert Morris, Dun & Bradstreet, Dodge, and many trade publications provide average ratios for industry groups. Although auditors should consult those publications for guidelines, experience also helps determine what relationships to expect. Common useful ratios are payroll to sales, payroll to employees, distribution of total payroll, profit margin, labor to materials, and payrolls by classification.

Payroll to Sales

The most obvious ratio to analyze is payroll to sales. Even if the audit does not require a sales figure, determining that ratio for the policy period is still important. No business can survive for any length of time if expenses exceed sales. Because payroll is an expense item, payroll cannot exceed sales, except

under unusual and temporary circumstances. The auditor should determine if raw materials are a factor in the expense of the business. If the business is essentially a "labor only" business, payroll will represent a significant portion of sales. Even so, a sufficient margin for overhead and profit should exist. Conversely, if both materials and labor are expense factors, the two combined must still allow for overhead and profit.

Examples: Payroll to Sales Ratio

Suppose that the policyholder, Luke, owns a restaurant. Also suppose that the auditor, Helen, has never done an audit on a restaurant and has no guidelines for restaurants. The general ledger shows gross sales of $600,000.

Helen examines the ledger and finds that rent, depreciation, and other fixed expense items amount to $140,000. She expects at least a 10 percent return on gross sales, or at least $60,000. Helen asks Luke what percentage of total sales he expects payroll to be. Luke does not know specifically but estimates that if payroll and food costs amount to two-thirds of sales value, the operation would be profitable if other expenses are tightly controlled. He estimates that labor and food costs will be about equal. Helen calculates that food and labor at two-thirds of sales would represent $400,000, and if they are about equal, the payroll should approximate $200,000.

The audit shows a payroll of $194,000, which is within an acceptable range of the expected payroll. A variation of 10 percent on that type of estimate would probably be acceptable. To double-check, Helen determines food purchases to be $214,000. Because the figures nearly match Luke's overall expectations, the audit appears to be in line based on this ratio analysis. Helen notes the payroll ratio in the file for reference in future audits as well as to develop a link of information for use in similar restaurants.

Another example involves a contractor, Lamont. The auditor, Jay, predetermines that for this type of insured, payroll and materials each run at about one-third of the contract price. However, in the audit, the actual payroll and material costs approximate only 10 percent each. Jay reviews the records to determine if any other accounts might contain payroll. While Jay discusses that possibility with Lamont, Lamont mentions that a year or so ago, when business slowed substantially, he changed how the business was operated. He let all but a few key people go when there were no jobs. Then, as a few jobs opened up, he subcontracted the work, with the subcontractors being responsible for both labor and materials. Some of Lamont's employees went site to site to ensure that the subcontractor was performing properly. Others did minor adjustments or cleanup after the job was complete, and the clerical employees continued as usual. Lamont knew that subcontract costs were about 60 percent of contract price but thought that this worked out well because it gave a fixed cost per job and eliminated the need to invest in equipment and materials. Jay was then able to verify the information and found the total result to be reasonable.

Payroll to Employees

Another ratio auditors use to verify data is a payroll to employees ratio. Obviously, the total number of employees and the total payroll should be directly related. With some exceptions, most businesses must pay at least the

minimum wage established by applicable wage and hour laws. Therefore, an auditor who knows the average number of employees can estimate the minimum payroll. The auditor must be sure to adjust payroll when a business has part-time employees and can do so by adjusting to an equivalent number of full-time employees required to perform the work on a full-time basis or by adjusting the expected payroll for the part-time employees on a ratio of actual hours worked versus full-time hours. With an industry average wage of $20 per hour, each employee on a full-time basis (forty hours) would receive at least $320 per week. For twenty full-time employees, the total payroll should be at least $832,000 ($20 per hour × 40 hours × 20 employees × 52 weeks = $832,000).

Of course, an insured rarely pays all employees the same rate. The wage paid for various tasks or functions depends on the knowledge and skills required as well as on competitive factors in the marketplace for obtaining employees with the required skills. The premium auditor can calculate the average wage rate for each occupational group or classification of the insured's employees. Remuneration of executive officers should be excluded from that calculation because to include them could substantially distort the average. If the insured's average wage reflects the average wage for that occupation published by the U.S. Department of Labor Bureau of Labor Statistics, then the auditor has an additional indication that the audit findings are reasonable.[2] An individual business can vary from an average for any number of reasons including location, availability of help, or specialized skills required.

Distribution of Total Payroll

A distribution of total payroll ratio can verify whether the portion of total payroll in each classification is reasonable for the business involved. The ratio of the clerical payroll to the total payroll depends on the particular operation. It varies not only by type of business but also by the size of the business. A small manufacturer might have six employees, one of whom is clerical. A similar manufacturer might have eighteen employees, but still only one employee is clerical. Those two cases present quite different ratios, but both are within reason. Generally, in a manufacturing operation an auditor would not expect the clerical payroll to exceed 10 percent of the total. If the insured exceeds that ratio, the auditor should investigate and provide an explanation. Some businesses have large accounts receivable departments to handle a large volume of credit business. On the other hand, some of the employees included in the clerical classification might perform other duties, and perhaps the auditor should reconsider their classification.

The auditor must analyze the business on the basis of experience, and perhaps specific guidelines issued by the auditor's company, to confirm that the clerical payrolls are consistent with expectations. The auditor should apply the same procedures to the other standard exception classifications. For example, the remuneration of salespersons should be consistent with the total payroll. That remuneration should also be consistent with the insured's method of marketing the products or services.

Likewise, the number of drivers or chauffeurs should correspond to the number of vehicles the insured owns. If the insured has one vehicle, there is probably only one driver. However, six people might share the driving responsibilities along with other duties. The auditor might not necessarily classify all six as drivers or chauffeurs. Conversely, if the insured has six vehicles, the auditors would expect six drivers. If the records indicate only one, the auditor should first confirm that the driver was properly classified. The auditor should also determine who drives the other vehicles, and if, in fact, they have other duties, that the proper classification was made.

Overtime Payroll to Total Payroll

Another useful data analysis ratio is overtime payroll to total payroll. The auditor should verify that the overtime adjustment is in line with the total payroll. Lacking any specific guidelines issued by the auditor's company, the auditor can accept a five percent ratio as reasonable. If the overtime adjustment exceeds that ratio, then the auditor should reexamine the adjustment and determine the reasons for the higher ratio. The auditor should also analyze the ratio of overtime for each classification. The analysis should also detail whether the overtime pay is recorded as time and a half, double time, premium time, etc. The way overtime pay is recorded will also affect the ratio.

Profit Margin Ratio

The profit margin ratio can sometimes alert an auditor to inconsistencies. A business usually intends to make a profit. Otherwise, it cannot exist for long. The ratio of profit to revenues depends on investment, turnover, and competition. Economic conditions or other factors specifically influencing a particular business might cause a temporary period of unprofitability. Nevertheless, over the long run a business must be profitable to survive.

Therefore, the auditor should reexamine any financial data that are not consistent with a reasonable profit for the business. The insured might be generating unreported income in a manner that could create an additional loss exposure. On the other hand, if the insured's records show extraordinary profits, there is the possibility of additional remuneration that does not show on the regular payroll.

Labor to Materials

The ratio of labor to materials offers another way to analyze audit findings. Once again, the auditor must consider the type of business and the prevailing conditions within its industry. In a service industry, materials are a less significant factor than labor. Conversely, for a business installing materials or products purchased by a customer, materials are a highly significant factor. Similarly, for a print shop, labor would probably be more significant than the paper products purchased. However, certain factors create differences among companies within the same industry. One company might have invested much more heavily in automated equipment than another, thereby reducing its labor costs. On the other hand, a company doing mostly custom work

would have a much higher labor-to-materials ratio. Knowledge of the insured's operation should enable an auditor to anticipate a reasonable ratio. Trade journals can be an important reference for guidelines in this area as in others.

Classification Ratios

When the policy bases premium on payroll, the auditor must compare the ratios of each classification to one another as well as to the total. It is highly unlikely, for example, that over 50 percent of the payroll of a manufacturing operation would be clerical. Likewise, auditors expect a construction company to have the largest percentage of payroll in the classifications applicable to the work it does. Payroll guidelines by classification are established based on experience. The auditor should always ask the insured to explain ratios that do not follow patterns the auditor expects for that business. Any unusual findings could indicate methods of operation that might have underwriting significance.

The ratios that the auditor analyzes can have acceptable variations. That is, just because a particular ratio does not meet some pre-established fixed figure does not indicate, in itself, any particular problem. Ratio analysis tests the reasonableness of the audit result. It is improbable that the insured's ratios are the exact average of others in the particular industry. However, if ratios deviate substantially from what is expected, the premium auditor should reexamine the audit figures to ensure they are correct and presented properly. The auditor must also be able to explain which aspect of the insured's operations caused the deviation.

Sampling Techniques

When a premium auditor wants to test the reasonableness of an aggregate figure, but the audit consists of many individual items, sampling techniques can be helpful. Rather than examine all of the items, the auditor can choose a representative sample. Within limits, the auditor can then project the whole from the sample data. Sampling also helps to ensure the accuracy of audit findings without the detail work that might otherwise be required.

When an insured pays employees on an hourly basis, the auditor generally compiles payroll from time records. For the premium auditor to check every payroll time record for the policy period is likely too time-consuming and probably of little value. An auditor might learn almost as much, however, from a one-month sample, which should include a holiday. To determine how the insured records the hours worked and regular, overtime, and holiday pay, the auditor must inspect a sufficient sample of the records. In addition, the sample might confirm that the classification of individual employees is consistent with actual operations.

Frequently, insureds enter pay for holidays not worked as overtime pay. The auditor should spot-check at least one week having a paid holiday to determine whether the insured has included holiday pay as an overtime item. If so, the auditor must adjust for each paid holiday during the policy period.

Many insureds group entries in their payroll records or payable systems by department and provide a subtotal for each group. That practice facilitates the classification of the insured's payroll, once the auditor determines that the insured properly includes individuals within each group. The auditor should take particular care that the insured does not automatically include supervisory or salaried personnel in a clerical class. The auditor must carefully verify each group and make any adjustments before using the insured's aggregate figures.

Because insureds make most payments for subcontractors, independent contractors, or hired trucks or equipment by check, the auditor might want to review the checkbook for a time period to determine payments made. This sample could specify the information to seek in the cash disbursements record and also reveal how the insured enters items in the cash disbursements record. Verification should precede use of the accounts. It might also be necessary to refer to a purchase record or accounts payable record, if they exist, to determine proper allocation and classification.

While reviewing the cash disbursements record, the auditor should carefully analyze the payments reflected under the miscellaneous or sundries column. Payments made infrequently or considered incidental are generally reflected in that column. Among other things, this could include commissions and payments made for casual labor, hired equipment, or even subcontractors or independent contractors.

An auditor should also review petty cash slips for a period of a month or more to determine if any cash payments should be included in the audit. The disbursements record might not show those payments in detail, and the auditor can more readily identify them right at the source. If the insured has made such cash payments during the sampled period, the auditor must review the petty cash accounts for the entire policy period.

By inspecting a sample of the receipts book, an auditor can determine whether it includes all income, that is, cash receipts, receipts on accounts receivable, and receipts from any miscellaneous sources of income. Analyzing receipts indicates how the insured keeps records and much else about the business. Renting equipment to others produces an entry in the receipts book. An entry for the sale of equipment or property could indicate a change in operations. The name of the account credited could suggest the work performed, particularly by a contractor.

Classification Review

Premium audits must determine the premium base and its classification. Because insurance rates can vary considerably based on the classification, a misclassification can substantially distort the premium. Therefore, premium auditors must review classifications to determine that the correct classifications are applied. Many of the previously mentioned methods used to analyze audit findings, such as comparing current and prior audit findings and comparing the insured's audit findings with industry averages, can also be used to

review classifications. To ensure that the classifications assigned are reasonable, a review of classifications should include a review of the following:

- Insured's operations
- Insured's employees
- Insured's exposure bases

Insured's Operations

The classification should be consistent with what the auditor expects for the insured's operations. If the insured does printing, then obviously the auditor should assign a classification that includes printing. If the insured uses automobiles, the appropriate classification should include automobiles. The audit should lead the auditor to expect a certain classification for the operation. The auditor should confirm the expectation or explain any deviation.

Examples: Confirming Classifications

Suppose that the insured manufactures only nuts and bolts. A review of the literature in the waiting room explains the quality and variety of the nuts and bolts available. In fact, one of the points made in an advertising brochure is that the insured makes no other products. As the audit progresses, nothing else indicates that the insured performs any other operation. The insured operates from this single location, as has been the case for the past eighty years. The records do not indicate any property having been bought, sold, or leased. The auditor previously verified that the classification on the policy was proper for nuts and bolts manufacturing in the insured's state. At that point, the auditor is satisfied that the appropriate governing classification is nuts and bolts manufacturing.

In a slightly different example, the auditor is dealing with the same insured, has read the same sales material in the reception area, and has become fully aware of the nuts and bolts manufacturing operations. The auditor also notes some other significant facts while conducting the audit. Just recently, the insured set up a rent account in the expense section of the general ledger, and it contains an entry for each of the past three months. At about the same time, the insured set up a separate payroll record that includes several new employees. Also, purchases in the purchase journal reflect the name of a plastics supplier.

In discussion with the insured, the auditor learns that the insured is still manufacturing nuts and bolts. In fact, the growth of that business has prompted the insured to look for additional plant space. The insured also states that the firm had done considerable market research, has rented a plant, and has begun manufacturing a new plastic "widget." The insured has not marketed that product yet. At this point, the insured has only printed promotional material but expects to make shipments shortly for an introductory marketing campaign to begin in the next thirty days.

In reviewing the entire operation, the auditor determines that this firm qualifies for more than one classification. (This was previously referred to in the workers' compensation manual as a "multiple enterprise.") The auditor classifies it as a plastics products manufacturer for the new operation, while still retaining the nuts and bolts classification for the original operations. Of course, the auditor must report that new operation to the underwriter.

The lesson to be learned from the application examples is that auditors should expect the unexpected. Using only payroll records, the auditor in the example might have considered the additional employees as an expansion of the existing operation. The insured at that point was unaware of the implications of the new operation, and a misclassification would have occurred. By considering all records, sampling and analyzing them, and then discussing them with the insured, the auditor can verify the information developed during the audit and determine proper classifications for the operations.

Auditors can use the same techniques to verify the exposure bases as they do to verify classifications. By sampling and using ratios, auditors determine whether they have assigned the proper classifications. Comparisons to prior audits or to the policy also help to verify classification accuracy. A complete analysis should give the auditor confidence in the selection of classifications.

Insured's Employees

Another area to review regarding classifications is the insured's employees. After having reviewed the insured's operations for proper classification, the auditor must still analyze what employees belong in what classification. For contractors, it is especially important to determine who does what and when.

Examples: Analyzing Employee Classifications

Suppose the nuts and bolts manufacturer from the previous example has twelve clerical employees who meet the requirements of physical separation and no interchange of labor. With no restriction on the nuts and bolts classification, the auditor should include those employees in the clerical class. In addition, the manufacturer has two salespeople on the road and an executive who calls on customers about 70 percent of the time and who is in the office the remainder of the time. The insurer has assigned those people to the outside sales class. The insurer has assigned the one individual who drives a company-owned vehicle to the chauffeur class. The remaining employees belong to the governing classification (defined later in this chapter), which is the nuts and bolts classification. The auditor finds that those remaining employees include a plant superintendent, several supervisors, the production employees, and employees incidental to the operation. The auditor confirms that the insurer has assigned the proper classifications and has allocated the proper payrolls to those classifications for the employees involved.

The insured that has recently started manufacturing plastic "widgets" is eligible for more than one classification. The plastic products manufacturing classification is appropriate for the additional operation. In reviewing the employees' duties, the auditor finds that the existing clerical staff absorbs whatever office and recordkeeping work needs to be done. As the operation grows, however, the insured might have to hire clerical staff for the support of that specific operation. The current plan is to sell the product exclusively through independent contractors. An additional chauffeur is not needed.

Among the employees recently hired is a plant manager. The manager and two supervisors spend their time in the plant overseeing the operation. The plant has one shipper-receiver and one person alternating between shipping and sweeping. In accordance with the manual rules, the auditor classifies the employees of the nuts and bolts division as in the previous example.

However, in the plastic widget division, all employees are directly involved in the plastic products manufacturing or an incidental process, and, therefore, the auditor allocates them to the plastic products manufacturing classification. After discovering the existence of an insured with more than one operation, the auditor should expect each operation will have some employees and allocate the payrolls accordingly.

If the insured operates several store locations, the auditor must apply the manual rules to determine the applicable classification at each location. Often store classifications have inclusions, and therefore certain standard exception classes are not allowed.

Sometimes the auditor must consider special rules while reviewing employees' duties. For example, in most cases, the auditor must assign warehouse employees to the classification applicable to the operations within the state. So, although confirming that these employees work at a separate location is important, the auditor must recognize the proper rules of classification and the specific inclusions or exclusions of a given class.

Contractors have unique classification rules. For example, for a contractor who installs sewer lines and water mains, the auditor should record what employees did the work and how much of those employees' payroll applies to the sewer job. In accordance with the rules of dividing an individual employee's payroll among applicable classifications, the records must adequately justify the payroll allocation. In addition, auditors must identify miscellaneous or incidental employees for proper classification.

Insured's Exposure Bases

The final area to review regarding classifications is the insured's exposure base. Depending on the coverage the policy provides, the auditor might encounter a variety of exposure bases for the insured. To treat each exposure base properly, the auditor must review and apply the appropriate manual rules for inclusions and exclusions for each.

The predominant exposure base that auditors encounter is remuneration, or payroll. The complexity of rules applicable to that exposure base requires that the auditor be aware of basic and governing classifications, standard exceptions, general inclusions and exclusions, and the amounts included for officers or owners.

All of the classifications listed in the workers' compensation manual, other than the standard exception classifications, are **basic classifications**. The auditor should assign the basic classification that best describes the business (operations, products, or services) of an employer within a state. The auditor's analytical review should indicate whether the correct basic classification was applied.

The **governing classification** at a specific job or location is the classification, other than a standard exception classification, that produces the greatest amount of payroll. The governing classification is relevant when more than one classification is permitted. The auditor should determine the governing classification early in a workers' compensation audit because the payroll of

Basic classification
Any classification of an employer's business listed in the *Basic Manual for Workers' Compensation and Employers Liability Insurance* that is not a standard exception classification.

Governing classification
The classification, other than a standard exception classification, that produces the greatest amount of payroll at an employer's location for the purpose of rating workers' compensation insurance.

employees not explicitly mentioned elsewhere in the rules must be included in the governing classification.

The preceding examples demonstrate that facts can differ from expectations. If the auditor determines that the insured's operations changed or were not what the insurer previously found them to be, the auditor must review the operations and properly substantiate any such change in classifications in the audit report. Many insurers require the auditor to submit that information to the underwriter when the auditor finally determines the proper classification.

One of the examples involved the nuts and bolts manufacturer who developed an additional product that created a business for which the manual permitted more than one basic classification. If the insured qualifies for more than one basic classification, the auditor must review the appropriateness of the original classification and determine what the additional classification should be. If the insured does not qualify for more than one basic classification, the auditor must review the appropriateness of the existing basic classification for the two operations. The workers' compensation manual gives instructions to determine the appropriate classification.

Audits for contractors frequently result in a change, addition, or deletion of classifications. Because several classifications might be used in the audit, auditors must correctly determine the governing classification to properly classify miscellaneous employees. Auditors should also determine the governing classification for the policy period and by job. Interim audits might have assigned miscellaneous employees to the classification with the largest loss exposure for the period audited or to the classification that the auditor presumes will be the governing classification for the policy period.

Sometimes the governing classification for the policy period can develop so that it is not the same as the classification with the largest loss exposure in any or all of the interim audit periods. The auditor should review the audits for the interim periods to ensure that the final audit for the policy period reflects all adjustments necessary and is consistent with the actual governing classification. Those adjustments might be because of the different type of work being performed during the particular interim period. At the final audit, the auditor must review the work performed during the entire policy year. The auditor determines the basic and governing classification or classifications that apply based on the loss exposures for the complete policy period.

Also, the basic or governing classification developed for the policy period might not be the classification that the auditor anticipated. Therefore, the auditor must make the appropriate adjustments for the governing classification applicable for the policy period.

Standard exception classification
A separate workers' compensation classification for an occupation or operation that is common to many businesses.

Some occupations or operations, such as clerical office employees, are so common to many businesses that the workers' compensation manual has established them as separate classifications. A **standard exception classification** is a separate workers' compensation classification for an occupation or operation that is common to many businesses. The basic classification

does not include employees who fall within the definition of a standard exception classification unless the basic classification specifically includes them. The National Council *Basic Manual* lists the following as standard exceptions:

- Clerical employees
- Drafting employees
- Drivers, chauffeurs, and their helpers
- Outside salespersons
- Collectors and messengers

If an insured has only a few employees in the standard exception classifications, the auditor should include a list showing the employees, their duties, and their remuneration in the audit report. If the insured has many employees in the standard exception classification, the list can be arranged by department, showing duties and remuneration for the entire department.

The auditor should list employees or departments for standard exception classifications, even though the basic or governing classification includes one of the standard exception classifications. For example, "Electrical Wiring—Within Buildings & Drivers" is a classification that includes the standard exception driver employees within it. The auditor should list those employees on the audit report as drivers and should include their remuneration in the electrical wiring classification. That listing confirms that the insured has employees who are drivers. Further, should some change in classification become necessary, the new classification might not include drivers. The auditor or insurer could make an adjustment without another visit to the insured.

The auditor should treat employees in each of the standard exception classifications in this manner and should also confirm that the premium overtime and payroll limitation rules, if applicable, have been properly applied to each of those classifications. Any special rules that apply, such as a classification description including a standard exception classification, should be explained so the insured clearly understands those rules.

To ensure that employees have been properly included in standard exception classifications, the auditor might ask to see the area where a particular group of clerical employees works, to verify that the insured has met all of the requirements of the classification. If three clerical employees appear in the records and all three are evident in the area where the auditor is working, it is easy to confirm the classification. If, on the other hand, the policy or insured's records list six clerical employees, but only three are present in the immediate area, the auditor should confirm the other three clerical positions. For example, one employee might be a timekeeper. The auditor must determine whether that timekeeper meets the manual requirements to be assigned to the clerical classification; if not, the auditor should explain the employee's correct classification to the insured. Similarly, the auditor must confirm that a salaried superintendent or an order clerk in the shipping department shown in the clerical classification is properly classified before allocating his or her payroll to the classification.

For sales personnel, the auditors may need to determine whether they should be included in the governing classification or whether they actually are outside salespersons or messengers. Employers generally pay salespersons in whole or in part on a commission basis. The auditor should investigate those cases in which an individual does not appear to be paid on a commission basis. Insureds might also pay route salespersons and store sales personnel through a sales remuneration or commission plan. Those people should not be included under the standard exception salespersons classification. Messengers also present a unique challenge. The auditor must ensure that an employee listed as a messenger is not, in fact, a driver or chauffeur.

General inclusion
A category of business operations that is common in many businesses and is, therefore, included in the scope of the basic classification in the *Basic Manual* for rating workers' compensation insurance.

General exclusion
A category of business operations that is so unusual that the *Basic Manual* excludes it from the basic classification for rating workers' compensation insurance.

General inclusions are operations that appear to be separate businesses but that the manual includes within the scope of all classifications other than the standard exception classifications. In contrast, **general exclusions** are operations of a business that are so unusual that the manual excludes them from the basic classification and requires separate classification.

General inclusions involve the operation of commissaries for the insured's employees, the manufacture of containers for use by the insured, the provision of medical facilities for employees, the maintenance or repair of the insured's buildings or equipment by the insured's employees, and the printing by the insured on its own products. If an operation appears to qualify as a general inclusion, the auditor should confirm that it is not a separate business. One way to confirm the operation's status is to determine whether the insured actually sells the products or results of the operation or just uses them within the business.

Examples of general exclusions include the operation of aircraft, construction or alterations performed by the insured's employees, and stevedoring. Unless specifically included in the classification wording, the auditor should separately classify those operations. The auditor should also provide details about the classifications. Those details help in premium development and often help the underwriter determine whether the policy properly reflects the loss exposures and provides the coverage the insured anticipated.

Any time a general inclusion or a general exclusion operation exists, the auditor should carefully review the manual wording of the basic classification describing the insured's operation to determine the manual rule's application. Auditors must remember in this instance that specific classification wording takes precedence. The auditor should fully document all items so that everyone clearly understands the audit.

To ensure that remuneration has been assigned to the proper classification, the auditors should list the corporate officers and their duties. If the policy provides coverage for the owners or partners, the auditor should list them. The list should include all officers, even those that might not be active in the business; the duties of each officer, owner, or partner; and the remuneration of each officer, noting those officers receiving no remuneration. Even in states that provide an executive officer classification, the auditor should clearly define the duties of the officers to determine whether the classification applies.

If questions arise about the list's accuracy or completeness, the auditor should check the annual filing of corporations required in the state or the minutes of the board of directors. That information helps verify the minimums and maximums applicable to executive officers. The auditor must also check workers' compensation policies for exclusion endorsements that might exclude any or all of the officers from coverage under the policy.

The auditor should complete the detailed list of corporate officers and their duties each year. Changes in executive officers and yearly changes in the duties of executive officers are not uncommon.

Most states allow workers' compensation coverage for owners and partners. Because they are not employees, owners and partners do not appear on the payroll. The premium base, however, includes them at a fixed amount. Auditors should list names and duties of those persons individually so that these fixed amounts can be allocated to the proper classifications.

To avoid misclassification, the auditor must exercise extreme care when verifying an individual's duties. The auditor must verify duties using whatever sources of information are available. Sources include loss control reports, claim reports, and people within the insured's organization who fully understand the duties of the owners and partners.

SUMMARY

Verification and analysis ensure that all aspects of an audit are appropriate in relation to the insured's actual loss exposures. The auditor should use all possible means to ensure that data are sufficient, accurate, and reasonable.

From the time the auditor arrives at the insured's premises, verification and analysis must confirm expectations developed in the initial audit planning and review. As questions arise, auditors must obtain additional information from the insured's records, from independent sources such as publications relating to the business or industry, and from discussions with the insured. Physically inspecting part or all of the insured's operations might also be required to resolve questions or problems. The audit figures must be verified and reconciled against independent records. Sources of verification and reconciliation can include the general ledger, accounting journals, tax returns, financial statements, regulatory reports, and other relevant information.

During the audit, the auditor must also analyze data reasonableness by reviewing policy coverages and changes, audit findings, and classifications. The auditor analyzes the relationship of the total loss exposure to other financial aspects of the business. The payroll should be correlated to total sales and to the number of employees. Other ratios help the auditor to determine that elements within the audit are aligned with one another and are also reasonable for the industry. The auditor should also sample records to determine how the insured maintains them and how the insured records various transactions.

The auditor must also review classifications to determine if there are any new classifications or classification changes. This analysis includes properly confirming inclusions or exclusions for officers, partners, and owners. Auditors must detail their analyses of officers and standard exception classifications in accordance with any restrictive wording contained in the classifications definitions. Similar analyses of general inclusions and exclusions must be consistent with manual rules and the requirements of other classifications used.

A final analysis is necessary to determine that the auditor has developed loss exposures for all coverages provided in the policies. Conversely, auditors should note loss exposures for which no apparent coverage exists and should advise the underwriter of such.

The auditor should also review the audit results with the insured. That review is essential not only as an additional step in verifying audit information but also in ensuring the insured's agreement and understanding. This step usually clarifies or eliminates any misunderstanding that might otherwise develop.

If the audit data are sufficient, accurate, and reasonable, the premium auditor can be assured that audit findings are also sufficient, accurate, and reasonable. The auditor can then prepare a complete audit report.

CHAPTER NOTES

1. "Analytical Review Procedures," *Statement on Auditing Standards*, No. 23 (New York: American Institute of Certified Public Accountants, 1978), §3.
2. Earnings by industry are available at the Bureau of Labor Statistics Web site: www.bls.gov.

Direct Your Learning 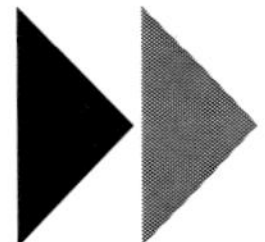

Premium Audit Report

Educational Objectives

After learning the content of this chapter and completing the corresponding course guide assignment, you should be able to:

- Describe the goals of an audit report.
- Describe the guidelines for preparing audit reports.
- Explain the nature of and/or why each of the following is an important component of an audit report:
  - Description of operations
  - Summary of loss exposures
  - Explanatory notes
  - Insured's signature
- Explain what audit report information is needed by other insurance company departments and why that information is needed.
- Describe audit report billing procedures.
- Given a case, apply appropriate guidelines and procedures for handling disputed audits.
- Define or describe each of the Key Words and Phrases for this chapter.

OUTLINE

Develop Your Perspective

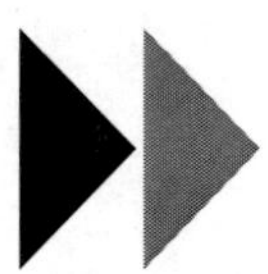

What are the main topics covered in the chapter?

The premium audit report is the documentation data collected in the audit process converted into a usable formula. This chapter emphasizes the goals of the premium audit report and presents guidelines for preparing effective reports.

Identify features of an effective premium audit report.

- Why must the results of the premium audit be recorded?
- What are the options available to handle a disputed audit?

Why is it important to learn about these topics?

Like the audit itself, the decisive ingredient of the written report is organization.

Consider the organization of the audit report.

- Why should unnecessary information be excluded from the report?
- Generally, why should the audit report follow a systematic format?

How can you use what you will learn?

While company procedures vary, certain elements are essential to any premium audit report. Evaluate the elements of a premium audit report.

- What information must be reported for premium determination?
- What information should be reported to other departments?
- How do other departments use the reported information?

Premium Audit Report

The audit report completes the audit process. The audit report records the findings, necessary explanations, and pertinent information for other departments and future auditors. In addition to recording figures extracted from the insured's records, much of what the auditor records stems from observing the insured's operations, premises, and equipment.

A complete audit report includes all communications resulting from a premium audit. Regardless of the format preferred by the company for the audit report components, those components should include the description of operations, the recapitulation for billing, all necessary explanatory notes, and any notices to other departments. This chapter describes the goals of an audit report and presents a format for systematically preparing the report.

GOALS OF THE AUDIT REPORT

The primary goal of the audit report is to record the data necessary to determine earned premium. Additional goals include documenting audit procedures and findings and providing ratemaking and other information. An auditor should keep all three of those goals in mind while preparing the audit report.

Record Data for Earned Premium Determination

The audit report is particularly important as the vehicle by which the insurer determines the premium. The final earned premium is generated from the audit data and resulting classifications of the insured's loss exposures in accordance with the policy terms. Therefore, the auditor must fully document all data pertaining to the audit, any deviations from what is normal practice, and the reasons behind those deviations.

Whether the auditor concludes with a premium calculation and billing or submits the report for premium calculation by a trained office staff member, the end result should be the same—an accurate premium billing determined in accordance with the insurance policy, the insured's operations, and the laws of the governing insurance jurisdiction.

If the auditor must refer decisions on classifications or other topics to an office staff member who is far removed from the audit, the auditor should fully explain the data and circumstances to that staff member. Auditors should produce reports complete and accurate enough so that anyone trained in premium audit billing could produce accurate billings from them.

Document Audit Procedures and Findings

During the audit process, the auditor uses a complex decision process and makes many judgments. The auditor must explain these procedures and judgments in the audit report. Should any questions arise about the audit, the report must show how the auditor arrived at the result. If an audit is not well documented, another auditor or manager might need to duplicate much of the original auditor's work.

Just as the auditor must document in the audit report *how* the audit was conducted, the auditor must also document *what* the audit found. A properly documented report leaves a trail for a subsequent auditor to follow. That trail has obvious value if the auditor cannot complete the audit or if the insured disputes the audit. No matter how well an audit has been conducted, insureds sometimes dispute audits, sometimes immediately, sometimes weeks, months, or even years later. The report documents information and provides a reference whenever disputes arise.

Auditors should document not only facts and conclusions but also the sources of information used. The persons interviewed, types of records examined, and sources of information are all significant indicators of the findings' accuracy. The findings in the report should pertain to the classifications, loss exposures, operations, and considerations that will help other departments or future auditors to use them.

Auditors can sometimes prevent disputes and re-audits if they review the audit report with the insured. Any copy of the audit report given to the insured should be written so that the insured can understand it.

Finally, each audit report becomes part of the permanent file, available for review by auditors before subsequent audits and as a useful guide.

Provide Ratemaking and Other Information

Audit reports provide statistics used to develop rates and provide information to other insurer departments. Ratemaking statistics are developed from the audit and the audit report. Accurate audits are those that are completely reported and properly billed by classifications, territory, and coverage. Those audits are essential in providing companies, bureaus and advisory organizations, and state jurisdictions with the statistical data necessary to calculate valid insurance loss costs and rates.

The audit report also disseminates information to other departments. The auditor must be aware of other departments' needs when gathering, recording, and communicating information. A later portion of this chapter describes that information and its relevance.

GUIDELINES FOR PREPARING AUDIT REPORTS

The following guidelines can help auditors prepare accurate and well-documented audit reports:

- Allow sufficient time
- Prepare the report promptly
- Be concise, clear, and credible
- Be action based
- Use a systematic format

Allow Sufficient Time

Sometimes auditors underestimate the time needed to conclude the audit and to prepare the supporting audit report. Whether using a computer or conducting a manual audit, the auditor must allow enough time to finish the audit, summarize it, prepare the audit report, and review the details of the report with the insured. Determining in advance exactly how much time that will take can be difficult because that depends on complexity, peculiarities, necessary explanatory remarks, individual speed, and company requirements. Nevertheless, with time, experience, and forethought, an auditor should be able to estimate the report writing time with a reasonable degree of accuracy. For renewal policies, the previous audit file usually provides some idea about the time that the report might require.

Prepare the Report Promptly

The audit report is most accurate when prepared while the facts are still fresh in the auditor's mind. Although many pressures combine to erode the time available to prepare the audit report, auditors should not delay completing it. Using a notebook computer, the auditor can complete the report while still on the insured's premises, compare loss exposures to the previous audit, and print a summary copy of the report for the insured to sign and date. The insured can keep a copy of the summary and compare it to the final audit statement or bill when either arrives. Some insurers require auditors to electronically transmit their audits each evening.

Be Concise, Clear, and Credible

Audit reports should be concise; that is, they should convey information in as few words as needed to be understandable. Mark Twain once said, "If I had had more time, I would have written a shorter letter." That quotation illustrates the inclination that most people have to start writing without really knowing what they want to say. For an audit report, that lack of planning could result in a lengthy, disorganized report with excessive and repetitive information.

Audit reports should also be clear (understandable). The auditor should focus on who will be reading and acting on the report and what the reader needs to know to complete the action. The auditor must make the information clear by, among other things, systematically presenting figures and defining technical words.

The audit report should also be credible (believable). The usefulness of the report depends mainly on how credible it is to the reader. People will not act on information or figures they do not believe to be correct. The information in the report must be verified, particularly when the report contains data or information contrary to normal or expected practice or contrary to prior reports or information on file. Irrelevant information in a report can also affect credibility by creating confusion and doubt that may erode confidence in the entire report.

Be Action Based

The audit report is not only to inform but also to prompt action, for example, a premium billing that leads to other actions. While preparing the report, the auditor should keep in mind the expected resulting action and should be aware that many people may have an interest in reading and acting on the audit report. The premium audit department needs logically and consistently presented facts and figures to facilitate a premium billing. The format should be clear to make checking and processing easier. If the report supplies figures recapitulated for a billing, then brevity is essential. If the report provides an account of the insured's operations on a month-by-month basis concluding with a recap, detail is necessary. For the claim, marketing, and underwriting departments, information in the report may fill in gaps or correct inaccurate file information. Many other individuals may also be interested in reading and acting upon the audit report, including insureds, producers, general managers, home office executives, accountants, attorneys, judges, and insurance regulators.

Use a Systematic Format

The auditor should systematically present the information in an audit report. Just as insurers need uniform standards of insurance auditing, so too do they need a uniform system of preparing the audit report. A systematic format makes reading, understanding, checking, and processing easy for the reader and helps eliminate omissions, avoid duplications, and streamline the preparation process for the auditor.

Report formats can vary by company and by individual. Exhibit 9-1 presents a format that can serve as a model. It follows the normal steps of the audit process, from the pre-audit investigation to the final report. The following items describe the corresponding items in Exhibit 9-1 (circled numbers in exhibit correspond to numbered items here):

1. Name, address, policy number(s), policy period, audit period, location of records, and phone number.

2. Description of operations. Ideally, the description should precede the record examination and figure extraction process because the classification should fit the description, rather than the description fitting the classification.
3. Gross payroll (or gross sales for general liability) and verification.
4. Analysis by classification.
5. Deductions (overtime, limitation excess, and so on).
6. Additions (board and lodging, amounts necessary to bring to minimum, and so on).
7. Additions (miscellaneous or casual labor not previously shown).
8. Additions (uninsured subcontractors, and those with inadequate limits in general liability).
9. Exposures for special jobs, increased limits, waivers, U.S. Longshore and Harbor Workers Compensation Act (USL&HW), and maritime exposures.
10. Ownership (names, duties, amounts included, and classification).
11. The **billing summary**, a recapitulation by classification and state, including rate changes and exposure breaks. Normally it should appear on a separate page so that there is no doubt about which figures to use in extending the premium.
12. Clearing of entities shown on policy. For each entity, the report should either show the exposure or show that no exposure exists. If there is no exposure, the auditor should explain the entity's relationship to the insured.
13. Clearing of classifications shown on policy. Similarly, the report should account for all classifications.
14. Clearing of states shown on policy. Again, the report should account for every state shown.
15. Explanatory remarks and notes concerning any policyholder peculiarities or deviations from normal auditing or classification procedures and reasons.
16. Notes for other departments.
17. Listing of records examined and notes for other auditors.
18. Insured's signature and date (most software programs will capture the date).
19. Auditor's signature.

Billing summary
A section in an audit report that summarizes an organization's classifications by state, rate changes, and exposure breaks used to extend the premium.

The auditor may modify this format, depending on the type of coverage audited, the jurisdiction involved, and the aspects of the audit that particular insurers want to emphasize. However, adhering to this or a similar format produces a thorough, readable report, and it can be used for all reports, regardless of the size of the audit.

Review the Audit Report

The importance of precise writing cannot be overemphasized. In conversation, ideas can be repeated, modified, and explained based on feedback from the listener. Written reports provide no opportunity for such feedback. What

EXHIBIT 9-1

Suggested Format for Audit Report

(1) Insured — Any Company, 112 Broad Street, Wichita, KS — Policy No. WC 102030 — Policy Period: 7-1-X5 to 7-1-X6 — Audit Period: Same

(Records at Able Accounting, 50 Riverside Drive, Wichita, KS 39301)

(2) Operations: Masonry contractor, new houses and commercial buildings. No subcontractors. No drivers. Part-time office help.

		Gross Payroll	Clerical-8810	Masonry-5022		Verification
7-20X5	(3)	$ 2,050	(4) $ 200	(4) ↑		(941 Reports)
8		2,210	200			3Q 20X5 $6,668
9		2,408	200			4Q 20X5 $6,564
10		2,396	200			1Q 20X6 $3,660
11		2,368	200			2Q 20X6 $7,183
12 (Bonuses included)		1,800	300	Balance		Total $24,075
1-20X6		1,260	250			Audit $24,075
2		1,200	250			0
3		1,200	250			
4		2,015	250			
5		2,550	250			
6		2,618	250	↓		
		$24,075	$2,800	$21,275		
	(5)	(1,280)		(1,280)	Overtime premium	
	(6)	0		0	Limitation excess	
		1,600		1,600	To bring Vice President Jones to required minimum	
	(7)	620		620	Casual labor, cash payment	
	(8)	0		0	Subcontractors	
		$25,015	$2,800	$22,215		

(9) Other loss exposures: No USL&HW — No special jobs

(10) Ownership:
- President—K. Jones — $12,000 included 5022
- Vice President—L. Jones — $3,600 included 5022; +$1,600 added to equal minimum
- Secretary-Treasurer—M. Jones — No salary, not active

(11) Billing Summary

Kansas Masonry -	5022	$22,215
Kansas Clerical -	8810	2,800

(12) No other entities

(13) No other classifications

(14) No other states

(15) No deviations

(16) No notes for other departments

(17) Records examined: payroll journal, cash book, individual earnings records, 941 Forms

Note: Oklahoma work expected next year.

(18) *R. Jones* — Signature of Insured — *7-15-X6* Date

(19) *M. Brown* — Signature of Auditor — *7-15-X6* Date

people read is what they will act on, whether or not what was written is what was meant. Therefore, premium auditors should review the audit report after it is written and revise as necessary to ensure that the report communicates what was intended. Auditors should check the accuracy of figures and information, fill in missing details, and clarify any aspects of the report that might not be obvious to readers. Auditors should check grammar and spelling. Reports with spelling and grammar errors raise questions about the accuracy of other aspects of the report.

COMPONENTS OF AUDIT REPORTS

The audit report presents the data gathered during the audit and contains the following four components, shown in Exhibit 9-1:

1. Description of operations
2. Summary of loss exposures
3. Explanatory notes
4. Insured's signature

Description of Operations

The first component of an audit report is the description of operations. It follows the standard identifying information on the audit report.

To prepare an accurate description of operations, ○ in the exhibit, the auditor should evaluate the overall operation of each entity the policy covers and should include descriptions of any of the entity's branch operations or departments that relate to the classifications or applicable coverages. For some coverages, such as workers' compensation, classifications are by state. For others, classifications are country-wide. The description of operations should also address the following questions regarding processes:

- How does the insured perform a particular operation?
- Does the insured use subcontractors?
- How does the insured sell or move products?

When appropriate, the description of operations should also note the absence of any operations that are usual in the insured's type of business. For example, the auditor should note that an audited restaurant has no takeout or delivery operations or that an audited gasoline station has no full-service pumps.

A description of operations need not be more than one paragraph covering the essential facts. Only the exceptional aspects of a particular operation require elaboration. To distinguish what is exceptional from what is normal for a particular type of business, an auditor might consult a source such as the Premium Audit Advisory Service's *Classification Guide*. That publication can also provide clues about particular matters to investigate during an audit.

Example: Description of Operations

Insured operates a retail cattle and poultry feed store. Operations include mixing, grinding, and packaging feed. Materials are received by rail and truck. Farmers phone in orders. Insured delivers orders by truck.

Special Note: The insured is adding a building material yard, which will handle lumber, sand, gravel, cement, brick, tile, and general line of building supplies. This is a separate location. Labor will not be interchanged. Customers will phone in orders for supplies. The insured will deliver orders by truck.

The insured's own advertising brochures can be an important source of information about its operations. Other sources of information include claim abstracts, loss control reports, bureau inspections, newspaper stories and ads, Dun & Bradstreet reports, and the yellow pages. Often, the auditor can attach those supplemental sources to the audit report and conclude the description with the notation, "See attached brochure."

The description of operations is the cornerstone on which classifications are based. Consequently, the description must accurately reflect what the auditor observes about the insured's operations and must describe, in detail, any change in the insured's operations that results in an additional classification not listed on the current policy. Underwriters need this information to endorse the policy if the operation is a continuing one, and bureaus and advisory organizations need it for approving the use of a new classification. Many insurers require their auditors to prepare a separate underwriting notice or advisory when the premium audit uncovers any material change to the insured's operations.

NCCI *Basic Manual* rules detail how insurers can change classifications after a policy is in force. If the insured's operations change, the insurer can change classifications as of the date of the change and make a pro rata adjustment. If the insurer determines that it assigned an improper class and that correcting that class would result in a decrease in premium, the insurer must make the change retroactive to the policy's inception date. If the change would result in an increase in premium, the change can be made as follows, depending on when the insurer discovers the error:

- If the insurer discovers the error during the first 120 days of the policy period, the insurer can make the change retroactive to the inception date.
- If the insurer discovers the error after the first 120 days of the policy period, but before the final 90 days, the insurer must make the change as of the date it discovers the error and make a pro rata charge.
- If the insurer discovers the error within the last ninety days of the policy period, manual rules do not allow a change in the classification for that policy period.

Of course, all of those rules assume that the insured did not misrepresent or conceal information from the insurer. If the insured did, the insurer should make the change as of the date on which the change should have applied if no misrepresentation had occurred.[1] Certain jurisdictions might have more stringent requirements. Timely audits and effective communication of the audit findings can at least prevent the same situation from recurring.

In addition to describing existing classifications, the premium auditor should explain classifications that are not applied but are normal for the operation. Consider a residential carpentry contractor with workers' compensation and commercial general liability coverage audited simultaneously. A description of operations reading "general contractor, new houses" might describe what the insured does and might support the corresponding carpentry classifications, but it does not explain the absence of the usual classifications associated with house building. A better description of operations might read as follows: "General contractor, new houses, all work sublet *except* rough-in carpentry. Certificates of insurance available for all subcontractors. No repair or remodeling, no commercial carpentry." Such a description, while not lengthy, supports the residential carpentry classification for private residences and various subcontracted work classifications. More important, however, is that the amplified description explains the absence of the related construction classifications and eliminates any questions about the applicability of the commercial carpentry classifications.

Summary of Loss Exposures

A second component of audit reports is the summary of loss exposures. The multiplicity of operations and numerous variations in accounting systems prohibit a standard format for this summary. Generally, however, the auditor should first develop and verify the total loss exposure. The verification should be clearly apparent on the audit report but separated from the calculation of the loss exposure.

The auditor should then develop the applicable classifications, carefully observing all classification procedure rules. Often, auditors must show miscellaneous employees separately until their governing classification can be determined and then assigned accordingly.

The auditor should devote a section of the summary to ownership, including names, titles, duties, amounts of payroll, and classifications. Some insurers prefer that this information appear immediately after the policy information on the audit report.

Questions often arise about the classification of a specific executive officer. Many re-audits or disputes stem from disagreements about the amounts and classification assignments of owners' and officers' payrolls. Displaying that information explicitly in the report helps prevent confusion and controversy, substantiates the premium charge, and provides a reference for any later explanations.

Once the total loss exposure by classification and ownership has been developed, the auditor should indicate deductions for overtime wages and payrolls in excess of manual limitations. At this point, the auditor should also indicate the additional amounts for board and lodging and unpaid employees and the amounts necessary to bring officers' remuneration to a required minimum. Another item to check and apply, if applicable, is the addition of miscellaneous day or casual labor and leased workers not previously included in the payroll. Finally, the auditor should include uninsured subcontractors, if any, in the appropriate classification.

Having determined a net exposure base by classification, the auditor might need to isolate special coverages and loss exposures. That could include policies with higher limits of liability; waivers of subrogation; and exposures related to occupational disease, miscellaneous liability, U.S. Longshore and Harbor Workers (USL&HW) Compensation Act, and maritime exposures. If the insured uses any aircraft, the auditor should show the name, use, and number of passenger seats for each aircraft.

The detail can become complicated on a sizable audit, especially to those who have not been involved in an audit before. Consequently, when the auditor determines the premium base by classification, or at any other premium base that is to be carried forward to the summary, the appropriate page and line should be indicated to alert the auditor and processors that the item should be brought forward to the summary.

The billing summary, Item 11 on the suggested format and in Exhibit 9-1, is where the auditor shows the final billing information. The summary can duplicate other portions of the audit report, but that duplication is necessary. Although the auditor underlines twice the net figures the insurer will bill, the person billing the audit could easily miss these figures among the details of the audit report.

The auditor should review and compare the estimated premium bases for each classification to those developed by the audit. For any significant change, up or down, the auditor should include an explanation, which is important to underwriters in evaluating the risk.

Another reason for the loss exposure summary is to locate all data for premium billing in one place. These data should be presented in proper billing order. For workers' compensation policies, data should be presented in summary form by entity and by state. For liability policies, data should also be separated by coverages. The billing order might vary by insurer, but, whatever the order, the summary should display the billing order.

The summary of loss exposures should be double-spaced to make reading easier and to avoid confusion in case corrections are necessary. For clarity, the summary should identify classifications with code numbers and with loss exposures. Locations, territories, and other required information should also be easily identifiable with the classifications. If the auditor is auditing two or more policies simultaneously, the distinction between policies and

loss exposures must be maintained. Any additional loss exposures, such as USL&HW Compensation Act, occupational disease, or special jobs, should be clearly shown in the summary and in proper sequence for billing.

Although circumstances sometimes dictate otherwise, the summary is ideally just that, a summary of loss exposures. Any additional calculations in the summary tend only to confuse the reader. Also, other remarks and notes have their place elsewhere in the report, and the auditor should not incorporate them into the summary.

Explanatory Notes

The third component of audit reports is the explanatory notes. Items 12 through 17 of the suggested format in Exhibit 9-1 consist of explanatory notes pertaining to the audit and the policy. The notes should show that the auditor has investigated the actual loss exposures and has accounted for (cleared) all (12) entities, (13) classifications, and (14) states shown on the policy, as well as (15) any explanatory remarks, notes, and deviations from normal auditing or classification procedures, (16) notes for other departments, and (17) listing of records examined.

Clearing of Entities

Clearing of entities means that an auditor either shows the actual loss exposure in the detail and summary sections of the audit or confirms the lack of loss exposure in that part of the report used specifically for clearing of entities. The audit report must clear, accounting for all entities shown on the policy and any that are not named but that are covered because of the wording of the named insured endorsement. When an insured firm conducts business under different names or, for some reason, comprises different legal entities, the policy might list several entities as named insureds. Loss exposures for all entities named on the policy must be shown.

The auditor should not merely clear those entities for which there is an estimated loss exposure. Operations change, and dormant or inactive entities have a way of reviving. Auditors can lose premium by failing to clear entities. Information about an entity that has become defunct or that has changed names should be included in the report and conveyed to the underwriting department so that the names on the policy can be revised. In some cases, the policy may have to be rewritten if the name change is precipitated by an ownership change.

Clearing of Classifications

The same reasoning applies to clearing (accounting for) all classifications on the policy that applies to clearing all entities. If classifications are not cleared, auditors might overlook classifications and coverages that apply, and the insurer might lose premiums. In addition, special job endorsements and classifications no longer applicable to an insured's operations could remain on an insured's policy for years, causing extra work for all involved.

Clearing of States

Although not as critical from the standpoint of premiums, clearing of states, nevertheless, is important from the standpoint of filing premium audit information with bureaus and advisory organizations. On the experience filing, the auditor must account for all states shown on an interstate-rated workers' compensation policy. The auditor's failure to clear the states leaves open the question of whether the insured is operating in other states.

Explanatory Remarks and Notes

Sometimes a classification or classifications actually used might not reflect the insured's loss exposures, based on the description of operations. The most common reasons for discrepancies are the following:

- Interchange of labor
- Lack of an accurate breakdown between classifications
- Bureau or advisory organization assignment of another classification

The auditor should settle discrepancies by explaining variations in classification and providing the documentation to answer any future questions about the discrepancies.

Deviations From Normal Auditing or Classification Procedures

For justifiable reasons, some audits deviate from standard audit procedure. Those deviations can have a small or a large effect on premium. Even if the effect is small, the auditor should explain the nature of the deviation and its reason as well as its probable effect on premium. Deviations made for the auditor's convenience might be acceptable when the premium effect is small and when the insured has concurred with it. A common example permitted by some insurers is when the policy period extends from the fifteenth of the month to the fifteenth of the same month the following year. Assuming little week-to-week payroll fluctuation, the auditor can save considerable time by auditing from the first of the month to the first of the same month the following year. That situation does not require a detailed explanation—only a brief comment, such as, "audit from first to the first for convenience, premium difference inconsequential."

Noting the deviations on the audit report can minimize future questions and controversy. If the deviation is the result of an insured's deficient recordkeeping practices, a note in the audit report can prompt an insured to take remedial action to rectify deficiencies. The auditor should discuss such deviations with the insured and make recommendations to correct the problem. It might also be appropriate to put some recommendations in writing for the insured, with a copy for the insurer.

Notes for Other Departments

Insurers differ regarding notes for other departments. Some insurers include all information for other departments in the premium audit report, but most only make a notation on the audit report and prepare a separate document. Regardless of procedure, auditors should make sure that the information includes or references any supporting documentation.

Listing of Records Examined

The premium audit report should list all records examined by the auditor. That list serves as a useful reference for the auditor if a question arises about the audit and for the auditor who performs the next audit. The records list should include notes about any difficulties in obtaining those records or any unusual features of the records.

Insured's and Auditor's Signatures

The fourth component of audit reports is the insured's and auditor's signatures. Item 18 in Exhibit 9-1 is the signature of the insured or the insured's representative with whom the auditor has reviewed the audit. Occasionally, insureds refuse to sign an audit report. Some insurers do not even ask for signatures because they have no legal effect, that is, they do not signify the insured's agreement with audit results. They do, however, establish that the audit actually occurred and that the audit data are authentic (from the insured's records).

However, obtaining the insured's signature is a good practice because it indicates that the auditor has taken the time to explain the audit to the insured. That step concludes the auditor's visit and establishes the identity of the person reviewing the audit in case questions should arise later. The report should also include the date the insured signed the report. Item 19 shows the auditor's signature and date.

OTHER INFORMATION

The auditor is usually one of the few insurer representatives who comes into contact with the insured and who views the insured's operations firsthand. Certainly the auditor is the only insurer representative who has access to the insured's confidential books of record. Consequently, auditors usually have access to more direct information about the insured than any other insurer department. An important secondary goal of the audit report is to provide other departments with information that relates to their functions and to answer the insured's questions.

Underwriting and Marketing Departments

The underwriter's fundamental responsibility is to select a book of business that produces a profit. That responsibility involves reviewing available information and often obtaining additional information about potential insureds. The selection process involves determining the proper classifications and price; reviewing the insured's past performance; evaluating hazards in relation to the operations, equipment, and materials used; and analyzing the character and experience of employees and management. In addition, the underwriter in some lines of business can modify the price by making special filings or can modify policy conditions such as restricting coverage on certain loss exposures. Underwriters must also consider the possibilities for loss control.

Once a policyholder is accepted, the underwriter must periodically monitor the account to determine continuing desirability and future action. Throughout that process, the underwriter bases most of the analysis on information furnished by someone else. Seldom does the underwriter inspect the insured's operations. Therefore, premium audit reports constitute a valuable source of the underwriter's information.

The auditor can also play a significant role in the area of production. To many insureds, the auditor is the insurer. The auditor's conduct and skill are often important factors in retaining an account. Often, auditors must demonstrate their proficiency by convincing an insured of the validity of an audit when the insured prefers having a lower-rated classification and a lower premium. The auditor can also directly serve the production or agency staff by being attuned to their needs for timely information.

The next section discusses the effects of the following on the underwriting and marketing departments:

- Incorrect classification
- Inadequate loss exposure estimates
- New or undisclosed loss exposures
- Underwriting desirability
- Classification or premium changes
- Additional business or improvements

Incorrect Classification

A critical part of the auditor's job is to classify the insured loss exposures correctly. Often, the auditor is the only source of information for proper classifications. At times, an auditor visits a prospective insured before it is accepted by the insurer, allowing the insurer to correct the classification before issuing the policy. Often, however, the auditor does not become involved until the policy has been written and the first interim audit or annual audit is due. At that time, the auditor should notify the underwriting department of any discrepancies between the classifications on the policy

and the classifications that the auditor has determined are appropriate for the insured's operations.

If the classification and rate on the policy are too high, the insured is being overcharged and may be placed at a competitive disadvantage when bidding for jobs or pricing products. Such a situation could have serious legal ramifications if insurer negligence is a factor. If the classification is wrong and the rate on the policy is too low, the account would probably not be profitable to the insurer.

Inadequate Loss Exposure Estimates

Another potential underwriting problem arises when the insurer bases premium on inadequate loss exposure estimates. When loss exposure estimates are inadequate, insureds are usually aware of that condition and may be reluctant to permit another audit. Conversely, insureds who expect a return premium because loss exposure estimates are too high are usually quick to make records available.

The auditor should give full loss exposure data to the underwriting department in those cases in which the estimates are inadequate. The underwriter usually has the responsibility of updating the loss exposures on the current policy.

New or Undisclosed Loss Exposures

New loss exposures are another area that can affect underwriting. New loss exposures can result from a change in the insured's operations or from a new venture. The insured often does not communicate such changes or new operations to the producer or insurer, or if reported, the information can be insufficient for underwriting purposes.

An auditor should not try to underwrite new operations but should supply the details about ownership and operations to provide complete rating information to the underwriting department. The auditor should also indicate the classifications for any new loss exposures. Other items of interest to the underwriting department include the previous track record of the new operation's management, financing, product marketing, source of income, and any information pertaining to unusual hazards.

The producer also has a particular interest in the insured's business and operations. Ideally, the insured communicates all changes in operations and all new operations beforehand to the producer. Often, however, in the rush of business pressure, insureds overlook notifying the producer. The auditor is in an excellent position to notify the producer of any changes or new operations. That notification serves two purposes: (1) It helps develop rapport between the auditor and the producer, and (2) it gives the producer time to contact the insured for information about the new operation and to provide insurance counseling before a new premium is developed. Because the auditor's notice to the underwriting department precipitates an inquiry to the insured, notifying the producer first allows him or her to contact the insured and possibly

arrange additional coverage immediately. Producers want to know in advance if an audit has generated a large additional premium so that they can prepare their insureds for the bill.

Underwriting Desirability

Underwriting desirability is highly complex and involves many considerations. The auditor is in a position to observe and communicate to the underwriting department information that affects an account's overall desirability as an insured, including hazard information.

Physical hazard
A tangible condition of property, persons, or operations that increases the probable frequency or severity of loss.

A hazard is a condition that increases the probable frequency or severity of a loss arising from an insured cause of loss. **Physical hazards** are tangible characteristics of the person, operations, or property insured that increase the probable frequency or severity of a loss. Premium auditors should use their own judgment, experience, and common sense to identify hazards and should report hazards that increase loss exposure.

Decaying buildings, unguarded stairways or elevators, poor lighting, poor housekeeping, cluttered aisles, overflowing refuse containers, and careless storage of combustibles are all physical hazards that affect loss exposure. The auditor should watch for overcrowding, use of unguarded saws and equipment, use of electrical equipment without proper grounding connections, and failure to use protective equipment such as hard hats or safety goggles. Other physical hazards the auditor should note are exposure to flood and exposure to harmful conditions from surrounding businesses or plants. Although it is not the auditor's responsibility to identify all hazards, the auditor should develop a habit of taking a critical look at potential loss-causing hazards and inform the underwriter about them.

Moral hazard
A condition that increases the likelihood that a person will intentionally cause or exaggerate a loss.

Moral hazards are intangible characteristics of an insured that increase the probable frequency or severity of a loss. Factors contributing to moral hazards include financial instability, business or industry failure, undesirable associates, and lack of moral character of the insured or its management. Illegal or unethical business practices, questionable losses, and unreported loss exposures are examples of possible moral hazards. The insurance policy is a contract of good faith based on complete honesty of both parties. Therefore, the auditor is obligated to report any observations indicating possible moral hazards.

Morale hazard
A condition of carelessness or indifference that increases the probable frequency or severity of loss.

Morale hazards are attitude problems that increase the probable frequency or severity of loss because of carelessness or indifference. Indifference to normal safety protective measures and to proper maintenance of property and equipment indicate possible morale hazards. Another indicator of a morale hazard can be careless recordkeeping. Low wages or a high turnover rate for the insured's employees could also be an indicator of poor business attitudes and morale hazard. Here, too, the auditor can report information that might not otherwise be available to the underwriter.

Another indicator of morale hazard can be an uncooperative insured. In addition to the possible increased potential for loss, the uncooperative insured

presents unique challenges to the auditor. Unless the lack of cooperation arises from a misunderstanding, which can be resolved, or from ignorance, which can be enlightened, it is doubtful that the auditor will be able to obtain the records required to correctly adjust premium. Failure or inability to obtain the records adversely affects underwriting.

Sometimes the producer can help to solve the problems of inadequate records. The producer may be in a position to influence the insured to cooperate, solving the problem before it involves the underwriting department. Therefore, problems with inadequate records or uncooperative insureds should be communicated to the agency or marketing staff to enlist their assistance.

If all attempts fail, the auditor should notify the underwriting department. The underwriting department should be used only as a last resort for resolving problems with insureds. Insureds that do not cooperate with premium auditors are also likely not to cooperate with the loss control department in implementing recommendations or with claim representatives in settling claims.

A final indication of a possible morale hazard is poorly kept records, which may suggest loss exposures of which the insurer is unaware. In addition to increasing loss potential, poor records waste the auditor's time and can obstruct a necessary premium adjustment. Although auditors can remedy poor recordkeeping by educating the insured, premium adjustment problems stemming from inadequate records may persist. In determining an account's desirability, the underwriter should consider such recordkeeping problems along with the probable premium effect in overcharge or undercharge and the extra time and expense involved in auditing.

The auditor can contribute significant information in many other areas of underwriting. By considering what information an underwriter needs about an account, the auditor can develop the audit report to convey that information.

Classification or Premium Changes

Producers prefer to be forewarned if one of their insureds is to receive a premium audit billing with a large additional premium because of a classification change. The producer then has time to plan the best way to collect the additional premium and to explain the classification change to the insured.

Another advantage of advance notice is that the producer can give an opinion about a classification change. At times, the producer might be aware of bureau inspections or other information that have an important bearing on the proposed classification change.

Ideally, the auditor should tell the producer of any classification change of consequence, whether or not it results in a major premium difference. Auditors should also communicate to the producer any large additional premiums due because of other reasons, such as an insured's underreporting or inadequate loss exposure estimates or deposits. The audit report should document that communication.

Additional Business or Improvements

When sending the producer and underwriter any information about potentially uninsured or underinsured loss exposures, auditors must be careful not to divulge confidential information. Generally, if the insured specifically mentions the need for coverage and a desire to be contacted, the auditor should notify the producer. Insurers may have specific policies about confidential information, of which the auditor should be aware.

The auditor can also communicate with the producer about possible improvements in the insured's insurance program. For example, installing a partition might qualify an employee for another classification and reduce workers' compensation premiums. Or maybe by a slight modification in process, the insured could avoid an interchange of labor and generate insurance savings. The auditor, by being aware of the insured's interest can consequently add value to the insured's insurance program.

Other Departments

Questions that the auditor cannot answer should be referred to someone else. The auditor should record such questions in the section of the audit report devoted to that purpose so that they can be forwarded to the person or department responsible for answering them. Sometimes insureds relate other experiences they have had with the insurer. The auditor should also include in the report any significant information in that regard, whether positive or negative.

Other departments, such as the claim and loss control departments, can benefit from the auditor's visit to the insured's premises and examination of the insured's records. How the auditor aids other departments can vary by insurer.

Claim information can help the auditor to verify employment of claimants and to assign classifications. The auditor can provide a return service by reviewing claim abstracts to verify or correct the classification codes assigned by the claims coder. Recently, various insurance regulators have emphasized the importance of improving accuracy in claim coding. No one is in a better position to review and to correct claim codes than the auditor. That review also ensures that claims and premiums are matched in the same classifications, improving the credibility of rates. Auditors should also review loss information to verify that claimants were the insured's employees and were injured during the coverage period. If claimants were not employees, the auditor should notify the claim department.

Inventory values, contractors' equipment lists and values, and automotive equipment values are other important facts that the auditor can furnish to the claim department. In addition, the auditor can facilitate claim adjustments by verifying periods or dates of employment and by providing or verifying average earnings for individual claimants.

The loss control or safety engineering department also has an interest in the auditor's observations. The loss control representative cannot visit every policyholder, but the auditor can serve as an additional source of information for loss control. The auditor should forward any information about unsafe procedures and working conditions so that the loss control department can investigate and make any recommendations.

The foregoing discussion by no means exhausts the list of potential beneficiaries of the audit report. General management, office administration, agency accounting—in fact, any department with an interest in the insured or the producer—can profit from the auditor's knowledge, experience, and position.

AUDIT BILLING

After the auditor completes the audit report, the audit is ready for billing and further processing. The procedure for processing the audit varies within the industry. In some cases, the auditor has the responsibility of preparing a tentative billing. However, the usual procedure is for inside staff to perform the task of billing and processing the audit. Whether or not premium auditors have billing responsibility, they should be familiar with billing procedures so that they can adequately respond to the producers' and the insureds' questions.

Audit Review Before Billing

The insurer should not issue a bill until the audit has been approved for accuracy, technical soundness, and professional excellence. The approval might come from an experienced auditor or from a professional reviewer. Some insurers also require the audit manager or supervisor to approve an audit before billing.

The reviewer should examine the audit for conformity to the policy, manual rules, regulatory agency rules, and insurer rules. Sometimes, portions of the report or report extracts must be communicated to other departments. Questions about classifications or coverages must be resolved before billing.

Although reviews of audits may appear to be a duplication of work, they may actually save both time and labor. The time and cost spent on a review is small in comparison to the cost of the extra time spent in rebilling, as well as to the loss of insureds and producers' goodwill.

The final review should do the following:

1. Verify the audit report's quality and completeness
2. Verify that the auditor has transferred all figures and classifications to the billing
3. Verify that the auditor has answered all questions and has or will communicate relevant information to other departments

4. Verify that rates transcribed from the policy are recorded correctly and that all rates for new classifications or coverages are correct
5. Review the accuracy of the billing and verify that the premium deposit was credited
6. Verify that the billing follows proper procedures
7. Verify adherence to insurer rules, approval procedure, and routing instructions
8. Include the initials of the person or persons responsible for the final review

Many computerized billing systems eliminate Items 4 through 7 of the final review.

Premium Calculation

An accurate premium billing results from a correct audit and a complete, accurate audit report. The following sections discuss the premium billings for workers' compensation and general liability insurance.

Workers' Compensation Insurance

The premium base for most workers' compensation insurance classifications is the payroll, and the unit of loss exposure is each $100 of payroll. Each entity is billed separately by state, and all entities are combined to obtain a total standard premium. Once the total standard premium is determined, the insurer applies any applicable premium discount based on the approved tables on a per-state basis. To aid the insured in allocating the insurance cost to each entity, the insurer can break down the discount not only by state but also by entity.

Following the proper order is important in billing workers' compensation insurance, both to calculate premium and to prepare statistical reports. A suggested order of application is shown in Exhibit 9-2, with accompanying comments. That suggested order of billing does not apply to every policy. Individual state exceptions might necessitate an addition to or a modification of the order. Other changes might be necessary for retrospectively rated policies, participating policies and companion policies, deductibles, or contractors' premium adjustment programs, or for individual company preferences or requirements. Billing procedures should correspond to the appropriate manuals covering the geographical area involved.

General Liability Insurance

Although the Insurance Services Office issues forms and files loss costs commonly used in the industry, liability insurance is less standardized than workers' compensation. Consequently, independent filings and exceptions tend to create greater variations in premium billings. Certain similarities in the billing of general liability audits are desirable, however, to facilitate the normal order of premium calculations and the proper coding and reporting of premium statistics.

EXHIBIT 9-2

Suggested Order for Determining Workers' Compensation Premiums

1. For each manual classification, multiply the units of exposure times the rate.
2. For the USL&HW exposure, multiply payroll times the surcharged, or "F," rates.
3. For voluntary compensation, multiply units of exposure times the rates. The insurer should indicate the employer's liability coverage limits of liability on the billing for rate verification purposes.
4. For an occupational disease surcharge, multiply units of exposure times the rate supplement.
5. Determine premium increase or decrease due to benefit changes. Sometimes, the insurer might use a graduated table to apply the premium charge; at other times, it is necessary to split the exposure and to apply the full premium increase to that portion of the premium developed after the benefit change. For specific cases, consult the bureau or state instructions. The increase or decrease normally applies to the following:
    a. Determine the premium developed from the manual classifications.
    b. Determine the USL&HW premium. The application of the benefit change to the USL&HW premium depends on whether the USL&HW rate loading is applicable to outstanding policies. If the loading changes, the USL&HW rate will generally decrease, thus making the premium increase applicable. The intent is to obtain the same amount of USL&HW premium that would have applied had the state benefits not changed.
    c. Determine voluntary compensation premium.
    d. Determine occupational disease surcharge premium.
6. Determine aircraft seat surcharge that should be developed by individual aircraft.
7. Determine charge for increased limits employer's liability coverage, if applicable. Increase applies to items 1, 2, 4, 5, and 6.
8. Determine premium for additional medical coverage, if applicable. It affects the same items as number 7. Because most states now have unlimited medical, this charge is becoming obsolete.
9. Determine waiver of subrogation premium.
10. Determine charge for maritime, Coverage I.
11. Determine charge for maritime, Coverage II.
12. Calculate short rate cancellation premium (if applicable).
13. Apply experience modification.
14. Apply loss constants on a per-state basis. See state manuals for applicability.
15. Apply expense constant on a per-policy basis. See appropriate workers compensation manual for rules on application.
16. Add loading to equal minimum premium.
17. Determine transition credit, if applicable.

Continued on next page

18. Apply premium discount, if applicable. After applying any transition credits, the insurer can determine the total standard policy premium and obtain the appropriate premium discount percentage factor by consulting the workers compensation Basic Manual or Premium Audit Reference Book.
19. Apply assigned risk surcharge.
20. Determine total premium and exposure.
21. Determine states named on the policy for which the insurer shows no exposure.
22. Determine deposit or reported premiums.
23. Calculate net additional or return premium.

Auditors should also recognize that the nature of the liability premium coding and statistical reporting system permits "change only" billings. In other words, the only items to be reflected in the billings, both charges and credits, should be those classifications or coverages that actually change during the policy period or billing period.

Other Billings

Numerous other types of insurance require billings because of either actual audited loss exposure or reported loss exposures or values. Among the more common types for which the auditor should know the billing procedures are automobile liability and automobile physical damage, garage liability, and property coverages, including fire and inland marine. In addition, in certain areas of the country, special policies and coverages might be audited and billed. The auditor should be familiar with those billing procedures common to the area in which the auditor works.

Report to Regulatory Agencies

An important part of the premium billing of final audits is the report that the insurer must file with regulatory agencies. For some types of insurance, the insurer files a copy of the actual billing so that the regulatory agency can verify adherence to manual rules and rates and can monitor the timeliness of audits. Generally, however, for insurance other than workers' compensation, all that the agency requires is an overall reporting of premium and losses by type of insurance and by classification.

A unit report filing is necessary for every workers' compensation policy. The insurer might make that filing to the National Council on Compensation Insurance or to the appropriate bureau in those states that require direct filing. The insurer must normally file the workers' compensation unit report within eighteen months of policy inception. However, insurers must file reports on three-year fixed-rate policies within forty-four months of policy inception. Insurers must file a unit report for each state shown on the policy, including those states for which no loss exposure develops.

The unit report must contain most of the information contained in the audit billing. That information includes the following:

- Insurer
- Policy number
- Policy period
- Pool surcharge
- Premium discounts
- Losses by state and classification
- Classification description and code
- Loss exposure by class, rate, and premium
- Experience modification
- Loss and expense constants
- Premium discount table used—stock or nonstock

Obviously, both losses and premiums should be accurate by classification and by state so that the statistical information derived from the unit reports are accurate. Insurers should reconcile all possible discrepancies before they file the reports.

DISPUTED AUDITS

No matter how careful the auditor is in conducting the audit, filing the report, and billing the insured, and no matter how great the auditor's expertise, some insureds disagree with the premium audit billing. Sometimes that disagreement is valid. However, sometimes insureds can use a dispute to obtain additional payment time while a re-audit is being negotiated. The insurer's insistence on immediate premium payment should nullify the effects of the dispute in the latter case. There are many ways that auditors can minimize the possibility of an audit dispute or can resolve any disputes that do arise.

Methods

Probably the best way to reduce the chance of a dispute is to make sure the audit classifications are correct. The auditor carefully reviews the duties of employees, the department functions, and everything else necessary to reach correct classification and then documents the records that were used to justify the assigned classifications. If disputes about classifications arise, the insurer should delay the billing pending resolution rather than bill the insured based on a potentially incorrect audit.

As part of the audit review process, some insurers compare the detail of the results of the prior audit to the current audit to discover any discrepancies. The person making that comparison should bring differences to the auditor's attention, and someone should resolve the differences if the report does not already do so. Some insurers provide the auditor with a copy of the prior year's report, so the auditor can resolve any discrepancies as part of the audit and not as part of the audit review.

Many insurers encourage their premium auditors to contact the state rating bureau to obtain assistance in determining classifications and applying the manual rules. However, insurers prefer auditors to work through the audit manager and the underwriting manager before requesting specific classification changes for an insured.

Auditors should inform the audit manager about the audit's results. If the auditor anticipates a dispute, the audit manager should become involved early in the dispute resolution. That gives the audit manager time to prepare the appropriate response and to involve other parties as necessary.

Sometimes the insured's disagreement results from the auditor's correct reassignment of supervisory employees from the clerical to the governing classification. For example, if the insured receives a premium billing that is much higher than expected, the insured might complain that the audit is incorrect, necessitating the extra work of a re-audit and perhaps creating ill feelings. It would have been better if the auditor, after making corrections in the insured's payroll or classifications, had reviewed and explained the payrolls and classifications with the insured before leaving the insured's office.

Ideally, auditors should eliminate all misunderstandings or questions before they become disputes. Valid questions about the audit usually arise from a lack of communication between the auditor and the insured or from the insured's lack of understanding of the insurance auditing procedure. Many of an insured's misunderstandings of the audit figures, classifications assignments, or coverages can be resolved during a review of the audit results at the audit's conclusion. The auditor can explain the classifications, how basis of premium was determined, and any additions to or deductions from the exposure base. It is especially important to explain any discrepancies (particularly those that result in higher premiums) and to convince the insured of the validity of those discrepancies. The auditor can use copies of loss control reports, Dun & Bradstreet reports, and claim reports to defuse a potentially disputed audit. For example, if the insured has filed a workers' compensation claim stating that a hammer fell on an employee's head, it would be difficult to argue that the employee belongs in the clerical classification. The auditor can make that argument with the necessary claim documentation.

A visit to the producer to explain potentially disputed audits and to obtain help in explaining the audit to the insured can also often prevent a dispute before billing. Certainly making all reasonable efforts to resolve questions should minimize the number of disputed billings.

Assuming that classifications are correct, the auditor should verify all payroll or other loss exposures to the extent possible. Double-checking totals catches many errors before, rather than after, billing. An incorrect audit result can occur when the insurer has not proofed and checked the audit and, consequently, the audit suffers from mechanical or mathematical errors. Incorrect audits also stem from inaccurate recording or transcription of figures, incorrect overtime or excess credit, or faulty classification of one or more employees.

Management Decisions

Sometimes all reasonable efforts to resolve differences between the auditor and the insured fail. If the insured refuses to accept what the auditor believes to be a technically correct audit, the matter should be referred to the management level. The auditor should submit all relevant information about the disagreement to the auditor's manager. The nature of the disagreement, pertinent background information, the insured's position, the producer's position, and the auditor's recommendations are all required before a manager can make a decision. The information should be as impartial as possible. The auditor should remember that the manager usually has only the auditor's information on which to base a judgment.

Sometimes the dispute can be resolved satisfactorily by the manager. Often, however, consulting other departments, such as claim or underwriting, is necessary. Occasionally, the manager might have to refer the matter to a higher level of management.

Regulatory Agency Settlement

When possible, disputes between the insurer and the insured should be settled by parties themselves. Insurers should take the insured's lack of familiarity of manual rules into account and should realize that courts generally interpret any ambiguous rules or provisions in the insured's favor.

If a private resolution is impossible, appealing to a regulatory agency for a decision might be beneficial. Usually, those cases arise because of disputes about classifications. The information submitted to the regulatory agency should be complete and accurate. An inspection of the insured's operations by the regulatory agency might be necessary before the agency can reach a decision. Because inspection is usually a time-consuming process, an interim agreement (such as having the insured pay any undisputed portion of the additional premium due), pending the regulatory agency's ruling, might be in order.

Court Settlement

Some disputes between insureds and insurers cannot be settled to the satisfaction of all concerned without litigation. No matter how sincere the attempt at resolution, sometimes the only recourse is to take legal action.

Generally, insurers tend to avoid a legal remedy, except in clear-cut and extreme cases. Those cases are usually collection cases, when the issue of who is right or wrong is not really in doubt, but the insured, for various reasons, refuses to pay the audit billing. If the auditor has properly documented the premium audit and the audit is correct, the insurer can usually collect without a lawsuit.

Occasionally, insureds initiate legal proceedings for retaliatory reasons or for damages they believe they have suffered because of the audit billing. Conceivably, negligence in making or billing an audit could damage the insured's reputation and financial standing, cause insurance cancellation,

and even possibly force bankruptcy. Such legal proceedings, regardless of who initiates them, involve the audit report and possibly the auditor in litigation.

Premium Audit as Evidence

One of the primary documents in the litigation of an audit is the premium audit report and its supporting documentation. Usually, the insurer's attorney requests copies of all documentation, along with the actual audit billing, before proceeding with the case. Also, the attorney might request an interrogatory (questions submitted to the auditor or the audit manager for written answers). For disputed audits involving assigned risk servicing carriers, the assigned risk pool manager might also request a sworn statement from an executive officer certifying the billing's accuracy. The insurer might also be asked to furnish copies of the billing and audit report to the opposing attorney and to the judge involved in the case.

Obviously, the auditor should prepare the audit report with that possibility in mind, verifying and documenting information and naming specific sources, records, and persons in the report. That verification and documentation is essential because the auditor who made the audit might no longer be available by the time of a court proceeding or the auditor might not recall all of the details and sources.

Auditor's Court Testimony

Few cases progress to the point of requiring the auditor's testimony. However, the court sometimes requires the auditor to testify to explain or clarify information on the report or to provide credible testimony. In a collection case, the premium auditor's testimony establishes the case's central elements, including the following:

- That the policy was issued and was auditable
- That the policy was issued and was in effect for a particular period
- That the proper earned premium for the coverage period was developed as set forth

Before appearing in court, the auditor should thoroughly review the case, become familiar with the legal concepts involved, and be prepared to explain the information contained in the report in concise, factual terms that those involved can understand. The appropriate manual rules and any regulatory authority rulings pertaining to the case constitute significant evidence. Obviously, the more knowledge, professional expertise, and auditing ability the auditor demonstrates, the more credible the testimony.

SUMMARY

The primary goal of the audit report is to record the data necessary to determine earned premium. Additional goals include documenting audit procedures and findings and providing ratemaking and other information. An auditor should keep all three of those goals in mind while preparing the audit report.

In preparing audit reports, a premium auditor should keep the following five guidelines in mind:

1. Allow sufficient time
2. Prepare the report promptly
3. Be concise, clear, and credible
4. Be action based
5. Use a systematic format

Components of the audit should contain a description of operations, a summary of loss exposures, the explanatory notes, and the insured's signature.

Some information discovered during an audit may have a substantial influence on the desirability of keeping the insured account. The premium auditor should inform the underwriting and marketing departments if any of the following occurs:

- An incorrect classification
- Inadequate loss exposure estimates
- New or undisclosed loss exposures
- Change in underwriting desirability
- Classification or premium changes
- Additional business or improvements

After the premium auditor completes the audit report, the audit is ready for billing and further processing. In some cases, the auditor has the responsibility of preparing a tentative billing. The usual procedure, however, is for the inside staff to perform the task of billing and processing the audit after it has been approved for accuracy and technical soundness. The premium calculation procedure varies among workers' compensation insurance, general liability insurance, and other billings. An important part of the premium billing of final audits is the report that the insurer must file with regulatory agencies.

Probably the best way to reduce the chance of an audit dispute is to make sure that audit classifications are correct. If a premium auditor cannot resolve a dispute, it should be referred to management to become involved. If private resolution is impossible, appealing to a regulatory agency for a decision might be beneficial, particularly in disputes about classifications.

Sometimes a dispute can be resolved only in a court. The premium audit report and its supporting documentation can be used as evidence. The premium auditor may be called on to testify that the policy was issued and was auditable, the policy was in effect for a particular period, and that the proper earned premium for the coverage period was developed.

CHAPTER NOTE

1. National Council on Compensation Insurance, *Basic Manual for Workers Compensation and Employers Liability Insurance*, Rule IV.G. 1-3, p. R-10, 4th reprint, effective 1 October 1992.

Direct Your Learning 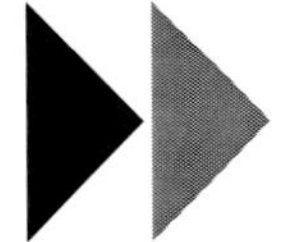

Communication and Premium Auditing

Educational Objectives

After learning the content of this chapter and completing the corresponding course guide assignment, you should be able to:

- Describe the four components of the communication process and explain how each of these components affects the quality of communication.
- Identify actions premium auditors can take to enhance their effectiveness through verbal communication.
- Given a case, recognize nonverbal channels of communication and interpret simple messages transmitted through such channels.
- Explain how perception and attribution influence communication between premium auditors and insured.
- Explain how premium auditors build cooperative relationships with policyholders.
- Describe the sources of confrontational relationships and methods of conflict resolution.
- Describe the advantages of a cooperative relationship between premium auditors and policyholders.
- Define or describe each of the Key Words and Phrases for this chapter.

OUTLINE

Develop Your Perspective

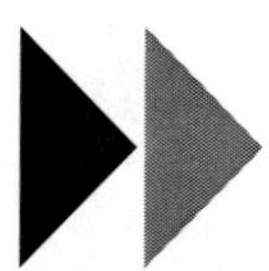

What are the main topics covered in the chapter?

Effective communication is an essential skill for premium auditors who must rely on interactions with others to access information and to perform an audit effectively. Premium auditors can take steps to overcome barriers to communication and to develop cooperative relationships with insureds.

Describe ways that premium auditors can improve communication with customers.

- Why is the quality of communication between auditors and insureds a key factor in influencing the success of an audit?
- How can an auditor avoid behavior that would likely obstruct effective communication during a premium audit?

Why is it important to learn about these topics?

The process of communication relies upon the sender's credibility.

Consider how a premium auditor can establish his or her credibility.

- What elements determine an auditor's initial credibility?
- How can an auditor uninentionally harm his or her credibility?

How can you use what you will learn?

Examine ways that trust and cooperation can be established in a premium audit.

- What proactive measures can an auditor take to avoid conflict?
- How can cooperative relationships be built?

Communication and Premium Auditing

Effective communication is vital to effective premium audits. It can relate to the quality and quantity of information an auditor receives from the insured. In an atmosphere of effective communication, insureds may be more willing to reveal additional loss exposures or explain apparent discrepancies, saving the auditor time. Auditors who understand good communication principles can selectively use them, not just when they encounter problems, but to enhance the quality in all interactions with the insured.

A full range of factors can affect the quality of communication between the auditor and the insured. For example, the insured may have misconceptions about the audit's purposes and probable outcome. Effective communication can overcome an insured's wariness or resistance and promote a positive and cooperative relationship between the insurer and the insured. The auditor can also use effective interpersonal skills to help correct negative perceptions the insured may have formed of the auditor.

THE COMMUNICATION PROCESS

The communication process, shown in Exhibit 10-1, has two phases: the transmission phase and the feedback phase.[1] The process also has several components. Understanding the functions of each of these components can lay a foundation for effective communication. The four main components of the communication process are:

1. Sender
2. Message
3. Medium
4. Receiver

EXHIBIT 10-1

The Communication Process

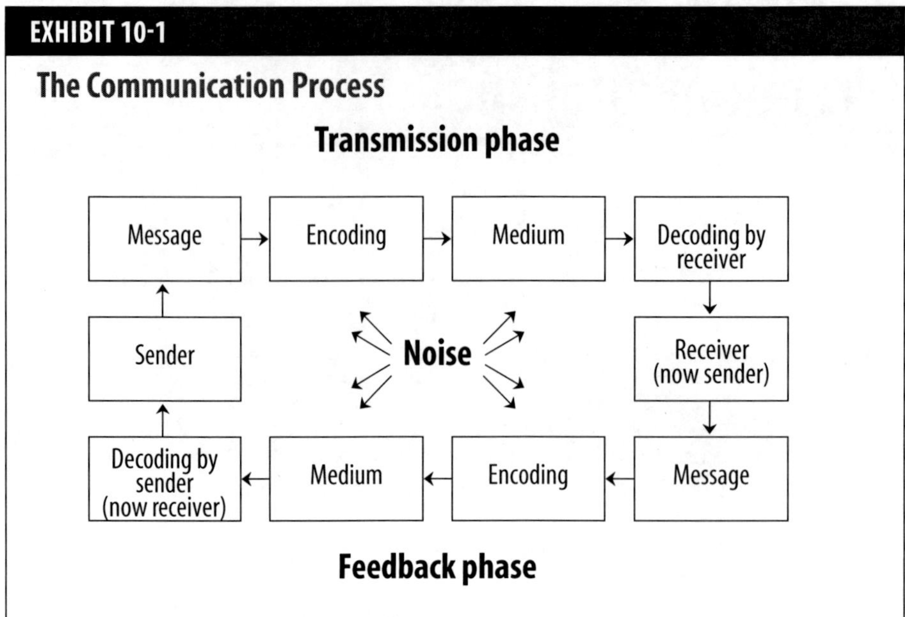

Gareth R. Jones and Jennifer M. George, *Contemporary Management*, 4th ed. (Boston: McGraw-Hill/Irwin, 2005), p. 571.

Any factor that results in a gap between the intended message and the perceived message reduces the effectiveness of communication. This factor is sometimes referred to as noise. To avoid noise, the sender must continuously monitor feedback from the receiver to determine whether intended and perceived messages differ.

Sender

Sender
The person who initiates the communication process.

Of the four components of the communication process, the sender and the receiver are primary. The premium auditor is usually the **sender**, the one who initiates communication at the beginning of a premium audit. The auditor becomes a receiver when the insured begins to provide information. To obtain detailed and accurate information, premium auditors must create a cooperative environment in which communication can occur.

Eliciting information from insureds can put the premium auditor's interviewing skills to the test. For example, an insured may initially refuse the auditor access to the necessary books and records. The auditor must explain why the books and records are needed. The insured might then give the auditor access but continue to watch over the auditor's shoulder. In this situation, effective communication skills can help reduce the insured's distrust of the auditor and of the process.

Credibility

The credibility of the sender is an important consideration in the communication process. The following three types of credibility can affect premium audit communications:

- **Initial credibility**, the degree of credibility an individual has *before* interpersonal communication begins. Initial credibility depends partly on the individual premium auditor's reputation and experience and partly on the perceived status of the premium audit profession.
- **Derived credibility**, an individual's perceived credibility during interpersonal communication. Auditors can enhance their derived credibility in many ways, described later in this chapter.
- **Terminal credibility**, an individual's perceived credibility *after* interpersonal communication in a given situation has occurred. Terminal credibility is the sum of the sender's initial credibility and derived credibility.

Initial credibility
The degree of credibility an individual has before interpersonal communication begins.

Derived credibility
An individual's perceived credibility during interpersonal communication.

Terminal credibility
An individual's perceived credibility after interpersonal communication in a given situation has occurred.

Message

The message is the second component of the communication process. The **message** consists of the words the sender uses and their underlying theme or idea. The process of translating a message into words is known as **encoding**. In encoding a message, the sender must make a number of decisions that determine the message's effectiveness. For example, the sender must choose those words that seem to express the intended meaning most clearly, arrange them to conform reasonably to grammatical rules, and decide the order or sequence for presenting different kinds of information or persuasive arguments.

Message
The words a sender uses in the communications process and their underlying theme.

Encoding
The process of translating a message into words.

Medium

The **medium** is the message's shuttle from sender to receiver. Speech and writing are both vital means of communication for premium auditors, who communicate with many people during the audit process. Media that can used by a premium auditor include letters, telephone conversations, e-mails, and face-to-face communications. The next section in this chapter examines how these various types of media are used for verbal and nonverbal communication.

Medium
The means by which a message is transmitted from sender to receiver.

Verbal Communication

Message types fall into two categories, verbal and nonverbal. All oral and written communications sent by the premium auditor are verbal messages.

Whether communicating face to face or in writing, the auditor's message should be clear and understandable to the receiver. Statements intended to inform or to elicit information are informative only if they are clear to both the sender and the receiver. Therefore, auditors should avoid overly technical language. For example, instead of asking an insured whether its "operations are physically separated," an auditor might ask, "Is there a wall between the foundry and the machine shop?" To ensure the message's clarity, auditors must carefully monitor the feedback to determine whether the insured has heard the message, processed the information, and interpreted the meaning accurately. What is perfectly clear to an auditor might not make sense to the insured.

Verbal messages from the premium auditor should also be verifiable. Because auditors are likely to ask many questions about an insured's finances, insureds want to be certain that the auditor needs the requested information. Auditors must make statements or give reasons that the insured can verify as factual or that the insured views as credible. To state "I always act discreetly" is to make a nonverifiable statement. In contrast, to assert that "my auditing firm is currently providing auditing services to United Insurance, Southeastern Insurance, and the Republic Insurance Company" is to make a verifiable statement. The latter assertion is probably more convincing to the insured and gives the auditor's message credibility.

Finally, verbal messages should have some demonstrable utility or relevance for the insured. A simple request for information without explanation might not be effective because it does not answer the implicit question that the insured wants answered: "Why should I give the information to you?" Therefore, the auditor must emphasize that the requested information serves the auditor's and the insured's mutual interests and that the information is relevant to the purpose of premium determination.

Paralanguage
The information conveyed through voice characteristics, such as pitch, rate, tone, and volume.

Paralanguage refers to the information conveyed through voice characteristics, such as pitch, rate, tone, and volume. These characteristics provide important cues about a person's psychological state. Premium auditors can greatly benefit by listening to and interpreting these cues. Vocal cues are distinctive because each individual has a "voice-print," just as each individual has a fingerprint. An individual's vocal print is the product of different sound qualities, such as pitch, rate, and tone. The distinctive combination of voice qualities is what makes a person's voice recognizable to others.

Pitch refers to the highness or lowness of the voice. Trained speakers can adjust the pitch of their voices to keep the audience's interest or stress important points. Generally, speakers use a natural voice pitch subconsciously when they are relaxed. Several factors influence pitch. Stress or excitement can raise a person's voice pitch. Suspicion or a desire for secrecy can lower pitch, as can illness, such as a cold. On becoming familiar with a person's natural voice pitch, a premium auditor will be able to detect changes in pitch that might indicate that a particular topic causes that person to become tense or uncomfortable. By identifying the source of tension or discomfort, the premium auditor might be able to ease it. Rather than address an isolated change in pitch, the auditor should listen for several changes or a pattern in pitch and determine whether they are connected to what is being discussed.

Rate of speech has two characteristics: speed and rhythm. Cultural and regional factors can influence the speed at which words are spoken. Voice speed can also indicate emotional states. Pressure or anxiety might increase voice speed. The fast-talking salesperson, for example, is operating under the pressure to make a sale. Increased speed can indicate that the speaker is under pressure to meet a deadline or to convince the listener of the speaker's point of view.

A decrease in the voice speed could indicate that the speaker is carefully weighing his or her words to ensure the meaning is clearly communicated. On the other hand, slower speech might indicate that the speaker is not recalling facts but is rather building a new version of a story or adding made-up details.

Rhythm is established by using pauses. Some people speak in bursts of words, with pauses between the bursts. Others speak with a fairly constant flow of words, with few pauses between thoughts. Some speakers respond immediately at the end of a question; others allow a significant pause.

Premium auditors can adjust their rate of speech to suit different situations. Sometimes, they can build rapport with customers by pacing, accomplished by mirroring others' speech rates. When dealing with people who speak English as a second language (ESL), speaking slowly can enhance communication. Speaking more loudly than usual is not necessary.

Tone refers to the inflection of the voice. Volume refers to the relative loudness of the voice. Changes in tone and volume can place emphasis on a particular word in a statement. Such emphasis can significantly alter the meaning of a message. To illustrate this, repeat the following sentence, each time placing emphasis on a different word: "I never said she was dishonest." At least five meanings can be inferred from the sentence depending on which word is emphasized. Paying attention to tone and volume can help premium auditors detect the unspoken meaning of messages.

Nonverbal Communication

The second category of messages is **nonverbal communication**, which is not spoken or written, and which can include eye movement, kinesics, appearance, and time and space. Individuals communicate not by words alone; many sensory mechanisms play a vital role in interpersonal communication. According to some studies, nonverbal communication conveys 93 percent of the meaning in communications; 35 percent originates from tone, and 58 percent comes from gestures and other body language. Tone is an aspect of both verbal and nonverbal communication.[2]

Nonverbal communication
Communication that is not spoken or written, including eye movement, kinesics, appearance, and time and space.

Using and understanding nonverbal communication can help premium auditors project the image of competent, confident, and trustworthy professionals; make accurate assessments of how the insured is reacting; and develop satisfying interpersonal relationships with insureds.

Nonverbal communication factors are often the major determinants of meaning in an interpersonal context. Usually, the feelings and emotions of communicators are more accurately exchanged nonverbally than verbally. The nonverbal aspect of communication conveys meanings and information that are relatively free from distortion and deception.

Nonverbal communication generally comprises more than half of all of business communication. This high percentage should encourage premium

auditors to learn how to use and interpret nonverbal communication effectively. People may communicate nonverbally by using the following:

- Eye movements
- Kinesics (body language)
- Appearance
- Space

Eye Movement

Eye movements are important in expressing interest and attention. In addition, the results of neurological studies suggest that eye movement is associated with activating different parts of the brain. Eye movements also offer hints about how a person is processing information. Premium auditors can use these hints to enhance their communications with others as they complete their auditing responsibilities.

The level of eye contact during communication signals the individual's level of attention. When premium auditors maintain eye contact with insureds during their discussions, they are showing the insureds that they are interested in what is being said. Furthermore, when people avert their eyes or look away from those they are speaking with, it can send the message that they are not interested or that they have something to hide. Appropriately maintaining eye contact is an excellent way of improving the effectiveness of any discussion.

Kinesics

Kinesics, often referred to as body language, includes facial expressions, gestures, and posture.[3] Kinesic behavior can be a valuable communication tool, and the ability to interpret it can help one understand others. Kinesic behavior might convey the following:

- Openness
- Confidence
- Defensiveness
- Nervousness

The face is the most meaningful nonverbal communication medium. The face reveals emotional states, reflects attitudes, and provides nonverbal feedback. Accurately interpreting an insured's facial expressions can help the premium auditor understand and respond to the moods, feelings, and emotions of the insured or the insured's personnel.

A sender can interpret emotional meaning from facial expressions. Some people, however, use their faces to disguise the true nature of their feelings. A person might add a second facial expression to the original to modify the effect. For example, an angry look immediately followed by a bewildered look might mean the receiver is really upset by the auditor's communication and wants to hide the anger and convey that the information is confusing.

Gestures are another distinct type of kinesic behavior that affects communication. Gestures are physical movements of a part or parts of the body. Whereas facial expressions indicate emotion, gestures reflect an individual's attitudes and disposition. Gestures can be emblems, illustrators, regulators, and adaptors, described as follows:

- **Emblems** are specific gestures substituted for words. They communicate a generally recognized meaning. For example, in American culture, a fist with the thumb pointing up is the "success" emblem.
- **Illustrators** are gestures that accompany the spoken word and that people use for purposes of emphasis or intensity. An example is pulling one's hair while saying, "This is driving me crazy."
- **Regulators** aid the flow of a conversation, for example, when the listener nods to encourage the speaker to continue.
- **Adaptors** indicate a communicator's probable behavior. Adaptors are particularly important because they frequently operate at the subconscious level and are not subject to the communicator's conscious control. Thus, adaptors may expose the communicator's level of confidence, attitude, and reaction to the message being conveyed.

Emblem
A gesture substituted for words.

Illustrator
A gesture that accompanies spoken words, used for emphasis.

Regulator
A gesture used to aid the flow of conversation.

Adaptor
A gesture indicating a communicator's probable behavior.

As a sender of communications, the auditor should be aware of adaptors that might reflect defensive or even hostile attitudes. The insured's adaptors might reveal attitudes towards the audit, the auditor, and the auditor's actions. The following four types of adaptor gestures are particularly important in the context of the premium audit:

- **Openness gestures** are motions or posture suggesting a positive reaction or receptivity. For example, uncrossed arms or legs and unbuttoned jackets suggest that individuals are reacting positively and are receptive to one another's ideas. When individuals are using openness gestures, they often move toward the edge of their chair and closer to party with whom they are communicating.
- **Confidence gestures** are motions or posture suggesting amicability and nondefensiveness. Confidence gestures include joining the hands with fingertips pointing upward ("steepling"), using expansive hand movements, or placing one's feet on the desk. A firm handshake and good posture communicate confidence and motivation. In contrast, weak handshakes and slouching may indicate lack of confidence.
- **Defensive gestures** are motions or posture suggesting suspicion, distrust, or dislike. For example, gestures such as the crossing of arms over the chest might signal that an individual is unreceptive to the other person's ideas and might actually dislike that person. An individual might also communicate defensiveness by turning his or her chair or body away from the other person.
- **Nervous gestures** are a person's motion or posture suggesting a tension level that is not conducive to effective communication. Nervous gestures can take a variety of forms, although hand-to-face gestures are a particularly

Openness gesture
A person's motion or posture suggesting a positive reaction or receptivity.

Confidence gesture
A person's motion or posture suggesting amicability and nondefensiveness.

Defensive gesture
A person's motion or posture suggesting suspicion, distrust, or dislike.

Nervous gesture
A person's motion or posture suggesting a tension level that is not conducive to effective communication.

reliable sign of nervousness. Nervousness is also manifested by frequent throat-clearing, playing with objects, and frequently adjusting one's clothing.

Openness and confidence gestures suggest that individuals are developing a satisfying working relationship, but defensive and nervous gestures warn that the communication is not going well.

Posture is another type of kinesics that affects communication. Gestures often reveal attitudes and behavioral predispositions, but posture can define the nature of the relationship between two or more individuals. In particular, the posture of the parties can indicate their relative status and might also suggest how strongly motivated they are to develop friendly and cooperative working relationships. In a two-person conversation, people see the individual who assumes the more expansive posture as having superior status. Not surprisingly, many individuals consciously assume an expansive posture in an attempt to project superior status.

Attempts to attain and maintain the appearance of high status include strategies such as sitting behind a large, elevated desk, using sustained eye contact to "stare down" and dominate other individuals, and placing others at a disadvantage by seating them at a small table. All of those actions reinforce the desired impression of superior status.

Posture can also indicate the degree of interest a person has in developing a friendly and cordial working relationship. The individual whose body posture is constricted and who rarely shifts from one posture to another is likely to be viewed as withdrawn, unresponsive, and difficult to approach. In contrast, the individual who frequently shifts from one posture to another, who leans forward frequently while talking, and who remains relaxed and expressive is usually signaling a friendly and cooperative intent.

Appearance

Personal appearance communicates an abundance of messages that define and establish a person's perceived social identity. That social identity can indicate how, when, and where people expect to engage in interpersonal communication.

Appearance can also affect an individual's behavior. People's behavior has been known to change after plastic surgery to correct a perceived or actual physical defect in appearance. Communicators have a vested interest in their personal appearance and can exercise control over it by carefully selecting their clothing and accessories. For premium auditors, dressing appropriately is important for at least two reasons: (1) it can convey a professional appearance that facilitates access to the insured's records, and (2) it can affect an auditor's credibility.

First impressions are important. General appearance, clothing, and neatness influence the way a person is seen by others. Premium auditors benefit when they dress appropriately for a given situation. An auditor might wear a suit for a meeting with the insured and an accountant. Casual attire might be more appropriate for meeting with an insured in a manufacturing plant or in an office where casual attire is the usual dress code.

Space

Another way people may communicate nonverbally is by use of space. The term proxemics refers to how individuals use interpersonal space. The arrangement of furniture in an office is an example of proxemics.[4] A premium auditor can take cues regarding proxemics based on where desks and chairs are positioned in an insured's office. Some individuals prefer to sit behind a desk facing the premium auditor. Other offices may have a separate table and chairs so that the parties can sit together and discuss the audit. Each of these arrangements sends a different message about how the individual feels about openness and status.

Premium auditors should remember that most insureds have well-developed expectations about acceptable spatial behavior in a business situation. Violating those expectations can undermine the auditor's credibility or trigger defensive behavior on the insured's part. Research has identified cultural norms that specify appropriate communication "distances" for different types of communication situations. For business communications, the usually accepted norm ranges from approximately four to ten feet. Moving closer than about four feet from a business associate suggests a familiarity that might be considered inappropriate for business transactions. However, a distance greater than twelve feet could give the impression of unapproachablility and the desire for formality in the interaction.

Many insureds assume that they have the right to control and regulate conversational exchanges in their own offices. While not relinquishing the right to share control of the conversation with the insured, the auditor should be sensitive to space considerations while on the insured's premises. If the auditor moves a chair closer to the insured or moves around the desk to share files or other information and the insured moves away, this is a sign that the insured is uncomfortable with the change in spatial distance. The premium auditor should recognize this sign and return to the original seating position.[5]

Receiver

The sender, message, and medium are the first three components of the communication process. The receiver is the fourth component. The **receiver** chooses from the verbal and nonverbal symbols in the sender's messages, selects the symbols that seem to convey the sender's intended meaning, and interprets the message's meaning. The process by which the receiver interprets the sender's message is called **decoding**. During the course of any exchange, a premium auditor must act as both a sender and a receiver.

Receiver
The person who chooses from the verbal and nonverbal symbols in the sender's message to interpret the message's meaning.

Decoding
The process by which a receiver interprets a sender's message.

Accurate decoding requires the receiver to know the language and be familiar with the sender's culture. Even with a single language and culture, many dialects and subcultures may exist, creating the potential for misinterpretation from encoding and decoding messages. Premium auditors must be aware of the possibility of encoding errors in the messages they receive and also of the possibility that messages they send might be improperly decoded.

Many of the factors that affect senders also affect receivers. Receivers' own perceptions are subject to the same types of distortions as those of senders. However, the communication skills required of senders and receivers also differ. One of the most critical skills for effective communication is the receiver's ability to listen and understand what is being communicated between the parties in the communication process.

Listening Skills

Successful communication requires the receiver to understand the sender's message. Therefore, listening is an essential skill in the communication process. Successful listening begins with the ability and willingness to listen actively and provide the sender with feedback.

Listening is a particularly important communication skill because people devote more time to listening than to any other communication activity. One study indicates that communication activities can be divided as follows:[6]

1. Listening—53 percent
2. Talking—16 percent
3. Reading—17 percent
4. Writing—14 percent

Several other studies have shown similar results regarding the amount of time communicators spend listening.

Active listening
The process of listening with mental and physical openness to more clearly determine a message's meaning.

Hearing words is easy, but translating their meaning can be difficult. Active listeners work at listening. Premium auditors who show that they are listening may obtain better cooperation from people. **Active listening** requires the devotion of mental and physical energy toward listening. The meaning of a speaker's message might be hidden between the lines. Consequently, listening beyond words is an essential skill of active listeners.

Listening speed and speaking speed differ. Most people can listen to and comprehend the meaning of more than 400 words a minute, but most speakers have difficulty exceeding 200 words per minute. That time differential can make it easy for a receiver to lose concentration and miss the meaning of a message.

A successful listener must have a mental attitude open to listening and free of distractions so that full attention can be given to the speaker. The listener must avoid the temptation to interrupt and should consider the question, "Am I really listening, or am I thinking about what I'll say next?" A listener who is waiting to speak or thinking about what to say next is not actively listening.

Allotting adequate time for communication is essential to maintaining a good mental attitude. Feeling rushed can jeopardize active listening because it fosters impatience, and the listener may tend to interrupt to hasten the conversation. Interruptions can cause the speaker to lose a train of thought and possibly omit important information.

Note-taking can distract one from active listening. However, the premium auditor may want to take brief notes to ensure that all important points are covered in the conversation. Note-taking might make some insureds uneasy because they do not know what the auditor is writing. The auditor can minimize that discomfort by keeping the notes brief and by explaining their purpose. To further alleviate any concerns, the auditor can offer to review the notes with the insured for accuracy at the end of the meeting.

Feedback

Feedback is the second of the two phases of the communication process, following transmission. **Feedback** is the information that the receiver sends back to the sender as a result of the communication. Through feedback, the receiver becomes a sender of communication. In a sense, feedback is the receiver's reaction to the communication. Senders can use feedback both to assess the adequacy of their messages and to determine the receiver's perception of the sender. Feedback serves several other important purposes, including clarity, corrective, and relational purposes, which are probably most important for premium auditors. They are described as follows:

Feedback
The information the receiver sends back to the sender in the communication process.

- Feedback serves the clarity purpose when the communication sender monitors feedback from the receiver to determine whether the messages are clear and to adjust the messages to clarify the intended meaning.
- Feedback serves the corrective purpose when it signals that the sender's behavior is unacceptable and the sender modifies that behavior accordingly. For example, if the feedback is an angry or defensive response, the sender would modify communication behaviors or the message that seemed to produce the response.
- Feedback serves the relational purpose when it enables the sender to assess the current state of a relationship. Feedback might suggest a lack of trust on the receiver's part, and, in response, the sender would modify both attitudes and actions to develop a more trusting relationship.

Verbal (oral and written) and nonverbal feedback can provide different types of information. Oral feedback reflects the adequacy or inadequacy of the sender's message from the receiver's perspective. The sender should monitor the receiver's oral feedback to determine whether the message is understandable and relevant, and if it is not, should modify the message. If the receiver's feedback is digressive and nonfluent (the receiver pauses frequently or stutters, for example), the sender should determine if the message was unclear and, if so, modify it.

Nonverbal feedback frequently provides information about how receivers view themselves and the message-sender. Research indicates that nonverbal feedback reflects the receiver's level of self-assurance, suggests the kinds and intensity of emotions the receiver is experiencing, and reveals how attentive the receiver is to the sender's communication efforts.

PERCEPTION AND COMMUNICATION

Perception
The means through which individuals gather information from their environment.

Perception is the means through which individuals gather information from their environment. Through the process of perception, the individual gathers the data received via the senses and sorts, evaluates, and analyzes the data based on inherent knowledge, beliefs, and value systems (the mental set or attitude). That perception process divides data into those absorbed by the brain (stimuli) and those that are not absorbed (the unnoticed remainder). Exhibit 10-2 shows the perception process.

EXHIBIT 10-2

Perception and Communication

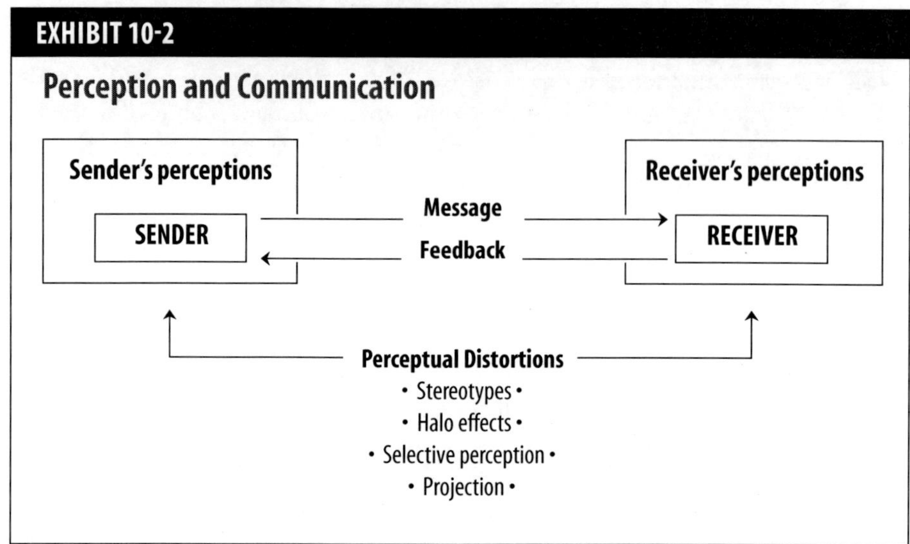

John R. Schermerhorn, Jr., *Management*, 7th ed., Copyright© 2002, John Wiley & Sons, Inc., p. 454. Reprinted with permission of John Wiley & Sons, Inc.

Because people rarely possess a detailed and factually accurate description of the people, events, and situations that shape their lives, perception and communication are inextricably linked. People frequently rely on their subjective impressions of people, events, and situations to determine their meaning and significance. The pervasive effect of perception on interpersonal communication is evident to anyone who has undergone marriage counseling, participated in a business interview, or observed a jury trial. Jury trials are good a example because the verdict is directly linked to the perceptions of the defense attorney, prosecutor, and jurors.

Perception is a complex activity that shapes a person's views of reality. It involves not only the observation of people and events in a given situation but also the attempt to determine the meaning and significance of what was observed.

Attribution
The process of assigning or ascribing a characteristic or quality to a person or an object.

Attribution

Attribution is the process of assigning or ascribing a characteristic or quality to someone or something. Attribution is an important component of perception. Attributions are made when people try to judge why other individuals

acted as they did. People often make attributional errors. For example, a lecturer may attribute a lack of interest to someone who has fallen asleep during a lecture. In reality, the person might be a diabetic who has fallen asleep because of low blood sugar levels.

Attributional errors can also pose a potential communication barrier in the context of a premium audit. Auditors should guard against the tendency to jump to conclusions. The insured's frown might not indicate a negative attitude toward the auditor but might instead be an indication of problems at home.

Perceptual Distortions

Attributional errors occur because people frequently base perceptions on subjective impressions, which can be inaccurate because they are affected by factors that result in perceptual distortion. Some of the more common perceptual distortions include stereotyping, halo effects, selective perception, projection, and the primacy effect.

Stereotyping

Stereotyping is the labeling of members of groups and placing them in categories that provide an incomplete or inaccurate description of a given individual. Common stereotypes are those of young people, old people, teachers, students, males, and females.[7] To a startling degree, stereotypes often control the impressions people have of others. People often expect an individual who belongs to a certain group to exhibit certain personal characteristics and to behave in certain ways.

Stereotyping
The act of labeling members of groups and placing them in categories that provide an incomplete or inaccurate description of a given individual.

Premium auditors might encounter insureds who have stereotyped them in ways that are misleading and not entirely flattering. On the one hand, the public is likely to believe that auditors possess a high degree of competence, and are well-educated, intelligent, analytical, precise, and mathematically inclined. On the other hand, some insureds might also attribute personal qualities to auditors that are hardly conducive to developing satisfying relationships. Auditors may be seen as emotionless, cold, unexciting, rigid, and excessively inquisitive. Effective communication can help to overcome such stereotypes. In addition, premium auditors can also improve the quality of communication by resisting the temptation to stereotype insureds.

Halo Effect

A **halo effect** occurs when one positive or negative attribute is used to form an overall impression of a person. The halo effect commonly occurs in performance evaluations when a manager who greatly admires one particular trait or ability rates an employee as outstanding overall because the employee does very well in that one skill area.

Halo effect
A perceptual distortion that occurs when a person uses a positive or negative attribute to form an overall impression of another person.

The reputation of an individual or a profession can also create a halo effect. The auditor's reputation will almost certainly affect the insured's perceptions as well as the auditor's initial credibility. The auditor's reputation may be based both on the status of the auditor's profession and on the auditor's past performance.

The auditor's individual reputation for competence and trustworthiness will probably have a greater effect on the insured's perceptions than will the status of the auditor's profession. Accordingly, the emphasis in this chapter has been on those steps the auditor can take to enhance the insured's perception of the individual auditor's level of competence and trustworthiness.

Selective Perception

Selective perception
The tendency to understand only those signals that are consistent with a person's past experiences.

Selective perception is the tendency to understand only those signals that are consistent with one's past experiences. To put it another way, individuals frequently see and hear only what their own beliefs and values will let them see and hear. The rest becomes the unnoticed remainder. Because people filter their perceptions through their beliefs and values, most people are highly susceptible to selective perception.

In the case of a premium audit, the frames of reference of the auditor and the insured can be different. In many cases, the insured might have had previous bad experiences with the insurer, the insurance agent, or even another auditor. Those experiences affect the insured's perceptions in ways that are not apparent or directly related to the auditor's own actions. The insured's uncooperative and even defensive actions might be the result of selective perception. With effective communication, the auditor can determine the reason for the insured's behavior and change the perception.

Projection

Projection
A perceptual distortion that occurs when a person assumes that other people share his or her values, beliefs, and goals.

Projection is a perceptual distortion that occurs when one person assumes that other people share the same values, beliefs, and goals. People distort perception by projecting their preferences onto others. Someone who likes a variety of challenging tasks might assume that others do also. People who want organization, direction, and close supervision might assume that others want the same. Auditors cannot assume that insureds are as eager and willing to determine the correct final premium as they are.

Primacy Effect

Primacy effect
A perceptual distortion caused by the influence of first impressions.

Another perceptual distortion is the primacy effect. In simple terms, the **primacy effect** is the influence of first impressions. First impressions can affect all subsequent perceptions because they are hard to change. Given their weight, premium auditors must make a special effort from the outset to create a positive impression. Many factors, both positive and negative, contribute to first impressions. However, personal appearance and voice probably have the greatest effect. Those two factors deserve particular attention because they can be controlled and modified.

Personal appearance plays a significant role in shaping first impressions because people begin making inferences about individuals as soon as they see them. Appearance is a particularly strong factor in perception when individuals do not interact on a regular basis, as is the case with the premium auditor and the insured.

Speech patterns and tone of voice are also important determinants of first impressions. For example, generally people perceive those who talk fast to be anxious. People may perceive individuals who increase the volume of their voice to emphasize the points they are making to be confident.

Implications

As the previous discussion suggests, many factors affect the perceptions of auditors and those with whom they interact. Auditors should be aware that the insured might have a distorted view of the auditor's image, attitudes, and anticipated actions because of the effect of stereotyping, the halo effect, selective perception, projection, and the primacy effect. At the same time, auditors should recognize that their own perceptions of the insured could be inaccurate because of the same kinds of factors.

Distorted perceptions can disrupt a premium audit. In the interest of effective communication, auditors can take steps to ensure the accuracy of their own and of the insured's perceptions.

Premium auditors should obtain as much factual information as possible about the insured's attitudes, motivations, and frame of reference. They can try to understand the perceptual perspective that shapes the insured's attitudes and actions. Finally, auditors should question whether their actions promote an open and honest communication that minimizes misperceptions and perceptual distortion.

RELATIONSHIPS WITH POLICYHOLDERS

Developing satisfying interpersonal relationships requires considerable effort, largely because people associate interpersonal relationships with action and reaction, with expectation and frustration, and with agreement and conflict. Indeed, developing satisfying interpersonal relationships is particularly challenging because two or more individuals share control of the relationship's outcomes. In the long run, however, the effort spent building cooperative relationships with insureds is well worthwhile.

Cooperative Relationships

Insureds and auditors do not need to be on opposing sides. Although their concerns naturally differ, they are not diametrically opposed. A friendly, mutually beneficial relationship is possible. To accomplish this, the auditor and insured must build a disclosing, assertive, and trusting relationship.

Disclosing Relationship

The less that people know about those with whom they are trying to communicate, the more difficult communication can be. The lack of knowledge forces people to guess about the person's intentions, expectations, and motivations and makes understanding the individual's behavior difficult.

People are forced to operate in an informational vacuum when the individuals with whom they interact are reluctant or unwilling to reveal how they view others, how they view the purposes of the communication, and how they view themselves. Consequently, some self-disclosure by interacting individuals is typically necessary if effective communication is to result. Self-disclosure means voluntarily sharing information about one's attitudes, perceptions, and needs that the receiver might be unable to learn from others.

If the insured seems to withhold information, the auditor should determine why. Of course, attempts to determine the reasons for nondisclosing behavior and to promote self-disclosure should be discreet and nonthreatening. Although not always successful, the attempts themselves can build a more open and satisfying relationship.

Assertive Relationship

Both parties must be assertive if a satisfying interpersonal relationship is to result. Among the rights that the assertive person recognizes are the right to act without continually justifying or apologizing for actions and the right to say "I don't know" and "I don't understand." Assertive individuals stand up for their rights, but only in ways that do not violate the rights of others. Defending one's own rights while violating the rights of others is aggressive, not assertive, behavior.

Nonassertive people avoid situations that require them to take a stand on an issue. By stating their views in a tentative and apologetic manner, if at all, they unwittingly relinquish their right to be treated as equals by those with whom they interact. Nonassertive individuals rarely focus on the specific offensive behaviors of those with whom they interact. They apologize frequently for their own actions even when apologies are not required. They do not sustain eye contact. They frequently assume closed and defensive bodily postures, and they speak softly.

Auditors who often find themselves at a disadvantage with insureds should assess their behaviors to determine whether they are sufficiently assertive.

Trusting Relationship

Trust is perhaps an important factor in developing a satisfying interpersonal relationship. In a trusting relationship, the parties involved work together to achieve mutually beneficial goals even when some degree of risk is involved. Communication in a premium audit necessarily involves some degree of risk. Attempts to be trusting that are not reciprocated can harden one's resolve not to be trusting again. Attempts to be trusting that do not immediately facilitate attaining one's goals can be frustrating. Nevertheless, efforts to build trust typically have a positive effect on the quality of interpersonal communication. As the level of trust between individuals increases, they become more relaxed and flexible in working to resolve disputes amicably.

Advantages of a Cooperative Relationship

Once both the premium auditor and the insured have fully disclosed information, asserted their interests without becoming aggressive, and learned to trust one another, the advantages of cooperation should become apparent to both. Those advantages may include the following:

- It may give the insured a better understanding of an audit.
- It encourages the insured to keep better records.
- It may result in improved customer service from the insurer.

Because the premium depends on the audit results, the insured must understand the audit procedure. If not, the insured might have questions when the premium bill arrives. In the long run, resolving those questions at the time of the audit is much easier. Every audit should include an explanation of the reason for the audit, definitions of special terms, classification procedures, and answers to any questions raised by the insured during the audit.

Auditors should explain why the audit is necessary and what procedures will be followed in ordinary language rather than in technical terms. Although some insureds might be able to follow the language of the manuals the auditor uses in performing the audit, many insureds might not. Therefore, the auditor must know the various manuals well enough to paraphrase the applicable provisions in each situation. For example, if a manufacturing operation includes printing labels for containers of the insured's own products, the auditor should not say that the "printing classification" did not apply because it was a "general inclusion." Rather, the auditor should tell the insured that for classification purposes, the manual considers printing of that type a normal part of the insured's operations. Because the insured prints only its own labels, a separate printing classification does not apply.

Some essential terms might be misleading to the insured, and the premium auditor should be prepared to define them. For example, insureds often do not realize that remuneration includes all bonuses, commissions, and possibly other forms of compensation, such as meals and lodging. Premium auditors should be able to clarify what the remuneration is so that the insured understands why the premium base includes such additional items. The auditor should also define terms that the rating manual restricts to certain operations or situations, such as "executive supervisor," "independent contractor," "casual labor," and "clerical employees."

Explaining the audit becomes crucial when the auditor discovers loss exposures or classifications differing from those shown on the policy declarations page and endorsements. The auditor should then be able to justify the difference to the insured. One approach is to show the relevant portion of the manual to the insured. Sometimes insureds perceive distinctions between their operations and classification definitions and expect the insurer to rate its operations separately. In that case, the auditor might need to explain the concept of pooling a large number of similar loss exposures.

The second advantage of a cooperative relationship is that it encourages the insured to keep better records. Many small businesses are operated by people with technical but not necessarily managerial skills. Although they may know their businesses well, they often have difficulty maintaining adequate records. Premium auditors, by virtue of their knowledge of accounting, can often assist such insureds in establishing or improving recordkeeping practices. Even though it might take some extra time, such assistance can benefit both parties. Future audits will be easier if the insured maintains better records. The insured might be able to reduce the premium by keeping the necessary records.

Many insureds do not realize that improved recordkeeping can result in lower premiums. Auditors have an obligation to notify them of that benefit. For example, the rules in most states exclude overtime premium pay from the payroll base for workers' compensation insurance. Naturally, the auditor cannot exclude such amounts if the insured's records do not show them. Therefore, the auditor should explain to the insured that recording overtime pay separately from regular pay will result in a lower premium.

Similarly, if the insured is in the construction or erection business, rules might allow division of a single employee's payroll when the records show how much time the employee spent on each job. If the records are inadequate, the auditor assigns payroll to the highest-rated classification.

Keeping proper records benefits both the insurer and the insured. The insurer benefits not only from the ease of future audits but also from the quicker resolution of claims and the improved underwriting desirability. The insured benefits from better managerial control of the business as well as from possible premium savings. Insureds might resent a request to keep more records solely for the insurer's benefit, but when an auditor communicates the clear advantages to the insured as well, the insured usually responds favorably. Such communication can therefore be a significant step toward forming a cooperative relationship with the insured.

The third advantage of a cooperative relationship is that it can improve the insurer's customer service. Because premium auditors are often the only insurer representative to visit an insured, they might encounter a barrage of questions and opinions about insurance matters of all sorts. Although auditors must be careful not to exceed their authority, they should respond to a policyholder's concerns in a manner that communicates a desire to help. A premium auditor who merely says, "That is not my department" reinforces an image of insurance as a one-way street. Insureds know the cost of insurance but tend to forget the benefits unless they have reminders. Therefore, every insurer representative should make a special effort to offer any assistance possible.

Many questions raised by insureds relate to premium determination. For example, insureds might ask about loss and expense constants, assigned risk surcharges, or minimum premiums. Premium auditors should be able to answer such questions, and failure to do so might cause the insured to doubt the auditor's competence or motives. A doubtful insured might hesitate to pay any additional premium due.

Cost consciousness is also at the center of more general questions or complaints. Insureds might accept the audit's accuracy but still believe that the premium is too high compared to past years. If the auditor can communicate specific events causing increased premiums, the insured might more readily accept the increased premium. For example, the auditor might identify changes in the composition of the insured's business. If rates have increased, the auditor should mention any corresponding increase in benefit levels. In any case, auditors should be prepared to listen sympathetically because insureds have few other outlets for their concern about rising insurance costs.

Other questions raised by insureds might involve technical areas outside the scope of the audit. A premium auditor is not an expert in claims or loss control and must therefore handle questions in those areas carefully so as not to mislead the insured or inadvertently commit the insurer. Many insurers instruct their auditors not to answer questions about coverage or other areas outside of the audit. Although such caution is clearly warranted, it should not be an excuse for indifference. When premium auditors cannot answer a question, they should explain why not. They can then record the insured's question or concern and refer it to the appropriate person as part of the audit report. To build a cooperative relationship, the auditor should provide a response to the insured's concerns. Any effort in that direction can go a long way toward keeping and increasing the good business written by the insurer.

Other advantages of the cooperative relationship between the insured and the auditor are less specific than the three described. Cooperation makes a thorough audit a much easier and more pleasant experience. Neither party is likely to think that it has won or lost. A cooperative relationship is more likely to produce an accurate audit—a benefit to both the insured and the insurer. The insured pays, and the insurer receives a premium commensurate with loss exposures. An accurate audit is crucial for the insurer to have adequate rates in the future. A cooperative relationship also increases the likelihood of retaining the insured for the future. Subsequent audits benefit as well from previous successful, cooperative audits.

The cooperative relationship also smooths the way for the insurer to handle any other aspect of the insurance program more effectively. The insured may be more receptive to suggestions and more willing to work with the insurer to maintain the relationship. In addition, the insurer, underwriter, and producer see the insured more favorably if the relationship is cooperative. The result is that the insured might obtain the benefit of the doubt in any borderline situations.

Confrontational Relationships and Conflict Resolution

Even with the best in communication efforts, premium audit relationships will occasionally become confrontational. Confrontation, if it arises, is most often centered around classification assignments, particularly those pertaining to proprietors, partners, or corporate officers. Insureds naturally want to minimize

their premium costs, so they might insist on assigning the lowest-rated classifications. A similar situation occurs when the insured insists that certain people are really independent contractors, not employees, and should not be included in the premium base. Auditors must be prepared for such possible confrontations and develop complete information describing the duties, operations, and responsibilities involved for those employees. Tactfully presenting all pertinent facts can often preclude disagreements.

An insured might initiate a confrontation in an effort to forestall an audit. An insurer's refusal to undergo an audit can stem from failure to understand the premium audit procedure or can reflect dissatisfaction with a claim settlement or anger over coverage cancellation. Confrontation might also arise because the insured knows that loss exposures have increased and is reluctant to pay additional premium. Whatever the reason, the auditor must be firm but not combative. If the problem cannot be resolved on the spot, the auditor should report as much specific information as possible to assist the ultimate resolution.

Another common source of confrontation in the premium audit is when the auditor and insured view their goals as incompatible. Such a view can only result in costly, nonproductive situations for everyone involved.

Because a confrontational relationship is not conducive to effective communication, both the auditor and the insured should make a concerted effort to develop a cooperative and trusting relationship. Auditors might begin by avoiding behaviors that could trigger the insured's defensive actions.

Integrative bargaining
A conflict resolution method by which two parties must first understand their relationship, their respective perceptions, and their attitudes in order to resolve their conflict.

When serious conflict does occur in a premium audit, both the auditor and the insured might consider the advantages of the **integrative bargaining** for conflict resolution. In this method, the two parties must first understand their relationship and their respective perceptions and attitudes. Such understanding is necessary before the problem or conflict can be resolved. The parties must then define the problem or conflict, making sure the problem and not the symptoms are identified. The two parties jointly search for a solution to the defined problem and reach a decision together. Exhibit 10-3 shows strategies that can be used for integrative bargaining.[8]

EXHIBIT 10-3

Negotiation Strategies for Integrative Bargaining

- Emphasize superordinate goals.
- Focus on the problem, not the people.
- Focus on interests, not demands.
- Create new options for joint gain.
- Focus on what is fair.

The exhibit draws on information from Gareth R. Jones and Jennifer M. George, *Contemporary Management*, 3rd ed. (Boston: McGraw-Hill/Irwin, 2003), p. 558.

SUMMARY

This chapter describes the principles of interpersonal communication that should prove useful to premium auditors. These principles are qualified generalizations rather than absolute communication "laws." Although not all of those principles are applicable to all auditing situations, when applied selectively, they should enhance an auditor's ability to communicate effectively.

The communications process has two phases, the transmission phase and the feedback phase. It also has four components: sender, message, medium, and receiver.

The auditor is one participant in the communication process, acting sometimes as a message sender and sometimes as a message receiver. The medium; the feedback given and received; the context of the premium audit; and the auditor's and insured's attitudes, perceptions, and behavior all affect communication and could impede effective communication. Auditors must understand the communication process and how their actions affect that process.

Verbal communications are messages that the auditor sends either face-to-face or in writing. When communicating verbally, the auditor should be clear and concise and should avoid using technical terms that the insured may not understand. Auditors should also be aware of how nonverbal communication can effect their interactions with insureds. Nonverbal communication can be conveyed through eye movements, body language, personal appearance, and the use of space. An understanding of not only how to use nonverbal communication appropriately but also how to interpret nonverbal messages from the sender will help to improve communications and reduce possible distortions and misinterpretations.

Perception has great influence on communication. Perception is the means through which individuals gather information from their environment. Attribution, which is the process of assigning or ascribing a characteristic or quality to someone or something, and which is an important component of perception was also described. Perceptual distortions may arise because of stereotyping, halo effects, selective perception, projection, and the primacy effect, as well as the implications of these perceptual distortions.

It is important that premium auditors build cooperative relationships with their customers. There will, however, be occasions when confrontation can arise in the premium audit process. Common sources of confrontation include differences of opinion on classification assignments, misunderstandings of the procedure, or dissatisfaction as the result of a claim settlement or policy cancellation. When these situations occur, the auditor can use integrative bargaining to help resolve the conflict and amicably complete the audit.

The Appendix to this chapter presents the premium auditor with communication principles based on the information contained in this chapter.

CHAPTER NOTES

1. Gareth R. Jones and Jennifer M. George, *Contemporary Management*, 4th ed, (Boston: McGraw-Hill/Irwin, 2005), p. 571.
2. Courtland L. Bovée and John V. Thill, *Business Communication Today*, 6th ed. (Upper Saddle River, N.J.: Prentice Hall, 2000), p. 36.
3. Kathryn M. Bartol and David C. Martin, *Management*, 3rd ed. (Boston: Irwin/McGraw-Hill, 1998), p. 447.
4. John R. Schermerhorn, Jr., *Management*, 7th ed. (New York: John Wiley & Sons, Inc., 2002), p. 454.
5. Gerard I. Nierenberg and Henry Calero, *How to Read a Person Like a Book*, (New York: Barnes & Noble Books, 1994), p. 150.
6. Joseph A. DeVito, *The Interpersonal Communication Book*, 9th ed. (New York: Addison Wesley Longman, 2001), p. 114.
7. John R. Schermerhorn, Jr., *Management*, 7th ed. (New York: John Wiley & Sons, Inc., 2002), p. 457.
8. The exhibit draws on information from Gareth R. Jones and Jennifer M. George, *Contemporary Management*, 3rd ed. (Boston: McGraw-Hill/Irwin, 2003), p. 558.

Appendix

Premium Auditor Communication Principles

PREMIUM AUDITOR COMMUNICATION PRINCIPLES

To improve communication with the insured, auditors should do the following:

1. Emphasize statements in their messages that are clear and verifiable and have some utility for the insured
2. State the audit's purposes explicitly and directly
3. Indicate how much time the audit will take and specify the nature of the information required
4. Identify the safeguards they will use to protect the confidentiality of information acquired
5. Use verbal feedback to assess the adequacy of their messages and nonverbal feedback to assess the adequacy of their presentation of self
6. Wear appropriate attire, which can significantly affect the first impression they make and facilitate their attempts to gain access to relevant audit information
7. Create a favorable first impression because that impression is a lasting one
8. Refrain from perceptual distortions that can be caused by stereotyping, the halo effect, selective perception, projection and the primacy effect
9. Be aware that gestures reveal an individual's attitudes and behavioral predisposition and avoid using closed, defensive, and nervous gestures
10. Be aware that postures tend to define the relative status of interacting parties and avoid postures that will have the effect of depressing their perceived status
11. Communicate at the prescribed consulting distance of four to ten feet
12. Use variations in speaking rate, pitch, and volume to present an image of one who is expressive, responsive, and interested in the insured's concerns
13. Develop their critical listening skills to become fully aware of both the explicit and implicit meanings that are part of the insured's messages
14. Develop their ability to interpret facial expressions to respond sensitively to the insured's emotions
15. Develop their ability to identify and interpret adaptor gestures to make informed judgments about the insured's behavioral predispositions and willingness to act cooperatively
16. Respect the insured's interpersonal space
17. Try to resolve interpersonal conflicts by using the integrative bargaining method of conflict resolution
18. Seek to obtain reliable information about the insured's intentions, expectations, and motivations by encouraging the insured to be self-disclosing
19. Protect their own rights as well as the rights of the insured by being appropriately assertive
20. Seek to build trust by exhibiting sensitivity to the insured's needs and feelings, by being coöperative, by honoring past commitments, and by indicating that trusting relationships are conditional

Direct Your Learning 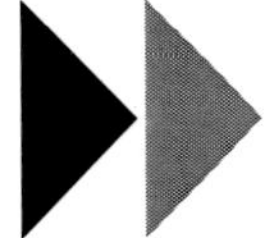

Professionalism in Premium Auditing

Educational Objectives

After learning the content of this chapter and completing the corresponding course guide assignment, you should be able to:

- Describe the elements of professionalism for premium auditors.
- Describe the ethical responsibilities of premium auditors and members of the National Society of Insurance Premium Auditors.
- Apply the ethical responsibilities of premium auditors and members of the National Society of Insurance Premium Auditors to a case.
- Summarize the purpose and evolution of professional organizations for premium auditors.
- Define or describe each of the Key Words and Phrases for this chapter.

OUTLINE

Develop Your Perspective

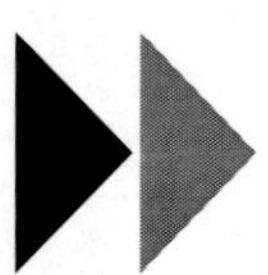

What are the main topics covered in the chapter?

Educational qualifications, technical proficiency, and high performance and ethical standards are marks of a professional auditor. Many organizations and services assist auditors in their professional development.

Identify the areas of technical proficiency that an auditor must develop.

- What skills are required beyond formal education?
- How can an auditor develop these skills?

Why is it important to learn about these topics?

Untrained auditors can be one of the most expensive employees on the insurer's payroll and professionalism in premium auditing is an important goal.

Consider why professionalism is important in an organization.

- Why are high performance standards for premium auditors important?
- What organizations promote professionalism in premium auditing?

How can you use what you will learn?

Examine your own professionalism and ethics.

- What steps can you follow to increase your professionalism?
- What can you do to ensure that you with be ethical in all your dealings?

Professionalism in Premium Auditing

Even into the mid-1990s, many premium auditors received little formal preparation for their careers. Many were given a set of manuals, a briefcase (if they were lucky), and some audit requisitions, and were pointed towards the door.

Insurers have since realized that an untrained auditor can be one of the most expensive employees on the insurer's payroll and that professionalism in premium auditing is an important goal.

ELEMENTS OF PROFESSIONALISM

Insurers need highly trained and skilled personnel to audit today's complex records and coverages. Coping with the demands of being a premium auditor requires a rigorous education, a high level of technical proficiency, high performance standards, and dedication to ethical standards.

Education

Although minimum educational qualifications vary by insurer, new premium auditors usually undergo considerable academic preparation, even before beginning their insurance careers. Most insurers require premium auditors to have a college degree with a concentration in accounting and business courses. Some insurers hire only accounting majors, and that trend is likely to continue. Courses in insurance are also considered beneficial.

Clearly, accounting knowledge is essential for premium auditors. They must be able to understand accounting systems developed by individual businesses and know what to look for and where to look for it. They must be able to analyze entries to obtain the information relating to the insurance premium. Perhaps most important, they must be able to evaluate the reliability of the accounting records by comparing sources to verify the accuracy of the information obtained.

A premium auditor's academic preparation should include other fields relating to the business environment, such as economics, finance, business law, information technology, management, and marketing. The humanities and sciences can add a broader perspective and help develop the capacity for critical thinking. Because communication skills are important for premium auditors, courses that develop writing and speaking abilities are valuable.

A sound, broad-based education prepares premium auditors to approach problems in a disciplined and systematic manner, to respond to changing conditions, and to understand and deal effectively with people.

After beginning an insurance career, premium auditors must become familiar with insurance principles and coverages. That knowledge usually comes from company training courses and an intensive study of insurance policies and manuals, and outside certification courses.

Premium auditors must be able to analyze a given insurance policy, including all its endorsements, and determine what the policy covers. They need to understand the exposure units on which the premium is based and to be able to identify and classify them from the insured's records and from observation of the operations. A clear understanding of how the insurance mechanism works enables premium auditors to perceive the importance of their role to that mechanism. In that way, they not only perform their own function more effectively, but they also effectively coordinate their efforts with other insurer functions.

Technical Proficiency

A premium auditor's technical proficiency depends on the knowledge acquired through formal education and training. However, that knowledge must be augmented by additional skills. The process of classifying loss exposures covered by a policy requires logical analysis and a broad knowledge of industrial processes. It also requires thorough familiarity with the content of applicable manuals, including the latest changes, so that the classifications can be applied uniformly. Auditors should be able to independently determine the correct classification rather than accepting a classification previously assigned. Accuracy in applying manual rules is the key to rate equity for all insureds.

With experience, premium auditors become skillful at interpreting accounting records for all types of businesses. They know what records they need and how to find them, and they can extract information they need for premium determination quickly. They can make sense of unorthodox or fragmentary records even without guidance from the insured's personnel. This skill involves not just a mastery of accounting principles but flexibility in applying them to a variety of recordkeeping systems.

Skilled premium auditors also become knowledgeable about the businesses they audit. They understand the processes involved in converting raw materials to finished products. They know which operations are normal for a business and can therefore identify unusual or incidental operations. They know where to look in the insured's premises and operations for significant deviations that might require further investigation.

The most important of all the premium auditor's skills may be the ability to organize the audit by following a logical, systematic process, resulting in a thorough, accurate audit. Using this skill ensures that matters that should be

investigated are investigated, and that explanations are provided when further investigation is not warranted.

Premium auditors must keep current with recent insurance industry developments. Most manual rule changes take effect on new and renewal policies that will not be audited until a year after the changes are published. By that time, the auditor might have forgotten that the rule ever changed. Local auditors' associations provide a forum for obtaining and exchanging information and for keeping current about what other auditors are doing. Self-study courses and insurance periodicals provide information about issues and changes in the industry.

Changes in the general business environment can affect an auditor's proficiency. New technology and changing accounting systems and software, for example, require auditors to learn new skills and update others. If appropriate courses and learning tools are not offered through insurer channels, the auditor might have to find other ways of learning the skills necessary to stay current.

Manual rule changes and changing accounting technology demonstrate the importance of continuing education as a requirement in maintaining technical proficiency. Many states now have mandatory continuing education requirements for insurance producers, similar to the requirements for other professions, such as accounting. Even if not required, continuing education is still important to the premium auditing profession. Article 3 of the National Society of Insurance Premium Auditors (NSIPA) *Code of Professional Ethics* (shown in the Appendix to this chapter) requires members to "continually strive to improve their professional knowledge, skills, and competence. . . ."

Performance Standards

Other attributes beyond a sound academic preparation and a high level of technical proficiency contribute to professionalism. Premium auditors must also ensure that their performance conforms to the standards for professionals who serve the public interest. Setting and achieving high performance standards requires premium auditors to recognize and competently fulfill their responsibilities to the public and to the insurer.

Responsibility to the Public

Insurance serves the public welfare by providing financial security against accidental losses at a reasonable price. That price reflects both the insurer's loss ratio and expense ratio. If premium auditors or any other employees of the insurer do not perform efficiently, the expense ratio will be higher, consequently raising the price the public pays for insurance protection.

Part of a premium auditor's responsibility to the public includes responsibility to the insured, and it relates to how the auditor interacts with the insured and with the insured's personnel. Courtesy, tact, and sensitivity to the insured's

concerns are qualities of professionalism incidental to competence and good service. Premium auditors who exhibit those qualities also benefit by earning the insured's confidence and cooperation.

The manner in which premium auditors approach policyholders strongly influences the image the policyholder has of the auditor. As discussed in previous chapters, premium auditors should always identify themselves and secure the insured's permission before collecting audit information. Throughout the audit process, they should explain the reason for the audit and the procedures involved, and they should respond to any questions as fully as the limits of knowledge and authority allow. They thus avoid answering questions about such issues as coverage adequacy, claim settlements, and loss prevention recommendations. In response to such questions, the auditor should promise to communicate them to the appropriate people.

Responsibility to the Insurer

Insurers expect a competent and conscientious effort from premium auditors, resulting in a thorough and accurate audit and audit report. If the auditor is unable to obtain records or investigate matters relevant to the audit, the audit report should explain why. When the auditor discovers information affecting the work of other departments, the insurer expects the auditor to report such information.

The insurer also expects premium auditors to function as part of a team by cooperating with other departments in achieving the insurer's overall goals. In some cases; the auditor is the only, or one of the few, direct personal contacts the policyholder has with the insurer, and, therefore, policyholders may base their opinion of the entire company on the experience with the premium auditor. The auditor has a responsibility, then, to represent the insurer with competence and professionalism. Premium auditors must also understand how their role fits into the overall insurance operation and become familiar with the functions and procedures of other departments in order to provide the best and most efficient service.

Premium auditors most often work unsupervised and are, therefore, responsible for managing their own time. Careful planning and scheduling can reduce nonproductive field time. Keeping appointments shows respect for the insured's time. Time management also helps minimize the expenses incurred in the course of field visits. In addition, time management means allocating sufficient time to certain tasks in order to save time later or avoid later problems. For example, when finishing an audit, the auditor should complete audit work sheets and, if necessary, explain them to the policyholder before departing. That expenditure of time at the end of the audit visit can prevent subsequent calls for revised audits or explanations. In addition, indicating on the audit report the location of the records, the name of the contact person, the telephone number, and the time required for the audit helps the next auditor to allocate time efficiently.

Ethical Standards

In addition to the other elements of professionalism, premium auditors must maintain high ethical standards. For several reasons, ethical considerations assume an even greater role in premium auditing than in many other business relationships. One reason is the sensitivity of the information obtained during an audit. Another is the sizable effect the audit has on insurance premiums, profits, and rates. Perhaps the most important reason is that, by determining earned premiums accurately, the premium auditor protects the integrity of the insurance contract and the insurance rating system.

Major obstacles to ethical conduct are indifference and inadvertence. A heightened awareness of the consequences of one's actions or inactions helps an auditor to make better and ethical decisions, even in unforeseen situations.

Statements of principle might appear idealistic, but the claim to professionalism includes a guarantee of conduct that is above reproach. Professional codes of ethics provide guidelines for behavior. Their importance lies in expressing the collective conviction of the profession that ethical considerations do matter. A code can never be a definitive guide to ethical conduct, but it can be a sign pointing in that direction.

Such codes have become important symbols of the ethical standards of many professions, including CPCUs (Chartered Property Casualty Underwriters), CLUs (Chartered Life Underwriters), attorneys, physicians, and CPAs. In all of those professions, breaches of the ethical code can lead to severe penalties, including loss of license or certification.

The **NSIPA *Code of Professional Ethics***, found in the Appendix to this chapter, identifies the principal ethical guidelines of premium auditors. In adopting a code of professional ethics, the NSIPA did not suggest that premium auditors are governed by ethical principles different from those governing other professionals. Rather, the *Code* embodies the ethical principles that have the most common application in the premium auditing profession. Each of the statements in the NSIPA *Code of Professional Ethics* summarizes a particular ethical principle as a guide to action.

NSIPA *Code of Professional Ethics*
The basic ethical principles in the discipline of premium audit practices.

The following sections are based on several of the articles of the NSIPA *Code of Professional Ethics* relating specifically to the ethical conduct of auditors. The remaining articles relate more to the other elements of professionalism described in this section, such as continuing education.

Confidentiality

A significant ethical responsibility for premium auditors is to treat the information obtained during an audit with total confidentiality. That strict responsibility follows directly from the audit's method and purpose. Premium auditors receive sensitive information from insureds for determining the earned premium. The insured gives the insurer permission to obtain and use such information for that purpose in the insurance contract for a policy with a

variable premium. The insured's permission for any other use of the information, however, is neither given nor presumed. The policy's audit condition is not a license for an open-ended investigation.

During their work, premium auditors encounter information that, for many reasons, insureds might prefer to keep private. Premium auditors examine insureds' books and learn the salaries of all the employees and the profits of the owners. To reveal such information to anyone else breaches social norms. Beyond that, other adverse consequences can occur; for example such a breach could generate employee relations problems for the insured.

Information about an organization's sales, profits, or cash flow can affect its relations with customers or creditors. That information, or specifics about customers' names or the size of their accounts, exposed to competitors, might give a competitor a considerable advantage. Even the insured's own producer could possibly derive information from the audit in an attempt to persuade the insured to purchase additional coverage. If the producer has obtained that information without the insured's consent, the insured could well decide to change producers and insurers.

Impartiality

Another ethical responsibility of particular significance for premium auditors is impartiality. Nondiscriminatory treatment ensures rate equity, but it is also a matter of principle. The insurance contract implies fair and impartial treatment by the auditor. Nothing in the contract allows variation in procedures according to incidental circumstances. Therefore, any insured legitimately expects the same treatment accorded all others with similar policies from the same insurer. Conversely, an auditor owes an ethical responsibility to the insurer to refuse to grant variations in procedures when requested to do so by an insured.

Prejudicial behavior is often unintentional. Premium auditors should ask themselves often whether they are being completely impartial.

A situation in which premium auditors may inadvertently exhibit partiality involves insureds in the residual market (that is, business that the insurer is required to write). Businesses in the residual market have had difficulty obtaining insurance in the voluntary market, and the insurer's underwriters do not voluntarily choose the business. A premium auditor might be inclined to regard such a business as less deserving of the quality of service extended to policyholders eagerly sought by the insurer, even though the fault might not lie with the insured.

Business cultural differences can also enter into a premium audit. A premium auditor might encounter rather disparate accounting systems in a neighborhood laundry and in a large commercial bank. Nevertheless, the responsibility to measure the insurance loss exposure fairly is the same. Premium auditors should be aware of and set aside any business cultural biases that might result in partial treatment of an insured.

Conflicts of Interest

A third ethical responsibility of auditors is to avoid conduct that others might view as a conflict of interest. Like many others in business, premium auditors are vulnerable to insureds' attempts to obtain favored treatment. Such attempts can range from ingratiating friendliness and a cup of coffee to blatant offers of money or valuable gifts and favors. Most insurers have strict guidelines for premium auditors about accepting gifts.

Mere adherence to rules or ethical guidelines does not necessarily constitute ethical behavior in itself. An individual can conform to the letter of guidelines while violating their spirit. Premium auditors must perform their tasks in a strictly objective manner. They should never give the appearance to an insured, or others, of being open to influence.

Another potential conflict of interest arises for premium auditors when they offer advice. Suppose, for example, that a policyholder expresses dissatisfaction with a producer. If the premium auditor has become friendly with another producer in the area who seems helpful and competent, the premium auditor might be tempted to recommend that producer to the insured. Then the premium auditor faces an ethical dilemma. On the one hand, improperly influencing the insured in the selection of a producer is possible. On the other hand, ignoring the insured's obvious need for assistance in an area in which a ready solution exists is also possible. Such choices are not made easily. They require sound judgment along with a deep commitment to honesty and integrity.

PROFESSIONAL ORGANIZATIONS

Standards of competence and ethical conduct are transmitted to the profession's members through a formal association. Formal organizations are important to professions; they enable professions to act collectively. Representing all members of the profession, a professional body can define the necessary underlying body of knowledge, establish standards for the practice of the profession, develop procedures for admitting new members, facilitate the exchange of professional information, and present the view of the profession in an influential manner.

The concept of an association can be traced to medieval times, when members of guilds gathered to promote their collective interest in a particular trade. Each guild set its own requirements for advancement from apprentice to journeyman to master. The guild also set quality standards for the work. Because of their importance for the advancement of learning, associations of masters and students won the special privileges of independence and self-governance that were characteristic of medieval universities. When universities won the recognition of church and state that only they could judge the qualifications of their members, they achieved the status of a self-governing profession.

During the nineteenth century, dentists, attorneys, architects, engineers, librarians, nurses, and accountants organized professional bodies. Differing employment relationships, however, limited various professions' degree of independence and self-regulation.

Professions indicate a degree of specialized training and skill such that the buyer cannot directly judge the quality of professional service received. Thus, licensing or professional accreditation procedures requiring specific educational qualifications and proficiency testing provide the public some assurance of competence and training. For example, certified public accountants have established high standards of competence and ethical behavior maintained by formal examination procedures for new members and by peer review for present members of the profession.

Local and Regional Premium Auditors' Associations

Premium auditors have played an important and highly specialized role in the insurance industry since the early 1900s. Eventually, they formed professional associations, first at the local level, then at the regional level, and finally at the national level when the National Society of Insurance Premium Auditors was formed.

In 1952 the first local auditors association began in Philadelphia. In the 1950s and 1960s, many local chapters were formed throughout the United States. From 1967 through 1973, five regional auditors' associations were formed.[1] Today, there are more than forty local chapters. Their monthly meetings provide an opportunity to discuss classification changes and other matters of common interest.

Many of the earliest associations restricted their membership to premium audit managers, while others welcomed premium auditors at all levels. Eligibility for membership thus became one of the most significant organizational questions for the premium auditing profession. Well-established associations hesitated to change their accustomed practices. The members had already achieved close bonds with counterparts in other companies, and those bonds enabled them to exchange ideas freely and communicate information to improve premium auditing practices. Members feared that a larger membership would weaken those bonds, possibly lessen members' status, and perhaps even diminish the association's effectiveness.

Others argued that the claim to professional status required a formal organization open to all premium auditors, that an association could not speak for premium auditors with one voice unless it actually represented all premium auditors, and that exclusive membership requirements implied a distinction of status and purpose alien to the concept of professionalism. Further, they argued, if field auditors were simply employees with closely supervised routine duties, then their managers had different interests. If, however, field auditors were expected to exercise independent judgment, to maintain a current knowledge of manual rules and classifications, and to determine the correct

earned premium to the best of their abilities, their purpose became identical with that of the premium audit managers.

Active local associations have developed in geographical areas containing significant concentrations of premium auditors. Most of them hold monthly meetings with an educational presentation. Speakers from bureaus and advisory organizations may explain specific classification problems relevant to a particular state. Those meetings also provide an opportunity for premium auditors to exchange information and to discuss problems.

During the 1960s, the perceived need for more educational presentations and seminars led to cooperative efforts among several local associations. Those efforts became formalized with the establishment of regional associations in five regions of the country—Northeast, Southeast, Southwest, Central States, and West. An association in each of those regions holds an annual seminar, which includes presentations by bureaus, discussions of auditing particular industries common to the region, and explanations of other topics of interest to premium auditors. Those five regional associations have become forums for the continuing education of premium auditors.

National Society of Insurance Premium Auditors

In 1975, a steering committee proposed the establishment of a national organization of premium auditors. Working with the presidents of the five regional associations, the steering committee planned a not-for-profit organization called the National Society of Insurance Premium Auditors (the Society). The Society's Articles of Incorporation included the following among the purposes of the organization:

- To develop a formal course of study and a proficiency testing procedure
- To provide a forum for the exchange of technical information
- To contribute premium auditing knowledge to the insurance industry
- To establish uniform standards of premium auditing
- To promote and develop the premium auditing profession

The Society's annual meeting brings premium auditors from across the country together for educational sessions and business meetings to discuss and resolve matters of common interest to the profession. In the interval between annual meetings, the Society's Board of Directors has authority to hold additional meetings and to manage the affairs of the Society.

The third annual meeting of the Society adopted the Code of Professional Ethics described previously in this chapter. The Society also serves a communication purpose. Its newsletter, *Newsline*, provides a forum for airing concerns of the profession, as well as a means of informing the membership. *Newsline* also contains articles on technical matters and audit problems. The Society also maintains a library of educational materials for premium auditors.

Premium Audit Advisory Service

In April 1978, the Premium Audit Advisory Service (PAAS) was established under the auspices of the American Insurance Services Group. Insurance Services Office, Inc. (ISO) purchased American Insurance Services Group from its parent company, American Insurance Association, in October 1997. The purpose of PAAS is to provide a forum for discussing general problems of common concern to premium auditors. That forum helps focus industry attention on the premium audit function through its involvement in education, staffing requirements, workload, legislative and insurance department developments, and the activities of industry boards and bureaus. Its services to member companies seek to promote the continuity, standardization, and improved administration of the premium audit function.

Participation in the Premium Audit Advisory Service is open to all property-casualty insurers and audit service companies. PAAS assesses subscribers according to their company's premium volume.

Educational bulletins
A series of bulletins developed by PAAS that provide timely information regarding education, legislation, and technology issues to premium auditors.

Classification guides
Guides developed by PAAS that provide detailed descriptions of workers' compensation and general liability classifications to assist premium auditors in assigning proper classification codes.

PAAS distributes current information affecting premium auditing. Its *Legislative Bulletins* discuss the premium audit implications of bills pending in each of the state legislatures and report on newly enacted laws. The **Educational Bulletins** provide information on coverage and classification changes along with additional clarifications and interpretations of existing rules. The **Classification Guides** offer extensive insights into operations contemplated by various classifications as well as indicating state exceptions. The guides, offered via a compact disk or through the Internet, are state specific for each of the classifications. The "Audit Information Summary" card and the "Summary of Outstanding Rate Changes" card, each issued quarterly, summarize the latest information concerning each of the fifty states. Specific state exceptions to NCCI *Basic Manual* rules are also listed in a "Chart of State Exceptions," published annually. PAAS has also published field auditors' training manuals covering workers' compensation, general liability, and commercial auto insurance. Also offered by PAAS is its Technical Achievement Program, a Web-based training program whereby the student receives the study material and takes a timed-exam on the Internet.

In addition to publications, the Premium Audit Advisory Service offers seminars throughout the U.S. on such subjects as workers' compensation, general liability, commercial automobile, trucking, credit and collection, and premium fraud.

All of the organizations of premium auditors just described have extended their influence within the insurance industry. Opinions or recommendations of those organizations are now often a part of the decision process when a bureau or an advisory organization revises its training manual. Although an individual premium auditor might not agree with all of those professional organizations' decisions, those decisions do give a premium auditing perspective to bureaus' actions that would otherwise be almost entirely absent.

SUMMARY

Insurers need highly trained premium auditors to review the complex records and coverages common in organizations. The following are marks of professionalism in premium auditors:

- Education—Most premium auditors have a college degree with a concentration in accounting and business courses. Accounting knowledge is essential. Courses in insurance and those teaching effective communication skills are considered beneficial.
- Technical proficiency—Logical analysis of loss exposures covered by a policy and as interpreted through relevant manuals is a required skill. Skillful interpretation of accounting records requires flexibility in applying accounting principles to a variety of recordkeeping systems. The auditor must be able to organize an audit by following a logical, systematic process to develop a thorough, accurate audit.
- Performance standards—Premiums auditors must ensure that their performances conform to the standards of a professional who serves the public interest as well as the insurer. Insurers expect a competent and conscientious effort from premium auditors and for auditors to function as part of a team by cooperating with other departments in achieving the insurer's overall goals.
- Ethical standards—Premium auditors must maintain high ethical standards because of the confidential nature of the information they obtain during an audit as well as the sizeable effect the audit has on insurance premiums, profits, and rates. Premium auditors' ethical standards relate to confidentiality, impartiality, and conflicts of interest. The premium auditor protects the integrity of the insurance contract and the insurance rating system.

The National Society of Insurance Premium Auditors supports premium auditors by providing standards for auditing, promoting education and exchange of information, and enforcing a code of professional ethics. The Premium Audit Advisory Service provides advisory information and guidelines to support the consistent application of premium auditing decisions.

CHAPTER NOTE

1. See the National Society for Insurance Premium Auditors Web site, http://www.nsipa.org (accessed July 15, 2005).

Appendix

National Society of Insurance Premium Auditors Code of Professional Ethics

NATIONAL SOCIETY OF INSURANCE PREMIUM AUDITORS CODE OF PROFESSIONAL ETHICS

Preamble

The provisions of the Code of Ethics cover basic principles in the discipline of premium audit practices. Premium Auditors shall realize that individual judgment is required in the application of these principles. Premium Auditors have the responsibility to conduct themselves so that their good faith and integrity shall not be open to question. While having due regard for the realistic limits to individual skills, Premium Auditors shall promote the highest professional premium auditing standards to the end of advancing the interest of their companies or organizations and of the insurance business.

The basic objective of the Code is to serve the public interest, not only by specifying minimum ethical conduct rightly expected of Premium Auditors, but by encouraging voluntary acceptance of standards of professional conduct far beyond minimal expectations.

Articles

1. Premium Auditors shall be prudent in the use of information acquired in the course of their duties.
2. Premium Auditors shall not use confidential information for any personal gain or in a manner which would be detrimental to the professional conduct of the insurance business. Premium Auditors shall not disclose to any other person any confidential information entrusted to or obtained by them unless a disclosure of such information is required by law.
3. Premium Auditors shall provide the same high standard of professional service to all policyholders regardless of color, sex, national origin, or type of business pursuit. Impartiality, integrity, honesty, and common courtesy shall be shown to policyholders, agents, accountants, and others with whom they may be in contact while carrying out their duties.
4. Premium Auditors shall continually strive to improve their professional knowledge, skills and competence, in the insurance business generally and in the practice of Premium Auditing specifically.
5. Premium Auditors shall conscientiously perform their duties in a manner that will assure equity and improve the efficiency of the insurance mechanism.
6. Premium Auditors shall perform their duties in a dignified and professional manner that will bring credit to the insurance business, and they shall assist in maintaining and raising professional standards in the insurance business.
7. Premium Auditors shall refrain from entering into any activity which may be in conflict with the interest of their employers or which would prejudice their ability to carry out objectively their duties and responsibilities.

8. Premium Auditors shall not attempt by direct or indirect means to injure maliciously or falsely the professional reputation or practice of another Auditor.
9. Premium Auditors will cooperate in extending the effectiveness of the profession by interchanging nonconfidential or nonproprietary information and experience with other Premium Auditors and encouraging fellow Auditors to improve and update their education.

Reprinted from the National Society of Insurance Premium Auditors Web site, http://www.nsipa.org (accessed July 15, 2005).

Index

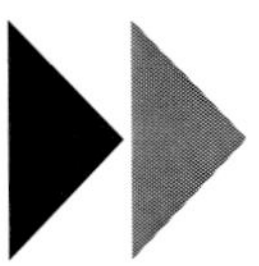

Page numbers in boldface refer to definitions of Key Words and Phrases.

E

F

G

H

I

O

P

Q

R

S

T

U

V

W